W9-AIA-149

Careers in Chemistry

Careers in Chemistry

Editor
Donald R. Franceschetti
The University of Memphis

SALEM PRESS
A Division of EBSCO Publishing
Ipswich, Massachusetts

GREY HOUSE PUBLISHING

Library of Congress Cataloging-in-Publication Data

Careers in chemistry.
    pages cm
 Includes bibliographical references and index.
 ISBN 978-1-58765-993-5 (hardcover)
 1. Chemistry--Vocational guidance.
 QD39.5.C243 2013
 540.23--dc23

                                                                    2012044523

ebook ISBN: 978-1-4298-3762-0

Contents

◎ - Designated as a Green Occupation by the US Department of Labor, Employment and Training Administration.

Appendixes

Indexes

Publisher's Note

It is estimated that the United States will have over 2.1 million job openings in STEM-related (Science, Technology, Engineering, and Mathematics) fields and occupations by 2020. More specifically, within that ten-year period, the US Bureau of Labor Statistics (BLS) projects that employment within the scientific, professional, and technical services industries will grow by approximately 29 percent. Along with these positive growth trends, employees in STEM occupations also earn higher salaries than workers in other fields and have lower unemployment rates than fellow college graduates, and STEM students are seeing an increase in grants and funding through burgeoning government and educational initiatives. Further, STEM students are highly targeted for recruitment by major cutting-edge companies such as Google, while companies such as Microsoft are starting to recruit for STEM careers at an early educational level by working to spark an interest in science and technology, especially among female students. The growth of STEM-related careers and the investment in science education will play a key role in the future of our nation.

Despite these trends and the steady growth across all STEM fields, the United States is experiencing a significant deficit in the number of STEM workers, or those holding technical jobs within the fields of science, technology, engineering, and mathematics. Not enough students are graduating with STEM backgrounds to fill the open positions in the marketplace, leading many schools across the country to engage in STEM advocacy campaigns to encourage student interest in STEM subjects.

To that end, this publication, *Careers in Chemistry*, contains over twenty alphabetically arranged articles describing specific fields of interest in chemistry with an accompanying discussion of a particular STEM-related career or occupation within that area. These occupational profiles provide a current overview and a future outlook, including green technologies where applicable. Merging scholarship with occupational development, this single comprehensive guidebook provides chemistry students and readers alike with the necessary insight into potential scientific pursuits and provides instruction on what job seekers can expect in terms of training and advancement, earnings, job prospects, working conditions, relevant associations, and more. *Careers in Chemistry* is specifically designed for a high school and undergraduate audience and is edited to align with secondary or high school curriculum standards.

Scope of Coverage

Understanding the interconnected nature of the different and varied branches of science and technology is important for anyone preparing for a career or endeavor in STEM fields. *Careers in Chemistry* comprises more than twenty lengthy and alphabetically arranged essays on a broad range of branches and subfields within chemistry and over twenty corresponding occupational profiles that highlight a particular career within that branch or subfield. The overview essays include traditional and long-established fields such as chemical engineering and pulp and paper chemistry to in-demand and cutting-edge fields such as green, environmental, and nuclear chemistry. This excellent reference work then presents possible career paths and occupations within high-growth and emerging fields as diverse as cosmetics chemistry, electrochemistry, femtochemistry, forensic science, geochemistry, pharmacology, and petrochemistry. While occupations requiring Green Enhanced Skills are marked with a "green leaf" symbol, the future applications of all occupations are thoroughly discussed.

Careers in Chemistry is also enhanced with numerous charts and tables, including US Bureau of Labor Statistics projections and median annual salaries or wages for applicable chemistry-based occupations. The Transferable Skills section notes those skills that can be applied across STEM occupations, and Interesting Facts provides insights into fields that are often overlooked. Rounding out these profiles are questionnaires completed by professionals in chemistry-related occupations. The respondents share their personal career paths, detail their potential paths for career advancement, and offer advice for students and readers—a must-read for those embarking on a career in science.

Essay Length and Format

Science overviews range in length from 3,500 to 4,500 words and all entries begin with ready-reference top matter, including fields of study and a clear definition of the chemistry branch or subfield. Essays then place the major field or area of study in historical or technological perspective by examining basic principles and core concepts, including the discipline's development, such as historic and current applications. The articles also cover the impact that each particular field has had on industry—a comprehensive section that includes private industry and business, government agencies and the military, and academic research and teaching, as well as the field's social context and future prospects and applications. Further reading suggestions and detailed author profiles accompany all articles.

Occupational profiles range in length from 1,500 to 2,000 words and include an "employment snapshot" in the top matter that presents the occupation's median yearly earnings; employment outlook (sourced from the BLS *Occupational Outlook Handbook*); O*NET-SOC Code (an eight-digit code assigned to each occupation through the US Department of Labor); and related "career clusters" that name occupations in the same field of work that require similar skills. Each occupation then receives the following detailed sections:

- **Scope of Work** presents a brief introduction to the occupation, including the applications of the work.

- **Education and Coursework** addresses the educational path and the basic coursework needed to go on to more advanced research or professional positions within this occupation or field.

- **Career Enhancement and Training** details the certification or licensing necessary to secure employment and advancement in a given occupation, if applicable, and discusses the benefits of professional associations and societies.

- **Daily Tasks and Technology** describes the typical set of daily activities of the occupation and the technology employed in the occupation.

- **Earnings and Employment Outlook** provides an overview of the wages and job growth associated with the occupation.

- **Related Occupations** lists similar or related occupations within the field.

- **Future Applications** discusses the impact this field or occupation will have on future jobs and careers.

- **More Information** lists websites that students can turn to for further research and information about the occupation.

In addition, unique highlights of these occupational profiles include:

- **Transferable Skills,** a list of six to eight commonly recognized skills considered to be transferable across multiple careers and work environments.

- **Careers Questionnaire,** a 150- to 300-word questionnaire completed by a professional within a particular field, relating his or her respective career path, advice, and possible advancement opportunities. This special feature canvasses a diverse range of professionals working in the fields of—or with a background in—chemistry, ranging from academia to the private sector, from small business owners to CEOs, and from young professionals to accomplished individuals.

Special Features

Several features continue to distinguish this reference series from other career-oriented reference works. The back matter includes several appendixes and indexes, including a general bibliography, a collated collection of annotated suggested readings, and an awards appendix listing the Nobel Prize winners in chemistry. Colleges to Consider presents an alphabetically arranged list of the most highly selective four-year colleges in the United States for pursuing and attaining a bachelor's degree in chemistry, using select criteria. A career guidance appendix presents a comprehensive listing of career-oriented portals maintained by preeminent and influential societies and organizations advocating on behalf of chemists and other scientists and science-related workers. Additionally, an occupational websites directory notes those websites with specific relevance to the pursuit of a career in chemistry.

Additional features are provided to assist in the retrieval of information. An index illustrates the breadth of the reference work's coverage, listing people, scientific concepts and theories, technologies, terms, principles, and other topics of discussion, while an occupational index directs the reader to all discussions of a specific occupation throughout both the science and occupational profile articles.

Acknowledgments

Many hands went into the creation of this work. Special mention must be made of consulting editor Donald R. Franceschetti, who played a principal role in shaping the reference work and its contents. Thanks are due to the many academicians and professionals who worked to communicate their expert understanding of chemistry to the general reader; a list of these individuals and their affiliations appears at the beginning of the volume. Finally, thanks are also due to the professionals who communicated their work experience through our careers questionnaires. Their frank and honest responses have provided immeasurable value to our careers product. The contributions of all are gratefully acknowledged.

440-637-5605 ? One on one

EYE ball Hard Hand

xvi   Elemnaiianeioning   it A No No No

Introduction

It is a truism that the pace of change in industry and technology has been rapidly increasing. The atomic nucleus was discovered a little over a century ago, the first primitive transistor built in 1947, and earth satellites a mere decade later. Today's student may use cell phone or VoIP technology to share information with a friend almost anywhere in the world, and the owner of an inexpensive computer has at his or her command more computing resources than the United States government had access to a scant sixty-five years ago. While the process of growth has experienced setbacks from time to time, the student who has some command of the hard sciences—particularly physics and chemistry—along with a modicum of communications skills, can expect to have an interesting and well-remunerated career.

This book is intended to serve as a guide to career options in these technical fields for students in high school or the early years of college. Generally, the careers available will depend on the breadth and depth of training. A few important general observations can be made at the outset. The most important outcome of schooling is learning how to learn. Today's high school graduates can expect a working lifetime of forty years or more and will need to acquire new knowledge throughout their careers from a wide variety of sources, many of them electronic. Communications skills—speaking, writing and the production of visual media—will continue to be important in the workplace, and basic computer competency will be essential. Additionally, understanding of mathematics is essential for any career in science. So in addition to the obvious courses in physics or chemistry, attention to coursework in English composition, computer programming, and mathematics is critical. Increasingly, people working in the sciences will find themselves working with individuals from different cultures and different nations. Courses that provide multicultural perspectives, including courses in foreign languages, might be a good investment.

The level of education obtained will help to delimit career prospects. Attending a vocational high school or community college could qualify you as a laboratory technician, but having a college degree will broaden career prospects considerably. Students interested in chemistry or physics should talk with science teachers about the programs available at the college of their choice. Students wanting to attain the bachelor's degree in chemistry should try to select a program accredited by the American Chemical Society and take advantage of this status to become student affiliates of that organization. The physics community in the United States has chosen not to accredit individual degree programs as some quite small departments have excellent programs. Finding a college with an active chapter of the Society of Physics Students, affiliated with the American Institute of Physics, is almost indispensible for the aspiring professional physicist. Student organizations in chemistry and physics have national and regional meetings, and plan field trips on a local level to industrial sites and national laboratories, while inviting speakers to campus to describe employment opportunities.

The Bachelor of Science degree takes the equivalent of four years to acquire and generally includes courses in the major, as well as in supporting areas such as mathematics, and includes a healthy dose of general education (English, history, foreign language, and social science). There are many employment opportunities for physicists and chemists at the bachelor's level, and many choose to enter the workforce at this point, though most employers will expect, and many will pay for, some amount of continuing education. Some graduates may go to professional school to become physicians, dentists, veterinarians, and optometrists, or to law school to enter one of the many fields of legal practice, including patent law (for which a bachelor's degree in one of the STEM areas is required). Additional opportunities for STEM graduates can be found in the armed forces, where they can obtain commissions as officers, and in secondary teaching, after obtaining an amount of professional preparation in pedagogy (the requirements differing greatly from state to state).

Further education for STEM graduates generally amounts to earning the Master of Science (MS) or Doctor of Philosophy (PhD) degree. This can be done on a full-time or part-time basis and often involves teaching or research duties that provide a stipend as well as remission of tuition, so that the graduate student can be a self-supporting adult. In contrast to bachelor's degree programs, which can involve taking courses in many different departments, graduate students generally take their advanced work in a single department or a few closely related ones. The majority of MS programs include a certain amount of graduate coursework in preparation for a comprehensive examination and a research project or thesis, which serves as the candidate's first introduction to research and often results in a scientific publication. MS programs require eighteen months to two years of full-time effort, but allow the student to enter the workforce at a more advanced level.

The doctorate degree has existed for many centuries though the requirements have changed vastly. In modern practice, the PhD requires passing a stringent general examination in the field of specialization and the submission of a PhD dissertation, a book-length manuscript describing a single research study. Obtaining the PhD can take four or more years beyond the bachelor's degree. The degree is required to teach on a permanent basis at most four-year colleges, and many universities will expect most of their new hires to have completed a stint as a paid postdoctoral research fellow before beginning the probationary period that leads to tenure. Many PhDs choose to enter industry instead, where the salaries are somewhat higher and there is greater opportunity to enter managerial positions and eventually become corporate executives.

Whatever career path is chosen, the young STEM student will find interesting work in the company of like-minded individuals. New fields of study will emerge and new research tools will appear. It is impossible to say now, in the second decade of the twenty-first century, where such careers will lead in thirty to forty years, but the probability of an engaging and satisfying career is high indeed for the student with an aptitude for science and math learning and the maturity to persist in a physics or chemistry career.

Donald R. Franceschetti
Departments of Physics and Chemistry
The University of Memphis

Contributors

Richard Adler
University of Michigan–Dearborn

Michael P. Auerbach
Marblehead, Massachusetts

Joseph Brownstein
Atlanta, Georgia

Daniel Castaldy
Marlborough, Massachusetts

Keith M. Finley
Southeastern Louisiana University

Molly Hagan
New York, New York

J. D. Ho
Independent scholar

Micah L. Issitt
Philadelphia, Pennsylvania

R. C. Lutz
Bucharest, Romania

Marianne M. Madsen
University of Utah

Steve Miller
Somerville, Massachusetts

Cassandra Newell
Somerville, Massachusetts

Robert J. Paradowski
Rochester Institute of Technology

Richard M. Renneboog
Strathroy, Ontario

Ruth Waddell Smith
Michigan State University

Max Statman
Eastman Chemical Company

Rose Young
Ipswich, Massachusetts

Careers in Chemistry

Agricultural Chemistry

FIELDS OF STUDY

Chemistry; biochemistry; biology; genetics; physiology; ecology; economy; soil and water sciences; molecular biology; chemical engineering; chemical biology; environmental chemistry; bioengineering; physical chemistry; synthetic chemistry; plant physiology; phytochemistry; entomology; cell biology; human toxicology.

DEFINITION

Agricultural chemistry is an interdisciplinary applied science that looks at the chemical processes that affect vegetable and animal food production, food protection, and food-yield optimization. The goal of agricultural chemistry is to understand the chemistry of crop and livestock production in order to safeguard and improve it for human uses. Important applications are the development and enhancement of fertilizers to accelerate production and increase yields; the development and enhancement of crop protection via chemical pesticides, herbicides, and fungicides; and the development of genetically modified crop varieties with improved resistance to pests and to herbicides that also possess higher nutritional value. Agricultural chemistry is essential to meet the food needs of the growing human population.

Basic Principles

The idea to improve plant growth and yield by using a variety of fertilizers, ranging from animal and human dung to Nile mud, for example, is almost as old as agriculture. Similarly, some of the earliest pesticides used were sulfur and arsenic in European antiquity. In this sense, humans intuitively used agricultural chemistry long before it would be understood as a science.

Modern agricultural chemistry began in Europe in the middle of the eighteenth century. Scottish physician Francis Home introduced the idea in his *Principles of Agriculture and Vegetation* (1757). This was followed up by English chemist Humphry Davy in *Elements of*

Agricultural Chemistry (1815). German chemist Justus von Liebig is generally considered founder of industrial agricultural chemistry. His *Agrikulturchemie* (1840; *Chemistry in its Application to Agriculture and Physiology*, 1847) presented the principle of industrially fabricated fertilizers. Its adoption caused a quantum leap in European agricultural production.

The development, manufacture, and continuous improvement of fertilizers as means to improve crop yield are the basic tasks of agricultural chemistry. Agricultural chemists have been instrumental in developing synthetic fertilizers and understanding and improving their effects. Great progress was made in the early part of the twentieth century on the basis of ammonium nitrate and ammonium sulfate.

Development of effective crop protection—namely pesticides, fungicides, herbicides, and insecticides—is another important task of agricultural chemistry. After World War II, development of effective pesticides in tandem with new fertilizers triggered the so-called green revolution, which vastly increased global food production.

Agricultural chemistry designed new hybrid plant seeds that provided higher yields at harvest. Further research led to creation of genetically modified foods and crop seeds, which have been sold commercially since 1996. Here, agricultural chemists have altered the genetic structure of some common crops, such as potatoes, corn, and soybeans, to create new plant varieties that offer higher yields, are more resistant to pests, and can provide extra nutrients. However, genetically modified foods have remained controversial due to fears about their safety, their ecological and environmental impact, and the fact that they are the intellectual property of the companies that create them.

Other basic goals of agricultural chemistry are to make fertilizers and pesticides as environmentally friendly as possible and produce them at low cost, leading to lower food prices. Developing feed supplements in plants used as animal fodder and identifying optimized soil, water, and air conditions for plant growth are also important.

Core Concepts

Agricultural chemistry is based on scientific understanding of plant and animal physiology. With this foundation, agricultural chemistry analyzes how certain chemical molecules and compounds can affect crop and livestock growth, plant yield, and resistance to infection or predators. The impact of soil, water, and air conditions on crops is analyzed. A key task of agricultural chemistry is to develop increasingly effective ways of applying beneficial chemical compounds that guide crop growth and boost resistance to outside threats with as little cost and negative environmental effects as possible. Since the late 1980s, genetics and genetic engineering have become very important for modifying crops at the microbiological level.

Plant and Animal Physiology. These two scientific fields provide knowledge of the functioning of plant and animal organisms down to the cellular and molecular level. Of special importance are the biochemical processes in plants, which are studied in phytochemistry, and a plant's power to resist infection, which is studied in phytopathology. Contemporary research focuses on the study of the chemical and biological processes at the level of plant cells and the interactions among these cells. How plants govern their internal functions and how they relate to their environment is researched as well. To carry out these studies, analytical and experimental tools from physics and chemistry are used. Animal physiology is used to analyze how animals convert plant feed and study the functioning of animal organisms from the molecular level upward.

Soil Sciences. The study of soil is important because it concerns a major influence on plant growth and strength. Through soil samples and remote sensing, soil is analyzed and classified with regard to its physical, chemical, and biological qualities. These in turn affect soil's fertility and various levels of plant-growth support. In addition, the water and climate conditions of specific regions are studied for their effect on vegetation and determination of crop options.

Analytical Chemistry. The tools of analytical chemistry are applied to understand the processes of growth and survival in plant and animal organisms. Classic tools include the separation of chemical compounds by distillation, extraction, or precipitation and their subsequent qualitative and quantitative analysis. Instrumental chemical analysis uses continuously optimized instruments to measure the physical qualities of a chemical compound. Spectroscopy, mass spectrometry, and chromatography, as well as electrochemical and thermal analysis, are contemporary tools that are used in agricultural chemistry to gain knowledge both of plant and animal organisms and the properties of chemical compounds developed to influence their behavior.

Chemical Research and Development. A core task of agricultural chemistry is research into the development of new beneficial chemical compounds to support enhanced food growth and security. Standard chemical-research methods are applied, first in the laboratory and then with an eye on industrial-scale production. New products are tested thoroughly during the development phase, which also involves incorporation of knowledge gained from human toxicology to avoid any harmful side effects for humans.

Industrial Production and Chemical Product Engineering. Production of agrochemicals uses methods for aligning chemical reactions with industrial chemical production, where there is an emphasis on economies of scale and cost efficiency. The methods of chemical product engineering also affect agricultural chemistry. Here, principles of unit operation, chemical process design, and transport phenomena are employed to design a process for manufacturing industrial agrochemicals.

Genetics and Genetic Engineering. Humanity has made intuitive use of the consequences of genetics since the prehistoric development of agriculture and animal husbandry. This was previously done through selective breeding and crossbreeding to obtain plants and animals with desirable traits. In contemporary agricultural chemistry, genetic engineering has become a major focus of research and development. Genetic engineering mimics the naturally occurring gene transfer but controls it more closely by directly adding or deleting specific genes in an organism. This became commercially feasible for plant modification in the 1980s. There are two methods of genetic engineering: cisgenesis transfers genes between organisms that could actually interbreed in nature, while transgenesis inserts genes from a different species. Gene transfer by scientists can be done physically, with a microsyringe or gene gun, or biologically, via a host bacteria or host

Interesting Facts about Agricultural Chemistry

- Sulfur dusting is the oldest known application of chemical crop production. It was practiced first in Mesopotamia (present-day Iraq) around 2500 B.C.E. and is still used to protect grapes all over the world.

- It is estimated that for each dollar spent on a pesticide, an additional four dollars' worth of food is produced on the treated land.

- The first documented use of poisonous plants to deter insects from attacking crops dates back to 2000 B.C.E. in India. This idea has made a comeback in organic farming, with agricultural chemists supplying knowledge about the chemical composition of substances that affect herbivorous insects.

- The agricultural biotechnological company Monsanto not only developed the herbicide glyphosate but also developed genetically modified plants and crop seeds that are able to survive this herbicide, thus allowing it to be used on any weeds springing up alongside these crops.

- Animals have been genetically modified for research. One spectacular modification is the insertion of a fluorescent protein from jellyfish that makes the modified animal glow green in the dark. Scientists use this fluorescence to track the activity and effects of the altered genes in modified animals, which have included pigs, chickens, and cats.

- The vastly underestimated negative effects of the herbicide DDT were lambasted in the book *Silent Spring* (1962) by American biologist Rachel Carson. Ten years later, DDT was banned in the United States.

- In 1992, China became the first country to permit commercial sale of a genetically modified plant, a tobacco plant made hardier against viruses.

virus. Scientists performing genetic engineering for crop plants must also determine where exactly to insert the new gene in the region of a target plant's DNA (deoxyribonucleic acid) structure, using a specifically designed promoter to ensure on-target gene delivery.

Biosafety. Because of the inherent dangers of chemically manipulating human food and animal feed, biosafety is a very important concern in agricultural chemistry. Biosafety seeks to prevent a major loss of biological diversity, which could occur through the massive spread of alien or transgenic genes, particularly those associated with genetically modified food crops. The Cartagena Protocol on Biosafety provides scientific guidelines and rules that have been in effect since September 11, 2003. At American universities and research institutes, a committee on biosafety evaluates and must approve agricultural chemistry research and experiments that may create a biohazard.

Applications Past and Present

Fertilizers. One of the oldest applications of agricultural chemistry is fertilizers to accelerate and increase plant growth and yield. They were used long before the science behind them was discovered.

The major breakthrough in scientifically understanding fertilizers was made by Justus von Liebig in 1840. Liebig discovered that nitrogen is an essential element of plant nutrition and that nitrogen-rich fertilizers can vastly improve plant growth. He propagated the use of ammonia and of chemical, rather than natural, fertilizers. Liebig found that plants require and thrive on phosphate, which they absorb best through the compound superphosphate (monocalcium phosphate). He sought to develop means of industrially producing such mineral fertilizers.

Liebig's scientific discoveries led to the industrial production of fertilizers. In 1842, English agricultural scientist John Bennet Lawes patented his process of obtaining superphosphate from phosphates in rock and coprolite (fossilized dinosaur feces) and set up a factory for its manufacture. In 1843, Lawes founded the Rothamsted Experimental Station, devoted to scientific study of fertilizers and other issues in agricultural science. In the twenty-first century, the institution still operates as Rothamsted Research.

More factories producing industrial fertilizers in England and Germany in the 1840s and 1850s greatly increased agricultural production in Europe and, soon, the United States. As their value as natural fertilizers became understood, guano (excrement of sea birds and bats deposited on lime rock) and sodium nitrate were also widely used.

To lessen dependence on natural fertilizers, European scientists looked at more chemical alternatives. In 1902, ethnic German chemist Wilhelm Ostwald patented the Ostwald process of producing nitric acid, an important feedstock for synthetic fertilizers, from ammonia. In 1903, Norwegian scientist Kristian Birkeland patented a method of producing nitric acid from nitrogen in the atmosphere and then using it to manufacture synthetic fertilizers. This method, known as the Birkeland-Eyde process, consumed a great deal of energy.

In 1909, German chemist Fritz Haber succeeded in obtaining ammonia from atmospheric nitrogen through its reaction with hydrogen gained from methane. In 1913, Haber collaborated with fellow German chemist and engineer Carl Bosch at Germany's BASF chemical company. They developed the Haber-Bosch process for industrial-scale production of ammonia. This finally provided sufficient feedstock for production of nitric acid under the Ostwald process. From this nitric acid, final nitrogen fertilizers were manufactured.

After these core chemical advances and discoveries, agricultural chemists began to devote their energies to creating fertilizers that would carry the desired nutrients to plants in most effective and concentrated form. To make fertilizers as environmentally friendly as possible, there has also been a drive to eliminate contamination, such as traces of cadmium or uranium, in less and less expensive processes.

By 2012, the Haber-Bosch process accounted for the annual production of one trillion pounds of fertilizer. Besides nitrogen, phosphorus and potassium are the most common industrial inorganic fertilizers. There was also a renaissance of organic fertilizers, and agricultural chemists sought to improve on their yield and production costs. The field of fertilizers has remained a primary application of agricultural chemistry.

Crop Protection. As with fertilizers, humans used pesticides long before their chemical and biological qualities were understood scientifically. In the eighteenth and nineteenth centuries in Europe and North America, scientists used plant extracts as insecticides, precursors to synthetic pesticides.

Chemical pesticides were discovered at the end of the nineteenth century. The first was dinitrocresol, invented by German chemical company Bayer in 1892. Since 1934, it has also been used as herbicide.

The 1930s were considered the golden age of pesticide discovery. In 1939, Swiss chemist Paul Hermann Müller, working for the Swiss pharmaceutical and chemical company Geigy, discovered the tremendous insecticide power of DDT (dichlorodiphenyltrichloroethane). DDT was used widely around the globe, with Müller receiving the 1948 Nobel Prize in Physiology or Medicine for his discovery. However, by the 1960s, DDT's severe environmental side effects became known, particularly its role in damaging eggshells of fish-eating birds, including the American bald eagle. As consequence, DDT was banned in the United States in 1972 and in most countries thereafter. DDT has seen limited use only as indoor insecticide against mosquitoes in some developing countries.

A key challenge for agricultural chemists working in the field of crop protection has become the continued development of increasingly environmentally friendly pesticides, herbicides, fungicides, and bactericides. Since 1970, the US Environmental Protection Agency (EPA) has closely supervised the use of pesticides. Its authority was strengthened by the Federal Environmental Pesticide Control Act of 1972, amended by the Food Quality Protection Act of 1996. However, human food production has become very dependent on crop protection. By 2012, about 5.6 billion pounds of pesticides were being produced globally.

Genetically Modified Food. In the early 1980s, agricultural chemists used genetic engineering to create the first genetically modified plants. The idea was to transfer desired genetic qualities directly. In 1983, the world's first genetically modified plant was presented by researchers. It was a tobacco plant designed to have a higher resistance to antibiotics. In 1986, in the United States and France, field trials began for genetically modified tobacco plants with increased resistance to herbicides. In 1987, the Belgian company Plant Genetic Systems introduced another genetically modified tobacco plant. This one was more resistant to insects due to the introduction of genes responsible for the production of insecticide toxins in the bacterium *Bacillus thuringiensis* (Bt). Bt-modification of plant genes has become a key application since.

In the United States, the first commercially sold genetically modified plant was the Flavr Savr tomato of 1994. It was modified to have a longer shelf life after harvesting. However, the high cost of production took this tomato off the market in 1997, a rare failure of a genetically modified plant.

In 1995 and 1996, genetically modified soybeans and canola were introduced in the United States. They were resistant to the widely used herbicides based on the chemical compounds glyphosate and glufosinate. By 2011, genetically modified soybeans accounted for 93 percent of the US harvest and 77 percent of the global soybean harvest. The canola harvest was also 93 percent genetically modified in the United States but only 22 percent worldwide. This made these two crops the most widely used genetically altered food of the era.

By 2012, genetically modified food had gone through two generations of applications. Plants of the first generation were modified to be more resistant to insects, having been given the added Bt toxin, or to be more resistant to herbicides used to kill weeds competing with the crops. In addition to soybeans and canola, alfalfa, cotton (for cottonseed oil), and sugar beets were also important crops that were genetically modified in this way. In the second generation, plants were modified to increase their nutritional value and overall quality. Vitamin-enriched corn achieved an 86 percent share of the US harvest but only a 26 percent global-harvest share in 2011. The commercial introduction of beta-carotene-containing golden rice was planned for 2013. In the future, plants of the third generation could be modified to increase their utility as biofuels or to make them grow ingredients for the pharmaceutical industry.

However, since its beginning, genetically modified food has been controversial. Critics have been dubious of its safety, expressed concern about negative environmental and ecological effects, and objected to the plants' status as commercial, patented food sources. By 2012, there had been numerous lawsuits against genetically modified foods, some temporarily banning its use. Particularly in England, test fields for genetically modified plants were routinely destroyed in acts of ecologically motivated vandalism.

Yet genetically modified foods have made food less expensive to grow and increased its quality and availability throughout the world. By 2010, 10 percent of the world's cropland was planted with genetically modified plant varieties, and trends predicted further growth in the future.

Impact on Industry

Despite the importance of agricultural chemistry in ensuring food quantity and quality for the growing world population, employment of agricultural chemists in the United States is expected to decline. According to calculations by the US Bureau of Labor Statistics (BLS), from 2010 to 2020, there may be a 22.2 percent decrease in the number of chemists employed by companies involved in the manufacture of pesticides, fertilizers, and other agricultural chemical products. According to the BLS, this is because chemical companies will increasingly combine or outsource their research and development to research universities and specialized companies, as well as moving some of their work activities abroad. However, employment of agricultural and other chemists was estimated to increase by 15 percent at universities, 10 percent in professional, scientific, and technical services, and 2.5 percent in federal, state, and local government by 2020.

Government Agencies. In the United States, there are three key government agencies requiring the work of agricultural chemists. The US Department of Agriculture (USDA) traces the effects of pesticides and herbicides on the environment. The USDA is also involved in some aspects of governmental oversight and regulation of genetically modified foods, especially those fed to livestock. The USDA's Animal and Plant Health Inspection Service (APHIS) is in charge of applying biotechnology regulations. The EPA employs agricultural chemists to track the effects of pesticides on the environment and in the food chain. All newly developed pesticides, herbicides, and other agrochemicals require EPA approval. The Food and Drug Agency (FDA) ensures the safety of human food and animal feed. This includes testing genetically modified foods in FDA laboratories.

Military. Military use of herbicides to destroy enemy crops was studied during World War II in the United Kingdom (1940) and the United

States (1944), though neither country actually used herbicides in combat at the time. In 1953, British forces used a herbicide to defoliate jungles and kill enemy crops when fighting a communist insurrection in Malaysia. During the Vietnam War, from 1961 to 1971, the United States used a variety of herbicides and defoliants, the most infamous being Agent Orange. The intention was to deprive the enemy of plant cover and crops grown in areas of their control. Agent Orange was found to be contaminated by a dioxin compound, a highly toxic carcinogen. In 1977, the US Air Force destroyed all of its remaining Agent Orange. The military use of herbicides and defoliants has been prohibited by the Environmental Modification Convention since 1978.

Academic Research and Teaching. In the United States, agricultural chemists are employed as faculty in major research universities. As agricultural chemistry is an interdisciplinary science, its faculty may be housed in different departments, primarily chemistry or biology, or in specific university programs. As many corporations seek partnerships with universities, there has been an increase in corporate funding for university research in agricultural chemistry. In addition to training future agricultural chemists through graduate and postgraduate study, faculty members active in the field of agricultural science perform both basic research, as in genetics, and more targeted work, as in the development of more environmentally friendly pesticides. The scientific work of American academic agricultural chemists on pesticides, fertilizers, and genetically modified food has had worldwide implications.

Major Corporations. By 2012, two major American corporations were active in the agrochemicals business. The leader was Monsanto, followed by DuPont. There has been considerable consolidation in the agrochemical industry, where research and development are capital intensive and there are great economies of scale. For this reason, the American Chemical Society has stated that employment opportunities for agricultural chemists in the industry will contract rather than expand. However, the industrial development of genetically modified food has continued to increase, and the quest for environmentally friendly and inexpensive fertilizer and pesticides has accounted for a considerable amount of the demand for agrochemicals.

Occupation	Chemists
Employment 2010	82,200
Projected Employment 2020	85,400
Change in Number (2010–20)	3,200
Percent Change	4%

*Bureau of Labor Statistics, 2012

The internationally active Missouri-based agricultural, chemical, and biotechnological company Monsanto achieved revenues of $11.8 billion in 2011, out of which $1.7 billion was net income. Worldwide, Monsanto employed a staff of 21,400 in 2010. One pillar of Monsanto's business has been glyphosate herbicides, marketed under the brand name of Roundup. Agricultural chemists at Monsanto working under organic chemist John Franz discovered glyphosate in 1970, and the company patented it as an herbicide. Even though Monsanto's US patent expired in 2000, Roundup products still accounted for about one-tenth of the company's revenues as late as 2009, based on the strength of its brand name. Since the 1990s, Monsanto has become the world's leading manufacturer of genetically modified crop seeds. One key modification gave Monsanto crops stronger resistance against glyphosate, so that its own herbicide could be used to kill weeds next to resistant crops.

As the world's third-largest chemical company, DuPont, headquartered in Wilmington, Delaware, has become very active in the production of genetically modified crop seeds that its scientists have developed. In 2008, DuPont held a global market share of 14 percent of all genetically modified crop seeds. In 2010, DuPont introduced a commercial product called Plenish soybeans, which have been genetically modified for high oleic-acid content as base for soybean oil.

Internationally, Germany's Bayer CropScience is the world's leading agrochemical corporation. In 2010, the company employed 20,700 people and earned revenues of €6.8 billion (then about $8.5 billion). In 2012, indicating some problems with the issue of genetically modified seeds and plants, Bayer CropScience paid a global $750 million settlement to rice farmers after the USDA charged that the company's genetically modified rice had contaminated regular American rice in Arkansas in 2006.

Social Context and Future Prospects

Understanding the chemistry of plant nutrition and crop protection has led to synthetic production of fertilizers. Together with the development of a vast array of chemically based crop-protection products, this triggered environmental movements in the twentieth century that vastly increased the amount of food produced.

Occupation	Agricultural and food scientists
Employment 2010	33,500
Projected Employment 2020	37,000
Change in Number (2010–20)	3,500
Percent Change	10%

Bureau of Labor Statistics, 2012

There has been widespread desire to make both of these applications of agricultural chemistry more and more environmentally friendly. This could be done by increasing their efficiency and accuracy. Despite a strong and growing social interest in organic farming, particularly in more developed countries, it became clear that the world's food needs could not be satisfied without the products of agricultural chemistry.

One of the most controversial applications of agricultural chemistry since the 1990s has been genetically modified food and the development of genetically modified crop seeds. Proponents have embraced the creation of crops that are more resistant to pests or allow the increased deployment of herbicides because

Occupation	Agricultural and food science technicians
Employment 2010	21,300
Projected Employment 2020	22,800
Change in Number (2010–20)	1,500
Percent Change	7%

Bureau of Labor Statistics, 2012

the crops themselves are immune to them. The scientific endeavor to increase the nutritional value of food through genetic modification has also been lauded and credited as an advance for humanity. However, there has been very strong opposition to this product of agricultural chemistry. Opponents cite a variety of reasons, including environmental, ecological, and anticapitalist arguments. There is some societal fear of genetically modified foods, even though agriculture has, since its beginning, sought to optimize its crops through human interventions such as selective breeding and hybridization. Overall, genetically modified food is the field of biotechnology in which most future development is expected. Eventually, agricultural chemistry may also enter the field of genetically modifying farm animals for commercial purposes, a step not yet taken as of 2012.

Further Reading

Deguine, Jean-Philippe, Pierre Ferron, and Derek Russell. *Crop Protection: From Agrochemistry to Agroecology.* Enfield: Science, 2009. Print. Proposes a supposedly more environmentally friendly alternative to agricultural chemistry, which the authors term *agroecology.*

Ferry, Natalie, ed. *Environmental Impact of Genetically Modified Foods.* Wallingford: CABI, 2009. Print. Comprehensive collection of balanced essays that present and probe varied risks and opportunities of genetically modified food.

Fukuda-Parr, Sakiko, ed. *The Gene Revolution: GM Crops and Uneven Development.* London: Earthscan, 2007. Print. Overview of how genetically modified foods affect agricultural development in a variety of sampled countries.

Haneklaus, Silvia, ed. *Recent Advances in Agricultural Chemistry.* Brunswick: Bundesforschungsanstalt fuer Landwirtschaft, 2005. Print. Collection of essays, about half in English, on topics ranging from precision farming to new tools such as yield maps of combinable crops.

Richmond, Nathan. "Agricultural Biotechnology: Public Acceptance, Regulation and International Consensus." *Chemistry for the Protection of the Environment 4.* Ed. Robert Mournighan. New York: Springer, 2005. 111–22. Print. Examines how public opinion in the European Union was shaped on the issue, with the resulting suspicion leading to conflict with the US position and influencing international attitudes toward genetically modified foods.

About the Author: R. C. Lutz, PhD, is an instructor of business English at an international consulting company. His students include professionals in science and engineering, particularly in the chemical, process, oil and gas, and petrochemical industries. He is the author of survey and encyclopedia articles in the applied sciences, among other subjects. After obtaining his MA and PhD in English literature from the University of California, Santa Barbara, he worked for a few years in academia before moving to a consulting company. He has worked across the globe in the United States, Oman, the United Arab Emirates, Turkey, and Romania.

Agricultural Chemist ✑ *

Earnings (Yearly Median): $58,450 (Bureau of Labor Statistics, 2012)

Employment and Outlook: Average growth (Bureau of Labor Statistics, 2012)

O*NET-SOC Code: 19-2031.00

Related Career Cluster(s): Agriculture, Food & Natural Resources; Government & Public Administration; Health Science; Manufacturing

Scope of Work

Agricultural chemists work to ensure and improve the quantity and quality of crops for human food and animal feed. A classic field of application within agricultural chemistry is the development of efficient fertilizers that promote plant growth, have as few negative side effects on the environment as possible, and are inexpensive to manufacture. A second key application is crop protection, in which agricultural chemists help develop and improve pesticides, herbicides, fungicides, and other chemical agents to support crop production. Agricultural chemists are also employed by government agencies to ensure food safety and track pesticides. They also work as scientists in academic settings.

---

* Designated as a Green Occupation by the US Department of Labor, Employment and Training Administration.

The most recent application sees agricultural chemists working to genetically modify food in order to make plants more resistant, provide increased yield, and add nutritional elements.

Education and Coursework

In high school, a student should take classes in chemistry, as well as in biology and physics. Good computer skills and proficiency in English are also necessary. Students should spend time in a chemistry laboratory and gain experience performing experiments. Interest in the genetic modification of food and other issues affecting agriculture could serve as motivation to pursue a career in the field.

The minimum educational requirement to work as an agricultural scientist is a four-year college degree. When choosing a college, students should look for an institution with a strong chemistry department and programs related to agricultural chemistry. Typically, students will pursue bachelor of science degrees in chemistry or biochemistry. However, as agricultural chemistry is an interdisciplinary science, students should take courses in biology, physics, water and soil chemistry, and physiology as well. Exposure to instruction in environmental and earth sciences is also useful.

General-education classes in computer science and English are beneficial for aspiring agricultural chemists. Many universities and colleges offer students the opportunity for undergraduate research, and a student should try to pursue this research with a faculty mentor who is active in agricultural chemistry. Work in laboratories or test fields offered by an agricultural and food science program is an excellent way to learn about practical applications of agricultural chemistry. An internship with an agricultural chemical company, or at a government agency employing agricultural chemists, would also be a wise choice.

For any type of advanced or research work as agricultural chemist, a master of science degree and a PhD are essential. Over two-thirds of US chemists have a PhD, as reported by the American Chemical Society for 2010. Among agricultural chemists, that percentage may be even higher. Students should choose a university with a good graduate program in chemistry and faculty involved in agricultural chemistry.

> ## Transferable Skills
>
> - Communication Skills – Reporting information
> - Interpersonal/Social Skills – Working as a member of a team (SCANS Workplace Competency – Interpersonal)
> - Research & Planning Skills – Creating ideas
> - Research & Planning Skills – Analyzing information
> - Organization & Management Skills – Managing people/ groups (SCANS Workplace Competency – Resources)
> - Organization & Management Skills – Organizing information or materials

After deciding on a field of agricultural chemistry to specialize in, the focus of postgraduate study should be aligned accordingly. The interdisciplinary nature of agricultural chemistry means students have a large degree of freedom; however, they also face the challenge of choosing a personal path of postgraduate courses and research, since there are many acceptable entry points to the field of agricultural chemistry. Fellowships and internships with agrochemical companies or government agencies can also be helpful opportunities to glean more experience and make networking connections during postgraduate work.

Career Enhancement and Training

Postdoctoral work in the form of research fellowships is recommended for agricultural chemists who want to do research and teaching in academia, but it is not required.

Membership in the American Chemical Society (ACS) is highly recommended for agricultural chemists. Even while working toward a master's degree or PhD, aspiring agricultural chemists have the opportunity to present their research at academic conferences. This is one of the best ways to network and learn more about career options and employment opportunities.

Because agricultural chemistry is a fast-moving science, particularly as regards genetically modified foods, an agricultural chemist is expected to keep abreast of the latest developments in the field. This can be done by subscribing to journals in the field and attending conferences. Agricultural chemists employed in the industry will have to observe the ethics concerning proprietary company knowledge in their interactions with fellow scientists and the general public. Those employed by government agencies will have to observe the rules of public service. In academia, a lifelong commitment to research and teaching is an absolute must, and publication is necessary for gaining tenure and professional advancement.

Daily Tasks and Technology

Daily tasks differ greatly, depending on whether an agricultural chemist works in industry, for a government agency, in academia, or as self-employed consultant. In industrial applications, an agricultural chemist is part of the business effort to develop a marketable product or to improve and enhance existing products. Usually, agricultural chemists work in teams involving scientists from other disciplines and technicians. The more senior and experienced scientist will lead the team, and there is an industry expectation that research will ultimately be of economic value to the company. The work location is typically a laboratory or some other open environment for experiments. The more advanced the position is, the more time will have to be spent on management issues, including presentations at company meetings.

In a government position, agricultural chemists typically share time between laboratory work and desk work. The former involves analyzing chemicals used in the agrochemical industry and soil samples from places where agrochemicals have been used. Working for the government, agricultural chemists present their analytical findings in internal and external reports. They carry responsibility for the safety of food and the environment and are expected to follow the highest ethical standards.

In academia, agricultural chemists perform laboratory and field research while maintaining a teaching schedule. An increasingly important task in this field is cooperation with academic institutions' industry partners. Writing grant applications is a necessity. And finally, an agricultural chemist contracting as an independent consultant typically works on a project basis for a variety of industrial clients.

The well-stocked laboratory of an agricultural chemist and research team employs the latest chemical measuring and analytical tools, ranging from Erlenmeyer flasks to centrifuges and vacuum pumps. The technologies for research and development include laser, spectrometer, and titration technology. There is a vast array of analytical and scientific software developed for applications in chemical analysis, in addition to database software and office and graphics software for presenting research results. Working with genetically modified foods also involves microtechnology in the case of syringe gene transfers, as well as nanotechnology in the use of gene guns.

Earnings and Employment Outlook

In spite of consolidation in the agricultural chemistry industry and a shift of jobs from the industry to academia in research partnerships, the estimated 10 percent job growth for agricultural chemists from 2010 to 2020 is about as fast as the average expected job growth in the United States. Traditionally, industry jobs have been the top payers, closely followed by government positions, with many academic employees averaging about only two-thirds of the industrial median wages. In addition, with federal and state budget cuts, there may be less funding for university research, including less money to hire academic personnel.

In spite of consolidation in the agricultural chemistry industry and a shift of jobs from the industry to academia in research partnerships, the estimated 10 percent job growth for agricultural chemists from 2010 to 2020 is about as fast as the average expected job growth in the United States.

For agricultural chemists beginning work in the industry in 2012, the ACS estimates an initial salary in the mid-$70,000s for a holder of a PhD, in the mid-$40,000s for agricultural chemists with a master's degree, and in the mid-$30,000s for holders of a BS. The ACS cautions that government and academic positions usually pay less, reporting a salary of $44,000 at a government GS-9 level and $47,100 at a GS-11-level position. In academia, median salaries for assistant professors were found to range from approximately $51,200 to $64,500, depending on the year, the location, the number of paid months in the annual contract, and whether an institution grants PhDs or not. It is not believed to be likely that these starting salaries will increase significantly over the next years.

Related Occupations

- **Agricultural and Food Scientists:** Agricultural and Food Scientists study all areas of agriculture and work to ensure overall food safety. Their occupation is built on interdisciplinary study leading to various specializations in their field.

- **Biochemists:** Biochemists need a PhD to qualify for their profession, which combines research of the chemical and biological principles of life.

- **Chemical Engineers:** Chemical Engineers utilize chemistry, biology, and physics to design processes for the effective industrial production of a variety of end products, which may range from food to fuel and from pharmaceuticals to specialty chemicals.

- **Environmental Scientists:** Environmental Scientists work to protect the environment from the vantage point of a particular skill in a natural science.

- **Natural Sciences Managers:** Natural Sciences Managers supervise the performance of other scientists, often administrating and coordinating large research-and-development projects. Many of them have backgrounds as practicing scientists.

Future Applications

As the human population grows and demands higher quantity and quality of food production, there is a natural demand for the work of agricultural chemists ensuring food production, protection, and improvement. There is a global desire for even more effective fertilizers to be developed to increase crop growth and yields and to minimize any negative environmental effects of fertilizers. Similarly, as insects, bacteria, and viruses become immune to one generation of pesticides, there is a constant demand for new crop protection solutions developed by agricultural chemists. Even though it has been controversial, the potential development of genetically modified plants, and perhaps even animals, provides a cutting-edge research field for agricultural chemists.

The challenge, however, is where the work of agricultural chemists will be performed. The US agricultural chemistry industry has consolidated considerably, which means there are only a limited number of employment positions. Some alternative job opportunities will emerge through partnerships between US universities and agrochemical corporations. Another growth area comes from smaller, specialized research companies providing professional, scientific, and technical services to large corporations. Thanks to the job openings estimated at these enterprises, the Bureau of Labor Statistics anticipates a job growth of around 10 percent from 2010 to 2020 for agricultural chemists.

R. C. Lutz, PhD

More Information

American Chemical Society
1155 Sixteenth Street NW
Washington, DC 20036
portal.acs.org

Biotechnology Industry Organization
1625 K Street NW, Suite 1100
Washington, DC 20006-1621
www.bio.org

CropLife America
1156 Fifteenth Street NW, Suite 400
Washington, DC 20005
www.croplifeamerica.org

United States Environmental Protection Agency
Ariel Rios Building
1200 Pennsylvania Avenue NW
Washington, DC 20460
www.epa.gov

Atmospheric Chemistry

FIELDS OF STUDY

Chemistry; physics; mathematics; geoscience; environmental science; meteorology; aeronomy; climatology; oceanography; fluid mechanics; fluid dynamics; inorganic chemistry; thermodynamics; atmospheric physics; volcanology; physical chemistry; hydrology; climate dynamics.

DEFINITION

Atmospheric chemistry is a subfield of atmospheric science that examines the chemical development and composition of atmospheric systems, that is, the layers of gases, liquids, and solids that surround the earth and other planets. Atmospheric chemists study how atmospheres form around developing planets and change over geological time, as well as the relationship between the biota (organisms living on a planet) and the atmosphere. Atmospheric chemists also provide important data to explain phenomena such as climate change, weather patterns, and seasonal temperature variation. These scientists work to develop solutions to various atmospheric problems, including pollution and ozone depletion.

Basic Principles

Key discoveries in the eighteenth and nineteenth centuries set the stage for the development of atmospheric science as a new branch of scientific inquiry, combining elements of chemistry, geology, and physics. The discovery of the atmospheric gas ozone by German chemist Christian Schönbein, often called the father of atmospheric chemistry, in 1839 and the discovery of the relationship between atmospheric gases and surface temperature by Swedish chemist Svante Arrhenius in 1896 were among the crucial discoveries that helped to stimulate interest in atmospheric composition.

During the twentieth century, enhancements in technology, including satellite measurements and computer modeling, allowed scientists to develop a more detailed understanding of atmospheric properties and processes. Gradually, atmospheric science became a branch of earth science or environmental science, the effort to develop a thorough scientific understanding of the earth's environment and evolution.

By the twenty-first century, atmospheric science was divided into a number of subfields, including atmospheric physics, climatology, aeronomy, and atmospheric chemistry. Atmospheric chemistry is itself a multidisciplinary field, drawing upon contributions from meteorology, inorganic chemistry, organic chemistry, environmental chemistry, oceanography, and volcanology. Unlike climatology, which studies aspects of the atmosphere involved in climate formation, or atmospheric physics, which studies the physical modeling of the atmosphere, atmospheric chemistry focuses on chemical reactions within the atmosphere. It also studies how the chemical properties of atmospheric gases, liquids, and solids contribute to atmospheric phenomena like weather and climate.

Core Concepts

In Situ Measurement Techniques. Atmospheric chemists use in situ (in position) measurements to evaluate the gas, liquid, and solid composition of the atmosphere within a localized area. In situ measurements can be collected by devices mounted to balloons or aircraft to sample atmospheric composition at high altitudes, or they can be taken at ground level. In situ measurements are limited in spatial dimensions, but they allow for the most accurate and detailed analyses of atmospheric properties. Samples collected in situ can be either analyzed immediately by the collecting device or trapped and carried to a laboratory for further analysis.

Remote Atmospheric Measurements. Remote-sample methods involve measuring gas compositions in areas relatively distant from the measuring apparatus. Atmospheric chemists can use equipment in balloons, aircraft, satellites, specialized long-distance spectrometers, and also in spacecraft to measure gas composition in distant areas. Remote measurements are necessary for studying the gas composition of other planets. They are also widely used to gain a better understanding of large-scale atmospheric patterns over the earth. Unlike in situ techniques, which are generally used to measure gas concentrations, remote-measurement techniques are more useful for modeling system-wide movements of gases. For instance, atmospheric scientists use radar measurements to track the movement of clouds and water vapor through the atmosphere, thereby producing a three-dimensional model of atmospheric movement.

Gas Chromatography. Chromatography is a common technique used in chemical analysis that involves determining the chemical composition of a sample by dissolving mixtures of gases within a liquid medium. The liquid is then passed through a device containing another liquid of known properties; this causes the various compounds within the mixture to separate at different intervals. The various constituents can then be measured, providing data on the composition of the original gas mixture. Chromatography is one of the most basic techniques used in atmospheric chemistry to determine the mixture of elements in atmospheric gases.

Mass Spectrometry. Mass spectrometry is a method used for measuring the atomic or molecular composition of a mixture or sample of material. The basic process entails converting the atoms contained within the mixture or sample to ions, or charged atoms, by bombarding the material with a stream of negatively charged electrons. The resulting ions, because of their charge, will interact with electrical fields. A spectrometer is used to separate ions according to their mass and charge; the separated ions are next filtered to a detector, where the relative composition of each type of ion is recorded. This data then allows chemists to reconstruct the chemical and atomic structures of the sample material. Spectrometry can be used to analyze gas, liquid, and solid samples of material.

Sources and Sinks. Atmospheric chemists investigate the life cycles of atmospheric components, including how these substances are produced and absorbed within the environment. A chemical source is a process or feature that produces atmospheric material. For instance, the metabolic processes within organisms produce methane, carbon dioxide, and water vapor, which then become part of the earth's atmosphere. A sink is a process that removes a particular type of material from the atmosphere, often to be stored in another environmental compartment. Plants and certain types of bacteria, for instance, absorb atmospheric carbon dioxide during photosynthesis, which they use to fuel growth and reproduction. These organisms therefore represent a carbon sink within the environment. They also produce oxygen as a byproduct, which is incorporated into the atmosphere.

Greenhouse Effect. The greenhouse effect is a model used to explain how the buildup of gases within the atmosphere interacts with solar radiation to influence the climate and surface temperature of a planet. Greenhouse gases such as carbon dioxide, methane, and ozone trap solar energy and heat reflected from the earth's surface, preventing this energy from escaping into space. Increases in greenhouse-gas levels in the atmosphere translate directly into increased surface temperatures; this plays a major role in determining climate variation.

Ozone Cycle. The ozone cycle is the process by which ozone is created from atmospheric oxygen and decomposes to release oxygen back into the atmosphere. Ozone is an unstable molecule containing three atoms of oxygen bonded together. Ultraviolet light originating from the sun impacts oxygen (O_2) molecules within the upper layers of the atmosphere, causing them to split into individual atoms of oxygen. These individual oxygen atoms then bond with molecules of oxygen, forming a molecule of ozone (O_3). The process also works in reverse, as ultraviolet radiation causes ozone to split into its constituent parts, yielding a molecule of oxygen and a free oxygen atom. By absorbing ultraviolet radiation and converting it to chemical energy through the ozone cycle, the ozone layer protects life on earth from the harmful effects of overexposure to solar radiation.

Chemical Transport Models (CTM). A chemical transport model (CTM) is a theoretical model used to emulate the creation and transport of specific species of atoms and molecules within a chemical system. Most CTMs are complex computer-aided systems that combine data taken from measurements of atmospheric concentrations with equations modeling known chemical reactions that occur in the system. There are a variety of CTM systems used to model the origin

Interesting Facts about Atmospheric Chemistry

- Approximately 78 percent of the atmosphere is made up of nitrogen, with oxygen accounting for nearly 21 percent. The remaining gases—including carbon dioxide, methane, and ozone—together make up only 1 percent of the air.

- Lidar (Light Detection and Ranging) uses infrared light to detect the position and movement of an object. NASA's Lidar Atmospheric Sensing Experiment (LASE) uses lidar to track water vapor as it travels through the atmosphere. Lidar is also used by police to measure automobile speed.

- American scientist John Jeffries conducted some of the first atmospheric experiments using a hydrogen-powered balloon. In 1784, he measured atmospheric humidity, water vapor, and temperature. Research balloons remained a cornerstone of atmospheric science into the twenty-first century. Modern versions are equipped with high-tech spectrographic or laser-aided measurement equipment.

- The MOPITT (Measurements of Pollution in the Troposphere) system is one of the world's most advanced tools for detecting pollution in the atmosphere. The machine was launched into orbit in 1999 aboard NASA's *Terra* satellite and uses spectroscopy to measure carbon dioxide levels. As the satellite orbits the earth, scientists are able to develop a global image of gas distribution.

- Chemiluminescence, the production of light from a chemical reaction, can be used to detect the presence of different gases in the atmosphere. For instance, nitric oxide (NO) reacts with ozone (O_3) to produce red light, and this reaction can be used to examine samples of gas for traces of ozone.

- Exobiologists use atmospheric chemistry to search for traces of life on other planets. Through respiration and photosynthesis, organisms alter the chemical composition of a planet's atmosphere. Using specialized scanning equipment, exobiologists examine gases on distant planets to search for characteristic signs of chemical fluctuations that may be indicative of life.

and transport of individual types of atmospheric materials. Various CTM systems, developed by both governmental and university-based research groups, measure the movement of atmospheric substances including carbon dioxide, methane, water vapor, and nitrous oxide.

The National Center for Atmospheric Research (NCAR) cooperated with researchers from a number of US universities to create a CTM known as MOZART (Model for Ozone and Related Chemical Tracers), which models various ozone concentrations within the atmosphere and can be used to create simulations of atmospheric conditions given differing concentrations of ozone. MOZART has been used in critical studies examining the role of ozone in climate change and temperature variation. Another CTM, called CAMx (Comprehensive Air Quality Model with Extensions), is an open-source system, allowing computer programmers and other specialists to participate in enriching the design of the system. The CAMx program primarily models air quality within a targeted modeling area.

Applications Past and Present

Atmospheric and Climate Modeling. Atmospheric chemistry is essential to climate modeling, which is the effort to create detailed computer models that predict the development of climate patterns. General circulation models (GCMs) use complex data involving chemical and physical properties and thermodynamic principles to model circulation patterns within either the atmosphere or the oceanic systems. These models can be combined into atmosphere-ocean general circulation models (AOGCMs), which attempt to emulate the overall movement of materials and energy between both the ocean and the atmosphere.

Atmospheric and climate modeling is used to predict the future development of the earth's climate given current conditions and likely future changes to composition, temperature, and other factors. To complete this task, scientists collect detailed data regarding atmospheric composition and then link different atmospheric states with corresponding conditions elsewhere in the environment. For instance, changes in atmospheric oxygen composition may be linked to reductions in tree cover in certain areas. These changes in oxygen levels will affect levels of carbon dioxide and ozone, thereby leading to alterations of temperature and climatic patterns on a planet-wide scale.

By creating detailed models that represent the state of the earth's current atmosphere, atmospheric chemists can perform experiments to study how atmospheric composition and chemical behavior would change under conditions involving increases in greenhouse gases, reduction or increases in ambient temperature, and a variety of other theoretical scenarios that might have global repercussions.

Climate Change. Climate-change science is an interdisciplinary effort to predict and understand the way that the earth's climate will change, given both current conditions and expected future influences on climate dynamics. One of the major debates of the twentieth and twenty-first centuries concerns whether the earth is currently experiencing a period of global warming due to the accumulation of pollutants and greenhouse gases in the atmosphere, and whether this trend is related to human activities, such as the burning of fossil fuels.

Atmospheric chemists use both in situ and remote detection and sampling equipment to measure atmospheric material around the globe and to compare this information with temperature measurements taken at the same locations. In this way, atmospheric chemists can make correlations between concentrations of atmospheric materials and relative temperatures both in the atmosphere and on the earth's surface. This data can then be used to test theories about future climate development and to predict how increases or reductions in atmospheric substances, like carbon dioxide and methane, will affect future climate development.

The Intergovernmental Panel on Climate Change (IPCC) is a group of scientists and researchers from more than sixty countries that conduct research on climate change and publish annual reports on the state of the world's climate. Atmospheric chemistry is a major part of IPCC research, because greenhouse gas concentrations are one of the most important factors precipitating climate change. Atmospheric chemists working for the IPCC were responsible for research indicating that, in addition to the direct release of greenhouse gases, chemical reactions in the atmosphere produce additional greenhouse gases that can contribute to the building greenhouse effect.

Ozone Depletion. The stratosphere is a layer of atmospheric gases located between ten to thirty miles from the earth's surface. The upper stratosphere contains the ozone layer, which is a thin membrane of ozone gas created by the interaction between solar radiation and atmospheric oxygen. In the 1980s, atmospheric scientists realized that ozone levels were dropping and that a hole had formed in the ozone layer over Antarctica. In 1987, the Antarctic Airborne Ozone Experiment sampled the atmosphere in the stratosphere and found compelling evidence that the ozone hole was related to the release of chlorine and bromine through human activity. The use of aerosol sprays and refrigerants containing chlorofluorocarbons (CFCs) was the key factor, as these compounds release gases that rise into the stratosphere and catalyze reactions that destroy the ozone layer.

Over the next decade, the use of CFCs and other ozone-destroying bromine and chlorine aerosols were restricted and banned in many countries in an effort to stem the destruction of the ozone layer. Without sufficient ozone coverage, increased solar radiation impacting the planet would have deleterious effects on life and would cause temperatures to rise. The loss of ozone over Antarctica could eventually lead to the melting of polar ice, which would destroy the ecosystem of Antarctica and flood other continents as ocean levels rise. Atmospheric chemists monitor ozone levels and sample atmospheric gases to test for the presence of ozone-destroying pollutants.

Acidic Deposition. Acidic deposition, also known as acid rain, occurs when atmospheric chemical reactions result in an increase of acidic chemicals within atmospheric discharge, such as rain, fog, and snow. Acid rain results from the buildup of gases like sulfur dioxide (SO_2) and nitrogen oxides, which are produced by a variety of industrial processes, including the burning of fossil fuels. These compounds react with water, carbon dioxide, and oxygen in the atmosphere. Fueled by energy from solar radiation, the reactions create sulfuric acid (H_2SO_4) and nitric acid (HNO_3), which fall to the earth along with normal precipitation. Acidic precipitation can damage trees and root systems, kill fish and other aquatic organisms, and poison water supplies. Large-scale environmental damage has been recorded in areas where pollution is severe.

Atmospheric chemists study the factors that lead to the development of acidic deposition and monitor levels of chemicals in the atmosphere to predict potential incidents of acid rain. In addition, experimental chemistry is involved in developing methods used to purify the atmosphere and to reduce levels of pollutants that cause acid deposition. Research in atmospheric chemistry has also be used in creating state and federal regulations to control pollutants released from industrial processes in an effort to reduce the severity and frequency of acid rain incidents.

Public Safety. Atmospheric chemistry is used to monitor conditions in the atmosphere that pose a risk to public safety. The air quality index (AQI) used by the Environmental Protection Agency (EPA) to monitor air quality in the United States was developed with the aid of atmospheric chemistry research. The AQI is set by measuring levels of gases such as carbon dioxide, methane, sulfur dioxide, ozone, and nitrogen dioxide, based on previously measured concentrations known to cause medical issues among the populace. Federal, state, and private organizations make daily or hourly AQI measurements available to the public in an effort to help the populace avoid dangerous atmospheric conditions.

The 1990 amendments to the United States' Clean Air Act states that the EPA must reevaluate the AQI every five years to adjust for new discoveries and research regarding air purity and the dangers of pollutants. The creation of AQI guidelines and changes to the AQI system are largely due to research conducted by atmospheric chemists. When pollutant levels rise above a certain level, federal and state regulations require certain measures to be taken, including the broadcasting of health advisories and the shutting down of traffic and industrial processes to reduce known sources of pollutants.

Paleoclimatology. As atmospheric materials cycle through the earth's systems, they leave traces of molecules in the terrestrial and oceanic environments. Atmospheric chemists can investigate the remnants of organisms and physical structures from the distant past. They can then use chemical signatures and concentrations of certain atoms fixed within these ancient materials to reconstruct a model of past climate systems. Information about past climatological systems can also be used to understand current climate-change patterns and the potential effects of changing atmospheric conditions.

In ice cores taken from deep within permanent glaciers, chemists have found pockets of atmospheric gases that were trapped when the liquid water became frozen in the distant past. Paleoclimatologists use chemical analyses of these gases to reconstruct the composition of the atmosphere during the period. In addition, different atmospheric conditions lead to the deposition of different types of chemical residues that can be incorporated into fossils. The proportions of certain types of isotopes and characteristic chemicals therefore provide clues to the nature of the earth's ancient atmosphere.

Impact on Industry

The fastest-growing facet of atmospheric chemistry research is in the field of climate-change science, including studies regarding anthropogenic (human-caused) changes in atmospheric properties. A majority of new jobs in atmospheric chemistry, atmospheric physics, and other facets of the environmental sciences are expected to be created in the fields of climate-change research and environmental protection. The goal is to prevent ecological damage from industrial and commercial development. This facet of the industry is also responsible for the development of a variety of new technological innovations that help to shape the field.

In 2010, the United States was the global leader in research into environmental and alternative technology, with Germany, the United Kingdom, Japan, and the Netherlands also ranking prominently in this branch of scientific development. According to the US Bureau of Labor Statistics (BLS), approximately 9,500 individuals were employed as atmospheric scientists or meteorologists in 2010, and the industry was growing at a rate commensurate with the national average, with the addition of one thousand jobs expected in the decade between 2010 and 2020.

Academic Research and Teaching. In 2010, approximately 15 percent of atmospheric scientists worked in university research and teaching positions. The number of university positions available is limited in comparison to the number of annual graduates in the atmospheric sciences, which is expected to increase competition for university positions in subsequent years.

University research programs are responsible for a wide variety of innovative developments in the field, including the development of atmospheric modeling programs. For instance, the Atmospheric Chemistry

Occupation	Atmospheric and space scientists
Employment 2010	9,500
Projected Employment 2020	10,500
Change in Number (2010–20)	1,000
Percent Change	11%

Bureau of Labor Statistics, 2012

Group at Stanford University conducts modeling research of aerosols and pollutants from human sources, attempting to learn how these materials affect atmospheric change. Similarly, the Massachusetts Institute of Technology (MIT) maintains research programs that investigate anthropogenic climate change and the way that chemical pollutants are transported within the lowest level of the earth's atmosphere.

Government Agencies. Since 2010, government agencies have provided more than 36 percent of employment opportunities to atmospheric scientists. The National Oceanic and Atmospheric Administration (NOAA) is the federal government's largest employer of atmospheric scientists, most of whom are meteorologists working at one of the organization's fifteen hundred weather stations around the country. The NOAA also supports a variety of research programs covering atmospheric modeling, pollution control, and climate change research.

The National Aeronautics and Space Administration's (NASA) Goddard Institute for Space Studies (GISS) employs hundreds of atmospheric chemists and physicists involved in the creation and operation of monitoring and measurement systems to gain a better understanding of global atmospheric development. NASA is one of the nation's foremost leaders in climate-change research and has developed a variety of technological advances in atmospheric modeling and measurement techniques. NASA also utilizes atmospheric chemistry in studies of extraterrestrial atmospheres, analyzing data from long-range spectroscopy telescopes and satellite imagery to determine atmospheric conditions on other planets.

Military. Both the US Department of Defense and the US Armed Forces employ atmospheric scientists to help monitor weather patterns. Most of the atmospheric scientists employed directly by the military are meteorologists. However, a smaller number of atmospheric chemists and physicists may be hired for the development of new military technology, including more precise measurement techniques for predicting developing weather patterns. In some cases, military investors may support pollution research and other facets of theoretical chemistry programs in an effort to develop new technology.

Private Industry Research and Technology. Privately owned corporations involved in research and technical services account for more than 15 percent of employment opportunities in the atmospheric sciences. Atmospheric chemistry and physics are important in the development of environmentally friendly technology, and many atmospheric chemists have found employment working on research that is used to develop commercial technology. The automotive industry, for instance, occasionally funds atmospheric-science studies in its efforts to monitor automotive emissions and pollutants and to develop new fuel and exhaust systems.

Social Context and Future Prospects

Atmospheric chemistry has frequently been at the forefront of environmental research. The field was essential for efforts to address ozone depletion and other atmospheric-pollution issues in the 1980s and 1990s, leading to government bans on a variety of substances known to cause atmospheric damage. In the twenty-first century, atmospheric chemistry and physics research has been playing a major role in the debate over climate change.

One of the most controversial issues in the global-warming debate concerns the degree to which current climate-change patterns are related to anthropogenic factors. This debate has numerous consequences for the future of governmental and industrial regulations and will have a consequent impact on national and international economic prospects. For this reason, atmospheric chemistry research is important in determining the degree to which greenhouse-gas emissions, climate change, and warming or cooling trends are related to human industry.

Occupation	Chemists
Employment 2010	82,200
Projected Employment 2020	85,400
Change in Number (2010–20)	3,200
Percent Change	4%

Bureau of Labor Statistics, 2012

In addition, the potential for new legislative and regulatory measures to reduce industrial pollution has created opportunities for atmospheric scientists, with numerous corporations seeking to market environmentally friendly products in the future. As the petroleum industry faces reductions in supply and profitability, atmospheric scientists will likely have increasing opportunities for employment in the automotive and energy industries, helping to design the next generation of technology to meet evolving standards in pollution control.

Further Reading

Dessler, Andrew E., and Edward A. Parson. *The Science and Politics of Global Climate Change: A Guide to the Debate*. New York: Cambridge UP, 2010. Print. Introduction to the issue of climate change, including atmospheric chemistry and other atmospheric properties research. Also discusses the potential future of research in the area of climate change.

Frederick, John E. *Principles of Atmospheric Science*. Sudbury: Jones, 2008. Print. Introductory text describing the various fields of atmospheric sciences, including atmospheric chemistry, atmospheric physics, and climatology. Describes techniques and research methods utilized in modern climate and atmospheric research.

Hoffmann, Matthew J. *Ozone Depletion and Climate Change: Constructing a Global Response*. New York: State U of New York P, 2005. Print. Detailed introduction to ozone depletion and various methods used to combat ozone-destroying pollutants in the atmosphere. Contains a historical review of ozone research and modern techniques to study ozone change in the twenty-first century.

Jacob, Daniel B. *Introduction to Atmospheric Chemistry*. Princeton: Princeton UP, 1999. Print. Comprehensive introduction to atmospheric chemistry. Provides detailed information on the essential technologies, techniques, and discoveries within the field, with overviews of environmental issues investigated through atmospheric chemistry research.

NASA GISS: NASA Goddard Institute for Space Studies. Natl. Aeronautics and Space Admin., n.d. Web. 21 Aug. 2012. Describes a variety of current research programs in the environmental sciences, physics, and atmospheric chemistry. Also contains descriptions of using atmospheric chemistry in the study of climate change and global warming.

NOAA: National Oceanic and Atmospheric Administration. US Dept. of Commerce, n.d. Web. 21 Aug. 2012. Contains information on a number of research projects investigating atmospheric properties in monitoring weather, pollution, and environmental hazards. Also contains information about research programs supported through the federal funding of NOAA.

About the Author: Micah L. Issitt, BS, is a professional freelance writer and journalist who specializes in the life sciences and sociology. He has written numerous articles covering the environmental sciences and the history of environmental science in the United States.

Atmospheric Chemist 🍃

Earnings (Yearly Median): $87,780 (Bureau of Labor Statistics, 2012)

Employment and Outlook: Average growth (Bureau of Labor Statistics, 2012)

O*NET-SOC Code: 19-2021.00

Related Career Clusters: Government & Public Administration; Health Science; Agriculture, Food & Natural Resources

Scope of Work

The work of atmospheric chemists ranges from detecting ozone levels and greenhouse gases to monitoring air-pollution levels in cities. It also includes studying acid rain or determining the chemistry of the atmospheres of other planets in order to learn about the formation of the galaxy.

Atmospheric chemistry can intersect with many other disciplines. For instance, atmospheric chemists sometimes work with soil scientists, ecologists, geologists, oceanographers, or hydrologists to determine how the atmosphere interacts with these other planetary elements.

Outside of research, atmospheric chemists can work in a policy-oriented role, advising the government on strategies to reduce pollution. They can also advise industry to change production methods, as they did in the 1990s with the elimination of ozone-destroying chlorofluorocarbons (CFCs) in aerosols.

Education and Coursework

Work in atmospheric chemistry requires a minimum of a bachelor's degree. Research-oriented careers will require a master's degree or PhD.

Atmospheric chemistry is an interdisciplinary field. With that in mind, it is important to build a strong and varied science foundation in high school. In addition to chemistry, physics, and advanced mathematics (including calculus), statistics and computer science will be invaluable for college-level studies. English and writing courses are also important because some applications of atmospheric chemistry include policy making or publishing research papers. Extracurricular activities that involve laboratory or field work provide hands-on experience and make for a stronger college application. Internship opportunities exist for precollege students, such as the National Oceanic and Atmospheric Administration (NOAA) student internship program. Such opportunities may also exist at nearby universities.

While some institutions offer undergraduate degrees in atmospheric science, it is more common to find programs in basic chemistry. A typical undergraduate course of study in chemistry includes introductory and advanced classes in inorganic and organic chemistry, biochemistry, physical chemistry, thermodynamics, and kinetics. Supplementary courses in physics, math, and computer science will provide a stronger foundation for continuing on with graduate work.

Graduate study in atmospheric chemistry generally requires a bachelor's degree in chemistry. However, a degree in biochemistry, physics, mathematics, environmental science, meteorology, or a related field may be acceptable with applicable supporting coursework, depending on the program and specialization. Entry into a graduate program requires the GRE general test. Some programs also require the GRE chemistry subject test. Others will accept the subject test in biochemistry instead. It is a good idea to check admission requirements for potential graduate institutions in order to register for the appropriate GREs before applying. A strong graduate-school application will contain research experience in either the field or a laboratory. This can often be done as part of undergraduate thesis work, but it can also be from an internship or other work experience.

Fellowships for graduate study are available through specific institutions, as well as through science or other organizations such as NOAA, the military, the National Science Foundation, the National Center for Atmospheric Research (NCAR), or the National Aeronautics and Space Administration (NASA). In many cases, there are minority fellowships to encourage entry into scientific fields.

Career Enhancement and Training

No certification or licensing beyond a college or graduate degree is needed to become an atmospheric chemist. To become a more desirable job candidate, however, there are a number of useful strategies for networking, learning about new careers, or enhancing skills.

Research experience is one of the primary résumé boosters in this field. To that end, internships and research fellowships can be invaluable. For postgraduate students, the Presidential Management Fellows (PMF) Program or postdoctoral work at an academic institution can provide experience and the opportunity to explore a research topic in more depth.

Professional organizations, such as the American Chemical Society or the American Meteorological Society, can assist with job hunting or networking via local chapter meetings or annual membership conferences. Other organizations, such as the International Global Atmospheric Chemistry Project or NCAR, assist with coordinating research

---

Transferable Skills

- Interpersonal/Social Skills – Teaching others (SCANS Workplace Competency – Interpersonal)
- Research & Planning Skills – Analyzing information
- Research & Planning Skills – Identifying problems
- Research & Planning Skills – Gathering information
- Research & Planning Skills – Solving problems (SCANS Thinking Skills)
- Technical Skills – Performing scientific, mathematical, and technical work
- Technical Skills – Working with data or numbers

---

efforts. Many of these organizations or branches of government also provide information on applying for grants and other funding.

In addition to the PMF Program, the federal government offers the Pathways for Students and Recent Graduates program, which provides mentorship, career planning, training, and job placement in specific fields. Postdoctoral research opportunities may also be found with branches of the military.

Daily Tasks and Technology

Atmospheric chemists spend time both in the laboratory and in the field. Much of their work involves computer modeling and analysis. Daily tasks are dependent upon the type of research being performed. Atmospheric chemists may work in partnership with geologists, oceanographers, meteorologists, ecologists, and policy makers.

Fieldwork includes some tasks associated with meteorology. One such task entails setting up instruments designed to collect and measure wind, rain, and water, such as rain gauges, anemometers, and hygrometers, and then gathering the samples and data collected by these instruments. Field studies also include measuring trace gases and particulates in the atmosphere. This can mean something as remote as measuring ozone in Antarctica or as near as measuring air pollution in local cities. Data can be gathered from satellites or instruments that measure absorption spectra to detect various pollutants and particulates. These methods can also be applied to the study of atmospheres on other planets.

Laboratory work includes experiments to study chemical interactions and reactions in the atmosphere, such as aerosol formation. Special smog chambers or flow tubes are used to simulate the environments in which these reactions occur in nature.

Computer modeling and data analysis complement field and laboratory work. Information such as data from different locations or the dispersal of chemical tracers can be mapped and integrated with data from hydrologists and other scientists to examine larger systems. Remote-sensing data from satellites can also be added to enhance the overall data. Software used includes rendering programs, graphics programs, Advanced Visual Systems (AVS), and map-creation software.

Earnings and Employment Outlook

Atmospheric chemistry is a field that is expected to grow at an average rate compared with other professions, despite increasing interest in climate and air-pollution issues. Candidates with advanced degrees are more likely to secure employment.

Atmospheric chemists are most commonly hired by government or academic institutions, but they can also be employed in industry. Both government agencies and academic institutions have been facing budget cuts, which result in greater competition for scarcer jobs; therefore, more opportunities may be available in the private sector.

Salaries, while dependent upon experience and level of education, are likely to be competitive. Salaries tend to be higher in government positions and in research and development, and slightly lower at academic institutions.

Atmospheric chemistry is a field that is expected to grow at an average rate compared with other professions, despite increasing interest in climate and air-pollution issues.

Government agencies such as NOAA and NASA employ atmospheric chemists to examine the causes and effects of various air pollutants. NASA, for instance, has employed atmospheric scientists to study the effects of supersonic transports and space shuttles on the atmosphere. Government funding supports research-and-development organizations such as NCAR. Branches of the military also employ atmospheric scientists in both civilian and active-duty capacities as part of the armed forces or the Department of Defense, due to the effects that climate and air can have upon sensitive technology and military operations. Many atmospheric chemists teach at universities while also conducting research in their area of expertise.

Related Occupations

- **Materials Chemists:** Materials Chemists combine chemistry and physics to develop and test new compounds and materials, such as plastics, alloys, and drugs, or to investigate properties of existing materials.

- **Hydrologists:** Hydrologists monitor and protect water quality, track stream flow and water cycles, assist with planning dams or reservoirs, and develop flood-management strategies.

- **Environmental Engineers:** Environmental Engineers work with the government and industry to design and maintain facilities in compliance with environmental regulations or to develop strategies to remediate toxic sites.

- **Environmental Chemists:** Environmental Chemists also work with the government and industry to protect or restore the environment. In addition, they monitor air, soil, and water and assess hazards to human health.

- **Geochemists:** Geochemists document, analyze, and assess various environments in order to produce reports for general knowledge, such as geologic mapping; for environmental protection and preservation; or for natural-resource exploitation, such as drilling for oil and natural gas.

Future Applications

In the past, atmospheric chemists have had a major impact on science, policy, and industry, particularly with regard to discovering the hole in the ozone layer over Antarctica and linking it to the use of CFCs in aerosol cans. As air pollution in cities and the anthropogenic effect on greenhouse gases increase, the work of atmospheric chemists will be important in monitoring air quality and greenhouse gases and coming up with scientific advances to mitigate the effects of human activity on the planet.

One expanding role of atmospheric chemists is to advise policy makers on legislation that will be effective in curbing emissions from automobiles, industry, and other sources. Nobel Prize–winning atmospheric chemist Mario Molina, for instance, has occupied both roles, citing the importance of communicating scientific knowledge and discoveries with both policy makers and the public.

Climate change, whether due to natural cycles or human activity, is another area of growing concern and one that will be the subject of increasingly greater future research. Atmospheric chemists will likely be in demand for studying past climates and for anticipating upcoming shifts in local and global climates. As a result, nongovernmental and nonprofit organizations may hire more atmospheric scientists and climatologists.

Historically, NASA has employed atmospheric scientists in various capacities. As technology enables greater space exploration, atmospheric chemists will have the opportunity to study the atmospheres of other planets.

J. D. Ho, MFA

More Information

International Global Atmospheric Chemistry Project
University of Colorado
CIRES
Box 216 UCB
Boulder, CO 80309
www.igacproject.org

Joint Institute for the Study of the Atmosphere and Ocean
University of Washington
3737 Brooklyn Avenue NE
Box 355672
Seattle, WA 98195-5672
www.jisao.washington.edu

National Center for Atmospheric Research
University Corporation for Atmospheric Research
PO Box 3000
Boulder, CO 80307-3000
www2.ucar.edu

National Oceanic and Atmospheric Administration
1401 Constitution Avenue NW
Room 5128
Washington, DC 20230
www.noaa.gov

World Climate Research Programme
c/o World Meteorological Organization
7 bis, Avenue de la Paix
Case Postale 2300
1211 Geneva 2, Switzerland
www.wcrp-climate.org

Biochemistry

FIELDS OF STUDY

Cell biology; cell regulation; chemistry; endocrinology; enzymology; general biology; genetics; immunology; mathematics; metabolism; microbiology; molecular biology; oncology; physiology.

DEFINITION

Biochemistry involves the study of chemical processes in cells and organisms, which may include metabolic pathways and the regulation of such pathways. Biochemistry may also focus on the study of enzymes that catalyze metabolic pathways. Because cell metabolism utilizes a complex interaction of enzymes and the molecules they act upon (called substrates), an understanding of metabolism is key to defining the cell itself. Disruption of metabolic pathways may result in metabolic diseases, either hereditary (genetic) changes or alterations that result from exposure to environmental factors. Since at the molecular level, cancer is the result of genetic and biochemical changes that take place in the cell, oncology can include the application of biochemistry in understanding the significance of these changes.

Basic Principles

While biochemistry encompasses the study of any cell process using either organic (carbon-carbon bonding) or inorganic substances, its eighteenth-century origins focused largely on the chemistry of plant and animal proteins. Scientists recognized that protein could be digested using stomach secretions and, later, observed that saliva would convert starch into simpler sugars. However, the mechanism behind these reactions remained a mystery. In the nineteenth century, French chemist Louis Pasteur hypothesized that the process of sugar converting to alcohol during fermentation must be catalyzed (sped up) by a substance synthesized in living cells. Some years later, the term "enzyme" was coined by German physiologist Wilhelm Kühne to explain the reaction. During the 1920s, James Sumner demonstrated the protein nature of most enzymes.

Biochemistry is most widely used in the field of cell metabolism, encompassing any chemical reactions that take place in cells. The concept includes a wide range of chemical applications of events in the cell, from regulation of gene expression to regulation of metabolic pathways. The biochemistry of cells is often likened or simplified to a series of chemical reactions that either synthesize metabolic compounds (anabolism) or break down metabolic compounds (catabolism). The processes may release energy, usually in the form of the molecule adenosine triphosphate (ATP), or utilize energy, commonly the breakdown of ATP, in the reaction. The series of reactions constitutes the metabolic pathway.

Metabolic pathways commonly begin with a simple sugar such as glucose, the complete oxidation of which produces water and carbon dioxide in a process called respiration. Depending on the type of cell, many of which carry out pathways unique to a specific organism, only portions of a pathway may be important. However, descriptions of the biochemical pathways of metabolism remain relevant because, regardless of the starting or stopping points of the metabolic reactions in cells, the steps commonly overlap with the respiration pathway.

Core Concepts

The principles of chemistry and biochemistry are applied in most areas of the biological sciences, including cell biology, metabolism and physiology, microbiology, genetics, and the regulation of each of these processes.

Cell Metabolism. Biochemical principles apply to metabolic pathways carried out in both eukaryotic cells (nucleated cells such as those of plants and animals) and in prokaryotic cells, such as bacteria or other microbes. Carbohydrates, proteins, and lipids are metabolized in specific pathways to generate compounds necessary for reproduction and growth as well as being sources of energy. Common to nearly all cells are the primary pathways such as glycolysis (the breakdown of simple sugars such as glucose to pyruvate) and the Krebs cycle (the further oxidation of pyruvate), generating both intermediates for other pathways and sources of energy through movement of electrons. Organisms that carry out respiration with oxygen as the terminal electron acceptor (plants, animals, and many types of bacteria) produce much of their energy "currency" in the form of ATP through a process called oxidative phosphorylation, which is the production of ATP through a shift of energy as molecules become progressively oxidized. Biochemistry involves the study of not only intermediates in these pathways but also enzymes that catalyze each step and of the regulation of those pathways.

Metabolic Regulation. Regulation of metabolic activity occurs largely through two processes: gene expression and production of enzymes. Gene expression in prokaryotes such as bacteria is commonly a "negative" process in which the regulator is a repressor that inhibits gene activity. The presence of an activator that binds the repressor, removing it from its site on the DNA, allows reexpression of the gene. An example is the regulation of the lactose operon in bacteria, a series of genes that regulate the uptake and breakdown of the sugar lactose. In the absence of lactose, a repressor blocks operon expression. When the cell is exposed to lactose, the sugar binds the repressor, altering its structure, which releases it from the DNA. The result is expression of the gene for an enzyme, beta-galactosidase, which hydrolyzes the lactose into the simpler sugars glucose and galactose, each of which enters glycolysis.

Regulation in eukaryotic cells involves "positive" control in which the regulator activates gene expression, usually through a multistep pathway beginning at the cell surface. An example of the process is regulation of cell replication. The process begins when a growth factor binds a receptor on the cell membrane. A cascade of reactions results that alters the structure of a specific DNA-binding protein: the activator for gene expression.

Metabolic regulation may also take place using the enzyme itself. The product of the reaction may provide feedback by binding a site on the enzyme that reduces its activity. Respiration pathways are regulated in this manner. The feedback mechanism may be competitive, in which the product resembles the initial substrate and competes for the active site on the enzyme (a process common in amino acid synthesis), or "allosteric," in which the product binds an alternative site on the enzyme, changing its shape and reducing the activity. Many antibiotics function as competitive inhibitors of bacterial enzymes. Enzyme study generally involves the isolation and purification of the enzyme in question, which allows direct analysis of the molecule, the effect of various substrates, and the physical changes that take place as the enzyme interacts with other molecules.

Genetics. The source of hereditary information in both eukaryotic and prokaryotic cells is DNA. Some viruses use RNA for genetic information, but the principles of expression remain the same. Biochemical principles govern the expression of DNA in a manner likened to information flow: The genetic information in DNA is transcribed to RNA and then translated into proteins; this information flow is known as the "central dogma" of molecular biology. All processes in the cell are regulated by proteins. Mutations (alterations in the genetic information) may cause significant changes in the regulation of cell processes. Cancer, for example, is, at its core, a disruption of the biochemistry of cell pathways. An understanding of these pathways and their regulation is among the critical discoveries in cancer research taking place since the 1970s.

Biochemical Techniques. The evolution of molecular techniques was among the greatest changes that took place in the field of biochemistry during the twentieth century. The studies carried out during the first decades of the century involved the partial purification of the molecule from the cell, followed by treatment to determine its structure; in this manner, enzymes were determined to be proteins. The changes in chemical properties of the substrate allowed biochemists to observe events that took place during the reaction. In 1942, Edward Tatum and George Beadle addressed what a "gene" is, using mutants of the bread mold *Neurospora* that were unable to utilize pathways in the synthesis of amino acids. Their conclusion was that a gene encodes an enzyme, the "one gene–one enzyme hypothesis." Their hypothesis was modified as it became clear that gene products are not only enzymes and that genes may also encode multiple proteins.

Biochemical methods developed since the 1970s have significantly "simplified" analysis of enzymes and their substrates. Whereas in earlier decades identification of compounds required comparison with known structures or an understanding of the chemical properties of molecules, techniques such as x-ray crystallography and methods of separation using chromatography have resulted in increased ability to visualize events at the molecular level.

Applications Past and Present

Structure and Function of DNA. A common misconception is that DNA, the genetic material for most forms of life, was discovered by James D. Watson and Francis Crick during the early 1950s. However, DNA was first isolated in 1869 by Swiss chemist Johann Friedrich Miescher, who named it "nuclein"; it was termed a nucleic acid because of its chemical properties. Until the 1920s, the chemical makeup of DNA was known only to the extent of its components—a five-carbon sugar, nitrogen-containing bases and phosphates—but its function was unknown. During the 1930s and 1940s, a biochemical team at the Rockefeller Institute (now Rockefeller University) led by Oswald Avery demonstrated that when DNA is hydrolyzed (broken down), solutions containing DNA lose their ability to change the genetic characteristics of cells; the team concluded correctly that DNA was the source of genetic information. In 1953, Watson, Crick, Rosalind Franklin, and Maurice Wilkins, relying largely on the technique of x-ray crystallography, determined the structure of DNA.

Cancer Chemotherapy. Increased understanding of metabolic pathways in cells coupled with serendipitous discoveries associated with the poisonous gasses of World War I led to chemotherapy as a treatment for cancer. Nitrogen mustards were initially developed as weapons, first by the Germans and later by the Allies. A German bombing of a ship docked in Italy during World War I released a cargo of mustard gas that had been stored on the ship. Physicians observed that in addition to casualties directly related to exposure to the gas, persons exposed to the gas had bone marrow cell numbers that were significantly depleted. This knowledge was applied in treating victims of leukemia and lymphomas to reduce the level of neoplastic cells, representing the first use of chemotherapy in controlling cancer.

Interesting Facts about Biochemistry

- The term "protein" was coined in 1838 by chemist Jacob Berzelius since because these molecules appeared as the "leading" food for nutrition.

- The model by which enzymes specifically bind substrates at an active site was termed "Schloss und Schlüssel," (that is "lock and key,") by biochemist Emil Fischer in 1894. The phrase is still in use.

- The amino acid aspartic acid was isolated from asparagus, hence the origin of the name.

- The biochemist who identifies a gene has the option of naming it. Some scientists do so with a sense of humor. Mutations in the "ken and barbie" gene in the fruit fly Drosophila result in a lack of genitalia, which correlates with the lack on the dolls with those names. The gene product is a DNA-binding protein that regulates the process of maturation of male and female genitalia. A homologous gene is found in humans, though mutations are less serious.

- American biochemist James Sumner confirmed the protein nature of enzymes during the 1920s and 1930s. Among the critics of Sumner's hypothesis were German chemists who argued that German chemistry was superior, and since they had not demonstrated the protein nature of enzymes, that Sumner's conclusions were invalid.

- Plants and many bacteria can convert fat to carbohydrates (sugars) or carbohydrates to fats; animals can do only the latter. The difference lies in the metabolism of acetyl co-enzyme A, an intermediate in both fat and carbohydrate breakdown. Only plants and bacteria can metabolize acetyl coenzyme A back to sugars, a process used by seedlings during growth.

The discovery of some metabolic analogs, drugs that resembled intermediates in biochemical pathways but that would inhibit enzymes in those pathways, resulted in the development of folic acid analogs—aminopterin and methotrexate—for treatment of other forms of cancer. By the beginning of the twenty-first century a large number of drugs had been developed for treatment of various types of cancers, most based on the same principle of inhibition of enzymes or pathways necessary for tumors to develop.

Biochemical Basis of Cancer. The ability of filterable agents, subsequently shown to be RNA viruses, to produce tumors or leukemia when injected into animals had been known since the 1890s. The molecular basis remained unknown until the end of the twentieth century. During the 1960s, while studying biochemical events that took place after infection by these viruses, Howard Temin suggested replication takes place through a DNA intermediate that integrates into the cell chromosome; the enzyme known as a reverse transcriptase was discovered several years later. The genetic information in the virus that caused the cell transformation from normal to neoplastic became known as an oncogene. In the 1970s, it was discovered oncogenes do not originate with the virus but are cell genes. Within twenty years, more than one hundred oncogenes were observed in cells, all related to regulation of cell replication.

Oncogene products were characterized according to their functions and were found to fall into four major categories: growth factors, growth factor receptors, enzymes involved in the signaling pathway, and DNA binding proteins. A separate category of oncogenes became known as tumor suppressors, molecules that function as "stop signs" by inhibiting cell replication. Transformation of normal cells into cancer requires the mutation or alteration of combinations of certain oncogenes, in effect causing a cell to "short circuit" in a way in which the cell loses control of the replication process. In some cases identical forms of cancers in different individuals result from specific types of mutations. For example, many forms of colon cancer originate with a mutation in the same signaling pathway within the cell. Many forms of prostate cancer are found to share a common deletion mutation, the loss of a portion of a gene, in the cells of the tumor. Eventually, it may be possible to monitor the risk for certain forms of cancer through genetic analysis of the genes in question. This type of monitoring is already possible for certain inherited forms of breast cancer in which mutations in one of two breast cancer genes, BRCA1 and BRCA2, place the woman at significant risk for early development of the disease.

In theory, the same form of genetic analysis could be applied in determining the risk for other forms of chronic illnesses such as heart disease, dementias, or metabolic diseases, in which samples of a person's genome could undergo analysis for mutations in the relevant sites. Proper regulation in applying any results would be necessary to avoid abuse by health care or insurance companies.

Immunosorbent Assays for Measurement of Molecules. Prior to the 1960s, biochemical assays to determine the concentration of molecules were largely colorimetric—reagents reacted with each other to produce color changes that could be measured with spectrophotometers or other such instruments. Measurements could be carried out only if the concentration of the substance was relatively high, so such assays were not particularly useful for measuring substances such as proteins in the blood. During the early 1960s, Rosalyn Yalow and Solomon Berson developed a much more sensitive method of measurement in which they monitored the binding of radiochemicals to the substrate in question. A modified form of the radioimmunoassay, as it was called, utilized a competitive assay in which the substrate of unknown concentration would compete with a radioactive molecule for binding. Comparison with known standards would allow an accurate determination of minute quantities of the unknown substance. During the 1980s, the technique was further modified by replacing the radioactive molecule with an enzyme; the level of activity was a function of the concentration of the unknown substance. Now known as the enzyme-linked immunosorbent assay (ELISA), the technique is utilized by most hospital or biochemical laboratories for measurement of minute quantities of materials.

Impact on Industry

The application of molecular techniques is one of the most significant advances that has taken place in our ability to understand biochemical processes. In the past, much of biochemistry was observational; reactions were observed, and products were analyzed. Events taking place at the molecular level were poorly understood. Reflecting the development of technology for analysis of molecular events, since the 1970s, no area in the biological sciences does not use some form of molecular biochemistry. However, because equipment and supplies can be prohibitively expensive, few countries outside the West can afford extensive programs in pure biochemical research.

The growth outlook as depicted by the United States Bureau of Labor Statistics reflects the importance of biochemistry as a growth industry. For 2010, the BLS estimated employment numbers of more than twenty-five thousand in biochemistry, with an estimated growth rate during the following decade of 31 percent, a rate much faster than average.

University Research and Teaching. Much of the pure research in biochemistry is carried out at the university level; some 20 percent of researchers defined as biochemists work in university settings, though if one includes workers in the life sciences in general who utilize biochemical techniques, such as microbiologists, molecular biologists, and physiologists, the proportion is significantly higher. There are several reasons why most biochemical work is undertaken at the university level, most involving the funding provided by government agencies, which is necessary for the work.

Most universities have biochemistry departments, though often these departments have merged with other science departments, both eliminating administrative duplication and recognizing that biochemistry is a component of nearly all biological research. In some cases, universities are associated with teaching hospitals, and the biochemical research reflects the goal of medical application of the work.

Biochemical research at universities generally focuses on several specific areas within the "central dogma" of DNA replication and regulation, transcription of the genetic information, and its translation into gene products. Many of these processes utilize biochemical pathways, and an increased understanding of the roles played by intermediates in these pathways is a primary goal of much of university research.

Government Agencies. Several US government agencies are sources for scientific funding, most notably the National Institutes of Health and its twenty-seven institutes and centers. Among its more prominent subdivisions are the National Cancer Institute and the National Heart, Lung and Blood Institute. The National Science Foundation is an independent government agency that funds both educational programs and research projects, particularly those at small academic institutions. Other areas in the category of public health services may be in the field of forensics, including work with the Federal Bureau of Investigation in the analysis of materials associated with crimes or in drug analysis, and similar jobs at state or local levels. Local public health departments also become involved in the investigation of issues related to the general health of the public, including toxic contamination of foods and other environmental issues.

Occupation	Chemical engineer
Employment 2010	30,200
Projected Employment 2020	32,000
Change in Number (2010–20)	1,800
Percent Change	6%

Bureau of Labor Statistics, 2012

Industry. Given the nature of industry and the necessity to translate expensive biochemical research into some form of profit, product application is often among the goals of biochemical programs. The nature of the program is a function of the company. For example, research at pharmaceutical companies is often focused on new or improved medicinal drugs or antimicrobial products such as antibiotics. Medicinal applications of research also include the study of metabolic effects on drugs or possible toxic substances to which individuals may be exposed. For example, the metabolic processing of compounds within the liver may render toxic a substance that on its surface appears harmless. Some such compounds may be used in foods or in agricultural applications, and the role of the industrial biochemist is to determine whether such substances may become harmful.

Biochemists in the pharmaceutical industry may also devise methods for improved or increased sensitivity in testing for the presence of possible illness. For example, early detection of some forms of prostate, colon, or breast cancers has increasingly relied on detection of small quantities of molecules released from such tumors. Improved diagnosis of chronic illnesses such as Alzheimer's disease may be possible through detection of proteins released into the blood of patients.

Military. The development of biological weapons had been among the biochemical and microbiological applications of biochemistry. Projects of this sort have not been undertaken since the 1970s. Advances in weaponry have resulted in increased exposure to possible chemical and otherwise toxic substances, and among the programs carried out by biochemists is the testing of such substances for a better understanding of their effects on individuals. Increased levels of drug abuse has required development of improved biochemical testing for the presence of such compounds in the body.

Social Context and Future Prospects

Biochemistry, indeed most of the biological sciences, has evolved from an observational science to one that focuses increasingly on events at the molecular level. Improved technology and instrumentation has impacted both pure research and the application of the research, particularly in medicinal biochemistry. The first antibiotics, including penicillin and streptomycin, appeared on the popular market in the years after World War II; dozens followed, most the result of widespread screening of soil bacteria. Most of these substances function in inhibiting bacteria growth, and microbes have become increasingly resistant. New methods are necessary to develop the next generation of antimicrobials, and much of the research has involved "designer drugs," chemicals artificially synthesized that focus on specific sites or chemical structures of bacteria.

With an aging population, chronic illnesses such as cancer, heart disease, and dementia are taking a toll on the elderly. Biochemical research is focusing on better understanding aging effects and molecular changes at the cellular level as well as studies that attempt to slow or reverse such processes. Some dementias are confirmed only upon autopsy; improved methods of molecular detection of byproducts of nerve damage at earlier stages may provide a means to recognize or slow such processes.

Improved understanding of the cellular processes that occur during the transformation of normal cells into cancers has led to the realization that certain cancers are characterized by specific mutations at the cell surface or in regulation pathways. Biochemical development of anticancer drugs will increasingly target specific sites on or within cancer cells in hopes of treating the disease specifically, while minimizing any harmful side effects to surrounding tissues. Sensitive assays will be necessary to discover or monitor molecules or pathway intermediates specific to the illness.

Further Reading

Gibney, Michael, Ian Macdonald, and Helen Roche. *Nutrition and Metabolism.* 2nd ed. New York: Wiley, 2010. Print. Summarizes both the body's various systems and the roles played by various nutrients in metabolism.

Jansen, Lee, and Marc Tischler. *The Big Picture: Medical Biochemistry.* New York: McGraw, 2012. Print. Review of basic biochemistry with emphasis on medical applications. The first portion of the book summarizes organic molecules in the cell, while later chapters address medical issues.

Schwartz, David, ed. *Medicine Science and Dreams: The Making of Physician-Scientists.* New York: Springer, 2011. Print. Collection of interviews with some dozen professionals, discussing their decisions to enter careers in science. While not all strictly biochemists, the subjects do describe their interests in biochemistry.

Tanford, Charles, and Jacqueline Reynolds. *Nature's Robots: A History of Proteins.* New York: Oxford UP, 2001. Print. Presents stories behind the discovery of proteins and their roles in metabolic reactions. Discusses many of the scientists who laid the framework for biochemistry.

Tymoczko, John, Jeremy Berg, and Lubert Stryer. *Biochemistry: A Short Course.* New York: Freeman, 2010. Print. Abbreviated text for a biochemistry course. In addition to descriptions of biochemical reactions, provides extensive clinical applications of errors that can occur in metabolic functions.

About the Author: Richard Adler, PhD, is a microbiologist at the University of Michigan–Dearborn, where he has studied the effects of viral infection on cells and taught courses in microbiology, immunology, and introductory biology for approximately thirty-five years. He received both his bachelor's degree and doctorate from Pennsylvania State University in microbiology. His career has included research at the Roche Institute of Molecular Biology in Nutley, New Jersey, and sabbatical at the University of Western Ontario in London, Ontario. He has authored three books and published extensively in his fields of expertise.

Biochemical Engineer🖋

Earnings (Yearly Average): $81,540 (Bureau of Labor Statistics, 2012)

Employment and Outlook: Slower than average growth (Bureau of Labor Statistics, 2012)

O*NET-SOC Code: 17-2199.01

Related Career Cluster(s): Agriculture, Food & Natural Resources; Education & Training; Health Science; Manufacturing; Transportation, Distribution & Logistics

Scope of Work

Biochemical engineering is a relatively new subdiscipline of chemical engineering. It emerged in the mid-twentieth century with the large-scale production of antibiotics. Biochemical engineering is a discipline that serves as a link between the scientific disciplines of biology and chemistry and the production principles of chemical engineering. Biochemical engineering takes the individual research scientist's discovery and manufactures it on a global scale. Biochemical engineers review and refine the principles of the scientific process, help manufacturers to design and build machinery for commercial production, and work with sales personnel to efficiently deliver the product to market. To this end, biochemical engineers help to develop and manufacture a wide array of products including medicines, fertilizers, food, biofuels, chemicals, therapeutic proteins, and paper.

Education and Coursework

The high school curriculum for a student interested in biochemical engineering should include the full course load of math classes recommended for most engineering programs, including algebra, geometry, trigonometry, and calculus. Suggested science courses include biology, chemistry, and physics. In addition, a student's high school

---

Transferable Skills

- Working as a member of a team (SCANS Workplace Competency – Interpersonal)
- Identifying problems
- Determining alternatives
- Solving problems (SCANS Thinking Skills)
- Analyzing information
- Managing equipment/materials (SCANS Workplace Competency – Resources)
- Working in a laboratory setting

---

portfolio should also include English, computer science, and foreign language studies, as a biochemical engineer must be able to communicate effectively with various personnel, and often with researchers in other countries. Aside from regular coursework, students are also encouraged to participate in science and engineering clubs and fairs.

The minimum degree prerequisite for persons entering the field of biochemical engineering is a bachelor's degree. The degree may be earned through a specialized biochemical engineering program or a chemical engineering program with a focus in biochemical engineering. Either way, the engineering program should meet the American Board for Engineering and Technology accreditation requirements. There are currently 158 approved chemical engineering programs in the United States.

A bachelor's degree typically consists of four years of study; however, many students opt to enroll in either a five-year cooperative education program or a joint bachelor's/master's degree program. Many companies prefer to hire an engineer who has already had practical engineering work experience; thus, the extra year of schooling or a summer apprenticeship is often worth the investment in time.

A standard biochemical engineering undergraduate program combines engineering with a basic biochemistry background. A typical program is comprised of calculus, biology, physics, basic and biochemical engineering courses and labs, organic chemistry, biochemistry, and microbiology. In the final year of undergraduate study, or shortly thereafter, students are advised to take the Fundamentals of Engineering (FE) Examination, administered by the National Council of Examiners for Engineering and Surveying. This is the first step toward future professional engineering licensure.

Junior engineering positions require the minimum of a bachelor's degree. Engineers seeking a managerial role should also pursue a master's degree in business, while those seeking to enhance their skills or continue on toward a doctorate will enroll in a PhD program. Engineers who possess a PhD are eligible for university faculty positions or senior posts within the government and industry.

Career Enhancement and Training

Professional licensure is required of any engineer who serves the public directly, and provides advancement opportunities for all biochemical engineers. The engineering licensure procedure varies from state to state, but typically involves four steps: first, to obtain a four-year degree from an accredited chemical/biochemical engineering program; second, to pass the Fundamentals of Engineering Exam; third, to work under the supervision of a professionally licensed engineer, and fourth, to pass the Principles and Practice of Engineering (PE) Exam.

In addition to licensure, many biochemical engineers enhance their career profile through participation in professional associations. Two such reputable organizations are the American Institute of Chemical Engineers (AIChE), and the American Chemical Society (ACS). Both organizations provide technical education resources and connections to chemical engineers worldwide. These organizations enable their members to stay current in an ever-changing technological field by providing a variety of resources, including an online library, free journal subscriptions, webinars, online courses, in-house training programs, international conferences, and online public forums. College students may join AIChE for a nominal fee, and use it as a resource for internships and scholarships.

Students can acquire practical biochemical engineering skills as early as high school, through membership in local science clubs or the national Junior Engineering Technical Society (JETS). JETS conducts contests at colleges throughout the United States with the overarching goal of providing high school students the opportunity to apply classroom knowledge to real-world engineering problems. In addition to extracurricular activities, a subscription to an engineering or biochemically oriented magazine, such as *ChemMatters* or *PRISM*, provides updates on recent developments in the field.

Daily Tasks and Technology

Biochemical engineering is considered one of the most versatile fields in engineering, with biochemical engineers working in such varied industries as food services, pharmaceuticals, biorenewable fuels, and waste management. The duties of a biochemical engineer mirror this range of expertise, as this field oversees a product from its inception in an individual lab through its distribution in the marketplace. Congruent with this, biochemical engineers are involved in a product's discovery and development, commercial-scale processing and manufacturing, and worldwide sales and distribution.

In the developmental stage, biochemical engineers are involved in assisting biologists and chemists in discovering and creating new biological products, and ensuring that reliable methods are used to optimize the production of the involved cell cultures. At this stage, and throughout their career, biochemical engineers need to stay abreast of the current science and technology literature.

Process and manufacturing tasks include designing and constructing new industrial plants, drawing up equipment specifications and operating procedures, utilizing pilot studies to determine the most efficient method of production, and solving problems regarding the quality and safety of plant operations and procedures.

Biochemical engineers work in a variety of settings as they collaborate with bench lab scientists in basic research laboratories, supervise junior engineers and technicians at industrial plants, and consult with marketing and sales personnel in corporate offices. In analyzing data and conducting computer simulations, biochemical engineers use databases and computer-assisted drafting programs (CAD). Bioreactors, chromatographs, centrifuges, and gel-electrophoresis systems are some of the tools used in cell culture proliferation, microorganism cultivation, and protein or DNA expression.

Earnings and Employment Outlook

The job outlook for biochemical engineers has been predicted to have a slower than average growth rate compared to other professions (6 percent growth from 2010 to 2020). However, biochemical engineering is a subspecialty of chemical engineering that experts claim may actually experience a stronger than average growth rate, particularly in companies specializing in nanotechnology and genetic engineering. According to the US Bureau of Labor Statistics, the field of biotechnology is one of the fastest-growing employment sectors.

Though the median salary for biochemical engineers was about $90,000 in 2010, individuals with doctoral degrees in executive and independent research positions earn up to $120,000 annually. Currently, biochemical engineers work in manufacturing industries (32 percent), research and technological services (25 percent), and government agencies (16 percent). The remainder work as consultants within professional companies, or as independent contractors. As in most fields, private industries such as pharmaceuticals offer a higher salary than government.

Biochemical engineering has been classified as a "green" occupation by O*NET Online, as it is involved in ensuring safe environmental practices by developing alternative bioremediation processes and clean energy options such as biofuels

Related Occupations

- **Chemical Engineers:** Chemical engineers develop chemical processes to manufacture industrial products on a large scale. They apply engineering principles to standardize and expedite the manufacturing process.

- **Biochemists:** Biochemists study the chemical makeup and reactions of living organisms. To this end, they research what happens on the cellular level in the cause and cure of diseases.

A Conversation with James L. Robinson

Job Title: Emeritus Professor of Biochemistry, Department of Animal Sciences and Division of Nutritional Sciences

What was your career path?

I had always been interested in education—my parents were both educational missionaries—and was even called to teach when one of our teachers became ill toward the end of one semester. I had always been interested in science and thought I would be interested in being a high school chemistry teacher, but when I got to college I decided that teaching at the college level would be much more enjoyable. To teach science at that level requires a PhD and so graduate school and specialization were the next steps after earning my BS in chemistry. I was drawn to biochemistry and after earning my PhD in biochemistry, I did a two-year postdoctoral stint to gain further research experience. I considered jobs in premier undergraduate colleges, as that reflected my own college experience, and interviewed at several. I was offered a job at a major university with heavy emphasis on research and graduate education; my appointment was in the Dairy Science Department. While I had no dairy experience other than drinking milk, biochemistry could be applied in any biological field and the department was interested in having a bona fide biochemist on staff that would work with other faculty and develop, in due course, a relevant research program. Eventually, I worked on inherited diseases in dairy cattle. My teaching was mostly at the graduate level, primarily a course on nutritional biochemistry which became the capstone course for nutrition graduate students. I also developed an undergraduate course that was writing intensive and dealt with animals, domestic and wild, and their use around the world depending on the climate, economic status, and culture of various countries. After thirty-two years at the same institution, I retired. While I retain an office in my department, attend seminars, and work on projects of my own choosing, I have done a lot of travelling.

What are three pieces of advice you would offer someone interested in your profession?

1. Gain experience in any field that you have an interest in—as an entry-level worker, as a summer intern, or as a volunteer. This will allow you to see what the field is really like. Undergraduate research was something that opened my eyes to the options in the field that I choose. Finding out that a field is not for you is a good thing to learn early rather than after you have devoted years in preparation for it.

2. Push yourself to be the best you can be. Don't settle for just getting by.

3. Be open to options that you might not have considered. In my case, going into a very applied department in a major research university was not my first choice, but I had a very fulfilling career and have no regrets about my career path.

What paths for career advancement are available to you?

While active at the university, I had the opportunity to be involved in the administration of my department on an interim basis. But, after that experience, I knew that I would rather be involved with teaching and research. That was a good thing to learn before making a permanent career change. I made full use of sabbaticals (leaves of absence to gain further research experience and to recharge one's batteries), spending full years in France, the Netherlands, and Australia/New Zealand. I developed the undergraduate course on world animals after my experiences abroad. I have done some consulting and have colleagues who have made that a second career.

- **Environmental Engineers:** Environmental engineers incorporate the principles of engineering and ecology in an effort to address today's current environmental issues, such as water quality, air pollution, refuse reduction, and waste treatment.

- **Biomedical Engineers:** Biomedical engineers offer engineering solutions in order to improve medical care. Biomedical engineers are involved in the production of medical products such as artificial limbs, prostheses, and diagnostic machines.
- **Chemical Technicians:** Chemical technicians study chemical processes with specialized instruments in order to help chemists and chemical engineers (including biochemical engineers) in researching and producing chemically-based products.

Future Applications

As scientists work to discover solutions to today's environmental and medical concerns, it is interesting that many of these answers may be found at the molecular level of life.

At its inception, biochemical engineering introduced the mass production of antibiotics to the world, which is still considered one of the greatest life-saving advancements of the twentieth century. Today, however, the World Health Organization has warned of the danger of antibiotic-resistant bacteria that are emerging as a result of widespread antibiotic abuse. As the world looks to a new method for fighting bacterial disease, bacteriophages, or "bacteria-eaters" may become a renewed topic of interest. Phage research will provide a new product market for biochemists and biochemical engineers alike to develop and refine.

Advances in biotechnology are placing medical experts on the cusp of targeting cancers with vaccines, curing blindness with stem cells, and providing early detection of diseases using engineered proteins. These products will all require commercial production, and thus will produce an increase in jobs for biochemical engineers.

Biochemical engineers are currently using enzymes as biocatalysts in food processes, DNA manipulation, and biofuel production. To date, enzymes have been limited by the fact that they require optimal conditions in order to remain viable. Gene-sequencing advancements, along with the discovery of extremophiles, will invariably bring about the discovery of more adaptable enzymes and corresponding products.

Rose Young

More Information

American Chemical Society
1155 Sixteenth Street, NW
Washington, DC 20036
http://portal.acs.org/

American Institute of Chemical Engineers
3 Park Avenue
New York, NY 10016-5991
http://www.aiche.org/

American Society for Biochemistry and Molecular Biology
11200 Rockville Pike, Suite 302
Rockville, MD 20852-3110
http://www.asbmb.org/

American Society for Engineering Education
1818 N Street, NW, Suite 600
Washington, DC 20036-2479
http://www.asee.org/

TryEngineering.org
445 Hoes Lane
Piscataway, NJ 08854-4141
http://www.tryengineering.org/

Chemical Engineering

FIELDS OF STUDY

Chemistry; mathematics; physics; electrical engineering; fluid dynamics; electronics; mechanical engineering; process control; material engineering; safety engineering; biology; communications; economics; critical path scheduling.

DEFINITION

Chemical engineering, sometimes also called processing engineering, is the field of engineering that studies the conversion of raw chemicals into useful products by means of chemical transformation. Chemical engineering applies engineering concepts to design, construction, operation, and improvement of processes that create products from chemicals. For example, chemical engineering converts petroleum into products such as gasoline, lubricants, petrochemicals, solvents, plastics, processed food, electronic components, pharmaceuticals, agricultural chemicals, paints, and inks. Chemical engineering relies on all the technologies used in the chemical and related industries, including distillation, chemical kinetics, mass transport and transfer, heat transfer, control instrumentation, and other unit operations, as well as economics and communications.

Basic Principles

Chemical engineering is the discipline that studies chemical reactions used to manufacture useful products that appear in almost everything people have and use in the twenty-first century. Chemical engineering also is involved with reduction and removal of waste, improvement of air and water quality, and production of new sources of energy. It is also the responsibility of chemical engineers to ensure the safety of all involved in a given process through design, training, and operating procedures.

The dividing line between chemistry and chemical engineering is hazy and there is much overlap. Primarily, chemistry discovers and develops new reactions, new chemicals, and new analytical tools. It is the role of chemical engineering to take these discoveries and use them to evaluate the economic possibilities of a new product or a new process for making an existing product. Chemical engineers determine what processes or unit operation are needed to carry out the reactions required to produce, recover, refine, and store a particular chemical. In the case of a new process, chemical engineers consider what other products could be made using the process. They also examine what products newly discovered chemicals can be used to make.

The largest field of chemical engineering applications is the petroleum and petrochemical industries. Crude oil, if merely distilled, would yield less than 35 percent gasoline. Through reactions such as catalytic cracking and platforming, these yields have come to approach 90 percent. Other treatments produce other fuels, lubricants, and waxes. The lighter components of crude oil become the raw materials used to make most of the plastics, fibers, solvents, synthetic rubber, paper, antifreeze, pharmaceutical drugs, agricultural chemicals, and paints that are seen in people's daily lives.

Core Concepts

The design, construction, and operation of chemical engineering projects are commonly divided into various unit operations. These unit operations, singly or in combination, require a basic knowledge and understanding of many scientific, mathematical, and economic principles.

Mathematics. Mathematics drives all aspects of chemical engineering. Calculations of material and energy balances are needed to deal with any operation in which chemical reactions are carried out. Kinetics, the study dealing with reaction rates, involves calculus, differential equations, and matrix algebra, which is needed to determine how chemical reactions proceed and what products are made and in what ratios. Control system design additionally requires the understanding of statistics and vector and nonlinear system analysis. Computer mathematics, including numerical analysis, is also needed for control and other applications.

Organic and Physical Chemistry. Chemistry, especially organic and physical, is the basis of all chemical processes. A full understanding of organic chemistry is essential in the fields of petroleum, petrochemicals, pharmaceuticals, and agricultural chemicals. A great deal of progress was made in the field of organic chemistry beginning in the 1880s. Physical chemistry is the foundation of understanding how materials behave with respect to motion and heat flow. The study of how gases and liquids are affected by heat, pressure, and flows is needed for the unit operations of mass transfer, heat transfer, and distillation.

Distillation, in which more volatile components are separated from less volatile ones, requires knowledge of individual physical and thermodynamic properties and how these interact with one another in mixtures. For example, materials with different boiling points sometimes form a constant-boiling mixture, or azeotrope, which cannot be further refined by simple distillation. A well-known example of this is ethyl alcohol and water. Although ethyl alcohol boils at 78 degrees Celsius as compared with 100 degrees Celsius for water, a mixture of ethyl alcohol and water that contains 96 percent (by weight) or 190-proof ethyl alcohol is a constant-boiling mixture. Further concentration is not possible without extraordinary means.

Inorganic Chemistry. Inorganic chemistry deals with noncarbon chemistry and is often considered basic, as it is taught in high school and the first year of college. Many of the chemical industries do make inorganic chemicals such as ammonia, chlorine, oxygen, salts, cement, glass, sulfur, pigments, fertilizers, and sulfuric, hydrochloric, and nitric acids. Catalysts are inorganic materials that influence organic reactions, and understanding them is very important. The effectiveness of any catalyst is determined by its chemical composition and physical properties such as surface area, pore size, and hardness.

Analytical Chemistry. Analytical chemistry was once strictly a batch process, in which a sample would be collected and taken to a laboratory for analysis. However, modern processes continually analyze material during various stages of manufacture, using chromatography, mass spectroscopy, color, index of refraction, and other techniques.

Mechanical, Electrical, and Electronic Engineering. The disciplines of mechanical, electrical, and electronic engineering are needed by the chemical engineer to be able to consider process design, materials of construction, corrosion, and electrical systems for the motors and heaters. Electronic engineering is basic knowledge needed for control systems and computer uses.

Safety Engineering. Safety engineering is the study of all aspects of design and operation to find potential hazards to health and physical damage and how to correct them. This work begins at the start of any project. Not only must each and every part of a process be examined, but also each chemical involved must be checked for hazards, either by itself or in combinations with other chemicals and materials in which it will come in contact. Safety engineering also is a part of operator training and the writing of operating procedures used for the proposed operation.

Communication. Communication is key to all progress. Chemical engineers must be able to interact with others; no idea—whether for a new process or product or an improvement in an existing operation—can be implemented unless others are convinced of its value and are willing to invest in it. Coherent and easily understood reports and presentations are as important as any other part of a project. Operating procedures must be reviewed with the operation personnel to ensure that they are understood and can be followed.

Economics. Economics is the driving force behind all design, construction, and operations. The chemical engineer must be conversant in finance, banking, accounting, and worldwide business practices. Cost estimates, operating balances to determine actual costs, market forces, and financing are a necessary part of the work of any chemical engineer.

Applications Past and Present

Chemical engineering is involved in every step in bringing a process from the laboratory to full-scale production. This involves determining methods to make the process continuous, safe, environmentally compatible, and economically sound. During these steps, chemical engineers determine the methods and procedures needed for a full-scale plant. Mathematical modeling is used to test various steps in the process, controls, waste treatment, environmental concerns, and economic feasibility.

Acetonitrile Process. The acetonitrile process demonstrates how these disciplines combine to produce a process. Acetonitrile is a chemical used as a solvent and an intermediate for agricultural chemicals. The chemistry of this process involves reacting acetic acid and ammonia to make acetonitrile and water. The reaction between these raw materials is carried out over a catalyst at 400 degrees Celsius. The reaction takes place in tubes loaded with a catalyst of phosphoric acid deposited on an alumina ceramic support, which allows the reaction to take place at high rates. The reaction tubes are located in a gas-fired furnace designed to provide even temperatures throughout the length of the tubes. The exiting gases are cooled and condensed by scrubbing with water. This mixture enters a train of distillation columns, which first removes a constant-boiling mixture of the acetonitrile along with some water. In another distillation column, an azeotroping agent is used to produce an overhead mixture that when condensed, produces two layers with all the water in one layer. The water layer is removed, and the other layer is recycled. The base material leaving the distillation column contains the water-free acetonitrile, which is then redistilled to produce the finished product, which is ready to package and ship.

Such a process involves chemical engineers in the design and assembly of all the equipment needed for the process: the furnace, reactor tubes, distillation columns, tanks, pumps, heat exchangers, and piping. The chemical engineers also create the controls, operating procedures, hazardous material data sheets, startup and shut-down instructions, and provide operator training. Once the plant is running, the role of the chemical engineer becomes operating and improving the unit.

Petroleum and Petrochemical Applications. Chemical engineering is used in the petroleum and petrochemical industries. At first, all petroleum products were produced by simple batch distillations of crude oil. Chemical engineering developed continuous distillation processes that permitted marked increases in refinery production rates. Then high-temperature cracking methods permitted the conversion of high-boiling petroleum fractions (end products of refining) to useful products such as more gasoline. This was followed by the use of catalytic cracking that improved the gasoline output even more.

Distillation can take many forms in addition to simple atmospheric distillation. Chemical engineers can determine the need to use pressure distillation for the purification of components that are normally gases. Vacuum distillation may be useful if there are high-boiling components that are sensitive to the elevated temperatures required for normal distillation. With the need for aviation gasoline and other high-octane fuels, chemical engineering developed such methods as platforming, which uses the addition of a platinum catalyst to speed up certain reactions, to convert lower-boiling petroleum components into high-octane additives.

Petrochemical industries convert surplus liquefiable gases into solvents, plastics, synthetic rubber, adhesives, coatings, paints, inks, intermediates for agricultural chemicals, food additives, and many more items.

Inorganics. Sulfuric acid is typical of a major inorganic product that requires the type of process improvement that is provided by chemical engineers. Sulfuric acid is a high-volume, low-profit-margin material that has been in production for more than a hundred years. The chemistry is well known. Sulfur is vaporized, mixed with air, and passed over a catalyst to make sulfur trioxide, which is then adsorbed into water to make sulfuric acid. Chemical engineers look for better catalysts and seek to improve the purity of raw materials and increase control over temperature, flows, safety, and environmental concerns.

Biological Applications. The ancient biological process of fermentation is best known for its role in producing alcoholic beverages and breads. Although many people do not realize that fermentation is a chemical reaction, it is much the same as other organic reactions. The biological component is a microorganism that acts as the catalyst. Biochemical engineering products that are created using fermentation

Interesting Facts about Chemical Engineering

- Chaim Azriel Weizmann developed a process to produce acetone and butyl acetate, chemicals in critical demand during World War I. In return, the British government supported the establishment of the Jewish state of Israel, which named Weizmann its first president in 1948.

- The pure organic chemical produced in the greatest quantity per year is sucrose, or table sugar. The process of converting raw sugarcane or beets into uniform-size sucrose crystals involves extraction, heat transfer, multieffect evaporation, adsorption, crystallization, filtration, and drying—not to mention mass transfer and instrumentation.

- One of the chemical byproducts of paper manufacture is synthetic vanilla. One paper mill could produce the world's annual demand in one day.

- The first synthetic plastic, Bakelite, was developed to be a substitute for ivory in the manufacture of billiard balls.

- Aluminum, once more costly than gold or platinum, was so expensive that Russia minted aluminum coins to demonstrate its wealth and power. The Hall electrochemical engineering process for producing aluminum has lowered the cost of aluminum to where it has become a very low-cost material.

- Latex paints were developed as a substitute for oil-based paints, not only to produce a water-based paint that would not contribute to air pollution but also to produce a drip-proof product.

- DuPont employee Roy Plunkett stored some tetrafluoroethylene gas in a container. The next day, he found it had polymerized, leaving a waxy substance called polytetrafluoroethylene, commonly known as Teflon.

- Water and the element gallium, a material used in semiconductor manufacture, are the only two significant substances known to expand when they are cooled and frozen.

include acetone and butyl acetate, chemicals that were in critical demand by the aviation industry in World War I.

Biochemical engineering also made antibiotics available on a large scale. In the 1920s, Sir Alexander Fleming discovered the antibiotic properties of penicillin, which was produced in laboratory flasks, a few grams at a time. During World War II, the need for penicillin increased, and chemical engineers developed a large-scale process for producing penicillin from corn. This process was adapted to produce other antibiotics, and chemical engineering processes were developed for the manufacture of many synthetic drugs. Genetic modifications are being developed that are expected to produce the drugs of the future.

Fibers. In 1905, the first synthetic fiber, reconstituted cellulose, commonly known as rayon, was developed. The second synthetic fiber, cellulose acetate, which was developed in 1924, is still manufactured in large amounts for use in cigarette filters. The first fully synthetic fiber was nylon, a commonly used polyamide, followed by polyesters. Chemically treated cotton, known as permanent press, is another product of chemical engineering. In addition to fibers, the textile industry uses lubricants, dyes, pigments, coatings, and inks, all derived by chemical processes.

Plastics. The first thermoplastic, a material that could be reheated and molded, were the cellulosics (plastics derived from cellulose) used to make large signs, toys, automobile parts, and other objects that can be easily fabricated. Acrylic polymers such as methyl methacrylate are formed into optically clear sheeting and used as a nonshattering replacement for plate glass and for eyeglass and camera lenses. Polyethylene, developed during World War II as a superior coating for the wiring needed in radar, is still used as an insulator. The most common use for polyethylene and polypropylene is as the thin film used in plastic bags. Molded items such as bottles, containers, kitchen items, and packaging are manufactured from these polymers as well as polyesters, nylon, polyvinyl chloride (PVC), polystyrene, Teflon, and polycarbonates. The manufacture of all these plastics was developed through chemical engineering and depends on it for operation and improvement.

Refrigerants. The first refrigerants were sulfur dioxide and ammonia. These substances were rather hazardous, so a new range of refrigerants was developed. These refrigerants, commonly known as Freon, are halogenated hydrocarbons that can be tailored to the needs of the application. Home air-conditioning, automotive air-conditioning, and industrial applications are examples of these uses.

Nuclear Energy. The nuclear energy industry requires many solvents and reaction agents for the separation and purification of the fuel used in nuclear reactors. Special coatings and other materials used in the vicinity of intense radiation were developed by the chemical industry. Recovery of the spent nuclear fuel requires specially developed techniques, again requiring solvents and reactions.

Coatings. A typical example of corrosion is the rusting of iron. Corrosion causes the loss of equipment as well as physical and health hazards, not only in the chemical industry but also in almost every aspect of modern life. Corrosion is avoided through metal alloys such as stainless steel and protective coatings. These coatings can be tailored to protective needs inside and outside of a product.

Water Treatment. Raw water—untreated water from the environment—especially for industrial purposes, requires processing to remove suspended solids and soluble organics as well as inorganic ions such as sodium, calcium, iron, chlorides, sulfates and nitrates. Chemical engineering is used to design and manufacture the ion-exchange resins, coagulants, and adsorbents needed, as well as the procedures for use and regeneration of ion-removal systems.

Waste Treatment. Many chemical processes produce byproducts or waste that may be hazardous to the environment and represent uncaptured value. The role of process improvement engineers is to first find ways to reduce waste and, failing that, to develop methods to convert these wastes into materials that will not harm the environment.

Agricultural Applications. Agricultural chemicals such as insecticides, herbicides, fungicides, fertilizers, seed coatings, animal feed additives, and medicines such as hormones and antibiotics all are produced by chemical means. Other chemicals are used in the

Occupation	Chemical engineer
Employment 2010	30,200
Projected Employment 2020	32,000
Change in Number (2010–20)	1,800
Percent Change	6%

Bureau of Labor Statistics, 2012

preparation of products for harvesting and transporting to market.

Food Processing. The manufacture of foodstuffs such as dairy products, breakfast foods, soups, bread, canned goods, frozen foods, and other processed foods, as well as meats, fruits, and vegetables, use engineering operations such as heat transfer to heat or cool.

Impact on Industry

Chemical engineering has an impact on almost every aspect of people's lives. The chemical engineering profession is international in scope. Chemical plants exist in almost every country in the world; however, almost all petrochemical industries are located in countries with or near petroleum refineries. The United States dominates this industry, followed by Europe and the Middle East. Industrial processes are developed throughout the world and are made available to others through licensing. Engineering research is carried out by government agencies, universities, and major industrial concerns.

Employment of chemical engineers is expected to grow slower than the average for all occupations through the year 2020, which means employment is projected to increase 3 to 9 percent. Chemical companies will continue to research and develop new chemicals and more efficient processes to increase output of existing chemicals, resulting in new jobs for chemical engineers. Among manufacturing industries, pharmaceuticals may provide the best job opportunities. Much of the projected growth, however, will be in nonmanufacturing industries, especially service industries, particularly for research in energy and the developing fields of biotechnology and nanotechnology.

Government Agencies and Military. The US government has many agencies and programs that promote the development of new energy products or the improvement of existing ones, the reduction of chemical byproducts, and the recovery of energy and useful products from existing waste sites. These agencies include the Bureau of Mines, the Environmental Protection Agency, the Department of Defense, the Department of Agriculture, and even the National Aeronautics and Space Administration (NASA). Government grants fund many academic research programs designed to develop new materials and processes

Occupation	Industrial engineers
Employment 2010	203,900
Projected Employment 2020	217,000
Change in Number (2010–20)	13,100
Percent Change	6%

Bureau of Labor Statistics, 2012

that use less energy and produce fewer and less hazardous byproducts.

The most relevant military branch for chemical engineers is the US Army Chemical Corps, responsible for detecting and preventing chemical threats. Chemical engineers are also contracted by the government and military for work on such projects as developing more stable explosives and blast protection materials.

Industry and Business Sectors. Chemical engineering affects almost every industry and business that manufactures, handles, transports, and sells chemicals. Chemical engineers are called on to help evaluate the practicality and earning potential of investment proposals in which the manufacture or use of chemicals is to be considered.

The major corporations in the chemical industry include DuPont, Union Carbide, the Dow Chemical Company, Celanese

Occupation	Chemical technicians
Employment 2010	61,000
Projected Employment 2020	65,100
Change in Number (2010–20)	4,100
Percent Change	7%

Bureau of Labor Statistics, 2012

Chemicals, Monsanto, Eastman Chemical, ExxonMobil, Texaco, BP, and Royal Dutch Shell. Other major producers of chemicals include Procter & Gamble, Kraft Foods, Quaker Oats, Sherwin-Williams, and PPG Pittsburgh Paints. Major pharmaceutical companies such as Pfizer and Eli Lilly require biochemical engineering to produce the medicines they sell.

Academic Research and Teaching. One example of government-funded academic research is the recovery of liquid and gaseous fuels from coal. During World II, the Germans developed a process to make aviation gasoline and other fuels from low-grade coal. At the end of the war, the US government confiscated the German data and gave it to Texas A&M University. In the 1970s, the Bureau of Mines and Texas A&M began converting this mass of literature into a program to design a research-scale plant to develop methods for the economic production of fuels from coal and oil shale. As naturally occurring petroleum becomes more expensive and harder to find, the recovery of fuel products from coal is likely to become practical and to lead to the creation of new industries.

Another area of government-funded academic research is the desalinization of sea water. Fresh water is becoming scarcer, and multiple studies are seeking to find ways to produce large quantities of fresh water.

A master's degree in chemical or computer engineering or a master's of business administration degree will help advance an academic career in chemical engineering; generally, a doctorate is required for those seeking jobs in colleges and universities.

Social Context and Future Prospects

Many of the major issues that face society, particularly those concerning the supply of energy and water, the environment, and global warming, require immediate and continuing action from scientists such as chemists and chemical engineers.

Energy. The predominant sources of energy are coal, liquid petroleum, and natural gas. Coal use produces air pollutants such as sulfur dioxide, nitrogen oxides, mercury, and more carbon dioxide per

British thermal unit of energy generated than any of the other energy sources. Liquid petroleum and natural gas also produce carbon dioxide and other air pollutants. Problems regarding the limited supply of all three sources of energy are causing worldwide economic and political disruptions. Chemical engineering may be able to provide economical answers, in that it can create clean oil and gas from coal and oil shale, produce better biofuels from nonfood agricultural crops, and develop materials to make solar energy and hydrogen fuel cells practical.

The Environment. Both air and water pollution are affected by chemicals that are the result of manufacturing, handling, and disposing of materials such as solvents, insecticides, herbicides, and fertilizers. Chemical engineering has reduced factory emissions through the development of water-based coatings. In addition, new methods of converting solid wastes into usable fuels will help the environment and provide new fuel sources.

Water Access. The supply of fresh water for personal and agricultural use is already limited and will become more so as the world population grows. Two methods for recovering fresh water are distillation and reverse osmosis. To become practical, distillation systems must use better materials to prevent corrosion. Chemical engineers are likely to develop new alloys and ways to manufacture them, as well as better heat-recovery methods to reduce cost and lower carbon dioxide emissions. Because of the long-term threat to the climate from increased concentrations of carbon dioxide, chemical engineers are striving to develop methods to control and reduce these emissions.

Reverse osmosis uses membranes that allow water to pass through but not soluble salts. Chemical engineers are working on improved membrane materials that will allow higher pressures to improve efficiency and membrane life.

Further Reading

Dethloff, Henry C. *A Unit Operation: A History of Chemical Engineering at Texas A&M University*. College Station: Texas A&M UP, 1988. Describes how chemical engineering helped create the petrochemical industry that dominates Gulf Coast industry.

Dobre, Tanase, and José G. Sanchez Marcano. *Chemical Engineering: Modeling, Simulation, and Similitude*. Weinheim, Germany: Wiley-VCH, 2007. Looks at how computer-aided modeling is used to develop, implement, and improve industrial processes. Covers the entire process, including mathematical modeling, results analysis, and performance evaluation.

Lide, David R., ed. *CRC Handbook of Chemistry and Physics: A Ready-Reference Book of Chemical and Physical Data*. 90th ed. Boca Raton, FL: CRC, 2009. A vital source of information for designing chemical processes, analyzing results, and estimating costs.

Perry, R. H., and D. W. Green, eds. *Perry's Chemical Engineers Handbook*. 8th ed. New York: McGraw-Hill, 2007. First published in 1934, this handbook provides information about the processes, operations, and equipment involved in chemical engineering, as well as chemical and physical data, and conversion factors. More than seven hundred illustrations.

Towler, Gavin P., and R. K. Sinnott. *Chemical Engineering Design*. Oxford, England: Butterworth-Heinemann, 2009. Examines how chemical engineers design chemical processes and discusses all the elements and factors involved.

About the Author: Max Statman, BS, MS, was employed as a chemical engineer with Eastman Chemical Division from 1952 through 1996. He also served in the US Army Ordnance Corps from 1952 to 1954. He received a bachelor's degree (1952) and a master's degree (1971) in chemical engineering from Texas A&M University. He holds fifteen United States patents plus eleven foreign patents and served as president of the East Texas Chapter of the American Institute of Chemical Engineers, 1980–1981.

Production Engineer

Earnings (Yearly Average): $79,840 (Bureau of Labor Statistics, 2012)

Employment and Outlook: Slower than average growth (Bureau of Labor Statistics, 2012)

O*NET-SOC Code: 17-2112.00

Related Career Clusters: Business, Management & Administration; Manufacturing; Architecture & Construction

Scope of Work

Production engineers combine knowledge of manufacturing processes with management science to develop efficient, cost-effective systems of production. They work on many levels within a company's infrastructure, overseeing the purchase of new machinery, the implementation of work-flow strategies, and the training of new hires. The production engineer works across a variety of departments, facilitating communication and collaborative planning.

Many production engineers work in the petroleum industry, designing systems for the extraction and refinement of crude oil, but principles of production engineering can be applied to any manufacturing process. The assembly line, a modern manufacturing staple developed during the early days of automobile mass production, is just one example of a system formulated by production engineers. Production engineers help companies meet goals by analyzing the mechanical and human elements of the production process, addressing any issues that arise, and assuring the effective application of new work-floor plans or equipment.

Education and Coursework

Students hoping to pursue a career in production engineering should build a strong foundation in physics and mathematics during high school. Advanced-placement courses in economics and statistics will teach the skills necessary for understanding the financial and market aspects of the production engineer's job. Courses that introduce students to the basics of blueprints and architecture, such as drafting and other industrial arts classes, are also highly useful. High school students should be aware of the entrance requirements for different university engineering programs and shape their course load accordingly.

Most entry-level production engineers have a bachelor's degree in manufacturing, mechanical, or industrial engineering. However, given the interdisciplinary nature of a production engineer's duties, a background in any number of industrial studies could be beneficial.

Students should not confine their coursework to cold numbers and machinery. Strong interpersonal skills are a must for any production engineer, given the social and collaborative nature of the position. The

---

Transferable Skills

- Interpersonal/Social Skills – Working as a member of a team (SCANS Workplace Competency – Interpersonal)
- Research & Planning Skills – Defining needs
- Organization & Management Skills – Managing equipment/ materials (SCANS Workplace Competency – Resources)
- Organization & Management Skills – Paying attention to and handling details
- Technical Skills – Understanding which technology is appropriate for a task (SCANS Workplace Competency – Technology)
- Technical Skills – Working with data or numbers

---

production engineer is tasked with fostering successful working relationships and facilitating effective interdepartmental communication. Prospective engineers should take classes in management and management science in addition to course work covering labor relations and ergonomics.

Students should seek out internships and opportunities to shadow working production engineers in order to get a better idea of day-to-day tasks. Pursuing an advanced degree in systems engineering, industrial design, or business administration could diversify an applicant's resume and open a wider scope of opportunities.

Career Enhancement and Training

Production engineers can build their professional networks through a variety of trade organizations. Membership in the Institute of Industrial Engineers, for example, means access to nearly a dozen conferences every year, online seminars, and industry awards programs. For production engineers looking to foster the management skills that are integral to their duties, the American Society for Engineering Management offers classes and certificate programs. Many professional organizations provide resources for learning about and implementing emerging technologies in manufacturing. Production engineers are required to keep abreast of new machinery and software that will allow them to design more efficient systems.

It is not as important for industrial or production engineers to become certified or licensed as it is for other engineering professionals. The US Bureau of Labor Statistics (BLS) does, however, encourage those production and industrial engineers who work for companies that have government contracts to obtain certification. The licensing process typically begins upon graduation from an Accreditation Board for Engineering and Technology–approved undergraduate program. Following graduation, prospective production engineers should take the National Council of Examiners for Engineering and Surveying (NCEES) Fundamentals of Engineering (FE) exam and gain work experience. At least four years should be spent in the field before moving on to the final step in the licensing process, the NCEES Principles and Practice of Engineering (PE) exam.

Daily Tasks and Technology

It is the production engineer's job to tune the instrument of manufacturing, making sure every part works in concert with the others. Production engineers are active in every stage of the production process and are responsible for seeing the implementation of new procedures through to completion. They will often be included on planning committees for the construction of new factory floors and other manufacturing facilities; they will often be brought in on the ground floor of development, working with designers and researchers to build a product that meets customer demands while remaining economical. From there, the production engineer determines what manufacturing capabilities already exist and whether or not new machinery, materials, or labor practices are required. Once production begins, engineers continually monitor the process, gathering data and statistics to identify problems and eliminate inefficiencies.

Off the manufacturing floor, production engineers must constantly monitor demand and market forces that might affect the cost efficiency of their systems. They must also keep tabs on the environmental impact and resource consumption of the production process.

Earnings and Employment Outlook

According to the BLS, industrial engineers made a median wage of $76,100 in 2010. The lowest 10 percent earned under $49,700, and the top 10 percent earned over $112,830.

The BLS estimates that employment of industrial engineers will increase at a slower rate than the average for all occupations, growing 6 percent between 2010 and 2020.

The BLS estimates that employment of industrial engineers will increase at a slower rate than the average for all occupations, growing 6 percent between 2010 and 2020. But because they are not as specialized as other engineers, industrial and production engineers have a wide range of options for employment, as almost any industry seeks to cut costs and improve internal efficiency. According to the BLS, a general slump in manufacturing is behind the projected slow employment growth.

Related Occupations

- **Industrial Engineering Technicians:** Industrial engineering technicians work to solve industrial layout or manufacturing production problems through the application of engineering theory.

- **Ergonomists:** Ergonomists design equipment meant to optimize worker productivity while minimizing operator fatigue.

- **Petroleum Engineers:** Petroleum engineers design systems to improve oil and gas extraction and production.

- **Civil Engineers:** Civil engineers plan, design, and oversee the construction and maintenance of facilities and infrastructure such as roads, bridges, power plants, and dams.

- **Mining and Geological Engineers:** Mining engineers survey a potential site and determine the production processes and equipment necessary to mine it efficiently and safely.

Future Applications

The Occupational Information Network (O*NET), maintained by the US Department of Labor Employment and Training Administration, lists industrial engineering as a field undergoing significant change as the result of environmentally conscious technology and institutional reform. Production and industrial engineers will play an important role in minimizing the environmental impact of manufacturing and making sure production processes are up to the standards of green technology.

As technology continues to streamline the manufacturing process, the duties of a production engineer are likely to change in scale but not importance. Robotics technologies have already begun to minimize the human-labor element of manufacturing, but production engineers will still be needed to design work-flow systems, even as they become increasingly automated. Future production engineers will need to remain on the cutting edge of emerging technology; an even greater understanding of computer science and software engineering may also prove beneficial. As newer and more advanced consumer technology becomes more affordable, production output will need to increase, and it is production engineers who will design the next generation of assembly lines and manufacturing floors.

More Information

American Society for Engineering Management
600 West Fourteenth Street
Rolla, MO 65409
www.asem.org

Human Factors and Ergonomics Society
PO Box 1369
Santa Monica, CA 90406
www.hfes.org

Institute of Industrial Engineers
3577 Parkway Lane, Suite 200
Norcross, GA 30092
www.iienet2.org

International Society of Automation
67 T. W. Alexander Drive
PO Box 12277
Research Triangle Park, NC 27709
www.isa.org

Chemical Genetics

FIELDS OF STUDY

Biology; biochemistry; developmental biology; chemistry; organic chemistry; medicinal chemistry; drug development; pharmacology; molecular biology; chemical biology.

DEFINITION

Chemical genetics involves using small molecules to manipulate and therefore better understand biological systems. While *small* in this context does not have a concrete definition, small molecules are typically organic molecules that, because of their structure and composition, bind to proteins and allow modification of gene expression. The molecules used may be either man-made or isolated from natural sources. Depending on the nature and needs of the experiment, this may be done at the molecular, cellular, or organismic level.

Chemical genetics as a field is a relatively recent development, with many of the tools and data needed to systematize its research only arising since 1990. However, many of the important developments and discoveries of small molecules central to the field date from before this time. Continuing research allows scientists to better understand the workings of those discoveries.

Basic Principles

Genes work by encoding for proteins, and in chemical genetics, the small molecules used are designed or chosen in order to target those proteins. While genetic manipulation and experimentation has been a part of the field of genetics since Gregor Mendel's experiments with plants, chemical genetics differs from classical genetics in that it focuses on targeting the proteins rather than the genes themselves.

Chemical genetics has several advantages over classical genetics in its study and application. These advantages are largely linked to the fact that chemical genetics is typically done with simple organisms. The smaller scale allows for better concentration on a single effect.

In addition, the effect is often reversible; whether or not that is the case is easier to ascertain on a smaller scale. Finally, using cell-based chemical-genetics testing avoids the problem of long gestation and generation times that come with animal and human testing. The major disadvantage of chemical genetics is that it can be unclear from testing how usable a potential treatment is. It can be difficult to find or create a molecule that will only react with one target, so there is a possibility of small molecules having unintended side effects.

The two basic types of research in the field are called forward and reverse chemical genetics. In forward chemical genetics, as in forward classical genetics, the research looks from the phenotype (outward appearance of a trait) of interest to the genotype (genetic coding for a trait), but in chemical genetics, that continues from the genotype to the encoded protein. In experimentation, a number of small molecules are added to cells or animals to be observed for the desired effect. The next step is to identify the protein to which the small molecules have bound themselves.

With reverse chemical genetics, research begins with the protein. The small molecule being used is added to a sample of the pure protein, with the result placed into a cell or animal. The resulting phenotype is observed and analyzed.

Chemical genetics also features many of the same elements and processes as drug discovery. In drug discovery, however, the molecules used must be screened for safety because of their potential use in living humans or other animals. In chemical genetics, the initial focus is on effects, and the nature of many experiments, at either the cellular or the molecular level, means that the ongoing viability of the cell is not necessarily a primary concern, and therefore human-subject protocols are not in play.

Core Concepts

Chemical genetics is a systemic method of making discoveries that previously were more the result of serendipity. A stepwise process, along with powerful libraries and computing tools, can find and eliminate potential candidates for an experiment much more quickly than was possible in the past.

Forward Chemical Genetics and Target Identification. In a forward chemical genetics experiment, the goal is to find the protein that will react with a small molecule. In order to do this, a plate is prepared with a number of wells that will hold the experimental bacteria. Into each of these wells a different small molecule is placed. The small molecule is immobilized and then tested to determine which, if any, of the proteins in the bacteria it bonded with. Research into the best way to immobilize a molecule is ongoing, with researchers seeking a route that does not involve doing anything to the small molecule itself.

Compound Libraries. In order to determine which small molecule will have the desired effect on a protein, numerous suspects must be tested. Part of the reason for the expansion of the field of chemical genetics has been both the growing number of molecules found for scientists to use and the increasing amount of data resulting from their effects. As more experiments are done, the knowledge base regarding the effects of particular small molecules widens. Ideally, researchers would have access to the small molecules that might affect a target, and all of these molecules would be available for possible use and could be tested.

Typically, scientists working in the science industry have had access to a much wider range of these molecules than those working in other fields. However, there are plans to close that gap. The National Human Genome Research Institute, a branch of the National Institutes of Health (NIH), plans to develop a wide library of five hundred thousand small molecules, held across a number of centers, for use by researchers.

Reverse Chemical Genetics. In reverse chemical genetics, the goal is to find which small molecule, after binding to the protein, will have the desired effect on a system or an organism. To do this, a purified form of the protein needs to be created, which then needs to be combined separately with each of the small molecules of interest. These combinations are then monitored in the cell to see if the desired phenotype occurs.

Chemical Genomics. Finding a small molecule that affects a protein in the desired way is only the first step. The molecule must have the potential to interact with numerous proteins other than the desired target. Once inside a living organism, the molecule may react in unexpected ways, and the disruption of the biological pathway may have some unforeseen detrimental impacts. Any discoveries yielded by chemical genetics must still be put to real-world use in order to determine if they are effective and if their side effects outweigh the benefit of the treatment. Numerous pathways in the body require proteins; one of the goals of chemical genetics is finding a way to activate or deactivate each and every one of them.

Applications Past and Present

Drug Discovery—Pain Relief. While the scientific discipline of chemical genetics is relatively new, the application of the principles underlying the field is thousands of years old. A great deal of the research in the field has been and continues to be focused on the development of compounds that affect the human body and can alleviate or cure illnesses. Early humans used various plants as medicines; chemical genetics provides even greater tools for determining the action of these plants and isolating and or purifying active compounds for use as pharmaceuticals.

A drug more than a century old provides a useful example for understanding the workings of small molecules and chemical genetics. First discovered in 1853, aspirin was synthesized by placing an acetyl group on salicylic acid, which was isolated from the bark of the white willow tree. In 1897, Felix Hoffmann, working for the company Bayer, was able to synthesize the compound, and in 1899, it began to be sold commercially. Aspirin has been and remains one of the most popular drugs taken, both by itself and combined with other ingredients in pill form, in part because of its utility. In addition to its original purpose as a pain reliever, aspirin has been found to have use as an anti-inflammatory and a fever reducer and to reduce certain heart risks. At the same time, it does have side effects, such as heartburn, stomach pain, nausea, and vomiting. These are among the reasons there are a number of other over-the-counter pain relievers, some of which avoid the side effects of aspirin, such as acetaminophen. The negative effects of aspirin were worse before it was chemically manufactured. In

Interesting Facts about Chemical Genetics

- The origin of the term *chemical genetics* is credited to a 1935 paper by Hans von Euler-Chelpin that examined chlorophyll production in strains of barley. Von Euler-Chelpin and Arthur Harden had been awarded the 1929 Nobel Prize in Chemistry for work in "fermentation of sugar and fermentative enzymes."

- Acetylsalicylic acid, better known as aspirin, is an example of a small molecule that works by its action on the enzyme cyclooxygenase (COX). Developed by Felix Hoffmann in a Bayer laboratory in 1897, it was the first synthesized drug to be widely sold.

- John Robert Vane discovered the mechanism by which aspirin inhibits prostaglandin formation and alleviates headaches. Along with Swedish researchers Sune K. Bergström and Bengt I. Samuelsson, he was awarded the Nobel Prize in Physiology or Medicine in 1982 for his work on prostaglandins.

- Rapamycin, an immunosuppressive drug used to prevent rejection of a transplanted kidney—and sometimes to treat psoriasis—is named for Rapa Nui, the local name for Easter Island, where it was discovered in 1975.

- FK-506, also known as tacrolimus, was discovered in 1984 in a Japanese laboratory. Obtained from a sample of the bacteria *Streptomyces tsukubaensis*, the molecule, which suppresses the immune system, is used to prevent rejection of an organ after donation, and sometimes to treat Crohn's disease.

- Cyclosporin, an immunosuppressant used in organ transplants and as a treatment for rheumatoid arthritis, was discovered in 1972 in the labs of Sandoz (now Novartis) in Basel, Switzerland. Credit for and the timing of the discovery remain matters of some dispute.

fact, part of the reason for Hoffmann's interest in synthesizing aspirin in the manner he did was that his father had been taking salicylic acid only, but it severely upset his stomach.

Aspirin was in use for many years before its mechanisms were understood. However, by using chemical-genetics techniques, scientists have been able to develop a better understanding of why aspirin has its anti-inflammatory and pain-relieving effects, as well as its unpleasant side effects. Aspirin works by binding to cyclooxygenase-1 (COX-1, or sometimes just COX), a naturally occurring enzyme that catalyzes the formation of prostaglandins (PGs), which are molecules produced by the body that cause inflammation. The binding action prevents inflammation from occurring. At the same time, PGs produced by the COX-1 pathway are also involved in protecting the lining of the stomach, kidney function, and blood clotting. The inhibition of this pathway can therefore cause stomach pain, kidney disease, or blood thinning in certain cases.

The British pharmacologist John Robert Vane did a great deal of the research that accounts for the knowledge of the mechanism of aspirin. In the course of his research, he also laid some of the groundwork for the discovery of other COX pathways. Vane's research also contributed to the development of ACE inhibitors, another small-molecule treatment, which are used to treat high blood pressure and heart failure.

One of the pathways discovered by Vane was COX-2, which led to a new class of pain-relieving drugs known as COX-2 inhibitors. These strong anti-inflammatory drugs were used as treatments for arthritis and were used off-label to treat other forms of pain. Because of the adverse effects that can accompany aspirin use, the hope was that these new drugs would provide pain relief without the gastrointestinal side effects. While the drugs are able to provide pain relief, they are accompanied by elevated risk of heart attack and stroke; therefore, two of the three approved COX-2 inhibitors have been pulled off the market, and the remaining one carries a warning. However, research into the potential applications of these small molecules is ongoing.

A third enzyme, known as COX-3, has also been discovered, and there was some speculation that it might explain the pharmaceutical action of acetaminophen (Tylenol). However, strong evidence suggests that it does not play a significant role in PG production in humans, although it appears to have some effect in dogs; thus, it may have some utility in veterinary medicine.

Drug Discovery—Immune Suppressors. Other drug treatments have played significant roles in the development of chemical genetics. Several immunosuppressant drugs were isolated from fungal samples and ultimately played a central role in successful organ transplantation. These drugs include cyclosporine A, rapamycin, and tacrolimus, also known as FK-506.

Drug Discovery—Cancer Treatments. The idea of a "cure for cancer" is discussed less often than before as the public comes to understand that cancer is, in fact, a disease with many different forms. Accordingly, many different strategies are being tried to target various strains of cancers that grow throughout the body, with some treatments arising from chemical genetics.

For example, one early attempt at treatment used chemical-genetics techniques to target MEK, an enzyme that contributes to cell division. The treatment significantly reduced tumor growth while avoiding some of the toxic effects common in cancer drugs with less specific targets. MEK continues to be a subject of research for the treatment of various cancers. One emerging prospect in many cases is combination therapy to inhibit a second molecular pathway at the same time, as many cancers mutate to avoid a single treatment. As an example, one treatment for melanoma targets the BRAF protein, as mutations of the BRAF gene have been strongly linked with development of cancer. However, it has been observed that after prolonged treatment, more of the BRAF protein is produced. Therefore, a prospective treatment option is combining the current treatment with an MEK inhibitor with the goal of preventing the increased production.

The use of small molecules in cancer treatments is likely to have some strong benefits for the field as a whole due to the utility of the large database of information on small molecules and proteins established by the National Cancer Institute's Initiative for Chemical Genetics.

Drug Discovery—Infectious Disease. While many pharmaceuticals focus on targets in the human body, another target of chemical genetics is the foreign invaders that doctors and patients seek to counter. For example, malaria, which is spread by mosquitoes infected with a pathogen, has proved difficult to contain. Researchers studying the disease found an enzyme called PfSUB1 that breaks protein bonds, leading to a crucial step in the spread of disease once a host is infected. Several chemical screenings of thousands of possibilities have yielded some candidate molecules to inhibit the activity of PfSUB1. A drug called NITD609, developed at the Novartis Institute for Tropical Diseases, yielded promising results in early testing.

Hepatitis C treatment has also proved challenging. Drugs used to combat hepatitis C often have harsh side effects, such as flulike symptoms, and patients sometimes cease to respond to treatments. Screening tests yielded cyclosporine A as a drug candidate, as it inhibited replication of the viral cells. However, the known side effects of cyclosporine A make use of the drug undesirable, prompting researchers to focus on other candidates from the cyclosporine drug family.

Plant Genomics. The original subjects of classical genetics research, plants have a continued place in the field of chemical genetics. Plants might prove especially useful for chemical-genetics purposes because they have genomes much larger than those of humans and because many of those genes repeat. As a result, the introduction of small molecules can more easily help determine the function of various genes than a classical approach, as it allows single genes that are duplicates to be targeted simultaneously rather than individually.

Impact on Industry

Chemical genetics is a relatively new field, and as a result, much of the jobs data is not separated from larger fields of which it is a part, such as genetics and medical science. Geneticists in the field overwhelmingly have PhDs. Chemical genetics also requires a strong knowledge base in multiple scientific areas.

Pharmaceutical Manufacturers. There are a number of avenues of research for pharmaceutical development. Many pharmaceutical companies are looking to chemical genetics to play a role in the development of new treatment options for illnesses and diseases.

There is growing concern about certain developments and the lack of progress in some areas of drug discovery. For example, the number of antibiotics available has not grown significantly, while many bacteria have become resistant to available treatments. There are also concerns that factors such as a low investment return and too-strict regulation are preventing the development of more antibiotics in the United States.

Government Agencies and Military. Government agencies have played a role in furthering chemical-genetics research. A prime example is the establishment of the Initiative for Chemical Genetics, funded by the National Cancer Institute with the goal of giving researchers better information on the

Occupation	Biological scientists, all other
Employment 2010	35,800
Projected Employment 2020	38,000
Change in Number (2010–20)	2,200
Percent Change	6%

Bureau of Labor Statistics, 2012

small molecules and proteins they study by allowing the results to be shared in a database called ChemBank. The database was created and is hosted by the Broad Institute, a collaborative enterprise of researchers at Harvard University and Massachusetts Institute of Technology (MIT). The NIH is also funding a number of studies examining potential small-molecule treatments for various cancers and a study examining small molecules and metabolism in healthy elderly people.

Budget proposals for 2013 reveal some interest from the Defense Advanced Research Projects Agency (DARPA), an agency in the Department of Defense that funds research of potential use to the military, in developing a system for observing small molecules in vivo. Other military-supported research has included examining the biochemical pathway of anthrax with the hope of finding a treatment.

Academic Research and Teaching. Because chemical genetics mostly encompasses basic science research, academia is likely to remain the primary source of future advances in the field. While drug discovery and opportunities for people with skill sets from chemical genetics are likely to remain strong in industry, the focus on a return in investment in the form of marketable pharmaceuticals means most of the basic science research is likely to be done in an academic setting.

Social Context and Future Prospects

The growth of chemical genetics has been facilitated by the sequencing of the human genome and by the increased computing power that allows for increasingly large, fast databases of information on the various proteins and molecules that are used in chemical-genetics testing. Chemical genetics provides a means of conducting large-scale testing and research for the action of large numbers of compounds on large numbers of proteins. As medical science identifies the various mechanisms of disease, more opportunities for the potential use of small molecules are likely to emerge.

However, while chemical genetics has yielded important advances, there have been some highly publicized setbacks. Introduced to the market in the late 1990s and early 2000s, the small molecules used as COX-2 inhibitors had great success in treating arthritis pain, and they were ultimately prescribed for some off-label uses, including pain relief from migraines and after operations. However, the action of the small molecules also seemed to produce a dramatic rise in heart attacks and strokes. Merck took Vioxx off the market in September 2004, and a scandal subsequently ensued when facts emerged that the company had ignored and possibly concealed strong evidence of the risks of taking the medication. Litigation resulted in the release of documents that revealed the depths of the problem, and the company paid $4.85 billion to thousands of litigants who had been harmed. The FDA requested that Pfizer take Bextra off the market in April 2005 because of similar concerns, and ultimately, the company paid billions in a settlement over deceptive marketing practices. Celebrex, also sold by Pfizer, is the only COX-2 inhibitor still on the market in the United States as of 2012, although it carries a strong "heart event" warning.

While Vioxx and Bextra, both popular drugs, are no longer available, some physicians believe that, for certain patients, the benefits of the powerful pain relievers would outweigh the heart risks that have been found. However, the impact of the cases went far beyond those who suffered as a result of the side effects of a drug from a class that had once seemed promising. The scandal surrounding the COX-2 inhibitors remains in the news years later, and the issues raised with the recall of these drugs still loom large when it comes to public trust in the pharmaceutical industry. While the small-molecule products produced by chemical genetics can have powerful effects, their use in humans means that undesirable effects can happen when these molecules connect elsewhere. Only with a better understanding of the full field and the workings of the proteins targeted will the field of chemical genetics reach its full potential.

Further Reading

Blackwell, Helen E., and Yunde Zhao. "Chemical Genetic Approaches to Plant Biology." *Plant Physiology* 133.2 (2003): 448–55. Print. Discusses why a chemical-genetics approach would be advantageous in plant biology and addresses some experimentation conducted with the *Arabidopsis* plant.

Bonetta, Laura. "What Is Chemical Genetics?" *Howard Hughes Medical Institute.* Howard Hughes Medical Inst., n.d. Web. 23 Oct. 2012. Provides a basic introduction to the field of chemical genetics, with links to a number of multimedia features illustrating specific examples of the field.

ChemBank: Initiative for Chemical Genetics. Broad Inst., 2006. Web. 23 Oct. 2012. Collaboration between the NIH and a number of other institutions that has information on numerous small molecules and screens to help researchers who might not otherwise have access to that knowledge.

Cong, Feng, Atwood K. Cheung, and Shih-Min A. Huang. "Chemical Genetics–Based Target Identification in Drug Discovery." *Annual Review of Pharmacology and Toxicology* 52 (2012): 57–78. Print. Explains how the process of chemical genetics is used to approach drug discovery.

Florian, Stefan, et al. "Chemical Genetics: Reshaping Biology through Chemistry." *HFSP Journal* 1.2 (2007): 104–114. Print. Presents a general outline of the relationship between chemical genetics and drug discovery and gives a number of specific examples.

O'Connor, Cornelius J., Luca Laraia, and David R. Spring. "Chemical Genetics." *Chemical Society Reviews* 40.8 (2011): 4332–45. Print. Provides an excellent overview of both the field as a whole and a number of detailed specific developments.

Spring, David R. "Chemical Genetics to Chemical Genomics: Small Molecules Offer Big Insights." *Chemical Society Reviews* 34.6 (2005): 472–82. Print. Details the specific information that might be gleaned about the workings of proteins by using small molecules to target them.

Vane, John R., and Regina M. Botting. "The Mechanism of Action of Aspirin." *Thrombosis Research* 110.5 (2003): 255–58. Print. Provides a history and a summary of the workings of aspirin from a researcher involved in many of the key discoveries.

About the Author: Joseph Brownstein, MS, is a science and medical writer.

Geteticist

Earnings (Yearly Average): $70,790

Employment and Outlook: Much faster than average growth (Medical scientists in general; Bureau of Labor Statistics, 2012)

O*NET-SOC Code: 19-1029.03

Related Career Clusters: Health Science; Agriculture, Food & Natural Resources

Scope of Work

Geneticists study the traits and characteristics passed via heredity from parent to offspring in an organism. The information they uncover about genes can help these scientists learn more about the development of an individual's physical traits at a molecular level. It can also reveal more information about a species, as well as how a given population of that species is interconnected. Geneticists conduct research on genomes (the complete set of an organism's genetic information), DNA, and other biological features, compiling large quantities of data to create models and analytical frameworks. Based on their research, they often generate scientific reports and literature, including books and scholarly articles, that they present to scientific peers at conferences.

Education and Coursework

Geneticists typically complete several years of undergraduate, graduate, and postgraduate education. At the undergraduate level (four-year college or university), they must take courses in a number of scientific disciplines. Among these are mathematics and chemistry, biology, and other physical sciences. Aspiring geneticists may major in one or more of these scientific disciplines, with an emphasis on biology. They also need to take courses in computer science and statistics, which will prove essential in doing genetic research. Undergraduates must also hone their writing, public speaking, and researching skills by taking courses in social sciences in addition to physical- and natural-science courses.

Upon graduating from college, future geneticists pursue graduate degrees, beginning with master's degrees and then PhDs. Although some genetics-oriented students may stop at the master's level, the majority of these scientists continue to their doctorates. Earning a PhD in genetics can take between four and six years, although the dissertation phase can take longer. For the first few years of PhD programs, students take advanced courses in fields of relevance to genetics: biochemistry, molecular biology, botany, and agricultural sciences (the latter two are useful in the study of the genetics of crops and plant life). This coursework is structured and accompanied by work in a laboratory setting, giving students knowledge of the latest research techniques. After completing this coursework and the laboratory-training phase of their graduate education, candidates must embark on independent research projects, which are usually funded by the universities at which they are enrolled, government or private scientific foundations, or pharmaceutical manufacturers. This research will culminate in an extensive document known as a dissertation, which if completed, would be published in a relevant professional scientific journal. The dissertation is also an important tool for a job candidate: The research conducted at this level may help geneticists obtain jobs with either one of their project funders or other organizations.

Transferable Skills

- Communication Skills – Reporting information
- Interpersonal/Social Skills – Working as a member of a team (SCANS Workplace Competency – Interpersonal)
- Research and Planning Skills – Analyzing information
- Organization and Management Skills – Managing people/ groups (SCANS Workplace Competency – Resources)
- Organization and Management Skills – Organizing information or materials
- Technical Skills – Using technology to process information (SCANS Workplace Competency – Information)
- Technical Skills – Working with data or numbers

Career Enhancement and Training

Most geneticists who begin their careers after graduate school obtain further training as entry-level laboratory or research assistants. In this capacity, they work with experienced scientists at universities, pharmaceutical, or other scientific research laboratory facilities. This training helps them apply the knowledge and experience they obtained in graduate school to researching genetics in specific fields of study (such as pharmaceutical development, crop genetics, and epidemiology). It will also help them develop new research techniques, formulate models, and write new scientific papers for publication.

In addition to their basic laboratory work, geneticists must become skilled in computer science. They need to be proficient in computer-modeling software, which is used to create multidimensional images and frameworks. Computer-modeling software is also essential in compiling and collating large quantities of data. Much of the fundamental knowledge and capability in this arena is obtained while at the undergraduate and graduate levels. However, as both software and technologies used for computer modeling evolve, biophysicists must keep abreast of these changes to conduct comprehensive research.

Geneticists must become highly proficient in computer software and related technologies. Much of their basic training should have been received at the undergraduate level, but as these computer applications continue to improve, it is useful for geneticists and their scientific peers to familiarize themselves with the latest in word processing, spreadsheet, presentation, and database software.

Like other scientists, geneticists benefit greatly from networking with their peers through professional societies and associations. The American Genetic Association, the Genetics Society of America, and the American Society of Human Genetics are among the many genetics-related networking organizations in the United States and around the world.

Daily Tasks and Technology

The daily responsibilities of geneticists vary based on the field in which they apply their knowledge. In general, however, they collect samples, conduct research on genomes and related biological subjects, collate data, generate models, and use the information to generate reports and scientific papers. These responsibilities include utilizing existing research practices to analyze DNA samples, gene expression, protein complexes, and other basic genomic components.

When geneticists' research fails to yield further information, they may modify their analytical techniques or introduce new ones. Among the many different technologies used by geneticists are "electron guns," automated liquid-handling systems, and microbiology analyzers. Computers also play an essential role in geneticists' daily activities; laptops, as well as larger personal and analytical computers, are used heavily in the laboratory. In this arena, geneticists use analytical and scientific software (such as SAS/Genetics and Ward Systems Group's GeneHunter programs), bioinformatics (the application of computer and statistics systems to biological research), and basic operating systems and suites.

Geneticists' work is performed mainly in laboratory settings at universities, hospitals, private research facilities, and medical and pharmaceutical manufacturing organizations. Senior-level geneticists supervise laboratory staff (including research assistants, interns, and technology operators), maintain lab records and notebooks, and review data collected by lab personnel. These genetic researchers carefully monitor the progress made by staff on their assignments and ensure that the tasks performed are consistent with the overall project's parameters and deadlines.

Many geneticists are also university professors, teaching related courses to undergraduate and graduate students. In this area, they develop curricula and course syllabi, grade papers and exams, and monitor students' projects in the laboratory. They also keep abreast of the work of their peers by reading scientific journals and other literature.

Furthermore, geneticists use the data and models generated through their research to write and publish reports, scientific papers, articles, and books. They must therefore use word processing, spreadsheet, and even presentation software to write these materials and present them for their superiors and their clients and to their peers at scientific conferences.

A Conversation with Dawn Laney

Job Title: Genetic Counselor

What was your career path (including education)?

When I entered college, I initially thought that I would enjoy being a scientific writer or journalist. Accordingly, I chose a small liberal arts school which would allow me to explore a variety of subjects (Trinity College in Hartford, CT). I found that the best path for me was to split my focus and major in history and biology, with a minor in European studies. During my biology coursework, I completed a thesis project that was based on molecular genetics research in a professor's laboratory. I quickly learned that I preferred working with people directly rather than working in a laboratory setting. Around the same time, I learned about genetic counseling as a profession. I researched the career and spoke with the staff at the National Society of Genetic Counselors. Genetic counseling as a career combined working directly with patients and translating complicated scientific information into understandable everyday terms. There was also the opportunity to do research and write journal articles as well as other patient-focused books and informational fact sheets. I was hooked. I made sure to take the required courses in statistics, psychology, biology, and biochemistry and applied for a genetic counseling master's degree program. Although I had several interviews and was waitlisted for one school, genetic counseling programs are very competitive and I was not admitted that year. Accordingly, I took the next year to work as a case manager at a paternity testing company and shadow genetic counselors in the area. I reapplied the following year and was admitted to the genetic counseling masters degree in human genetics program at Sarah Lawrence College. The training program combined working with experienced genetic counselors in the field with intensive class work in human development, genetics, psychology, and biochemistry. After obtaining my masters degree, I began my genetic counseling career working with pregnant patients and their partners. Around this time, I obtained my board certification as a genetic counselor. After several years in the prenatal arena, I moved into newborn screening follow-up for the state of Georgia and finally into the very specialized field of lysosomal storage diseases. Working as a genetic counselor in lysosomal storage diseases has been a great opportunity for me to perform clinical research, write scientific articles, and work with patients. After two years of working on clinical research studies I was also able to obtain my certification as a certified clinical research coordinator. Currently, I am a genetic counselor, an investigator, a research coordinator, an instructor, infusion center manager, and the Emory Lysosomal Storage Disease Program Leader.

What are three pieces of advice you would offer someone interested in your profession?

1. One of the most important things I would suggest before applying for a genetic counseling program is to volunteer with a genetic counselor. In this way you can learn about the daily activities of a genetic counselor and obtain a better understand of the profession. This experience will help prepare you for the competitive graduate degree application process.

2. Research each genetic counseling program carefully and speak to recent graduates. Each program has a slightly different curriculum, specialty, and focus. In order to find the best programs for you a little legwork is needed.

3. Genetic counseling is a career on the rise given the increased amount of genetic information available in medicine and availability of inexpensive genetic testing options. There are plenty of genetic counseling jobs available if you are flexible in your location. However, if you are only interested in working in a specific city, you may not have a job waiting for you when you graduate from school.

What paths for career advancement are available to you?

The vast majority of genetic counselors have a master's degree in genetic counseling or human genetics. A genetic counseling master's degree is very flexible degree. Within the realm of genetic counseling you can become a program leader, genetic counselor supervisor, lead genetic counselor, program leader, or academic faculty. Depending on your interests you could also move into clinical research and become an investigator or primary study coordinator. Other genetic counselors work in the pharmaceutical and laboratory industries as team leads, directors, or patient advocates.

Earnings and Employment Outlook

Geneticists' annual earnings vary based on both the arena in which they work and the level of their experience. For example, entry-level geneticists may earn about $30,000 per year. On the other hand, some senior-level geneticists working in the private sector earn nearly $110,000 annually. The average salary for scientists in this field is about $71,000 per year.

Many biophysicists receive their pay through grants (one-time payments from a foundation or the government), which means that annual budgets can be subject to dramatic changes if the anticipated grants are not approved. Pay offered by pharmaceutical or medical manufacturers, for example, is more consistent.

Genetics is a relatively new scientific field, with enormous implications for the modern world. Geneticists can help predict and address hereditary diseases and conditions as well as birth defects. They also make it possible for medical and pharmaceutical researchers to better understand and treat diseases. The technologies and research practices utilized in this field continue to unearth new information about the human genome. In light of this fact, genetics has expanding implications in the health care, agriculture, and even archeological and paleontological arenas (as geneticists are sometimes called upon to analyze specimens from millions of years ago). As a result, geneticists will continue to be in demand, with opportunities available in a wide range of industries.

Related Occupations

- Biochemist/Biophysicist: These professions focus on the chemical and mechanical aspects of a living organism.

- Epidemiologist: Epidemiologists study the root causes and spread of disease among humans and other organisms.

- Agricultural and Food Scientists: These researchers study the development and use of crops and food products, sharing a number of common areas of research with those of geneticists.

- Medical Doctor: Physicians obtain a wide range of coursework during their training, including genetics. In many situations, medical doctors and geneticists work together on research projects as well as with individual patients.

Future Applications

The life sciences fields, which include genetics, continue to grow, due in no small part to the need to understand inherited conditions such as high cholesterol and cancer. Additionally, new technologies are being developed that are capable of analyzing genomic samples in greater detail than ever before. In light of these trends, demand for geneticists is growing at a significant rate, particularly for those with the knowledge and capability of utilizing this technology.

These scientists are already in demand for researching disease treatments and birth defects; growth in research regarding genetic disorders and conditions will add to this demand. The advances this field has taken, particularly with regard to researching diseases such as cancer and heart disease, demonstrate the continued relevance of genetics. Geneticists will be increasingly called upon to continue this research for the pharmaceutical and medical industries.

In addition to health care applications, geneticists will be in demand as scientists research both genetically modified crops and the impacts of climate change on life on Earth (both in the past and present). Genetics has clear implications for these growing research areas as well as for those in the health care arena.

Michael P. Auerbach

More Information

American Genetic Association
2030 SE Marine Science Drive
Newport, OR 97365
Tel. 541-867-0334
www.theaga.org

American Society of Human Genetics
9650 Rockville Pike
Bethesda, MD 20814-3998
Tel. 301-634-7300
Fax. 301-634-7079
http://www.ashg.org

Association of Professors of Human and Medical Genetics
9650 Rockville Pike
Bethesda, MD 20814
www.aphmg.org

European Society of Human Genetics
Vienna Medical Academy
Alserstrasse 4
1090 Vienna, Austria
Tel. 43-1-405-13-83-20
Fax. 43-1-407-82-74
https://www.eshg.org

Genetics Society of America
9650 Rockville Pike
Bethesda, MD 20814-3998
Tel. 301-634-7300
Fax. 301-634-7079
www.genetics-gsa.org

Chemical Technology

FIELDS OF STUDY

Chemistry; biochemistry; biology; mathematics; physics; engineering; electronics; fluid dynamics; statistics; analytical chemistry; metrology; quality assurance and control.

DEFINITION

Chemical technology focuses on the application of technological procedures and devices to the practice of chemistry and its related disciplines. In the narrowest sense, this relates to practices and processes in which chemical transformations are carried out, usually for the production or processing of specific materials. Chemical technology also encompasses the use of technology and devices for the monitoring and control of procedures and applications in any of the various disciplines of chemistry.

Basic Principles

Chemical technology is concerned with the physical environment and devices in which chemical transformations or reactions are carried out, as well as the instrumentation and control systems that are used to monitor, analyze, and control those reactions. Working as part of a team, chemical technicians ensure that processes and experiments are carried out correctly and that equipment is properly maintained. Processes may be carried out on any scale, ranging from a few milligrams of material in a batch to bulk quantities of material in continuous operation. The former is typical of laboratory experiments, while the latter is common in industrial settings.

Such chemical processes are generally carried out in a fluid medium, either in the gas phase or in solution. Solid materials are also often involved, as are combinations of solid, liquid, and gas phases. Each process requires a corresponding set of procedures for monitoring its condition and progress, and chemical technicians are generally responsible for carrying out this aspect of the work as well.

The chemical technician is a valuable member of the team with which he or she works. While not normally involved in the initial design of experiments and procedures, the technician is trusted to ensure that those procedures are carried out as specified, and any observational information that the technician acquires in that process is important to future functions. Typically, the more experience a technician gains in a specific role, the more that individual is relied upon in the continuing performance of that role within an organization.

Core Concepts

Much work in the field of chemical technology is hands-on "wet chemistry" or bench work. In such a research environment, a number of key techniques are used to measure specific chemical and physical properties and monitor chemical processes. The principal means of analysis in research and other sectors include nuclear magnetic resonance spectrometry, infrared spectrophotometry, high-pressure liquid and gas-phase chromatography, and mass spectrometry.

Spectrophotometry. All spectrophotometers function on the same basic principles. Materials interact with light of specific wavelengths, each assortment of wavelengths being associated with some specific molecular or atomic characteristic of the particular material. Thus, measurement of the interaction can be used to monitor the extent to which a specific compound is formed or consumed and can provide structural information about the molecules involved in a process. A single-beam spectrophotometer uses a single beam of light that passes through or reflects off of a sample of a material. The material absorbs some of the wavelengths of that incident light, and measurement of the transmitted light reveals which wavelengths have been absorbed. In a double-beam spectrophotometer, a single beam of incident light is split and passed through both a test sample and a reference sample, and the resultant transmitted light is compared to determine the specific wavelengths that have been absorbed. The nature of the material being measured determines which type of spectrophotometer is used. Enhanced versions of both types of spectrophotometers are used to perform specialized tasks; for example, Fourier transform infrared spectrophotometry is used to obtain high-precision measurements of absorption spectra.

High-Pressure Liquid and Gas Chromatography. In all forms of chromatography, a sample of a mixture of different materials dissolved in a fluid medium passes through a column of some solid particulate material. Different materials have different affinities for adhesion to solid particles and dissolution in a fluid medium, so as the fluid medium is passed through the column, the materials become separated from each other according to their respective abilities to adhere to the solid material before being redissolved in the fluid medium. The most common solid media in chromatography are silica gel and alumina. In gas chromatography, the fluid medium is typically an inert gas such as nitrogen or argon. As the gas passes through a long, narrow column packed with silica gel or alumina, the components of a mixture of materials that has been injected into one end of the column enter into an equilibrium between adhering to the solid particles and reentering the gas phase as vapors. They thus become separated and exit the column individually. Depending on the purpose of the experiment, the amounts of materials and their retention times may be recorded, or the individual components may be collected for further use. In high-pressure liquid chromatography, also known as high-performance liquid chromatography, the fluid medium is typically a high-purity solvent that is pumped through the column under high pressure, carrying the components of the mixture along with it.

Mass Spectrometry. The mass spectrometer functions on the rigidly defined mathematics of the motion of an electrically charged particle passing through a magnetic field. Given the strength of the magnetic field, a charged particle passing through that field follows a very specific circular path with a radius that depends directly on the mass of the particle. Thus, varying the strength of the magnetic field allows researchers to identify and measure the mass of particles. Mass spectrometry devices function under high vacuum, and that system is an essential component in the structure of any such device. While many mass spectrometers are commercially manufactured, some of the most sophisticated devices are built in-house to meet the specific requirements of individual researchers.

Combined Technologies. As the field of chemical technology encompasses a wide variety of processes and procedures, researchers in the field must often work with tools that combine elements of different technologies, such as the separation capabilities of chromatography and the identification and detection capabilities of mass spectrometry. Thus, mass spectrometry is often used in tandem with gas chromatography in the analysis of mixtures of materials. Combining mass spectrometry with high-pressure liquid chromatography is less common due to the necessity of dealing with massive solvent interference in the mass-spectrometry segment of the process.

Industrial Technologies. Industrial applications of chemical technology use many of the same tools that are used in research settings, but the primary chemical technology of industrial settings is that of process control. Reactions that work well on a small scale in the laboratory often do not produce the desired results when scaled up to large quantities. In addition, for industrial applications such as material production, it is generally preferable for materials to be produced in a continuous stream rather than in individual batch lots. It is necessary that the product be recovered cleanly and side reactions be eliminated so that unreacted materials can be recycled through the process for conversion into desired products. In industrial settings, then, chemical technology falls into two main categories: analytical technology for process monitoring and environmental technology for process control. The former relies on devices that are used to ensure that materials meet quality specifications and that the correct composition of process streams is maintained throughout the process. The latter category comprises bulk-material handling equipment such as compressors, condensers, and distillation towers.

Services and Quality-Control Technologies. Services based on chemical technology tend to be more specialized in the technology that they employ, and the degree of sophistication of the technology used mirrors the type of service being provided. A water-analysis service, for example, must have equipment capable of detecting and

Interesting Facts about Chemical Technology

- A device called a masticator cuts and blends natural rubber, after which the rubber forms a solid, coherent mass. The device was originally called "the pickle" by its inventor, Thomas Hancock.

- Louis Bernigaud, Comte de Chardonnet, devised the first artificial silk substitute by forcing liquid collodion, a nitrocellulose composition, through fine glass capillaries.

- Lyophilization is a process for removing water from a material by freezing it and placing it under vacuum. The process is generally known as freeze-drying and has been used for various purposes, from the preparation of biological materials to the recovery of priceless books, papers, and other archaeological artifacts.

- Nuclear magnetic resonance (NMR) measures the differences in the response of individual atoms in a molecule to an applied magnetic field according to their position within the molecular structure. The technology allows chemists to determine the three-dimensional shape of a molecule and is the basic principle of magnetic resonance imaging (MRI).

- Modern chemical analysis methods can detect and identify a compound from as little as ten picograms of material, an amount that is much too small to detect with the naked eye.

- Scanning tunneling microscopes and atomic force microscopes allow direct measurement and manipulation of individual atoms.

identifying contaminants to the level specified by regulation. Such a service would require mass-spectrometry technology but would have no need for nuclear magnetic resonance (NMR) spectrometry. Similarly, a forensic-analysis service might require DNA sequencers, NMR and infrared spectrophotometers, mass spectrometers, and chromatography devices. Quality control in chemical operations is more concerned with the measurement of what should not be present than with the composition of input and output process streams. Extraneous materials in a reactive stream can severely limit, and even ruin, the viability of the process by encouraging the formation of undesired products and preventing desired reaction processes. Thus, technicians working in quality control must analyze materials used as process inputs as well as those produced by or obtained from those processes to ensure that the material compositions are correct.

Applications Past and Present

Polymers. One of the most useful applications of chemical technology is the synthesis of material to produce new materials such as polymers. Polymer materials have become both ubiquitous and essential to modern society. One of the first devices used in this field was a machine called the masticator, used to "chew" raw rubber from natural sources. The mastication process brings about a change in the properties of the rubber, through which it becomes able to form a coherent mass rather than a crumbly mixture. In the development of other polymeric materials, typical small-scale laboratory ware was and continues to be used to prepare and determine the nature of the materials of interest. The nature of new polymeric materials also demands that specialized analytical methods and procedures be developed so that large-scale production can be monitored effectively. Polymerization reactions obey the same stoichiometric rules as any simple chemical reaction, and in many cases reaction stoichiometry has been determined empirically, particularly in the case of thermosetting polymers such as those used in advanced composite materials (ACM). This growing area of application requires ACM technicians to have a working knowledge of the stoichiometric properties of complex and exotic resin mixtures, effectively making them practicing chemical technicians.

Pharmaceuticals. All pharmaceuticals are produced through the work of chemical technicians. The field is generally divided into the two areas of drug discovery and development and drug manufacturing. In the discovery and development area, chemical technicians work to isolate and identify chemical compounds from natural sources and synthesize specific compounds that are expected to have certain desirable properties that can be tested. Both of these tasks rely heavily on manipulative and analytical techniques. Chromatography is one extremely versatile and important methodology used in the isolation of compounds; it encompasses a number of specialized techniques, including gas chromatography and high-pressure liquid chromatography. Distillation is another important practice in preparative chemical procedures. As liquids have varying boiling points, distillation enables their separation accordingly. The boiling point of any given liquid is also dependent on atmospheric pressure, becoming lower as the pressure decreases. Thus, reduced-pressure distillation is often used to remove excess solvents from a solution of a desired compound or to purify a material that suffers decomposition at elevated temperatures.

Other techniques used in pharmaceutical preparations rely on a particular compound's different solubilities in different solvents or on its acid-base properties. The most important aspect of drug development, however, is determining the absolute identity and molecular structure of the compound under study once it has been obtained in its pure form. Often, a specific compound with useful pharmaceutical properties can be obtained from a natural source only in extremely small quantities. Identifying its molecular structure allows synthetic chemists to determine how best to prepare the compound on a scale large enough to enable proper testing and use of the compound as a pharmaceutical agent.

Forensics. Chemical technology has become an indispensable aspect of forensic analysis in law enforcement. Some of the most sophisticated chemical technology is put to use in this field, including devices such as high-resolution spectrophotometers, chromatographic systems, and mass spectrometers. Such devices are generally used to identify compounds from even very minute samples. In 2007, for example, randomly selected Irish banknotes were all found to have trace quantities of cocaine on them when analyzed using a combination of liquid chromatography and mass spectrometry. The chromatography stage isolated the individual compounds obtained from the banknotes, and the mass spectrometry stage revealed the identity of each compound by determining the molecular masses and the pattern of masses of the fragments obtained by breaking apart the molecular structure.

Other devices used in forensic analysis measure the wavelength or frequency of energy associated with specific electronic or structural transitions that occur within a molecule. Each different molecule absorbs or emits light in a specific pattern and at specific wavelengths. Because of this feature, instrumental techniques such as infrared and NMR spectrometry are often sufficient to identify a material that has been recovered from a crime scene or victim. Such analysis is also pertinent in biological examinations, as witnessed by the use of DNA in forensic analysis.

Biofuels. Biofuels is a rapidly expanding field of application that seeks to produce combustion fuels from renewable sources, specifically plant matter, using chemical technology. This is achieved through two primary methods. The first is fermentation, in which microorganisms consume vegetable matter and produce alcohols as a by-product. The alcohols are then recovered for use as combustible fuel, and the remaining material is recycled as animal feedstock or fertilizer accordingly. In the second method, commonly referred to as biodiesel, seed and other plant-sourced oils are recovered and reduced chemically to esters of long-chain fatty acids, which can be used directly as fuel in diesel engines. This application is rapidly being adopted in many areas, notably the public and private transportation industries, and is also being tested for commercial aircraft and naval purposes. The ultimate benefit of this chemical technology is the end of reliance on fossil fuels throughout the world, which would have environmental implications and also alter economics significantly on a global scale.

Impact on Industry

Chemical technology is a crucial part of many industries, from government to academia. According to the US Bureau of Labor Statistics, employment of chemical technicians is expected to increase by 7 percent between 2010 and 2020, a slower growth rate than the average for all occupations. However, this statistic refers to overall employment of chemical technicians and does not take into account the differing rates of growth of the industries in which they are employed. In the growing biofuels industry and other industries concerned with the environment and green energy, for instance, employment is expected to increase more dramatically.

Government Agencies. Many government agencies rely heavily on chemical technology. For instance, the US Environmental Protection Agency, Environment Canada, and similar federal, state, and provincial agencies throughout the world depend on analytical and toxicological studies to assess the dangers associated with various toxic agents in the environment. This information allows them to make informed decisions when proposing environmental regulations such as

Occupation	Chemical technicians
Employment 2010	61,000
Projected Employment 2020	65,100
Change in Number (2010–20)	4,100
Percent Change	7%

Bureau of Labor Statistics, 2012

those limiting exposure to certain compounds. As the technologies and methodologies employed become more sophisticated and sensitive, and as observation of environmental effects over time provides a more detailed set of empirical data, the legislated exposure limits are often adjusted to account for new knowledge that has become available. Thus, an exposure level that was considered safe at one time may be severely reduced, and the material may even be banned from use. Prime examples of this are the elimination of tetraethyl lead from gasoline after the long-term effects of exposure to the lead from exhaust gases became apparent and the elimination of the pesticide DDT, chlorofluorocarbons (CFCs), and polychlorinated biphenyls (PCBs) from common use. Government agencies also use chemical technology for a variety of applications related to geological assays and materials science. Because all matter is chemical in nature, including that of living systems, medical agencies such as the Center for Disease Control and law-enforcement agencies such as the Federal Bureau of Investigation rely on the biological and biochemical information obtained by specialist technicians in their respective fields.

Military. Military applications of chemical technology focus on the offensive and defensive aspects of materials and medical practice.

Many military aircraft are constructed from advanced composite materials, a growing practical area of applied chemical technology, and such materials are becoming increasingly used in naval applications as well because of their intrinsic strength, their ability to be formed into desired shapes, and their nonmetallic character. Advanced composite materials have completely replaced wood and metal in many traditional applications and present numerous potential applications suitable for both military and police use; for example, they are increasingly being used in vehicle and body armor. The military does not maintain production facilities of its own except for research purposes, however, and the actual work involved in producing military-grade goods is normally contracted out to reliable domestic manufacturers and specialty companies.

Academic Research and Teaching. Chemical technology is an essential aspect of university research and teaching, both as a supporting function and as a field of instruction. Students undertaking courses of study in any of the branches of chemistry are required to learn at least the basic principles of laboratory technology and techniques, as well as more advanced methodologies such as instrumental analysis as their programs progress. A university or college may employ several technicians for the purpose of maintaining teaching laboratories. Individual research groups within an institution may also employ technicians to assist with laboratory operations. As a field of instruction, chemical technology typically falls under the umbrella of chemical engineering. In this field, students are taught the principles of chemistry and the application of those principles in industrial settings. Research in this field focuses on development of new methods of material manipulation on an industrial scale and improvement of existing methods. This typically includes electronic controls and monitoring methods as well as the physical equipment required for those functions.

Social Context & Future Prospects

Everything in the world is chemical in nature, whether it is an animal, a vegetable, or a mineral. Therefore, all technology that examines, consumes, or produces any material must function on the principles of chemistry, as chemical technology. This in turn means that modern society is founded on chemical technology and relies upon the field for its very existence. The role of chemical technology is changing, however. In the past, it served to produce various materials, most notably plastics, that have become an environmental concern. Concern has also grown in regard to the effects of by-products of chemical technology that have been expelled into the environment, such as carbon dioxide and various pesticides and other residues. Chemical technology is now called upon to remedy the situations that it has engendered, first by identifying the extent of the effects and the environmental mechanisms that are affected and then by devising means of reconfiguring or eliminating the identified problems. At the same time, chemical technology is required to maintain its essential role in medical applications and new product development in response to demands for new and better goods and services. The importance of chemical technology will increase as focus continues to shift toward renewable resources such as biofuels and away from nonrenewable resources such as oil and coal.

Further Reading

Askeland, Donald R. *The Science and Engineering of Materials*. New York: Chapman, 1996. Print. Provides a background for many of the chemical-process technologies associated with diverse materials, including polymeric and advanced composite materials.

Fenichell, Stephen. *Plastic: The Making of a Synthetic Century*. New York: Harper, 2009. Print. Chronicles the documented and anecdotal history of polymers and plastics and provides a critical analysis of their environmental and economic effects.

Georgius Agricola. *Georgius Agricola: De Re Metallica*. 1556. Trans. Herbert Hoover and Lou Henry Hoover. New York: Dover, 1950. Print. Discusses early methods of working with metals and chemicals and provides insight into the origins of the field of chemical technology.

Strobel, Howard A., and William R. Heineman. *Chemical Instrumentation: A Systematic Approach*. New York: Wiley, 1989. Print. Explores the importance of instrumentation, an essential feature of chemical technology that is fundamental to the control and monitoring of chemical processes in all disciplines, and provides a comprehensive background on the operating principles of numerous instrument types.

About the Author: Richard M. Renneboog holds a master's degree in organic chemistry from the University of Western Ontario in London, Canada, and an associate's degree in electronics engineering technology from Loyalist College in Belleville, Canada. He worked for several years as a chemical technologist before becoming a writer and technical consultant.

Chemical Technician

Earnings (Yearly Median): $42,070 (Bureau of Labor Statistics, 2012)

Employment and Outlook: Slower than average growth (Bureau of Labor Statistics, 2012)

O*NET-SOC Code: 19-4021.00

Related Career Clusters: Agriculture, Food & Natural Resources; Education & Training; Health Science; Manufacturing

Scope of Work

Chemical technicians have a wide variety of career options in many fields. Since all matter is chemical in nature, the production and use of materials in any field or application can represent a career opportunity. Generally, chemical technicians work in industrial fields involving the manufacture, development, and manipulation of synthetic and natural materials, with their primary responsibilities being to carry out the work required for a particular process. This normally ranges from performing routine laboratory and work-space maintenance to monitoring sensitive operational processes. Academic institutions employ chemical technicians to prepare and maintain material supplies for use in teaching laboratories and perform routine sample preparation and spectroscopic examination. Medical facilities employ chemical and biochemical technicians for similar functions in their respective work environments. In industry, chemical technicians work in production, materials manufacturing and processing, recycling, health and safety monitoring, and similar areas within a broader employment context. As the negative effects of many chemicals on the environment become more apparent, chemical technicians play an increasingly important role, working to assess the damage and determine new, more environmentally friendly ways of working with and disposing of chemicals.

Education and Coursework

The minimum educational requirement for a chemical technician is an associate's degree in chemical technology. Such programs are often categorized by area of specialization, such as general chemistry, biochemistry, or medical laboratory assistance. Programs leading to a bachelor's degree generally have a similar focus on a specific area, with a more in-depth theoretical focus; a bachelor's degree more appropriately prepares an individual for an advanced career than does an associate's degree, and graduates of two-year programs who seek to advance in such a career will typically be required to undertake more advanced formal education to upgrade their qualifications.

In both cases, an aspiring chemical technician will be required to take courses in basic chemistry and the branch of chemistry relevant to his or her specific area of focus, as well as mathematics and statistics, analytical methodologies, and basic physics. Students may also be required to take courses in occupational health and safety, electronic control and monitoring systems, and computer science. More specialized fields such as medicine, biochemistry, and biology will also require courses of study in organic chemistry, biochemistry, biology, medical terminology, and biophysics. Training in some specialized areas, such as the manufacture of advanced composite materials (ACMs) from various chemical substances and resins, is available at only a small number of facilities in North America; such materials have become crucial components in the manufacture of aircraft, spacecraft, and military vehicles.

Career Enhancement and Training

Professional organizations in many different fields exist to support the work and careers of chemical technicians. Each organization has a

---

Transferable Skills

- Research & Planning Skills – Creating ideas
- Research & Planning Skills – Identifying problems
- Research & Planning Skills – Identifying resources
- Research & Planning Skills – Gathering information
- Research & Planning Skills – Solving problems (SCANS Thinking Skills)
- Research & Planning Skills – Analyzing information
- Organization & Management Skills – Managing equipment/materials (SCANS Workplace Competency – Resources)
- Technical Skills – Performing scientific, mathematical and technical work

segment of its operations devoted entirely to those who work as technicians and technologists within that field, and many stand-alone organizations exist as well. In North America, the American Chemical Society and the Chemical Institute of Canada are the primary organizations for chemists working in all branches of chemistry, and both are linked to subsector organizations devoted to chemical technicians and technology. Such support groups encourage young people to consider the field as a career choice and provide information and resources through their respective websites. Many organizations offer associate memberships for students.

Professional organizations such as the American Chemical Society expect their member technicians and technologists to maintain a certain standard of practice in their work, often requiring a program of continuing education. Membership also carries annual membership dues that go toward the publication of member-focused newsletters and other information of relevance, as well as the presentation of conferences and symposia. Such meetings are particularly valuable to individual members because of the professional networking opportunities that they provide.

Daily Tasks and Technology

The daily work of a chemical technician varies depending on the nature of the position held within an organization. In most cases, chemical technicians provide technical support and services related to research, analysis, and quality control. Often, a technician specializes in a single specific role within an organization and is not expected to provide services outside of that role. For example, a mass spectrometry technician in an analytical laboratory typically only services and maintains the spectrometers that he or she routinely uses, prepares samples for spectrometric mass analyses, and obtains the corresponding mass spectrographs that will be interpreted by the individuals who requested them. In an industrial production setting, chemical technicians may be responsible for testing the quality of input and output materials for a process stream to ensure that they are within the specified quality limits. This applies generally in a number of varied and specific applications, such as paint preparation, food processing, pharmaceutical synthesis, and plastics production, among others.

Regardless of the field in which they work, chemical technicians are expected to maintain a properly clean and safe working environment, write technical reports appropriate to the work that they carry out, clean and maintain laboratory equipment such as glassware that is used in their work, and maintain the stock of supplies and materials that are required in their work.

Earnings and Employment Outlook

Due in large part to the development of automated laboratory technology, the demand for chemical technicians is expected to experience slower-than-average growth between the years 2010 and 2020. Tasks that once required the work of several technicians over a period of days can now be carried out by a single automated system in a matter of minutes, and new systems are continually being developed. However, the increasing focus on green or sustainable chemistry is not only changing the ways in which chemistry-based processes are carried out but also opening entirely new fields of employment. One such field is the developing biofuels industry, which will provide more employment opportunities for chemical technicians who have a broad knowledge of biochemical processes and biology. Similarly, the pharmaceutical and medical-research industries are expected to provide many opportunities for chemical technicians with a background in biochemistry and bioorganic chemistry.

Due in large part to the development of automated laboratory technology, the demand for chemical technicians is expected to experience slower-than-average growth between the years 2010 and 2020.

According to the US Bureau of Labor Statistics, wages for chemical technicians vary based on the field in which they work. As of May 2011, average wages for chemical technicians were highest in the oil and gas industries, followed by the federal government and the electrical power industry; however, the estimated number of technicians working in those fields was correspondingly low. Average annual wages were lowest in the architectural and engineering industry, which was estimated to employ a significant number of workers. Technicians in other fields earned significantly more on average, no doubt due to the greater degree of specialized knowledge and education required. For most fields, employment is expected to remain fairly constant, while employment opportunities in areas related to environmental protection and the production of ACMs and biofuels are expected to increase significantly.

Related Occupations
- **Environmental Science and Protection Technicians:** Environmental science and protection technicians work with environmental scientists and others to analyze pollution levels and prevent contamination in all sectors.

- **Chemical Equipment Operators:** Chemical equipment operators maintain and operate equipment used to perform chemical research or manufacture products.

A Conversation with Judith Steininger

Job Title: Professor Emeritus at the Milwaukee School of Engineering and President of Language Arts for Business

What was your career path?

Serendipity or chance has directed much of my chemistry career. First, I worked as a research chemist, then as an educator in Kenya and the US. Writing and communicating about science has been the biggest surprise, publishing in magazines, journals, as well as corporate brochures and advertising. Lately, I have been reading my chemistry essays for a public radio program. I have a bachelor's degree in chemistry and a master's degree in literature as well as an education certificate.

What are three pieces of advice you would offer someone interested in your profession?

1. Learn your subject well. The beauty of science is that it advances but the laws are fundamental. You can apply them to new information.
2. Be able to communicate your discipline in writing and speaking for a variety of audiences especially non-scientists.
3. Be willing to try something different. I have enjoyed the range and diversity of my career. I'm never bored.

What paths for career advancement are available to you?

As a scientist you have at least two primary paths: becoming the go-to expert in your discipline or the generalist through a management career or by using the discipline and rigor you learned in science to help you in something entirely different.

- **Soil and Plant Science Technicians:** Soil and plant science technicians collect and analyze samples of soil and plants in order to determine the effects of various environmental and human factors, including soil composition and pollution, on plant growth.

- **Food Science Technicians:** Food science technicians analyze the chemical makeup of food in order to maintain and improve the quality of food materials for both human and animal consumption.

- **Pest Control Technicians:** Pest control technicians use various chemical substances to manage or eliminate pest populations in homes, businesses, and other locations.

Future Applications

Chemical technicians are not confined to a particular industry or set of responsibilities, and as such, the opportunities for such workers will likely continue to expand even as growth in some industries slows. As public and industry interest in the environment and environmental regulation increases, chemical technicians will be needed to analyze and counteract the effects of outdated practices and technology on the natural world. In the field of site remediation, for example, sites contaminated by chemical waste represent the failure of previous industries to adequately understand the intimate relationships between their activities and the environment, and the contaminants at such sites must be identified and removed to eliminate their toxic effects. Such clean-up efforts will likely continue for some time, as the widespread use of harmful chemicals for industrial and household applications persists. Advancements in the field of ACM production and the biofuels industry will provide additional opportunities for individuals with chemistry-based training.

Richard M. Renneboog, MS

More Information

American Chemical Society
1155 Sixteenth Street NW
Washington, DC 20036
www.acs.org

American Chemistry Council
700 Second Street NE
Washington, DC 20002
www.americanchemistry.com

Chemical Institute of Canada
130 Slater Street, Suite 550
Ottawa, Ontario K1P 6E2
Canada
www.chemistry.ca

Cosmetics Chemistry

FIELDS OF STUDY

Chemistry; chemical engineering; biology; microbiology; polymer science and engineering; composites engineering; physics.

DEFINITION

Cosmetics chemistry is the science behind the creation of products designed to alter a person's external appearance or natural odor. Although the finished products created by those working in the field are part of a multibillion-dollar beauty industry, the scientists who formulate the products must be as versed in chemistry as their peers who work in major research facilities. Practitioners in the field must be familiar with the hundreds of different raw materials that are permissible in cosmetic formulations. Everything from hair- and skin-care products to deodorants and perfumes fall under the aegis of cosmetics chemistry.

Basic Principles

From their earliest history, human beings have adorned themselves to improve their appearance or augment physical attributes deemed desirable in a given culture. In the pictographs left by the ancient Egyptians thousands of years ago, people applied darkening compounds around the eyes to accentuate their features. The twenty-first-century cosmetics industry might utilize different materials than the Egyptians did, but the purpose of such adornment—improving one's appearance—remains the same. At their core, cosmetics attempt to improve the external appearance or odor of the body. They are not, however, involved in curing ailments or improving bodily functions.

In the twenty-first century, scientists working with cosmetics occasionally face derision from their peers who deem the end result of cosmetics chemistry something less than hard science. Some claim that researchers in the field spend more time trying to copy the products of industry leaders than they do creating new items. In actuality, product production requires extensive knowledge of a myriad of substances and what results from their interactions. Furthermore, chemists in the field must also keep in mind functionality and cost. A chemical mixture produced in the lab that improved the elasticity of skin would not revolutionize the industry if it proved so expensive as to be out of reach of most consumers or if it smelled unpleasant. Cosmetic chemists must often balance science with marketing and an oftentimes fixed budget in their work. Larger firms that employ scientists are typically the best financed. Their teams of chemists are the most highly paid in the industry, just as their research is often exhaustive and cutting-edge.

Core Concepts

Emulsions and Emulsifiers. Cosmetics chemistry covers a variety of applications, including skin and hair care products, makeup of every variety, perfumes, colognes, and other items designed to alter one's natural odor. Which area a cosmetics chemist works in will determine the nature of the employment experience and expectations. For those employed producing skin-care products, the most common medium is some form of emulsion. Emulsions are the result of one unmixable substance being suspended in droplet or globule form in another liquid. These immiscible (unmixable) products—usually some form of oil and water—are agitated so that they are dispersed in what is called the continuous phase. The two substances are still not completely mixed together but they are more evenly spread out. An emulsifier must be added in order to prevent the immiscible liquids from completely separating into what is called the dispersed phase. Emulsifiers thus bind oil droplets and keep them in place instead of allowing them to separate as they naturally would from the liquid. Each emulsifier molecule contains a hydrophilic (water loving) section and a lipophilic (oil loving) section. The hydrophilic-lipophilic balance (HLB) between these two sections will determine their use in the manufacturing of various creams and ointments. Product specifications will ultimately determine the type of emulsion employed. If a company seeks a greasier, longer-lasting product, it will utilize water suspended in oil mixture; when a less long-lasting formula is required companies will adopt an oil suspended in water mixture. At every stage of the process a chemist is needed to determine which mixtures to create and which emulsifier will best keep the consistency of the mixture. Trial-and-error experimentation serves as the principal means of creating a lotion blend that is agreeable both in terms of performance and in texture, but that also retains its stability for an extended period of time.

Fragrance. Almost as important as altering appearance through the use of cosmetics is the use of assorted perfumes, colognes, and deodorants to mask the body's natural odor. Most fragrances consist of an assortment of ingredients blended to create the desired scent. Plant oils painstakingly extracted from organic matter are most often the key ingredient, followed by synthetic components—typically called fixatives—that ensure the oils utilized in the solution do not spoil and that impart a fragrance of their own. Numerous experiments are performed at this stage to ensure that the oils utilized will have the longest shelf-life possible. The oil mixture is next blended in a solvent. What percentage of the new compound is comprised of the oil mixture will ultimately determine its use. Perfumes, for examples, have a more concentrated oil composition in relation to solvent than do colognes. The quality of the finished product is a direct result of the raw materials employed in its creation. Despite the claims of companies that assert that their far cheaper formulation smells just like the higher priced original, perfume chemists know that the longevity and stability of the compound will erode far faster than if more expensive ingredients been employed.

Creating Color. Many of the cosmetic formulations are designed to change the appearance of the eyes, lips, hair, and other parts of the body through the application of color. Chemists employed by the cosmetics industry are always being pushed to produce more vibrant colors in long-lasting formulations that are superior to those produced by rival firms. Ingredients to make such colors vary depending on the nature of their use. Newer formulations such as certain skin tanning products react with proteins in the skin to create richer and darker hues. Lipsticks utilize a water-insoluble dye that can retain its hue even when exposed to saliva. There are a limited number of pigments available, with thousands of derivative color shades based on them. Consistent replication of each shade requires advanced chemical knowledge of the type of raw materials, along with the fillers and stabilizers needed that to reproduce a shade over and over again. Not only must chemists replicate the color palate, they must place it in a formulation that will not degrade and can be delivered in a usable format.

Cleaning the Body. Soaps, shampoos, and other cleaning agents are designed for the purpose of cleaning the body. Many such products do more than clean; they also include fragrances meant to enhance the freshness associated with bathing. Cleaning formulas utilize surface-active agents, or "surfactants," that, like emulsions, contain water-soluble and fat-soluble components. By design, the lipophilic portion binds with dirt on the skin and the hair, while the hydrophilic portion carries the otherwise water-insoluble debris away. As in all phases of the cosmetics industry, chemists are needed to perfect the formulations and to research newer and more powerful ways to clean and deodorize the body.

Applications Past and Present

People, even ancient people, have always attempted various means of making themselves physically more appealing. The drive—whether an instinctual need to procreate or a more complex emotional need—to alter appearance is undeniable, and external appearance has been a crucial factor in shaping human evolution. Depending on the era, certain physical traits have been considered particularly desirable. The effort to achieve a certain look or accentuate a certain physical feature has led to a long history of efforts to adorn the body with colors and scents. Time and place have determined the nature and extent of body alteration deemed normal.

Ancient Egyptian Cosmetics. Thousands of years ago, the ancient Egyptians enhanced their eyes and added color to their cheeks through the application of natural agents. Assorted scented oils were employed by many to soften the skin and to mask the body's natural odor, but most often such formulations served a religious purpose. Naturally occurring compounds such as red ochre were widely used, as were any moisturizing agents that would protect the skin and the hair from the consequences of prolonged exposure to the sun. Egyptians did not

Interesting Facts about Cosmetics Chemistry

- Cosmetics were widely used in the ancient world. In Egypt, perfumes and body adornment often assumed a spiritual dimension.

- In 2012, natural cosmetic products accounted for slightly less than 10 percent of the global beauty care market. Interest in safer and more environmentally friendly products is growing, however, and they are expected to take up a greater future share of the market.

- The cosmetics industry has proven remarkably durable. Despite wars, economic downturns, and even natural disasters, demand for beauty and skin-care products remains strong.

- The Romans gave the world the word "perfume," which derives from the Latin verb *fumare*, meaning "to smoke." It is believed the term stems from the use of incense at religious observances. Pleasant aromas were coveted for spiritual observations and became associated with all nice smelling compounds.

- Although cosmetics are meant to enhance and protect the surface of the skin, many modern formulations are defined as "cosmeceuticals" for their ability to bring about positive change below the outer layer of the skin.

- Many toxic ingredients are permitted in cosmetics formulas. The color Red #40, most often used in lipsticks, is produced from coal tar, a known toxic compound.

limit their attention to the skin and the hair. They even found fresh breath important, and often chewed tamarisk leaves to keep the mouth free of offensive odors. Perfumes were widely worn, and creators of a given fragrance guarded their compounds with the same diligence as modern multimillion-dollar manufacturers.

Ancient Greek Cosmetics. Evidence suggests that the ancient world almost universally embraced appearance- and odor-altering agents. Emerging global powers such as the Greeks used a sizable volume and variety of cosmetics. Living in a largely mountainous landscape with soil poorly suited to agriculture, ancient Greeks developed intricate trading networks in order to procure the raw materials and foodstuffs not available in their native land. Cosmetics of all sorts were one of the major trade items in the Hellenic world. As with any trading people, exotic products of all types were introduced and sold in Greek communities. Perfumes and makeup from throughout the known world were available in cosmopolitan city-states such as Athens. When Greek civilization was overrun by the Romans, the importance of cosmetics remained strong, and their export throughout the rapidly expanding the Roman Empire continued apace. Even more so than the Greeks, the Romans removed the last vestiges of the spiritual from perfuming rituals, making the practice just another means of making oneself more physically attractive.

By time the Christian era dawned, a more modern conceptualization of cosmetics existed. They were often cost-prohibitive, making them a symbol of status, just as their use was now largely ornamental in nature. Perhaps the only limiting factor in their use was the availability of the raw materials utilized to make cosmetic formulations. Before the widespread availability of synthetic compounds, ancient cosmetics producers needed to keep their finger on the pulse of international trade to always stay one step ahead of demand for a given pigment or fragrance. Should they lose sight of the latest source of good-quality raw materials, they would find themselves quickly without the commodities needed.

Cosmetics in Western Europe. Greek and to a greater extent Roman territorial aggrandizement brought with it not only the spread of political and military traditions, it also brought the expansion of other social and cultural customs, such as the use of cosmetics and perfumes. In the emerging European order, both men and women employed assorted cosmetic agents to make their skin appear whiter and their body smell fresher in a time when bathing was uncommon. People applied makeup to appear younger and more attractive, as well as to create the appearance of physical health. In the wake of assorted disease outbreaks that pockmarked the skin, some attempted to conceal the damage with cosmetic agents.

White skin was especially prized, as it served as an important indicator of social status. The paler the complexion, the more desirable
the appearance for much of European history. In the entirety of world
history, most people who have ever lived have engaged in some type
of outdoor work, typically in agricultural pursuits. Those who toil all
day in the fields will inevitable develop tanned skin commensurate
with their laborer status. In contrast, a pale appearance indicated a life
spent mostly indoors, a sign of leisure brought about by wealth. Pale
skin thus carried with it an important social cue regarding class and
lifestyle. To be rich and pale was more desirable than being poor and
sunburned. Cosmetics helped enhance this reality for some, just as it
created the illusion of opulence for others.

Over time, however, European tastes changed, and the fascination
with pale skin diminished; once deemed the epitome of beauty, pasty
white skin came to be regarded as synonymous with sickness and disease. Taking its place was a desire for rosy cheeks and a healthy glow
that was imparted through the use of cosmetics. Items such as lipstick
and rouge first appeared in France during the 1700s before briefly
gaining popularity in the rest of the continent.

As was common in Europe, intense national rivalries prompted
equally strong prejudices against other nations. French makeup,
which was once the rage in England, fell into disfavor. Queen Victo-
ria in the 1800s belittled the use of makeup, considering it something
more worthy of a prostitute than a proper English lady. Lipstick and
rouge were temporarily shelved in exchange for a more modest cosmetic appearance.

Regardless of the desired result, whether French opulence and sen-
suality or English austerity and restraint, the cosmetic formulations in
wide use contained an array of potentially life-threatening substances.
In an age where the link between certain chemicals and health were
not well understood, toxic substances such as mercury and lead were
commonly employed in cosmetic creations.

Industrialization Modernizes Cosmetics. Industrialization changed
everything about the European landscape, including cosmetics. The
transportation and printing revolutions that emerged with industry

helped create markets for cosmetic manufacturers and advertising firms that attempted to sell the women of the world an image of beauty that only makeup could create. Aside from creating modern, global economies, industrialization spawned the emergence of societies founded on mass production and mass consumption of goods. Industrial capitalism in places like the United States and Europe created a consumer culture in which advertising firms promoted Western ideals

Occupation	Chemical technicians
Employment 2010	61,000
Projected Employment 2020	65,100
Change in Number (2010–20)	4,100
Percent Change	7%

Bureau of Labor Statistics, 2012

of beauty. In an effort to achieve the norms defined by the producers of commodities such as cosmetics, twentieth-century women—and, to a lesser extent, men—spent much of their disposable income on cosmetic items to alter their natural appearances. Selling an idealized sense of beauty proved to be a competitive business, with new products continually appearing on the market.

Cosmetics Today. The major cosmetics firms in existence today emerged at the start of the twentieth century. As the health risks associated with certain staple ingredients used to produce cosmetics became widely understood, it was imperative for manufacturers to hire skilled chemists to look for newer compounds capable of safely producing the results yielded by more toxic substances. Mass production also required careful scientific scrutiny of the formulation of cosmetics to ensure that formulas remained consistent and that they could survive travel across great distances, sometimes under less than optimum conditions. Cosmetic chemists who are employed by the world's major makeup and fragrance firms continue to do what their less scientifically trained predecessors have done for centuries: They are still seeking out new compounds and designing new products to make people look younger and healthier.

Impact on Industry

Cosmetics chemistry has always struggled with the perception that it is not a "real science." To some, the very notion that a scientist would be engaged in extensive laboratory work to produce compounds to improve superficial appearances seems unimportant when other chemists in the field are working to cure diseases or to enhance food yields. However, in cultures where youth is celebrated, cosmetic chemists produce the visual and olfactory stimulation that generates enormous revenue for the firms that employ them.

Occupation	Chemists
Employment 2010	82,200
Projected Employment 2020	85,400
Change in Number (2010–20)	3,200
Percent Change	4%

Bureau of Labor Statistics, 2012

Private Industry. International cosmetics firms such as L'Oréal, Esteé Lauder, Elizabeth Arden, and Revlon have benefitted most from cosmetics chemistry. Manufacturing, advertising, and selling cosmetics remains almost entirely a profit-driven enterprise. Other institutions such as the government or major research firms focus their funding on such pursuits as space exploration or disease treatment and prevention. Research dollars for cosmetic chemists come almost exclusively from corporate executives who want their scientists to make products at a cost that will not bankrupt the company. Other chemists in the field who work for smaller firms tend to direct most of their efforts toward replicating popular products manufactured by bigger companies with large-scale research and development initiatives.

US Military. One of the few constituent components of the federal government with any interest in the production of cosmetics is the nation's armed forces. Camouflage has long been worn by combat soldiers as a means to obscure skin and prevent detection by enemy combatants. In much the same manner that scientists are engaged in producing formulas directed at women, some are exploring ways to produce skin-obscuring makeup that will better stand the rigors of use in a combat zone.

Finding a Job. The prospects for employment in cosmetics chemistry remain good. If recent evidence is any indicator, the cosmetics world seems impervious to economic developments that impact other businesses and industries. Even a dramatic economic downturn does little to dampen the sales of the major cosmetics firms. Indeed, consumers seem willing to spend money on vanity items that will improve their appearance even as they struggle to provide necessities for their families. Job prospects in the field will thus remain strong as long as America and much of the rest of the world continue to hold youthful ideals of beauty and health.

Social Context and Future Prospects

Opponents of the cosmetics industry come from a variety of ideological angles. Some find the youth-oriented marketing of cosmetics firms unnecessarily demeaning to women. These opponents argue that advertisements depicting underweight models with dense makeup application—often digitally altered—are misleading and send a negative message to young women about beauty standards. A less obvious but equally troubling notion has emerged in the second half of the twentieth century, positing that the beauty industry is meant to keep women subservient to men. Since the pioneering efforts of activists such as Betty Friedan, modern feminists have urged women to turn away from the corporate male-generated image of female beauty to embrace a natural and unadorned appearance. However, despite Friedan's efforts and that of many modern feminists, the cosmetics industry remains a potent international economic force.

Questions of body image are often linked to charges that the cosmetics industry traffics in inherently dangerous products. It is certainly hard to deny that since people first began utilizing cosmetics, there have been a long series of unfortunate and often preventable health risks resulting from their use. Whether a chemical causes cancer or just a rash, the responsibility for poor and limited testing rests with the beauty industry. On some occasions the desire to rush a product to market has eclipsed the careful experimentation and research necessary to ensure the safety of the product before it is released to the general public. Critics of the industry have asserted that many chemicals currently approved for cosmetics usage by the Food and Drug Administration are potential carcinogens when used over long periods. Some evidence suggests that the use of certain antiperspirants, for example, increases the risk of breast cancer.

Although some want even more testing to take place in the industry, others question the testing methods employed by the world's large firms. Animal rights activists have aggressively attacked the research and development tactics of many cosmetics companies for their use of animals to test new products.

Further Reading

Dayan, Nava, Lambros Kromidas, and Gaurav Kale. *Formulating, Packaging, and Marketing of Natural Cosmetic Products*. Hoboken: Wiley, 2011. Print. Discusses the shift toward natural beauty products as consumers grow more aware of the potentially toxic substances found in the cosmetics produced by the major firms.

Downing, Sarah Jane. *Beauty and Cosmetics, 1550–1950*. Oxford: Shire, 2012. Print. A history of changing ideals of beauty and the cosmetics that were used to achieve it. Includes illustrations and analyses of different eras.

Malkan, Stacy. *Not Just a Pretty Face: The Ugly Side of the Beauty Industry*. Gabriola: New Society, 2007. Print. Reports on the wide array of potentially deadly chemicals found in makeup and perfumes despite some limited federal oversight.

Pointer, Sally. *The Artifice of Beauty: A History and Practical Guide to Perfumes and Cosmetics*. Stroud: Sutton, 2005. Print. Chronicles the historical evolution of the modern cosmetics industry and also offers an important philosophical discussion of who and what defines beauty.

Romanowski, Perry, and Randy Shueller. *Beginning Cosmetic Chemistry*. 3rd ed. Carol Stream, IL: Allured, 2009. Print. Provides interested students with insight into what a budding cosmetic chemist can expect if employed in the field.

About the Author: Keith M. Finley, PhD, is instructor of history and assistant director of the Center for Southeast Louisiana Studies at Southeastern Louisiana University. He has written extensively on twentieth-century American politics, society, and ecology, including the 2010 D. B. Hardeman Prize–winning *Delaying the Dream: Southern Senators and the Fight Against Civil Rights, 1938–1965*. Finley has also cowritten two award-winning documentary films on coastal erosion and environmental degradation in south Louisiana.

Perfume Chemist 🖋

Earnings (Yearly Median): $69,790 (Bureau of Labor Statistics, 2012)

Employment and Outlook: Slower than average growth (Bureau of Labor Statistics, 2012)

O*NET-SOC Code: 19-2031.00

Related Career Clusters: Manufacturing; Marketing; Agriculture, Food & Natural Resources; Health Science

Scope of Work

From the fine mist of Chanel No. 5 to the pine-tree air freshener hanging from a trucker's rearview mirror, perfume chemists craft the scents of life. They synthesize aromas from man-made chemicals and natural compounds, bottling scents for a multiplicity of uses. Beyond the expected applications, fragrances designed by chemists are used in any number of household cleaning supplies, hair-care products, and even processed foods.

Fragrance is one of the more creative specializations within the chemistry field. It requires hands-on laboratory skills, the physical ability to discern minute olfactory differences between often-complex chemical compounds, and a flair for composing evocative—and marketable—scents. The discipline has existed since antiquity, and while technology has changed the science of it all, the art is still inherent. Perfume chemistry is one of the integral but often-overlooked ways in which science touches everyday life.

Education and Coursework

At the very least, an entry-level perfume chemist is required to have a bachelor's degree in chemistry. A specialization in synthetic, organic, or physical chemistry is often helpful, and an applicable master's degree is required for higher-level and managerial positions. While few universities have dedicated fragrance chemistry programs, many offer classes on the subject. For example, William and Jefferson College in Pennsylvania has offered a course on perfume chemistry. Continued postgraduate training is offered by a variety of professional organizations, including the American Chemical Society, the Flavor and Extract Manufacturers Association, and the Research Institute for Fragrance Materials. But there is no substitute for in-lab apprenticeship; a perfume chemist must have an abnormally acute sense of smell, a skill best developed and nurtured through firsthand experience.

The International Federation of Essential Oils and Aroma Trades (IFEAT) offers a diploma in aroma trades studies. In partnership with the International Centre for Aroma Trade Studies (ICATS) and the University of Plymouth in Great Britain, the IFEAT course gives an overview of the fragrance industry, covering the intricacies of the trade from the chemist's lab to the marketer's campaign pitch. The remote-learning course is available to anyone who is interested, though the majority of people who take the course are perfumers-in-training.

Career Enhancement and Training

Since perfumery is such a specific discipline within the field of chemistry, it is often difficult to find relevant instruction in the traditional academic setting. Many fragrance companies run in-house schools

---

Transferable Skills

- Communication Skills – Expressing thoughts and ideas
- Research & Planning Skills – Creating ideas
- Organization & Management Skills – Selling ideas or products
- Technical Skills – Applying the technology to a task (SCANS Workplace Competency – Technology)
- Technical Skills – Working with your hands
- Work Environment Skills – Working in a laboratory setting
- Work Environment Skills – Working in an odorous atmosphere

to train future employees, with course work typically spread out over four years. The Institut Supérieur International du Parfum de la Cosmétique et de l'Aromatique Alimentaire (ISIPCA) in Versailles, France, is the most prominent independent school for the study of perfumery in the world. The ISIPCA trains about four hundred students every year, offering thirteen different courses for students and working professionals, taught by a team of industry veterans.

A well-rounded perfumer should be familiar with more than just the science of the business, for in the fragrance industry, the customer and the chemist are not as far apart as one might expect. A chemist needs to know what consumers look for in a product. Knowledge of the post-production sales-and-marketing process gives any perfumer a distinct career advantage. The Fragrance Foundation, an international trade group, offers certificate courses in sales and marketing in addition to a variety of other educational and networking resources.

Daily Tasks and Technology

Perfumery is an age-old craft, but it has come a long way since the days of mashing up orange peels to create pungent oils of citrus and animal musk. Today, perfume chemists spend most of their time in the lab, composing aromas from bottles of synthetic ingredients, rather than working out in the field. In fact, fewer than 5 percent of the roughly three thousand ingredients used by a perfume chemist are of organic composition.

A perfume chemist's day could be spent performing any of the many steps in the scent-making process. Some perfume oils are indeed obtained from raw natural material, using a variety of chemical and physical techniques in which a perfume chemist must be versed; solvent extraction and odor isolation (a method of extracting aroma from a source in the field) are just two examples. But the majority of a chemist's work deals in the mixing of synthetic aroma compounds to create the desired scent. Laboratory equipment of all sorts is integral to the perfumery process, so an aspiring chemist should have hands-on experience in such a setting.

Perfumery, like most scientific pursuits, involves frequent interdisciplinary collaboration. A perfume chemist should have well-developed teamwork skills and be a facilitator of effective collaboration. Successful product development, especially in a consumer-goods industry like perfumery, requires clear communication between those in every stage of the process. A perfume chemist will work with creative developers, marketers, and company executives in the course of creating a new scent. Additionally, a perfume chemist needs to remain engaged with consumer trends and demands so as to further inform decisions made in the laboratory.

Earnings and Employment Outlook

The average wage of a perfume chemist varies in relation to location, amount of experience, and position within the company. According to the Bureau of Labor Statistics (BLS), the median salary for a chemist or materials scientist—a category that includes perfumers—was $69,790 per year in 2010. Perfume chemists who hold managerial positions within their company are likely to receive much higher wages commensurate with their prior experience and educational qualifications.

Job growth in the field, while increasing, is slower than average for all occupations. According to the BLS, the employment of chemists and materials scientists is only expected to increase 4 percent by 2020. Though employment growth may be minimal, BLS adds that chemists are perpetually in demand due to the continued need for monitoring the quality of chemicals in consumer products. The possible applications of perfume chemistry are so wide ranging that the industry is economically secure even during recession.

BLS recommends pursuing a master's or doctorate degree to improve employment prospects and reports that many companies are expected to partner with research universities and smaller research-and-development firms rather than employing in-house chemists.

Related Occupations

- **Flavor Chemists:** Similar to perfume chemistry in both process and application, a flavor chemist, also known as a flavorist, uses chemistry to modify the gustatory properties of food products.

- **Cosmetic Chemists:** Cosmetic chemists synthesize raw materials, formulate recipes, and test products for the cosmetics industry.

- **Environmental Scientists:** Environmental science is an interdisciplinary field that uses science to find solutions to problems endangering the environment.

- **Organic Chemists:** Organic chemists work with carbon-based molecules that are used in a variety of industries, especially pharmaceuticals.

- **Analytical Chemists:** Analytical chemists work in research-focused positions, studying the structure, composition, and nature of substances for a wide breadth of applications.

Future Applications

Perfumes and other cosmetic products become more advanced and chemically complex every day. Perfumeries on the edge of innovation are experimenting with nanotechnology, which is technology aimed at controlling individual atoms and molecules. Already it is estimated that one thousand cosmetic and personal-care products utilize nanotechnology in their composition.

Nanotechnology has the potential to change the very nature of perfumery. Industry experts predict that it will allow them to create time-released, more durable scents with a longer shelf life through a process called nano-encapsulation, in which microscopically small particles are coated with different substances to dictate their behavior. One potential future application is a "perfume pill" product called Swallowable Parfum, which would cause users to sweat out atomized fragrance that, as the sweat evaporated, would remain on the skin.

Steve Miller

More Information

American Chemical Society
144 Sixteenth Street NW
Washington, DC 20036
www.acs.org

The American Society of Perfumers
PO Box 1551
West Caldwell, NJ 07004
www.perfumers.org

Fragrance Foundation
545 Fifth Avenue, Suite 900
New York, NY 10017
www.fragrance.org

International Fragrance Association
Chemin de la Parfumerie 5
Vernier, Geneva
Switzerland
www.ifraorg.org

Research Institute for Fragrance Materials
50 Tice Boulevard
Woodcliff Lake, NJ 07677
www.rifm.org

Electrochemistry

FIELDS OF STUDY

Physical chemistry; thermodynamics; organic chemistry; inorganic chemistry; quantitative analysis; chemical kinetics; analytical chemistry; metallurgy; chemical engineering; electrical engineering; industrial chemistry; electrochemical cells; fuel cells; electrochemistry of nanomaterials; advanced mathematics; physics; electroplating; nanotechnology; quantum chemistry; electrophoresis; biochemistry; molecular biology.

DEFINITION

Electrochemists study the chemical changes produced by electricity, but they are also concerned with the generation of electric currents due to the transformations of chemical substances. Whereas traditional electrochemists investigated such phenomena as electrolysis (using electricity to generate a chemical reaction), modern electrochemists have broadened and deepened their interdisciplinary field to include theories of ionic solutions and solvation. This theoretical knowledge has led to such practical applications as efficient batteries and fuel cells, the production and protection of metals, and the electrochemical engineering of nanomaterials and devices that have great importance in electronics, optics, and ceramics.

Basic Principles

As its name implies, electrochemistry concerns all systems involving electrical energy and chemical processes. More specifically, this field includes the study of chemical reactions caused by electrical forces as well as the study of how chemical processes give rise to electrical energy. Some electrochemists investigate the electrical properties of certain chemical substances; for instance, these substances' ability to serve as insulators or conductors. Because the atomic structure of matter is fundamentally electrical, electrochemistry is intimately involved in all fields of chemistry from physical and inorganic through organic and biochemistry to such new disciplines as nanochemistry. No matter what systems they study, chemists in some way deal with the appearance or disappearance of electrical energy into the surroundings. On the other hand, electrochemists concentrate on those systems consisting of electrical conductors, which can be metallic, electrolytic, or gaseous.

Because of its close connection with various branches of chemistry, electrochemistry has applications that are multifarious. Early applications centered on electrochemical cells that generated a steady current. New metals such as potassium, sodium, calcium, and strontium were discovered by electrolysis of their molten salts. Commercial production of such metals as magnesium, aluminum, and zinc were mainly accomplished by the electrolysis of solutions or melts. An understanding of the electrical nature of chemical bonding led chemists to create many new dyes, drugs, plastics, and artificial plastics. Electroplating has served both aesthetic and practical purposes, and it has certainly decreased the corrosion of several widely used metals.

Electrochemistry played a significant part in the research and development of such modern substances as silicones, fluorinated hydrocarbons, synthetic rubbers, and plastics. Even though semiconductors such as germanium and silicon do not conduct electricity as well as copper, an understanding of electrochemical principles has been important in the invention of various solid-state devices that have revolutionized the electronics industries, from radio and television to computers. Electrochemistry, when it has been applied in the life sciences, has resulted in an expanded knowledge of biological molecules. For example, American physical chemist Linus Pauling used electrophoretic techniques to discover the role of a defective hemoglobin molecule in sickle-cell anemia. A grasp of electrochemical phenomena occurring in the human heart and brain has led to diagnostic and palliative technologies that have improved the quality and length of human lives. Much research and development is being devoted to increasingly sophisticated electrochemical devices for implantation in the human body, and some even predict, such as American inventor Ray Kurzweil, that these "nanobots" will help extend human life indefinitely.

Core Concepts

Primary and Secondary Cells. The basic device of electrochemistry is the cell, generally consisting of a container with electrodes and an electrolyte, designed to convert chemical energy into electrical energy. A primary cell, also known as a galvanic or voltaic cell, is one that generates electrical current via an irreversible chemical reaction. This means that a discharged primary cell cannot be recharged from an external source. By taking measurements at different temperatures, chemists use primary cells to calculate the heat of reactions, which have both theoretical and practical applications. Such cells can also be used to determine the acidity and alkalinity of solutions. Every primary cell has two metallic electrodes, at which electrochemical reactions occur. In one of these reactions the electrode gives up electrons, and at the other electrode electrons are absorbed.

In a secondary cell, also known as a rechargeable or storage cell, electrical current is created by chemical reactions that are reversible. This means that a discharged secondary cell may be recharged by circulating through the cell in a quantity of electricity equal to what had been withdrawn. This process can be repeated as often as desired. The manufacture of secondary cells has grown into an immense industry, with such commercially successful products as lead-acid cells and alkaline cells with either nickel-iron or nickel-cadmium electrodes.

Electrolyte Processes. Electrolysis, one of the first electrochemical processes to be discovered, has increased in importance in the twentieth and twenty-first centuries. Chemists investigating electrolysis soon discovered that chemical reactions take place at the two electrodes, but the liquid solution between them remains unchanged. An early explanation was that with the passage of electric current, ions in the solution alternated decompositions and recombinations of the electrolyte. This theory had to be later revised in the light of evidence that chemical components had different motilities in solution.

For more than two hundred years, the electrolysis of water has been used to generate hydrogen gas. In an electrolytic cell with a pair of platinum electrodes, to the water of which a small amount of sulfuric acid has been added (to reduce the high voltage needed), electrolysis begins with the application of an external electromotive force, with bubbles of oxygen gas appearing at the anode (due to an oxidation reaction) and hydrogen gas at the cathode (due to a reduction reaction). If sodium chloride is added to the water, the electrochemical reaction is different, with sodium metal and chlorine gas appearing at the appropriate electrodes. In both these electrolyses the amounts of hydrogen and sodium produced are in accordance with Faraday's law, the mass of the products being proportional to the current applied to the cell.

Redox Reactions. For many electrochemists the paramount concern of their discipline is the reduction and oxidation (redox) reaction that occurs in electrochemical cells, batteries, and many other devices and applications. Reduction takes place when an element or radical (an ionic group) gains electrons, such as when a double positive copper ion in solution gains two electrons to form metallic copper. Oxidation takes place when an element or radical loses electrons, such as when a zinc electrode loses two electrons to form a doubly positive zinc ion in solution. In electrochemical research and applications the sites of oxidation and reduction are spatially separated. The electrons produced by chemical processes can be forced to flow through a wire, and this electric current can be used in various applications.

Electrodes. Electrochemists employ a variety of electrodes, which can consist of inorganic or organic materials. Polarography, a subdiscipline of electrochemistry dealing with the measurement of current and voltage, uses a dropping mercury electrode, a technique enabling analysts to determine such species as trace amounts of metals, dissolved oxygen, and certain drugs. Glass electrodes, whose central feature is a thin glass membrane, have been widely used by chemists, biochemists, and medical researchers. A reversible hydrogen electrode plays a central role in determining the pH of solutions. The quinhydrone electrode, consisting of a platinum electrode immersed in a quinhydrone solution, can also be used to measure pH (it is also known as an indicator electrode because it can indicate the concentration of certain ions in the electrolyte). Also widely used, particularly in industrial pH measurements, is the calomel electrode, consisting of liquid mercury covered by a layer of calomel (mercurous chloride), and immersed in a potassium chloride solution. Electrochemists have also created electrodes with increasing (or decreasing) power as oxidizing or reducing agents. With this quantitative information they are then able to choose a particular electrode material to suit a specific purpose.

Applications Past and Present

Batteries and Fuel Cells. Soon after Italian physicist Alessandro Volta's invention of the first electric battery around 1800, investigators found applications, first as a means of discovering new elements, then as a way to deepen understanding of chemical bonding. By the 1830s, when new batteries were able to serve as reliable sources of electric current, they began to exhibit utility beyond their initial value for experimental and theoretical science. For example, the Daniell cell was widely adopted by the telegraph industry. Also useful in this industry was the newly invented fuel cell, which used the reaction of a fuel such as hydrogen and an oxidant such as oxygen to produce direct-current electricity. However, its requirement of expensive platinum electrodes led to its replacement, in the late nineteenth and throughout the twentieth century, with the rechargeable lead-acid battery, which came to be extensively used in the automobile industry. In the late twentieth and early twenty-first centuries, many electrochemists predicted a bright future for fuel cells based on hydrogen and oxygen, especially with the pollution problems associated with widespread fossil-fuel use.

Electrodeposition, Electroplating, and Electrorefining. When an electric current passes through a solution (for instance, silver nitrate), the precipitation of a material (silver) at an electrode (the cathode) is called electrodeposition. A well-known category of electrodeposition is electroplating, when a thin layer of one metal is deposited onto the surface of another. In galvanization, for example, iron or steel objects are coated with rust-resistant zinc. Electrodeposition techniques have the advantage of being able to coat objects thoroughly, even those with intricate shapes. An allied technique, electrorefining, transforms metals contaminated with impurities to very pure states by anodic dissolution and concomitant redeposition of solutions of their salts. Some

Interesting Facts about Electrochemistry

- Alessandro Volta, often called the father of electrochemistry, invented the world's first battery, but he did not understand how it worked (he believed in a physical-contact theory rather than the correct chemical-reaction theory).

- English physicist Michael Faraday, with only a few years of rudimentary education, later formulated the basic laws of electrochemistry and became the greatest experimental physicist of the nineteenth century.

- Swedish chemist Svante August Arrhenius, whose ionic theory of electrolytic solutions became fundamentally important to the progress of electrochemistry, was nearly drummed out of the profession by his skeptical doctoral examiners, who gave him the lowest possible passing grade.

- The electrochemical discovery that charged atoms or groups of atoms in solution have a distinct electric charge (or some integral multiple of it) led to the idea that electricity itself is atomic (and not a fluid, as many believed), and in 1891, Irish physicist George Johnstone Stoney gave this electrical unit the name "electron."

- Charles M. Hall in the United States and Paul L. T. Héroult in France independently discovered the modern electrolytic technique of manufacturing aluminum in 1886; furthermore, both men were born in 1863 and both died in 1914.

- Many molecules in plants, animals, and humans have electric charges, some with two charges (called zwitterions), others with many (called polyelectrolytes).

- In the second half of the twentieth century, many academic institutions in the United States taught courses in electroanalytical chemistry and electrochemical engineering, but no American college, university, or technical institute taught any courses in applied electrochemistry.

industries have used so-called electrowinning techniques to produce salable metals from low-grade ores and mine tailings.

Advances in electrochemical knowledge and techniques have led to increasingly sophisticated applications of electrodeposition. For example, knowledge of electrode potentials has made the electrode-position of alloys possible and commercial. Methods have also been discovered to provide plastics with metal coatings. Similar techniques have been discovered to coat such rubber articles as gloves with a metallic layer. Worn or damaged metal objects can be returned to pristine condition by a process called electroforming. Some commercial metal objects, such as tubes, sheets, and machine parts, have been totally manufactured by electrodeposition (sometimes called electromachining).

Electrometallurgy. A major application of electrochemical principles and techniques occurs in the manufacture of such metals as aluminum and titanium. Plentiful aluminum-containing bauxite ores exist in large deposits in several countries, but it was not until electrochemical techniques were developed in the United States and France at the end of the nineteenth century that the cost of manufacturing this light metal was sufficiently reduced to make it a commercially valuable commodity. This commercial process involved the electrolysis of alumina (aluminum oxide) dissolved in fused cryolite (sodium aluminum fluoride). During the century that followed discovery of this process, many different uses for this lightweight metal ensued, from airplanes to zeppelins.

Corrosion Control and Dielectric Materials. The destruction of a metal or alloy by oxidation is itself an electrochemical process, since the metal loses electrons to the surrounding air or water. A familiar example is the appearance of rust (hydrated ferric oxide) on an iron or steel object. Electrochemical knowledge of the mechanism of corrosion led researchers to ways of preventing or delaying it. Keeping oxidants away from the metallic surface is an obvious means of protection. Substances that interfere with the oxidizing of metals are called inhibitors. Corrosion inhibitors include both inorganic and organic materials, but they are generally categorized by whether the inhibitor obstructs corrosive reactions at the cathode or anode. Cathodic protection is used extensively for such metal objects as underground pipelines or such structures as ship hulls, which have to withstand the corrosive action of seawater. Similarly, dielectric materials with low electrical conductivity, such as insulators, require long-term protection from high and low temperatures as well as from corrosive forces. An understanding of electrochemistry facilitates the construction of such electrical devices as condensers and capacitors that involve dielectric substances.

Electrochemistry, Molecular Biology, and Medicine. Because of the increasing understanding of electrochemistry as it pertains to plant, animal, and human life, and because of concerns raised by the modern environmental movement, several significant applications have been developed, with the promise of many more to come. For example, electrochemical devices have been made for the analysis of proteins and deoxyribonucleic acid (DNA). Researchers have fabricated DNA sensors as well as DNA chips. These DNA sensors can be used to detect DNA damage. Electrochemistry was involved in the creation of implantable pacemakers designed to regulate heartbeats, thus saving lives. Research is under way to create an artificial heart powered by electrochemical processes within the human body. Neurologists electrically stimulate regions of the brain to help mitigate or even cure certain psychological problems. Developments in electrochemistry have led to the creation of devices that detect various environmental pollutants in air and water. Photoelectrochemistry played a role in helping to understand the dramatic depletion of the ozone layer in the stratosphere and the role that chlorofluorocarbons (CFCs) played in exacerbating this problem. Because a large hole in the ozone layer allows dangerous solar radiation to damage plants, animals, and humans, many countries have banned the use of CFCs.

Nanomaterials in Electrochemistry. Miniaturization of electronic technologies became evident and important in the computer industry, where advances have been enshrined in Moore's law, which states that transistor density in integrated circuits doubles every eighteen months. Electrodeposition has proven to be a technique well-suited to the preparation of metal nanostructures, with several applications in electronics, semiconductors, optics, and ceramics. In particular, electrochemical methods have contributed to the understanding and applications of quantum dots, nanoparticles that are so small that they follow quantum rather than classical laws. These quantum dots can be as small as a few atoms, and in the form of ultrathin cadmium-sulfide films they have been shown to generate high photocurrents in solar cells. The electrochemical synthesis of such nanostructured products as nanowires, biosensors, and microelectroanalytical devices has led researchers to predict the ultimate commercial success of these highly efficient contrivances.

Impact on Industry

Because electrochemistry itself is an interdisciplinary field, and is a part of so many different scientific disciplines and commercial applications, it is difficult to arrive at an accurate figure for the economic worth and annual profits of the global electrochemical industry. More reliable estimates exist for particular segments of this industry in specific countries. For example, in 2008, the domestic revenues of the United States battery and fuel cell industry were about $4.9 billion, the lion's share of which was due to the battery business (in 2005, the United States fuel cell industry had revenues of about $266 million). During the final decades of the twentieth century, the electrolytic production of aluminum in the United States was about one-fifth of the world's total, but in the twenty-first century, competition from such countries as Norway and Brazil, with their extensive and less expensive hydropower, has reduced the American share.

Career opportunities for electrochemists range from laboratory technicians at small businesses to research professors at prestigious universities. The battery business employs many workers with bachelor of science degrees in electrochemistry to help manufacture, service, and improve a variety of products. Senior electrochemical engineers with advanced degrees may be hired to head research programs to develop new products or to supervise the production of the company's major commercial offerings. Electrochemical engineers are often hired to manage the manufacture of electrochemical components or oversee the electrolytic production of such metals as aluminum and magnesium. Some electrochemists are employed by government agencies, for example, to design and develop fuel cells for the National Aeronautics and Space Administration (NASA), while others may be hired by pharmaceutical companies to develop new drugs and medical devices.

Government Agencies. In the United States during the decades after World War II, the National Science Foundation provided support for many electrochemical investigations, especially those projects that, because of their exploratory nature, had no guarantee of immediate commercial success. An example is the 1990s electrochemical research on semiconducting nanocrystals. The United States Office of Naval Research has supported projects on nanostructured thin films. It is not only the federal government that has seen fit through various agencies to support electrochemical research, but state governments as well. For example, the New York State Foundation for Science, Technology, and Innovation has invested in investigations of how ultrathin films can be self-assembled from polyelectrolytes, nanoparticles, and nanoplatelets with the hope that these laboratory-scale preparations may have industrial-scale applications.

Government agencies and academic researchers have often worked together to fund basic research in electrochemistry. The Department of Energy through its Office of Basic Energy Sciences has supported research on electrochromic and photochromic effects, which has led to such commercial products as switchable mirrors in automobiles. Researchers at the Georgia Institute of Technology have contributed to the improvement of proton exchange membrane fuel cells (PEMFCs), and scientists at the University of Dayton in Ohio have shown the value of carbon nanotubes in fuel cells. Hydrogen fuel cells became the focus of an initiative promoted by President George W. Bush in 2003, which was given direction and financial support in the 2005 Energy Policy Act and the 2006 Advanced Energy Initiative. However, a few years later, the Obama administration chose to de-emphasize hydrogen fuel cells and emphasize other technologies that will create high energy efficiency and less polluting automobiles in a shorter period of time.

Industry and Business. Because of the widespread need for electrochemical cells and batteries, companies manufacturing them have devoted extensive human and financial resources to the research, development, and production of a variety of batteries. Some companies, such as Exide Technologies, have emphasized lead-acid batteries, whereas General Electric, whose corporate interest in batteries goes back to its founder, Thomas Alva Edison, has made fuel cells a

Occupation	Engineering technicians
Employment 2010	451,900
Projected Employment 2020	476,500
Change in Number (2010–20)	24,600
Percent Change	5%

Bureau of Labor Statistics, 2012

significant part of its diversified line of products. Some businesses, such as Alcoa, the world's leading producer of aluminum, were based on the discovery of a highly efficient electrolytic process, which led to a dramatic decrease in the cost of aluminum and, in turn, to its widespread use (it is second only to steel as a construction metal).

Academic Research and Teaching. Electrochemistry is an immense field with a large variety of specialties, though specialized education generally takes place at the graduate level. Certain universities, technical institutes, and engineering schools have programs for students interested in theoretical electrochemistry, electrochemical cells, electrodeposition, nanomaterials, and many others, affording the opportunity for select teaching positions.

Social Context and Future Prospects

Even though batteries, when compared with other energy sources, are too heavy, too big, too inefficient, and too costly, they will continue to be needed in the twenty-first century, at least until suitable substitutes are found. Although some analysts predict a bright future for fuel cells, others have been discouraged by their slow rate of development. As advanced industrialized societies continue to expand, increasing demand for such metals as beryllium, magnesium, aluminum, titanium, and zirconium will necessarily follow, forcing electrochemists to improve the electrolytic processes for deriving these metals from dwindling sources. If Moore's law holds well into the future, then computer engineers, familiar with electrochemical principles, will find new ways to populate integrated circuits with more and better microdevices.

Some prognosticators foresee significant progress in the borderline field between electrochemistry and organic chemistry (sometimes called electro-organic chemistry). When ordinary chemical methods have proved inadequate to synthesize desired compounds of high purity, electrolytic techniques have been much better than traditional ones in accomplishing this, though these successes have occurred at the laboratory level and the development of industrial processes will most likely take place in the future. Other new fields,

Occupation	Chemists
Employment 2010	82,200
Projected Employment 2020	85,400
Change in Number (2010–20)	3,200
Percent Change	4%

Bureau of Labor Statistics, 2012

such as photoelectrochemistry, will mature in the twenty-first century, leading to important applications. The electrochemistry of nanomaterials is already well underway, both theoretically and practically, and a robust future has been envisioned as electrochemical engineers create new nanophase materials and devices for potential use in a variety of applications, from electronics to optics.

Further Reading

Bagotsky, Vladimir, ed. *Fundamentals of Electrochemistry*. 2d ed. New York: Wiley-Interscience, 2005. Provides a good introduction to this field for those unfamiliar with it, though later chapters contain material of interest to advanced students.

Bard, Allen J., and Larry R. Faulkner. *Electrochemical Methods: Fundamentals and Applications*. 2d ed. Hoboken, NJ: Wiley, 2001. Provides comprehensive treatment of the theory and applications needed to understand this field's fundamentals.

Brock, William H. *The Chemical Tree: A History of Chemistry*. New York: Norton, 2000. Previously published as *The Norton History of Chemistry*; shows how the development of electrochemistry forms an important part of the story of chemistry; includes an extensive bibliographical essay, notes, and index.

Ihde, Aaron J. *The Development of Modern Chemistry*. New York: Dover, 1984. Makes available to general readers a well-organized treatment of chemistry from the eighteenth to the twentieth century, of which electrochemical developments form an essential part. Illustrated, with extensive bibliographical essays on all the chapters; author and subject indexes.

MacInnes, Duncan A. *The Principles of Electrochemistry*. New York: Dover, 1961. Paperback reprint of a classic text that treats the field as an integrated whole; author and subject indexes.

Schlesinger, Henry. *The Battery: How Portable Power Sparked a Technological Revolution*. New York: HarperCollins, 2010. Provides an entertaining, popular history of the battery, with lessons for readers familiar only with electronic handheld devices.

Zoski, Cynthia G., ed. *Handbook of Electrochemistry*. Oxford, England: Elsevier, 2007. Surveys most modern research areas of electrochemistry, such as reference electrodes, fuel cells, corrosion control, and other laboratory techniques and practical applications.

About the Author: Robert J. Paradowski, MS, PhD, is a historian of science and technology who specializes in the history of chemistry with a special emphasis on the life and work of Linus Pauling. He is a summa cum laude graduate of Spring Hill College, with a master's degree in chemistry from Brandeis University and a doctorate in the history of science from the University of Wisconsin. He has taught at Brooklyn College, Eisenhower College, and the Rochester Institute of Technology.

Fuel Cell Engineers

Earnings (Yearly Average): $79,230 (O*NET Online, 2012)

Employment and Outlook: Slower than average (O*NET Online, 2012)

Fuel Cell Engineer: 17-2141.01

Related Career Clusters: Manufacturing; Health Science; Transportation, Distribution & Logistics

Scope of Work

Fuel cell engineers work in research institutions, private engineering companies, small businesses, and for the federal government. Fuel cell engineers design fuel cells: energy conversion mechanisms that generate power with chemical reactions using hydrogen and oxygen.

By means of this chemical reaction, a fuel cell produces an electric current that can be harnessed as a source of electric power.

Fuel cell engineers oversee the complex process of developing and testing fuel cells. In addition to designing fuel cell systems—the motors, chemicals, and components of the cell—they are responsible for analyzing data gathered from testing cells and accessing progress and setbacks. Engineers implement experiments to develop new and more efficient fuel cell designs and technology. Writing reports evaluating experiments, as well as reading the literature of new advancements in fuel cell technology, is an important aspect of this occupation.

Education and Coursework

Fuel cell engineers need at least bachelor's degree in an engineering specialty—chemical, electrical, mechanical, or civil—or a degree in materials science, a field that applies the study of matter and atomic particles to engineering. There are also masters and PhD programs in engineering. An engineer's four-year education consists of not only engineering classes, but courses in physical science, mathematics, the humanities, and social sciences. Most programs require specialized design classes in a computer lab.

Admission into an engineering program is competitive, and a candidate should have a strong interest and aptitude for math and science in order to succeed in this field. It is not uncommon for an engineering school to offer a five-year joint bachelor's and master's program. A master's degree will potentially lead to an increase in salary and augment an applicant's marketability in the competitive engineering industry.

In the United States, a master's in engineering (MEng) is often a two-year degree consisting of specialized engineering and laboratory courses. A comprehensive research project (a graduate thesis) is required at the end of the second year. Classes related to business and management may also be required in order to prepare graduates for managerial positions within the engineering industry. There is a networking advantage to a master's degree—it improves contacts within the field and may lead to internships and co-ops with engineering companies.

Transferable Skills

- Communication Skills – Speaking effectively (SCANS Basic Skill)
- Interpersonal/Social Skills – Working as a member of a team (SCANS Workplace Competency – Interpersonal)
- Research & Planning Skills – Solving problems (SCANS Thinking Skills)
- Organization & Management Skills – Managing equipment/ materials (SCANS Workplace Competency – Resources)
- Technical Skills – Performing scientific, mathematical and technical work
- Work Environment Skills – Working in a laboratory setting

Joining a professional engineering society or organization is a great way to make valuable connections with other professionals and learn more about the engineering industry. The National Society of Professional Engineers, for example, is an organization for working professionals that offers full-time engineering students a unique membership package, which is a great opportunity for students to make connections and learn more about their profession. The American Association for Fuel Cell Engineers is an organization devoted to promoting further education and networking opportunities for fuel cell engineers. Both of these organizations aim to educate the public on the benefits of fuel cells.

Career Enhancement and Training

Engineers are required to have a license in the United States if they offer services to the public, but the requirement for licensure varies depending on each individual state's regulations. In order to receive an engineering license, a candidate must hold least a bachelor's degree, pass a comprehensive eight-hour exam, and complete four years of professional engineering experience. A college graduate from an accredited engineering program is eligible to take the initial Fundamentals of Engineering exam (FE), and, if they pass, they can move on to the Principles and Practice of Engineering (or PE) exam. The PE examination will test engineers' knowledge and skills in their concentration, such as chemical or electrical engineering. Upon successful completion of this exam, an individual will have earned his or her license and be officially considered a professional engineer, also known as a PE.

"Engineers in training," or EIT, is the term the National Council of Examiners for Engineering and Surveying (NCEES) uses to refer to college graduates who have passed the eight-hour FE exam. An EIT completes his or her training under the direct supervision of a professional engineer. The training is complete after four years of supervision and upon passing the comprehensive PE exam.

An engineer must be a US citizen in order to work for the federal government. In addition to obtaining a license, a high-security clearance may be required by the federal government, but this mainly applies to nuclear and aerospace engineers or those involved in confidential defense system technology.

Daily Tasks and Technology

In addition to designing the various mechanisms and technology that compose a fuel cell, the daily tasks of a fuel cell engineer include constantly evaluating the results of experiments and keeping track of progress and failures. Problem-solving skills are exercised on a daily basis: Engineers seek to develop new and more efficient fuel cell components, and they are constantly making changes to designs and experimenting with new technology. They research and develop new and more efficient testing procedures for evaluating a fuel cell's performance. Discovering new applications for fuel cells—such as in electric vehicles—is something engineers are constantly exploring.

Fuel cell engineers are obligated to keep up with the growth of fuel cell technology. This means reading the current literature, taking additional courses, and contributing to the field logging information gathered from experiments and writing reports on experiments. Unlike fossil fuels, fuel cells are a form of green energy, a renewable (or naturally rejuvenated) and environmentally safe source of power. The green nature of fuel cells is an appealing aspect of this energy source, and engineers are perpetually exploring new ways to make the cells more green, sustainable, and cost-effective.

The daily tasks for fuel cell engineers vary depending upon their level of experience. More experienced PEs, for example, coordinate schedules, validate designs for cells, and authorize the release and implementation of fuel cell parts for production. Less experienced engineers—especially EITs—assist PEs in research, testing, and the development of new technology for the cells. EITs are not authorized to approve a product for production.

Fuel cell engineers use a variety of technologies to develop and test a fuel cell. A piece of equipment called a homogenizer, for example, is used to create compounds by combining chemicals. The fuel cell itself is a technological innovation. Similar to a battery, a fuel cell uses a chemical reaction to produce energy. Unlike a battery, however, a fuel cell produces energy with the supply of hydrogen, thus continuously producing power.

A fuel cell strips hydrogen and oxygen of their electrons and uses this positive charge to generate energy as it passes through a converter. There are a few different types of fuel cells. Alkaline cells use a more expensive form of technology that, in addition to generating electricity, can provide drinking water—for example, the National Aeronautics and Space Administration (NASA) has used these to provide astronauts with water. Molten carbonate fuel cells use sodium and magnesium at high temperatures, and other cells use phosphoric acid, a type of inorganic acid.

Earnings and Employment Outlook

The demand for fuel cell engineers is expected to grow at a slower than average rate (approximately 5 percent) through 2020. The energy generated from fuel cells, however, is both cost-effective and environmentally sound. This lack of a carbon footprint makes fuel cells an appealing form of green energy in a world threatened by global warming.

As the momentum of the green movement increases, green energy, including fuel cells, may become a more prevalent source of energy. The number of fuel cell engineers, therefore, is expected to increase with the greater demand for environmentally safe energy. There is considerable competition in the green industry, however, including cost-effective wind, solar, geothermal, and nuclear power. These other forms of power may take precedence over fuel cells, as they are capable of producing affordable power on a larger scale.

According to information accessed from Recruiter.com in 2012, the average salary for fuel cell engineers ranges from $64,000 to $96,000. Annual salaries also vary by the employer, with engineers working in the private sector and for the federal government earning the most, with an average of $118,180. But the American Solar Energy Society rated fuel cells as the third-fastest growing form of green energy, with the first two being biomass and solar. The push for green energy, therefore, may lead to increases in salary as the demand for fuel cell engineers grows.

Related Occupations

- **Nuclear Engineers:** Nuclear engineers develop the instruments and systems needed to produce nuclear energy.
- **Chemical Engineers:** Chemical engineers design manufacturing plants and oversee the chemicals used in production.
- **Physicists and Astronomers:** Physicists and astronomers develop technology and conduct research by studying space and matter.
- **Electrical Engineers:** Electrical engineers oversee the design and production of electrical technology, including computer hardware and circuit boards.
- **Chemists and Materials Scientists:** Chemists and materials scientists study the properties of chemical substances and develop new technology.

Future Applications

Fuel cells are expected to come into higher demand and become an important source of energy. Hydrogen, the chemical used in fuel cells, is the most prevalent element in the universe, and it is ideal for

A Conversation with Kevin Desrosiers

Job Title: Fuel Cell Engineer

What was your career path?

I started out as an environmental engineering undergraduate interested in material recycling, hazardous waste cleanup, and energy, and became interested in fuel cell systems that ran off biogas from landfills. I did not participate in any internships, but I did work one summer as an undergraduate researcher in a National Science Foundation Sponsored REU program. Then I pursued a Master's degree in mechanical engineering in order to learn more about hydrogen fuel cell systems in the automotive field.

What are three pieces of advice you would offer someone interested in your profession?

1. I would recommend research opportunities such as an REU program, or internship at a company in order to get as much hands-on job experience as possible.
2. Think about graduate degrees that are similar to your undergrad degree in order to get some breadth of exposure to your field, while at the same time learning even more about some subjects and refining your interests.
3. Visit or speak with industry professionals in order to help find a field you really enjoy. Involvement with clubs in school will also expose you to many interesting, possible career paths.

What paths for career advancement are available to you?

I have been fortunate to work in R&D (research and development) since starting as a test technician. In my current position I would likely become a senior engineer, but I also see many opportunities to branch out into similar fields such as algae biofuel development (combining both of my degrees and turning waste into energy), and even solar or wind power. The energy market is diversifying, and I see that there is demand for professionals with general energy industry experience that can analyze energy systems and help integrate grid power, backup power, and energy storage into economical solutions.

producing energy due to its abundance and green nature—releasing no environmentally detrimental fumes. The sustainability of hydrogen fuel cells will also help decrease the dependence on expensive foreign oil.

In the near future, fuel cells may be used to power and heat buildings and homes. They may also be used to power many portable electronic devices and electric automobiles. The US Army's Engineer and Research and Development Center (ERDC) is exploring ways to use fuel cells in the military. Fuel cells, for instance, are lighter and easier for troops to transport than large batteries. Fuel cells may also be used to power military vehicles.

Fuel cells may also play an important role in health care. The Massachusetts Institute of Technology (MIT), for example, has recently experimented with fuel cells that generate power with glucose (sugar). Scientists at MIT have used these sugar-powered fuel cells to power brain implants in mice. In the future, this neural technology could be used in paraplegics to help them regain control of their body and walk.

The green energy component of fuel cells is an appealing aspect of this technology, and engineers are continually exploring new ways to make the cells more green and cost-effective. Hydrogen fuel cells may also become a more efficient source of energy than wind and solar due to the abundance of hydrogen and its sustainability.

Daniel Castaldy

More Information

Fuel Cell and Hydrogen Energy Association
1211 Connecticut Avenue NW, Suite 600
Washington, DC 20036
www.fchea.org

Fuel Cell Today
Gate 2 HQ Orchard Road
Royston Hertfordshire, UK
www.fuelcelltoday.com

National Council of Examiners for Engineering and Surveying
280 Seneca Creek Road
Seneca, SC 29678
www.ncees.org

National Society of Professional Engineers
1420 King Street
Alexandria, VA 22314
www.nspe.org

Society of Chemical Industry
14 Belgrave Square
London, UK
www.soci.org

Environmental Chemistry

FIELDS OF STUDY

Chemistry; chemical engineering; bioengineering; physics; physical chemistry; organic chemistry; biochemistry; molecular biology; electrochemistry; analytical chemistry; photochemistry; atmospheric chemistry; agricultural chemistry; industrial ecology; toxicology.

DEFINITION

Environmental chemistry is an interdisciplinary subject dealing with chemical phenomena in nature. Environmental chemists are concerned with the consequences of anthropogenic (human-created) chemicals in the air people breathe and the water they drink. They have become increasingly involved in managing the effects of these chemicals through both the creation of ecologically friendly products and efforts to minimize the pollution of the land, water, and air.

Basic Principles

Environmental chemistry is the science of chemical processes in the environment. It is a profoundly interdisciplinary and socially relevant field. What environmental chemists do has important consequences for society because they are concerned with the effect of pollutants on the land, water, and air that humans depend on for their life, health, and proper functioning. Environmental chemists are forced to break down barriers that have traditionally kept chemists isolated from other fields.

Environmental chemistry needs to be distinguished from its later offshoot, green chemistry. As environmental chemistry developed, it tended to emphasize the detection and mitigation of pollutants, the study of the beneficial and adverse effects of various chemicals on the environment, and how the beneficial effects could be enhanced and the adverse effects eliminated or attenuated. Green chemistry, however, focuses on how to create sustainable, safe, and nonpolluting chemicals in ways that minimize the ecological footprint of the processes. Some scholars define this field simply as sustainable chemistry.

The work of environmental chemists is governed by several basic principles. For example, the prevention principle states that when creating chemical products, it is better to minimize waste from the start than to later clean up wastes that could have been eliminated. Another principle declares that in making products, chemists should avoid using substances that could harm humans or the environment. Furthermore, chemists should design safe chemicals with the lowest practicable toxicity. In manufacturing products, chemists must minimize energy use and maximize energy efficiency; they should also use, as much as possible, renewable materials and energy resources. The products chemists make should be, if possible, biodegradable. Environmental chemists should use advanced technologies, such as computers, to monitor and control hazardous wastes. Finally, they must employ procedures that minimize accidents.

Core Concepts

Chemical Analysis and the Atmosphere. Indispensable to the progress of environmental chemistry is the ability to measure, quantitatively and qualitatively, certain substances that even at very low concentrations pose harm to humans and the environment. By using such techniques as gravimetric and volumetric analysis, various types of spectroscopy, electroanalysis, and chromatography, environmental chemists have been able to accurately measure such atmospheric pollutants as sulfur dioxide, carbon monoxide, hydrogen sulfide, nitrogen oxides, and several hydrocarbons. Many governmental and nongovernmental organizations require that specific air contaminants be routinely monitored. Because of heavy demands on analytic chemists, much monitoring has become computerized and automatic.

Atmospheric particles range in size from a grain of sand to a molecule. Nanoparticles, for example, are about one-thousandth the size of a bacterial cell, but environmental chemists have discovered that they can have a deleterious effect on human health. Epidemiologists have found that these nanoparticles adversely affect respiratory and cardiovascular functioning.

Atmospheric aerosols are solid or liquid particles smaller than a hundred millimicrons in diameter. These particles undergo several possible transformations, from coagulation to phase transitions. For example, particles can serve as nuclei for the formation of water droplets, and some chemists have experimented with particulates in forming rain clouds. Human and natural biological sources contribute to atmospheric aerosols. The chlorofluorocarbons (CFCs) in aerosol cans have been factors in the depletion of the earth's ozone layer. Marine organisms produce such chemicals as halogen radicals, which in turn influence reactions of atmospheric sulfur, nitrogen, and oxidants. As marine aerosol particles rise from the ocean and are oxidized in the atmosphere, they may react with its components, creating a substance that may harm human health. Marine aerosols contain carbonaceous as well as inorganic materials, and when an organic aerosol interacts with atmospheric oxygen, its inert hydrophobic (water-repelling) film is transformed into a reactive hydrophilic (water-absorbing) layer. A consequence of this process is that organic aerosols serve as a conduit for organic compounds to enter the atmosphere.

Carbon dioxide is an example of a molecular atmospheric component, and some environmental chemists have been devoting their efforts to determining its role in global warming, but others have studied the earth's prebiotic environment to understand how inorganic carbon initially formed the organic molecules essential to life. Using photoelectrochemical techniques (how light affects electron transfers in chemical reactions), researchers discovered a possible metabolic pathway involving carbon dioxide fixation on mineral surfaces.

Water Pollution. Because of water's vital importance and its uneven distribution on the earth's surface, environmental chemists have had to spend a great deal of time and energy studying this precious resource. Even before the development of environmental chemistry as a profession, many scientists, politicians, and citizens were concerned about water management. Various governmental and nongovernmental organizations were formed to monitor and manage the quality of water. Environmental chemists have been able to use their expertise to trace the origin and spread of water pollutants throughout the environment, paying special attention to the effects of water pollutants on plant, animal, and human life.

A particular interest of environmental chemists has been the interaction of inorganic and organic matter with bottom sediments in lakes, rivers, and oceans. These surface sediments are not simply nonreactive sinks for pollutants but can be studied quantitatively in terms of how many specific chemicals are bonded to a certain amount of sediment, which in turn is influenced by whether the conditions are oxidizing or reducing. Chemists can then study the bioavailability of contaminants in sediments. Furthermore, environmental chemists have studied dissolution and precipitation, discovering that the rates of these processes depend on what happens in surface sediments. Using such techniques as scanning polarization force microscopy, they have been able to quantify pollutant immobilization and bacterial attachment on surface sediments. Specifically, they have used these methods to understand the concentrations and activities of heavy metals in aquatic sediments.

Hazardous Waste. One of the characteristics of advanced industrialized societies has been the creation of growing amounts of solid and liquid wastes, an important proportion of which pose severe dangers to the environment and human health. These chemicals can be toxic, corrosive, or flammable. The two largest categories of hazardous wastes are organic compounds such as polychlorinated biphenyls (PCBs) and dioxin, and heavy metals such as lead and mercury. Environmental chemists have become involved in research on the health and environmental effects of these hazardous substances and the development of techniques to detect, monitor, and control them. For example, they have studied the rapidly growing technology of incineration as a means of reducing and disposing of wastes. They have also studied the chemical emissions from incinerators and researched methods for the safe disposal of the ash and slag produced. Because of the passage of the Resource Recovery Act of 1970, environmental chemists have devoted much attention to finding ways of reclaiming and recycling materials from solid wastes.

Pesticides. The mismanagement of pesticides inspired conservationist Rachel Carson to write her classic *Silent Spring* in 1962, and pesticides continue to be a major concern of industrial and environmental chemists. One reason for the development of pesticides is the great success

Interesting Facts about
Environmental Chemistry

- At life's beginning, single-celled cyanobacteria made possible the evolution of millions of new species; however, what modern humans are doing to the atmosphere will result in the extinction of hundreds of thousands of species.

- More than 99 percent of the total mass of the earth's atmosphere is found within about 30 kilometers (about 20 miles) of its surface.

- Although 71 percent of the earth's surface is covered by water, only 0.024 percent of this water is available as freshwater.

- According to a National Academy of Sciences study, legally permitted pesticide residues in food cause 4,000 to 20,000 cases of cancer per year in the United States.

- From 1980 to 2010, the quality of outdoor air in most developed countries greatly improved.

- From 1980 to 2008, the EPA placed 1,569 hazardous-waste sites on its priority list for cleanup.

- According to the US Geological Survey, even though the population of the United States grew by 16 percent from 1980 to 2004, total water consumption decreased by about 9 percent.

- Because of global warming, in February and March 2002, a mass of ice larger than the state of Rhode Island separated from the Antarctic Peninsula.

- The United States leads the world in producing solid waste. With only 4.6 percent of the world's population, it produced about one-third of the world's solid waste.

- Each year, 12,000 to 16,000 American children under nine years of age are treated for acute lead poisoning, and about 200 die.

farmers had in using them to control insects, thereby dramatically increasing the quantity and quality of various agricultural products. By 1970, more than 30,000 pesticide products were being regularly used.

This expansion in pesticides is what alarmed Carson, who was not in favor of a total ban of pesticides but rather their reduction and integration with biological and cultural controls.

Because pesticides are toxic to targeted species, they often cause harm to beneficial insects and, through biomagnification, to birds and other animals. Pesticide residues on agricultural products have also been shown to harm humans. Therefore, environmental chemists have become involved in monitoring pesticides from their development and use to their effects on the environment. They have also helped create pesticide regulations and laws. This regulatory system has become increasingly complex, costing companies, the government, and customers large amounts of money. The hope is that integrated control methods will prove safer and cheaper than traditional pesticides.

Applications Past and Present

Anthrosphere. The anthrosphere—that part of the environment used or modified by humans—is of particular interest to environmental chemists. They want to know how humans and their activities, especially making and using chemicals, affect the larger environment. Building homes and factories, producing food and energy, and disposing of waste all have environmental consequences. Whereas some environmentalists study how to create ecologically friendly dwellings, environmental chemists study how chemical engineers should design factories that cause minimum harm to the environment. Specific examples of applications of environmental chemistry to industry include the creation of efficient catalysts that speed up reactions without themselves posing health or environmental hazards.

Because many problems arise from the use of hazardous solvents in chemical processes, environmental chemists try to develop processes that use only safe solvents or avoid their use altogether. Because the chemical industry depends heavily on petroleum resources, which are nonrenewable and becoming drastically diminished, environmental chemists study how renewable resources such as biomass may serve as substitutes for fossil fuels. They are also creating products that degrade rapidly after being discarded, so that their environmental impact is transient. Following the suggestions of environmental chemists, some companies are developing long-lasting, energy-saving batteries, and others are selling their products with less packaging than previously.

Hydrosphere. The hydrosphere consists of all the water found on the earth. Throughout history, water has been essential in the development of human civilizations, some of which have declined and disappeared because of deforestation, desertification, and drought. Water has also been a vehicle for the spread of diseases and pollutants, both of which have caused serious harm to humans and their environment. Environmental chemists have consequently been involved in such applications as the purification of water for domestic use, the monitoring of water used in the making of chemicals, and the treatment of wastewater so that its release and reuse will not harm humans or the environment. For example, such heavy metals as cadmium, mercury, and lead are often found in wastewater from various industries, and environmental chemists have developed such techniques as electrodeposition, reverse osmosis, and ion exchange to remove them. Many organic compounds are carcinogens and mutagens, so chemists want to remove them from water. Besides such traditional methods as powdered activated carbon, chemists have used adsorbent synthetic polymers to attract insoluble organic compounds. Detergents in wastewater can contribute to lake eutrophication and cause harm to wildlife, and some companies have created detergents specially formulated to cause less environmental damage.

Atmosphere. In the twentieth century, scientists discovered that anthropogenic greenhouse gases have been contributing to global warming that could have catastrophic consequences for island nations and coastal cities. Industries, coal-burning power plants, and automobiles are major air polluters, and environmental chemical research has centered on finding ways to reduce or eliminate these pollutants. The Clean Air Act of 1970 and subsequent amendments set standards for air quality and put pressure on air polluters to reduce harmful emissions. For example, chemists have helped power plants develop desulfurization processes, and other scientists developed emission controls for automobiles.

The problem of global warming has proved difficult to solve. Some environmental chemists believe that capturing and storing carbon dioxide is the answer, whereas others believe that government regulation of carbon dioxide and methane by means of energy taxes will lead to a lessening of global warming. Some think that the Kyoto Protocol, an international agreement that went into effect in 2005, is a small but important first step, whereas others note that the lack of participation by the United States and the omission of a requirement that such countries as China and India reduce greenhouse gas emissions seriously weakened the agreement. On the other hand, the Montreal and Copenhagen Protocols did foster global cooperation in the reduction and phasing out of CFCs, which should lead to a reversal in ozone layer depletion.

Agricultural and Industrial Ecology. Agriculture, which involves the production of plants and animals as food, is essential in meeting basic human food needs. Fertilizers and pesticides developed by chemists brought forth the green revolution, which increased crop yields in developed and developing countries. Some believe that genetic engineering techniques will further revolutionize agriculture. Initially, chemists created such highly effective insecticides as DDT, but DDT proved damaging to the environment. Activists then encouraged chemists to develop biopesticides from natural sources because they are generally more ecologically friendly than synthetics.

Industrial ecology is a new field based on chemical engineering and ecology; its goal is to create products in a way that minimizes environmental harm. Therefore, environmental chemical engineers strive to build factories that use renewable energy as much as possible, recycle most materials, minimize wastes, and extract useful materials from wastes. In general, these environmental chemists act as wise stewards of their facilities and the environment. A successful example of ecological engineering is phytoremediation, or the use of plants to remove pollutants from contaminated lands. Artificially constructed wetlands have also been used to purify wastewater.

Impact on Industry

From the 1970s on, environmental chemists devoted themselves to the management of pollutants and participation in government policies and regulations that attempted to prevent or mitigate chemical pollution. In the 1990s, criticism of this command-and-control approach led to the formation of the green chemistry movement by Paul Anastas and others. These chemists fostered a comprehensive approach to the production, utilization, and termination of chemical materials that saved energy and minimized wastes.

By the first decade of the twenty-first century, environmental chemistry had become a thriving profession with a wide spectrum of approaches and views. Industries are involved in a wide variety of processes that have environmental implications, from food production and mineral extraction to manufacturing and construction. In some cases, such as the renewable energy industries, the environmental influence is strong, but even in traditional industries such as utilities and transportation companies, problems such as air and water pollution have become corporate concerns.

Government Agencies and Military. Environmental chemists can pursue careers in such government agencies as the EPA, the Food and Drug Administration, the Natural Resource Conservation Services, the Forest Service, and the Department of Health and Human Services. Additionally, since the beginning of the modern environmental movement, state and federal governments have increased grants and fellowships for projects related to environmental chemistry. For example, the EPA's Green Chemistry Program has supported basic research to develop chemical products and manufacturing techniques that are ecologically benign. Sometimes government agencies cooperate with each other in funding environmental chemical projects; for instance, in 1992, the EPA's Office of Pollution Prevention and Toxics collaborated with the National Science Foundation to fund several green chemical proposals. These grants were significant, totaling tens of millions of dollars.

In the military, the relevant branch for environmental chemists is the US Army Corps of Engineers, specifically the Environmental Chemistry Branch of the Engineer Research and Development Center, which provides expertise in environmental sciences to government agencies.

Industry and Business. Environmentalists and government regulations have forced leaders in business and industry to make sustainability a theme in their plans for future development. In particular, the US chemical industry, the world's largest, has directly linked its growth and competitiveness to a concern for the environment. Industrial leaders realize that they will have to cooperate with officials in government and academia to realize this vision. They also understand that they will need to join with such organizations as the En-

Occupation	Chemists
Employment 2010	82,200
Projected Employment 2020	85,400
Change in Number (2010–20)	3,200
Percent Change	4%

Bureau of Labor Statistics, 2012

vironmental Management Institute and the Society of Environmental Toxicology and Chemistry to minimize the environmental contamination that has at times characterized the chemical industry of the past.

Besides government and academia, professional organizations have also sponsored green research. For example, the American Chemical Society has established the Green Chemistry Institute, whose purpose is to encourage collaboration with scientists in other disciplines to discover chemical products and processes that reduce or eliminate hazardous wastes.

Major Corporations. Top American chemical companies, such as Dow, DuPont, Eastman Chemical, and Union Carbide, have vowed to use resources more efficiently, deliver products to consumers that meet their needs and enhance their quality of life, and preserve the environment for future generations. Nevertheless, these promised changes must be seen against the background of past environmental depredations and disasters. For example, Dow is responsible for ninety-six of the worst Superfund toxic-waste dumps, and Union Carbide shared responsibility for the deaths of more than 2,000 people in a release of toxic chemicals in Bhopal, India. Eastman Chemical, along with other companies, is a member of Responsible Care, an organization devoted to the principles of green chemistry, and the hope is that the member industries will encourage the production of ecologically friendly chemicals without the concomitant of dangerous wastes.

Academic Research and Teaching. Because of the many increasing environmental concerns in industry, government, and academia, numerous careers are possible for environmental chemistry graduates, especially in academic research. Graduates have found research positions in business, law, marketing, public policy, government agencies, laboratories, and

Occupation	Environmental scientists and specialists
Employment 2010	89,400
Projected Employment 2020	106,100
Change in Number (2010–20)	16,700
Percent Change	19%

Bureau of Labor Statistics, 2012

chemical industries. After obtaining a doctorate, some environmental chemists become teachers and researchers in one of the many academic programs devoted to their field.

Social Context and Future Prospects

In a world increasingly concerned with environmental quality, the sustainability of lifestyles, and environmental justice, the future for environmental chemistry appears bright. For example, analysts have predicted that environmental chemical engineers will have a much faster employment growth than the average for all other occupations. Environmental chemists will be needed to help industries comply with regulations and to develop ways of cleaning up hazardous wastes. However, other analysts warn that, in periods of economic recession, environmental concerns tend to be set aside, and this could complicate the employment forecast for environmental chemists.

Some organizations, such as the Environmental Chemistry Group in England, have as a principal goal the promotion of the expertise and interests of their members, and the American Chemical Society's Division of Environmental Chemistry similarly serves its members with information on educational programs, job opportunities, and awards for significant achievement, such as the Award for Creative Advances in Environmental Chemistry. These organizations also issue reports on their social goals, and documents detailing their social philosophy emphasize that environmental chemists should be devoted to the safe operation of their employers' facilities. Furthermore, they should strive to protect the environment and make sustainability an integral part of all business activities.

Further Reading

Baird, Colin, and Michael Cann. *Environmental Chemistry*. 4th ed. New York: Freeman, 2008. A clear and comprehensive survey of the field. Each chapter has further reading suggestions and websites of interest. Index.

Carson, Rachel. *Silent Spring*. 1962. Reprint. Boston: Houghton, 2002. Originally serialized in *The New Yorker* magazine, honored as one of the best nonfiction works of the twentieth century; criticizes the chemical industry and the overuse of pesticides.

Girard, James E. *Principles of Environmental Chemistry*. Sudbury, MA: Jones, 2010. Emphasizes the chemical principles undergirding environmental issues as well as the social and economic contexts in which they occur. Five appendixes and index.

Howard, Alan G. *Aquatic Environmental Chemistry*. 1998. Reprint. New York: Oxford UP, 2004. Analyzes the chemistry behind freshwater and marine systems. Also includes useful secondary material that contains explanations of unusual terms and advanced chemical and mathematical concepts.

Manahan, Stanley E. *Environmental Chemistry*. 9th ed. Boca Raton, FL: CRC, 2010. Explores the anthrosphere, industrial ecosystems, geochemistry, and aquatic and atmospheric chemistry. Each chapter has a list of further references and cited literature. Index.

Schwedt, Georg. *The Essential Guide to Environmental Chemistry*. 2001. Reprint. New York: Wiley, 2007. Provides a concise overview of the field. Contains many color illustrations and an index.

About the Author: Robert J. Paradowski, MS, PhD, is a historian of science and technology who specializes in the history of chemistry with a special emphasis on the life and work of Linus Pauling. He is a summa cum laude graduate of Spring Hill College, with a master's degree in chemistry from Brandeis University and a doctorate in the history of science from the University of Wisconsin. He has taught at Brooklyn College, Eisenhower College, and the Rochester Institute of Technology.

Environmental Chemist

Earnings (Yearly Average): $63,920 (Bureau of Labor Statistics, 2011)

Employment Outlook: Average growth (Bureau of Labor Statistics, 2010)

O*NET-SOC Code: 19-2031.00

Related Career Clusters: Agriculture, Food, & Natural Resources; Architecture & Construction; Government & Public Administration; Health Science

Scope of Work

Environmental chemists study the various chemicals found in nature and the effects of human-introduced chemicals on the environment. This may involve gathering and studying samples, establishing remediation programs, providing guidance and management during emergency response efforts, and helping companies comply with federal regulations. Although environmental chemists initially focused on determining which chemicals and reactions might be harming particular ecosystems, later advancements in technology made it possible for chemists to analyze not only the chemicals but also the environmental damage itself. For instance, after an oil spill, an environmental scientist might analyze the damage, determine that a certain type of dispersant is essential to the cleanup effort, and recommend a course of action. Environmental chemists examine the origin, transfer, and ramifications of chemicals driven into the environment, determine solutions, and work to restore the environment and preserve it from further destruction.

Education and Coursework

The interdisciplinary nature of environmental chemistry requires training in a broad range of areas, and those pursuing a career in the field must undertake coursework in a number of disciplines. An aspiring

---

Transferable Skills

- Communication Skills – Speaking effectively (SCANS Basic Skill)
- Interpersonal/Social Skills – Working as a member of a team (SCANS Workplace Competency – Interpersonal)
- Research & Planning Skills – Identifying problems
- Research & Planning Skills – Determining alternatives
- Organization & Management Skills – Organizing information or materials
- Technical Skills – Using technology to process information (SCANS Workplace Competency – Information)
- Technical Skills – Performing scientific, mathematical, and technical work
- Work Environment Skills – Working both indoors and outdoors

---

environmental chemist should take advanced placement courses in chemistry in high school, along with any additional courses in environmental studies that may be available. At the undergraduate level, a student of environmental chemistry should develop a solid foundation in several sciences, including biology, ecology, mineralogy, and engineering. Courses that build strong interpersonal and communication skills are recommended as well, as chemists must communicate scientific information to a diverse set of individuals and audiences through oral briefings, written documents, training sessions, and public hearings.

Though an associate's or bachelor's degree may prove adequate for some, many experienced professionals recommend that aspiring environmental chemists obtain a master's degree from a program approved by the American Chemical Society. Environmental chemists interested in teaching at the university level or obtaining certain research positions should pursue a doctorate in the discipline. Though doctoral programs typically emphasize research, they differ significantly in subject matter and methodology. For instance, in the doctoral program at the Nicholas School of the Environment and Earth

Sciences at Duke University, doctoral students choose from subjects including marine science and conservation, earth and ocean sciences, and environmental studies and policy. Students at the Yale School of Forestry and Environmental Studies have options ranging from hydrology to tropical ecology and water resource management.

Career Enhancement and Training

Many environmental chemists begin as research assistants, field analysts, or technicians and work their way toward increased responsibility and autonomy as project leaders. Others pursue degrees in public policy, law, or business. For instance, an individual might use his or her knowledge of chemical processes to serve in a corporation's regulatory affairs department, ensuring that government standards are upheld.

A career in environmental resource management is a natural fit for individuals with specialized environmental science degrees looking to take on more responsibility and perhaps effect more positive change. An environmental manager oversees large-scale operations to improve areas that have been damaged in some way by people or industry. They plan and supervise projects, manage researchers and technicians, and measure progress during the effort. Other environmental chemists move up to positions in research or academia, joining the faculty at a college or university or becoming full-time researchers.

Daily Tasks and Technology

Environmental chemists fill a number of roles. Those working for state and local governments may help to write and enforce regulations to protect citizens and the environment. They may perform inspections and scrutinize complaints regarding air quality, water quality, and food safety. Scientists working for private consulting firms may oversee projects to ensure that they adhere to environmental standards and comply with regulations.

Regardless of the industry, environmental chemists typically determine collection methods for research projects, collect environmental data, analyze that data, and prepare reports to explain the findings. After assessing threats to the environment, they may develop remediation programs to prevent, manage, or repair the problems. For instance, an individual may construct a plan to restore a contaminated body of water. Work is primarily performed in a laboratory, except when a situation requires the study of chemicals in the environment. Some companies use indoor ecosystems to conduct experiments and test their products.

Earnings and Employment Outlook

The employment of environmental scientists and related specialists, including environmental chemists, is projected to experience average growth between 2010 and 2020, increasing by 19 percent. According to the US Bureau of Labor Statistics, average wages for such scientists vary widely, in part because the designation "environmental scientist" encompasses a wide range of workers with different specialties, job titles, and responsibilities. Wages also vary greatly based on industry of employment.

The employment of environmental scientists and related specialists, including environmental chemists, is projected to experience average growth between 2010 and 2020, increasing by 19 percent.

Changing technology and increased government environmental intervention have led to greater opportunities for environmental chemists. In 2012, the *New York Times* reported that the Environmental Protection Agency (EPA) was beginning to undertake several of the most expensive and technically complex cleanups in the history of the organization, intending to transform massive stretches of polluted urban waterways in Oregon, Washington, Massachusetts, Connecticut, New York, and New Jersey. Such initiatives provide ample opportunities for environmental chemists, who may use their skills to analyze the nature and severity of the pollution in the water and surrounding land, determine how best to remove the pollution, and report their findings to the EPA and other government organizations. As more time and money are put into such cleanup projects, new technology will be

A Conversation with Ann L. Franke

Job Title: Product Analyst, Information Services industry

What was your career path?

After majoring in chemistry I went on for a Master of Science in public management and policy. I have worked as a health policy analyst in government and as a research analyst and chemist in consulting firms in the environmental area. My experience working with hazardous chemical data led to my current position as a product analyst at EBSCO Publishing. My role includes identifying hazardous chemicals cited in documents contained in the databases of Expert Publishing, a product that provides decision-support chemical information for the environmental health & safety community. I also process the documents for inclusion in the indexed databases.

What are three pieces of advice you would offer someone interested in your profession?

A background in science or engineering is a good basis for a variety of professions, including information services. Although I have not worked as a chemist in a laboratory setting, I have found that the technical nature of the chemistry degree was useful both for getting into graduate school and for finding jobs requiring analytical skills. Computer skills also are essential for participating in electronic publishing. Keeping up with current events and breakthroughs in health and science is also important.

What paths for career advancement are available to you?

Possible opportunities for advancement include taking on more responsibilities for the maintenance, expansion, and marketing of the product and training and supervising new staff as the product grows.

needed to analyze and eliminate pollutants more efficiently, providing further opportunities for environmental chemists working in the research and development sector of the field.

Related Occupations

- **Environmental Engineers:** Environmental engineers work to solve environmental problems by designing and supervising the creation of environmentally friendly structures and systems.

- **Hydrologists:** Hydrologists work to reduce water pollution, develop methods of water conservation and preservation, and oversee the construction of hydroelectric power plants and waste treatment facilities.

- **Geoscientists:** Geoscientists study the earth's physical composition, construct detailed geological maps, and work to locate natural resource deposits.

- **Environmental Science and Protection Technicians:** Environmental science and protection technicians investigate the causes of pollution, often working alongside environmental chemists.

- **Materials Scientists:** Materials scientists examine substances to identify their chemical and physical makeup and apply this information to the production of new materials.

Future Applications

While interest and advances in environmental chemistry have been somewhat slow to develop, the effects of the field on academia and industry are now widespread. Many universities throughout the world have programs that emphasize environmental chemistry, producing graduates with high expectations about what can and should be accomplished with regard to sustainable products and practices. This, along with increasing knowledge of the hazards created by chemical waste and ever-expanding technological advances, has prompted increased corporate interest in environmental chemistry and a push toward developing environmentally friendly processes and technologies in a variety of industries. To do so, such industries will continue to require the skills of environmental chemists, who may work in a number of areas.

Consulting firms will need to hire chemists to help clients interpret increasingly complex environmental laws and regulations and ensure that necessary changes are made. Other environmental chemists will be needed to assist with the planning and construction of new utilities to ensure that they meet new standards. In the manufacturing and technology industries, chemists will be needed to design cost-effective methods for meeting environmental regulations, while others will work to reduce inefficiencies and develop new products. Regardless of specialty or industry of employment, environmental chemists will play a crucial role in moving technology forward and raising further awareness of the effects of human actions on the natural world.

Molly Hagan

More Information

American Chemical Society
Division of Environmental Chemistry
1155 16th Street NW
Washington, DC 20036
www.envirofacs.org

Environmental Protection Agency
1200 Pennsylvania Avenue NW
Washington, DC 20460
www.epa.gov

Royal Society of Chemistry
Burlington House
Piccadilly, London W1J 0BA
www.rsc.org

Femtochemistry

FIELDS OF STUDY

Chemistry; physics; physical chemistry; spectroscopy; optics; photonics; quantum mechanics; statistical mechanics; electromagnetism; condensed-matter physics; fluid physics; solid-state physics; computational chemistry; atomic and optical physics; biophysics; mathematics; calculus; differential equations; linear algebra; statistics; numerical analysis; ultrafast spectroscopy; nonlinear optics; signal processing; computer science.

DEFINITION

Femtochemistry is the study of chemical reactions occurring on a femtosecond timescale, that is, from tenths of a femtosecond to hundreds of femtoseconds. A femtosecond (fs) is 10^{-15} seconds, or one-quadrillionth of a second. To conceptualize how short a femtosecond is, consider that there are more femtoseconds in a second than there are seconds in thirty million years. Femtochemistry's importance stems from the fact that many reaction processes occur on the order of hundreds of femtoseconds and move through a number of intermediate stages. The ability to study events on such short timescales is greatly enhancing scientific understanding of such crucial processes as how protons move through water and how energy moves through photosynthetic systems.

Basic Principles

Chemical reactions occur over a wide range of timescales. The study of chemical kinetics, or the rate at which a chemical event occurs, is a relatively new one; the first actual measurement of a reaction rate was performed by Ludwig Wilhelmy in 1850. The Arrhenius equation, used to predict reaction rates, debuted in 1889 and has since become a mainstay of introductory chemistry courses. The first Nobel Prize in chemistry was awarded in 1901 to Jacobus H. van 't Hoff, who expanded upon Svante Arrhenius's work. Over the next few decades, different experimental techniques were developed, reaching the millisecond (10^{-3} s) and then the microsecond (10^{-6} s) timescales.

The next major event in the study of chemical kinetics was Theodore Maiman's invention of the ruby laser in 1960. The subsequent developments of Q-switching (1961) and mode-locking (1964) enabled the production of nanosecond- and picosecond-scale pulses of light. Each light pulse takes a snapshot of a sample, with the length of the pulse determining the time resolution of the "photograph." Thus, a picosecond-long laser pulse provides information about what a system looked like at a given picosecond in time.

Femtochemistry developed in the mid-1980s, when Egyptian American scientist Ahmed Zewail and his colleagues studied the dissociation (a kind of splitting) of a simple molecule, iodine cyanide (ICN). Zewail and his team succeeded in viewing the transition stages of the reaction, which occurred on the femtosecond timescale, in 1987; Zewail was later awarded the Nobel Prize in chemistry for his work. Over the next decades, femtochemistry has continued to be refined, achieving much shorter pulses with higher energies, and applied to myriad systems.

While the prefix "femto-" is not commonly used in everyday speech, terms such as "micro-" and "nano-" are. These terms tend to be used interchangeably to mean "small"; however, their precise meanings should not be forgotten. There are one thousand milliseconds in a second, one thousand microseconds in a millisecond, one thousand nanoseconds in a microsecond, one thousand picoseconds in a nanosecond, and one thousand femtoseconds in a picosecond. Each order of magnitude corresponds to different types of chemical processes, and they should not be confused.

Core Concepts

As a field that combines elements from several disciplines, femtochemistry relies heavily on a number of key concepts related to chemistry and physics as well as to subfields such as optics.

Spectroscopy. Spectroscopy is the use of light to investigate the properties of matter. When light passes through or is reflected by matter, its intensity, wavelength, orientation, and direction are changed. By studying the light before and after it interacts with the sample, scientists can learn things about the properties of the sample material. For example, the concentration of a solution can be determined by calculating how much of the light passing through the sample is absorbed, and the thickness of some thin films can be determined based on the change in the orientation of the light after deflection. These properties cannot be measured directly by the naked eye and thus must be determined indirectly using the response of light. In femtochemistry, femtosecond-length light pulses are used to study the structures of transition-state compounds and other "invisible" structures and processes.

Chemical Reactions and Vibrational Spectroscopy. One of the major applications of femtochemistry is in determining precisely how a given chemical reaction involving bond breaking or bond making occurs. Many different timescales are relevant for chemical reactions, but femtochemistry's unique contribution lies in the study of molecular vibrations, which tend to occur on a femtosecond timescale. To understand why these vibrations are important, consider that molecules are best imaged as balls connected by springs. In a water molecule, two smaller balls (hydrogen atoms) are connected to a larger ball (the oxygen atom). However, these connections are not static; this V-shaped molecule bends, stretches, and scissors in every possible way, with the distances and angles between the atoms varying around some average. This motion is important, because it tells scientists something about the molecule's environment. If one of the hydrogen atoms is being pulled toward another molecule, the beginnings of a chemical reaction involving an atom transfer, the vibrations slow because the atom is spending more of its time farther away from the parent molecule and thus must travel a longer distance. After it transfers and becomes part of the neighboring molecule, it vibrates at a different frequency determined by its new environment.

Scientists can calculate the vibrational frequencies expected for specific systems of molecules and use the measured vibrational frequencies to identify the routes that the different atoms take as they rearrange to form new molecules in chemical reactions. Vibrational spectroscopy, the use of light to measure these vibrations, was developed long before it became possible to take femtosecond measurements; however, slower measurements are unable to take snapshots frequently enough. These slower measurements result in blurry pictures that show only the initial and final molecular arrangements, whereas femtochemistry allows snapshots to be taken frequently enough for scientists to determine exactly how the atoms in the molecules have rearranged themselves.

Transition States and Reaction Control. Most reactions are more complicated than an atom transfer. Although it may not seem as if it would be difficult or important to predict how such a reaction occurs, reactions tend to involve larger molecules, and changes in neighboring molecules, such as the solvent, can be crucial. Furthermore, this discussion has omitted information about electronic energy levels and spin states for the sake of accessibility; these details make the overall description of a chemical reaction even more intricate. Femtochemistry allows researchers to gain information about how reactions occur in more detail than ever before. For example, many transition states, which had previously been theoretical, unmeasurable concepts, have been identified. The transition state is the arrangement of the atoms and electrons at which point the reaction must proceed to the products instead of slipping back to the reactants. Identifying this state and other information about a given reaction may allow for future reaction control. Chemical reactions generally produce numerous products, many of which are undesired, and scientists continue to search for ways to synthesize some compounds. The ability to control reactions would allow researchers to apply a given set of conditions to ensure that a reaction proceeds efficiently to the desired product, minimizing waste and expanding their ability to create any desired molecule.

Coherence. Coherence refers to creating synchronous chemical events. Because any given sample contains many, many molecules, it is useful to have all of the reactions occur at the same time when attempting to record how a reaction occurs using femtosecond "photographs." One common way to create coherence is to use a "pump-probe" laser experiment. The "pump" laser pulse sets up the system, putting the molecules in an excited state or liberating the target molecules from a surface. The "probe" pulse is then used to measure the properties of interest, acting as the camera in the photography analogy. In addition to creating a defined start time, coherent experiments are useful in signal amplification. Molecules are so small that almost any measurement actually contains information about a very large number of molecules. Depending on the experiment, sometimes the signals from molecules undergoing reactions other than the reaction of interest, reacting at different times, or even reacting in different directions can make it difficult to record the signal for the reaction of interest. Controlling the start time of the reactions can help prevent this.

Applications Past and Present

Femtochemistry has applications in almost every area of chemistry because of its ability to provide "snapshots" of chemical reactions while they are in progress. Through such applications, femtochemistry furthers science and technology in a number of industries.

Water. One might assume that water is one of the best understood substances, due to its ubiquity. However, the opposite is actually the case: Water is as unique and complex as it is common, and much about how it interacts with substances dissolved in it (that is, its properties as a solvent) is only poorly understood. Water is a dynamic network of hydrogen bonding; the hydrogen atoms in each H_2O molecule also form loose bonds, known as hydrogen bonds, with nearby oxygen molecules due to the hydrogen's slightly positive charge and the oxygen's slightly negative charge. These bonds are not stationary; hydrogen atoms can jump from one oxygen atom to the next, and any change to one water molecule affects all surrounding molecules. The structure of water is different depending on whether it is completely surrounded by other water molecules on all sides (referred to as being in the bulk solution), at an interface (such as the interface between water and air), or near other molecules. This structure is important because it determines which molecules will dissolve in water and how important biological compounds, such as proteins, will function. Because these rearrangements occur on a femtosecond timescale, they can only be accessed using femtochemical techniques.

Interesting Facts about Femtochemistry

- There are as many femtoseconds in a second as there are seconds in about 31.7 million years.

- The distance that light travels in one hundred femtoseconds is equivalent to the thickness of a relatively fine strand of human hair (roughly thirty micrometers).

- The term "jiffy," originally used to describe a short period of time, was introduced as a scientific term by chemist Gilbert N. Lewis early in the twentieth century. Lewis used the word to describe the amount of time it takes a photon to travel a centimeter, which is thirty-three picoseconds or thirty-three thousand femtoseconds. Thus, femtochemistry is chemistry on a subjiffy timescale.

- The concept of hours was developed circa 1500 BCE, minutes and seconds circa 1500 CE, milliseconds circa 1900, and femtoseconds circa 1980. It took thousands of years for humans to progress from hours to minutes but only about one hundred years to improve millisecond resolution by a factor of one trillion.

- The optics systems required to generate femtosecond laser systems are quite complex and very sensitive; some components require cooling to 4 Kelvin, which is 4 degrees Celsius above absolute zero, the lowest possible temperature.

Atmospheric Chemistry and Combustion. Research related to atmospheric chemistry and combustion tends to focus on very small molecules; however, many bond-breaking and bond-making processes remain unclear, even for triatomic molecules. Femtochemistry is used in atmospheric chemistry to determine what molecules form during the intermediate stages of a reaction. For example, the reaction of OClO to produce Cl (chlorine), which is partially responsible for the depletion of the ozone layer, has been studied in numerous ways using femtosecond spectroscopy. Combustion chemistry entails the study of the reactions and products associated with combustion, such as ketones, of which acetone is the simplest example. Acetone can dissociate in different ways depending on the amount of energy applied.

Some of these mechanisms are fairly straightforward, but others have yet to be clearly defined. Femtochemistry again provides a means to take very quick snapshots of the structure of the molecules after inducing dissociation in different ways. Using this knowledge, scientists are better able to predict global-scale changes in the atmosphere's composition and help regulators enact more effective policies.

Biological Processes. Femtochemistry has been used to shed light on many biological processes that were previously inaccessible because of their speed. For example, femtochemistry has been used to determine how the compound retinal, which is crucial for vision, reacts so efficiently with light. Within two hundred femtoseconds of irradiation, retinal twists, acquiring a new structure, and then continues to oscillate. The details of this process allow the retinal molecule to respond to light energy with high efficiency. Chlorophyll has been studied in a similar fashion. In both of these examples, femtochemistry allows the reactions of these molecules with light to be studied with unprecedented time resolution; instead of just seeing the initial and final structures, researchers can identify each step in the process. In this way, scientists can determine exactly how these molecules convert light energy into chemical energy able to be used by organisms.

Catalysts. Catalysts represent a key element of modern chemistry. By definition, catalysts are materials that accelerate chemical reactions and, most important, are regenerated at the end of each reaction for use in the next. Catalysts have improved the scale and speed of chemical manufacturing and decreased waste by reducing the need for large amounts of solvent. However, much about how these catalysts work and how they become inhibited or poisoned (a temporary or permanent reduction in efficiency, respectively) is unknown. Femtochemistry experiments are helping to elucidate these mechanisms, which will in turn help scientists develop better catalysts.

Superconductors. When most materials conduct electricity, some of the electrical energy is lost in the form of heat. Superconductors, in contrast, transmit electricity with no loss, making them extraordinarily useful, with applications ranging from transportation (such as electric rail systems) to improved power distribution. Superconductors can also be used to create very powerful electromagnets, which are required for magnetic resonance imaging (MRI) in medicine and nuclear magnetic resonance (NMR) spectroscopy in chemistry, the latter of which is a crucial technique used to determine the structures of molecules ranging from several atoms to hundreds of atoms. Femtosecond laser pulses can be used to generate terahertz radiation, a useful but difficult-to-access range of frequencies that is uniquely suited to studying superconductors.

Impact on Industry

Femtochemists work at the intersection of chemistry, physics, and often engineering. According to the US Bureau of Labor Statistics, the employment of chemists and materials scientists is expected to increase by 4 percent between 2010 and 2020, while employment of physicists and astronomers is projected to increase by 14 percent. Considering that femtochemistry is an expanding subfield of chemistry and is heavily influenced by physics, a reasonable estimate for the employment growth rate for femtochemistry is 10 percent. In addition to researchers whose primary focus is femtochemistry, there will be an increasing demand for scientists with a background in femtochemistry and another field, such as biochemistry, who can apply femtochemical principles to other areas of study.

Government Agencies. The US Department of Energy maintains a series of national laboratories that carry out federally funded research. Argonne National Laboratory, located near Chicago, Illinois, has facilities capable of producing femtosecond x-ray pulses, the uses of which include determining the structures of proteins. Femtochemistry is relevant to the Environmental Protection

Occupation	Chemists and materials scientists
Employment 2010	90,900
Projected Employment 2020	94,900
Change in Number (2010–20)	4,000
Percent Change	4%

*Bureau of Labor Statistics, 2012

Occupation	Chemical technicians
Employment 2010	61,000
Projected Employment 2020	65,100
Change in Number (2010–20)	4,100
Percent Change	7%

Bureau of Labor Statistics, 2012

Agency due to its applications in atmospheric chemistry. Indeed, because of femtochemistry's wide range of applications, essentially every government agency that conducts chemical research has begun work in the field or is expected to do so as the field continues to develop.

Military. Femtochemistry has a number of potential applications in security and explosives detection. One subfield of femtochemistry, terahertz spectroscopy, can be used to differentiate between many common explosives and is beginning to see applications in airport security. Femtosecond pulses are also very useful for determining the mechanisms related to the detonation of explosives due to their ability to take very quick snapshots and thus gather data on the chemical changes that happen before the sample (and, often, the surrounding equipment) is destroyed. The military will likely continue to fund femtochemistry research and employ femtochemists well into the future in order to develop these applications further.

University Research and Teaching. Femtochemistry is of great interest to many chemists and physicists and has spawned university-level research efforts in many different subfields, including materials science, biochemistry, inorganic chemistry, physical chemistry, theoretical chemistry, atomic and molecular physics, and electrical engineering. As the instrumentation required for femtosecond spectroscopy becomes less costly, a greater number of research groups will be able to afford to carry out femtochemistry experiments.

Other Industries. Femtochemistry is a key science in a number of industries. In the pharmaceutical industry, femtochemists study how potential new drugs interact with their intended targets on a short timescale. A variety of industries employ femtochemists to develop new materials, such as solar panels and superconductors. Corporations involved in manufacturing the components used in femtosecond spectroscopy setups also employ engineers and sales representatives with femtochemistry backgrounds.

Social Context and Future Prospects

Although the field of femtochemistry is relatively new, it has already improved scientific understanding of many key biological processes, which in turn provides an understanding of the causes of and suggests potential treatments for various illnesses and disorders. Femtochemistry has also shed light on how water behaves around biomolecules, allowing scientists to make more accurate predictions about how potential drugs will behave in the body. The application of femtosecond measurements to atmospheric chemistry has and will continue to improve scientific understanding of the gas-phrase reactions that contribute to global warming and respiratory issues. Finally, the knowledge gained by applying femtochemistry to catalysts and superconductors will advance the development of new materials with countless important applications.

In the long term, improvements in instrumentation will increase access to femtosecond pulses with highly specified energies and durations, which will in turn allow femtochemical techniques to be applied to a wider range of chemical systems. Reaction control is also of great interest; the ability to control reactions could be used to reduce waste, generate the desired products in higher yields, and probe complex molecules in new ways. Finally, as the study of reactions occurring on the femtosecond timescale becomes more common and affordable, scientists will likely seek to carry out research on even shorter timescales. Attosecond spectroscopy (1 attosecond equals 10^{-18} seconds, or $1/1000$ of a femtosecond), is currently in very early development but is already offering interesting insights into chemical and physical phenomena.

Further Reading

"The Nobel Prize in Chemistry 1999: Advanced Information." *Nobelprize.org*. Nobel Media, n.d. Web. 26 Aug. 2012. Provides a detailed, accessible overview of Zewail's founding of femtochemistry, the field's importance, and its applications.

Telle, Helmut H., Angel González Ureña, and Robert J. Donovan. *Laser Chemistry: Spectroscopy, Dynamics and Applications.* Hoboken: Wiley, 2007. Print. Introduces concepts on which a solid understanding of femtochemistry may be based, providing a broader context for the science.

Zewail, Ahmed H. "Femtochemistry: Past, Present, and Future." *Pure and Applied Chemistry* 72.12 (2000): 2219–32. Print. Provides an overview of femtochemistry and future research directions and includes several diagrams that help to place femtochemistry in the context of the broader field of chemistry.

---. "Femtochemistry: Recent Progress in Studies of Dynamics and Control of Reactions and Their Transition States." *Journal of Physical Chemistry* 100.31 (1996): 12701–24. Print. Discusses various developments in the field of femtochemistry and provides an overview of Zewail's key work in the field.

---. *Voyage through Time: Walks of Life to the Nobel Prize.* Hackensack: World Scientific, 2003. Print. Interweaves Zewail's personal life and scientific contributions, focusing in particular on the research for which he was awarded the Nobel Prize.

About the Author: Cassandra Newell, BA, graduated from Colby College with a bachelor's degree in chemistry and Russian and then attended MIT, completing 2.5 years of work toward a PhD in physical chemistry before leaving to pursue other interests. She worked as a research assistant at both institutions, studying such topics as molecular recognition, guest-host chemistry, computational chemistry, terahertz spectroscopy, acoustic spectroscopy, and proton/electron transfer in chemical systems. She also has experience as a teaching assistant and tutor in the fields of spectroscopy and quantum mechanics. Since leaving academia, she has pursued projects pertaining to science communication, such as editing scientific manuscripts and writing about science for nonspecialists.

Experimental Scientist

Earnings (Yearly Average): $84,600 (Bureau of Labor Statistics, 2011)

Employment and Outlook: Slower than average growth (Bureau of Labor Statistics, 2010)

O*NET-SOC Code: 19-2032.00

Related Career Clusters: Agriculture, Food & Natural Resources; Health Science; Manufacturing

Scope of Work

Experimental science is based on the principle of the scientific method, a system of investigating a substance or phenomenon in which a scientist defines a distinct question or problem, develops a hypothesis, performs experiments and collects data, and analyzes the data to determine whether the hypothesis is correct. This method is applicable to a wide variety of hard sciences as well as to various social sciences. Thus, in its broadest sense, the title of experimental scientist can apply to researchers in a number of different fields. However, it most generally is used in reference to the field of chemistry, which itself encompasses a large number of specialized branches.

The work carried out by experimental scientists can generally be divided into two classes: pure research and applied research. The former can be thought of as developing and testing hypotheses for the sake of increasing knowledge about a particular field of study. The latter can be thought of as performing research in order to develop practical applications of the resulting knowledge. Although there is some overlap between these two areas, pure research tends to be carried out in academic settings, while applied research is typically carried out in industries seeking to develop new products and services.

Education and Coursework

A bachelor's degree is the minimum educational requirement for a career in experimental science. Undergraduate programs often require completion of an individual research project, in which a student demonstrates that he or she has acquired the ability to design and carry out experiments in a particular discipline. This educational and practical experience is typically sufficient for those seeking an entry-level position in the field, from which a more advanced career can be developed in time.

Higher-level research positions generally require an advanced degree, and a doctorate is preferred or required in many areas. A doctorate

> ## Transferable Skills
>
> - Managing equipment/materials (SCANS Workplace Competency – Resources)
> - Performing scientific, mathematical, and technical work
> - Creating ideas
> - Identifying problems
> - Identifying resources
> - Gathering information
> - Solving problems (SCANS Thinking Skills)
> - Analyzing information

in any scientific field typically demands between one and seven years of specialized study and experimentation under the mentorship of a senior educator, often a tenured staff member. Individual degree programs vary based on the nature of the discipline, the research project being undertaken, and the specialty of the mentor. Most degree programs culminate in the defense of a thesis that describes a research project in detail and provides a valid interpretation of the results obtained in accord with the theoretical principles of the discipline.

There are many opportunities to learn more about a particular field of study and the careers that are possible within it before deciding on an educational path. Internships may be available in both educational and industrial environments, and some college and university research groups allow students to work as unpaid assistants for a limited period of time in exchange for practical experience in a functioning laboratory. There are also various professional organizations that exist to support the work of experimental scientists in nearly every field, many of which offer associate memberships for students.

Career Enhancement and Training

No certifications are required for a career as an experimental scientist. However, certification in a particular area or completion of additional training such as occupational safety courses may be required by some employers. In addition to advanced degree programs, there are numerous opportunities for experimental scientists to obtain new skills and refresh their knowledge of their chosen discipline. Professional organizations such as the American Chemical Society promote continuing education as well as communication and collaboration among members working in the same field and make available a collection of resources for the benefit of their members. The vast majority of professional organizations and associations publish peer-reviewed reports of work that has been carried out, allowing members to remain knowledgeable about advances in the field. Membership in any professional organization carries a fee that supports the activities of the organization, such as the publication of journals and reports and the hosting of conferences. Admission to specialist conferences is perhaps the most important benefit to members of professional organizations, as such events are the primary means of networking personally with other members. Building a network of professionals within one's field of specialization enables an individual to identify new opportunities for both career development and educational advancement.

Daily Tasks and Technology

Experimental scientists are responsible for conducting experiments and maintaining the laboratory environment in accordance with established procedures and standards. In an academic environment, experimental scientists may keep basic records, review experimental work being carried out, teach the techniques required of the particular field of study, administer examinations, read and grade laboratory reports, and ensure that the proper equipment and materials are available. When tasked with carrying out original research, experimental scientists design the experiments to be performed, collate and interpret the results, and write reports for peer-reviewed journals. Other tasks may include teaching academic courses, adjudicating at the defense of an academic thesis, or assuming an administrative position within a particular department. In an industrial environment, experimental scientists design and carry out experimental procedures and report the results to the managerial body of the organization. As industrial research is typically carried out with the expectation that the resulting knowledge or discoveries will be economically useful to the organization, it is generally necessary for scientists to justify experimental procedures before they can be carried out.

Regardless of employer or industry of employment, it is necessary for experimental scientists to keep abreast of the appropriate literature of the field, including research papers, patent literature, and reports published by relevant scientific, government, or industry organizations. Conducting experiments requires expertise in numerous analytical and preparative techniques as well as the use of the corresponding equipment, and scientists must at times design and construct equipment to meet a planned experiment's specifications. Personal computers and related technology have revolutionized and simplified many of these tasks and devices, and new applications that will further this process are continually being developed. Thus, experimental scientists must also remain up to date in regard to technological advancements relevant to their work.

Earnings and Employment Outlook

Employment of experimental scientists is expected to experience slower than average growth between 2010 and 2020. Positions at the leading edge of pure research in any area of experimental science are limited and are almost without exception reserved for those who both hold a doctorate in that particular field and have a documented track record of successful research. These positions are typically found in academic environments and are normally funded by grants. The majority of experimental science positions, though perhaps not as prestigious, are economically important jobs that drive industry, technology, medicine, and many other fields. These positions, typically held by salaried employees in corporate environments, tend to be focused on finding solutions and applications for specific problems rather than advancing knowledge for the sake of knowledge. Such positions are far more numerous than positions in pure research and are expected to remain a constant component of the corporate sector as new products, technologies, and methodologies are constantly being developed to improve or replace existing ones. Overall, employment of qualified

A Conversation with Jennifer Gibson

Job Title: Pharmacist; President, Excalibur Scientific, LLC

What was your career path?

I earned a Bachelor of Science degree in biochemistry. I completed an undergraduate research project which led me to a job in a high through-put DNA sequencing and genomics research lab. In this position, I gained real-world, hands-on science experience, but also developed skills for communication in science, personnel management, and project management. When I desired more flexibility in my career, I returned to school and earned a Doctor of Pharmacy degree. While in pharmacy school, I worked as an intern in a university's drug information center where I became proficient at researching, reporting, and presenting drug-related topics to a variety of audiences. After graduation, I became a licensed pharmacist and worked as a clinical pharmacist in a hospital setting. At the same time, I completed medical writing and editing projects on a freelance basis. After three years in a hospital setting, I founded my own medical communications company and now write clinical textbooks, prepare continuing education programs, and consult on practices within the healthcare community.

What are three pieces of advice you would offer someone interested in your profession?

1. Gain real-world, hands-on experience in science. Academic learning is important, but the experience gained from actually working in a lab or hospital or pharmacy setting is invaluable and will help determine your likes and dislikes when it comes to a career.

2. Network. Get to know people who have jobs that you are interested in and use their connections, when appropriate, to open doors for your own career.

3. Build your communication and social skills. An interest or expertise in medicine or healthcare can only get you so far. You must be able to translate that knowledge to usable information for your patients or clients. Learn how to communicate with people from a variety of age groups and cultural backgrounds.

> **What paths for career advancement are available to you?**
>
> Nearly limitless. With a license to practice pharmacy, I could easily return to a traditional pharmacy setting with a part-time or full-time schedule. Depending on lifestyle preferences, I could remain a staff pharmacist or advance to management positions. In my current company, I am the owner and president, so my career decisions are entirely my own. I have 100% flexibility in the projects I take on and the clients I work with. I work as much or as little as I want. I can grow the company to whatever size I choose in the future.

experimental scientists is expected to increase much more rapidly than average in the biochemical and medical fields, while employment of experimental scientists in the fields of chemistry and materials science is expected to increase at a rate that is slower than average.

Employment of experimental scientists is expected to experience slower than average growth between 2010 and 2020.

Related Occupations

- **Biochemists:** Biochemists conduct research regarding the physical and chemical properties of plants, animals, and other organisms.

- **Natural Sciences Managers:** Natural sciences managers supervise the application of experimental science in a field, managing projects and the research carried out by various scientists and technicians.

- **Soil and Plant Scientists:** Soil and plant scientists study plants and soils to determine the effects of soil composition, pollution, and other factors on plant growth.

- **Medical Scientists:** Medical scientists perform research to develop treatments for medical conditions and produce new pharmaceutical compounds and biomaterials.

- **Agricultural and Food Scientists:** Agricultural and food scientists perform experiments and collect data regarding food in order to improve the safety and productivity of food production.

Future Applications

Experimental scientists play an essential role in a number of fields, expanding knowledge, developing new uses for materials, creating new medicines and medical devices, and working toward advancements in many other areas. As the scientific community and industry become increasingly interested in environmentally friendly technology and methods, the work of experimental scientists will be crucial to developing "green" solutions for problems that affect society. In the growing biofuels industry, for instance, experimental scientists play a vital role in developing efficient processes for converting raw organic materials such as algae and vegetable oils into usable combustion fuels. Other scientists work to reverse or negate the environmental presence of discarded plastics that have accumulated around the world as well as develop new and better plastics and polymers. This trend toward sustainable energy and environmentally friendly production is expected to continue, providing ample opportunities for experimental scientists to use their skills.

Richard M. Renneboog, MS

More Information

American Chemical Society
1155 16th Street NW
Washington, DC 20036.
www.acs.org

Materials Research Society
506 Keystone Drive
Warrendale, PA 15086
www.mrs.org

National Science Foundation
4201 Wilson Boulevard
Arlington, VA 22230
www.nsf.gov

Food Chemistry

FIELDS OF STUDY

Food science; food technology; chemistry; biochemistry; biology; microbiology; nutrition; toxicology; human health and safety; medicine; pharmacy; engineering; chemical engineering.

DEFINITION

Food chemistry, the largest branch of food science, is the study of the basic biological components of food, including the interactions and processes involving lipids, carbohydrates, and proteins. The field also includes the understanding of nonbiological components—such as preservatives, additives, or flavorants—and their effect on manufactured foodstuffs. A food chemist is charged with improving the taste and quality of food, the development of packaging that safely preserves food, and studying the effects of industrial processing on the vitamin and mineral contents of food.

Basic Principles

Food chemistry can be dated to the eighteenth century, when a Swedish pharmacist named Carl Wilhelm Scheele (who discovered chlorine, glycerol, and oxygen) studied the properties of lactose. By the time Scheele died in 1786, he had isolated a number of chemical compounds found in plants and animals. However, the study of food chemistry as a means to create new food products did not arise until a century later. Most food chemistry institutions, including the *Journal of Agricultural and Food Chemistry*, published by the American Chemical Society, and the Institute of Food Science and Technology in London, were established in the 1950s.

Food chemistry requires a strong understanding of the principles of biochemistry. The two fields are built on the study of chemical compounds known as macronutrients, which include carbohydrates, proteins, and lipids (more commonly known as fats). Cells use these macronutrients as a source of chemical energy. Food is primarily made up of these three components. An understanding of the interactions of these three components provides the basis for home cooking as well as the manufacture of food products on a large scale. For instance, fats like meat or milk can go sour because of the chemical makeup of lipids and the effects of oxidation. Food chemistry also encompasses an understanding of water, vitamins, minerals, and enzymes.

Core Concepts

In addition to the organic chemical compounds that occur in food, food chemistry makes use of concepts from several other subjects, including: food rheology, food fortification, aseptic processing, and water activity.

Food Rheology. The study of rheology examines the movement and flow of unusual materials, like mayonnaise or peanut butter. Rheology also applies to nonfood substances like paint or molten plastic. Rheology as it applies to food is particularly important when it comes to processing. When developing a product, food chemists need to think about how that product might behave within the structure of a package and in transport. In addition to the logistics of a product, rheology dictates much of the consumer experience, including the texture of a product and how it feels to the mouth (referred to as the "mouthfeel"). For instance, is that product juicy, smooth, brittle, or creamy? Rheology is also involved in a food's structure and appearance, as well as the characteristics of the food's components. Does a particular food product contain a paste? Can it retain its shape? All of these characteristics relate to a food product's rheology.

Food chemists (and food rheologists) aim to develop instruments of production that address the complexity a food's rheological behavior. In this way, industrially produced foods with unusual textures can be manufactured to taste and feel the same from factory to consumer.

Food Fortification. Food fortification, or enrichment, is the addition of essential vitamins, or micronutrients, to a food product. Food fortification was first practiced in the 1920s after two Ohio doctors found that sodium iodine was effective in the treatment of goiter (an enlarged thyroid gland). This discovery led to the introduction of iodized salt, which has become commonplace, as have fortified foods in general. Today, for example, you can buy milk that has been fortified with vitamin D. Food fortification is becoming a matter of public health policy as well as a commercial endeavor. In developing countries, several companies are working to fortify staple foods, like grains, with vitamin A; the staple foods in these countries lack proper nutrients due to either the poor quality of soil in the region or an insufficient diet nationwide. The World Health Organization (WHO) cites micronutrient deficiencies as the cause of blindness, anemia, and mental retardation in children. In 2003, the Global Alliance for Improved Nutrition (GAIN) announced that they would assist recipient countries in fortifying foods and condiments like salt, flour, oil, sugar, and soy sauce with iron, iodine, vitamin A, and folic acid.

There are four methods commonly used in fortifying foods. The first is biofortification, or the process of breeding genetically modified crops to increase their nutritional value. Microbial biofortification, or synthetic biology, is the addition of probiotic bacteria to foods. Commercial fortification refers to the processes that create the products at the grocery store, including fortified milk and salt. Lastly, home fortification can be achieved by the application of drops containing micronutrients like vitamin D.

Aseptic Processing. Aseptic processing refers to the process of safely packaging food products to ensure that they are kept fresh. Philip Nelson, a professor of food science at Purdue University, developed the modern process in which foods are sterilely processed and then placed in a similarly sterile container. (Aseptic processing was used before Nelson, but he was the first to apply it on a larger scale.) Nelson made it possible for companies to process foods, namely liquids and semi-liquids like pudding, safely and at a much faster rate. During aseptic processing, the food product passes through a very thin pipe where it is quickly heated (to kill pathogens) and then quickly cooled. After passing through the pipe, the food product is packaged in a pressurized and pathogen-free compartment.

The old method, which Nelson's has largely replaced, required a larger amount of energy to heat the food product after it had already been packaged; companies also ran the risk of ruining the product if left in the heat for too long. Still, the inception of aseptic processing, which began in the wine industry at the turn of the twentieth century, has ensured that food products, from canned soup to orange juice, can be mass-marketed safely.

Water Activity. Another important element of food chemistry is water activity. Water activity is widely defined as the measure of free or unbound water available for chemical or biological activity. The amount of water a food contains influences the food's texture and, in some cases, how susceptible it is to spoilage or the growth of microbes. Food chemists are able to remove water through concentration, or through freezing, salting, or drying a food product. These methods are helpful in food processing.

Much as the interactions of carbohydrates, proteins, and lipids are the building blocks of food chemistry, water's interactions with a food's chemical makeup has an extraordinary influence on the properties of that food. Food in which water is tightly bound to surrounding protein molecules has a very low water activity; foods with low water activities include crackers and dried vegetables. Fresh fruit is an example of food that has a high water activity. Moisture allows for the rapid growth of bacteria, which is why fresh fruit left out for too long will soften and attract insects. The mathematics of water activity is not useful for frozen foods, but is widely used for dried, salted, and fresh foods.

Applications Past and Present

Food Preservation. The earliest endeavors in food chemistry were in an effort to preserve food. In the early 1800s, the French chef Nicolas Appert answered a challenge from Napoleon Bonaparte to invent a way to keep food from spoiling when being shipped to the French army. After years of experimenting, Appert found that if he sealed food in an airtight container and then soaked that container in hot water, food would stay fresher, longer. Appert's discovery, of course, was the canning technique that would affect food consumption worldwide. (An Englishman named Peter Durand was the first to apply Appert's technique to tin cans; Appert had used glass bottles.)

Of course, humans had been preserving or slowing the fermentation process of food for thousands of years by drying, smoking, salt-curing, or salt brining meats and vegetables to be consumed later or out of season. Early American settlers handed down techniques for home canning, pickling, and making jam. In the 1800s, Americans made use of cellars and occasionally caves as an early means of refrigeration. At the turn of the twentieth century, New York inventor Clarence Birdseye discovered that flash-freezing foods preserved their taste better; Birdseye found a way to effectively deliver these frozen foods to the public, creating a precursor to the extensive modern frozen food industry.

The visible effects of temperature on food were understood early, but even Appert was not entirely sure why the food he had sealed in bottles (and then heated) did not go bad. The first person to fully understand why certain foods were susceptible to spoilage and under what conditions was French chemist Louis Pasteur. Pasteur realized that microorganisms were responsible for spoiling food and causing illness. His contributions to food chemistry are more fully discussed in the next section.

Food Safety. Louis Pasteur took a more scientific approach to food less than fifty years after Appert fed Napoleon's army. He discovered that bacteria were responsible for souring the wine and beer made by local alcohol manufacturers in Lille, France. Pasteur reasoned that heating a liquid to just below its boiling point and then cooling it would kill bacteria. He later famously applied this approach to milk, and the process came to be known as pasteurization. Pasteur recognized that bacteria came from the environment (and further, that when food was left in the environment, it was susceptible to that bacteria) at a time when most scientists thought that bacteria spontaneously generated.

In 1888, during an outbreak of meat poisoning in Germany, August Gärtner discovered a food-borne bacterium called *Bacillus enteritidis*. It seemed that people were getting sick after consuming meat from a cow that had been sick when it was slaughtered. Gärtner's discovery influenced what safety precautions are taken when food is processed. Consumers and producers were more educated about food safety at the dawn of the Industrial Revolution, but it became clear that there would need to be public policies put in place to address the expansion of the business of food.

The United States enacted a historic piece of public health legislation in 1906 when Congress passed the Pure Food and Drug Act. The law is a testament to the work of journalists, including author Upton Sinclair and a government official named Harvey W. Wiley. Journalists known as muckrakers raised public awareness of careless food preparation and questionable business practices in the food industry. Sinclair's novel *The Jungle* was published in 1906; it shocked the nation with horrific descriptions of the Chicago meat packing industry. Wiley, who had been commissioned to research the adulteration of food products in 1902, presented further evidence that poisonous and harmful additives were being used by food companies to meet demand. President Theodore Roosevelt passed the Meat Inspection Act the same year. The Pure Food and Drug Act was amended several times before being extended in scope in 1933.

The US Food and Drug Administration (FDA)—first created as the Bureau of Chemistry in 1862 by President Abraham Lincoln—and other regulatory agencies continue to monitor the food industry as the processes of food production continue to change.

Food Technology. Food technology refers to the actual production processes of food. Though the term is relatively new, scientists have been contributing research to the field for centuries. Appert and Pasteur can be credited as early innovators in modern food technology; canning and pasteurization are processes that are widely used today, though they have also been improved. As the twentieth century progressed, people enjoyed better public health information and were able to store food for longer; it then became the endeavor of food technologists, as mass-marketed foods were on the rise, to also improve a product's overall quality and taste.

The 1940s saw a boom in the mass production of food during World War II. Like Appert and his glass bottles, practices were invented to satisfy wartime needs and then later applied commercially. Companies developed ways of concentrating, freezing, and drying foods (such as frozen concentrated orange juice) to ship overseas. Flour was fortified with iron as the country survived on rations, and an early form of aseptic processing came into use. The same era also gave rise to homogenized milk, which is blended intensively so that the fat does not separate. In the 1950s, controlled atmosphere packaging (CAP) was developed to ensure a longer shelf-life for products. Mechanized food production reigned. In the 1960s, the bottling industry put local soda fountains out of business by selling popular beverages—like Coca-Cola, developed by a pharmacist in the late 1800s—at the grocery store. Mechanization led to a boom in processed foods, some of which contained synthetic or chemically enhanced ingredients.

Trans fat, largely in the form of partially hydrogenated vegetable oil, became popular with producers in the early 1900s because it served as a preservative, giving food products a longer shelf-life; consumers liked it because it tasted good, and often improved a product's texture. It was not until the 1990s that scientists found that trans fats can cause health problems like high cholesterol, heart disease, and diabetes. Along with such information came a wealth of diet products—Healthy Choice began selling frozen dinners in the late 1980s— and products that purported to be healthy imitations of the real thing. Artificial sweeteners, which are generally seen as safe, are added to a number of food products in lieu of sugar. High fructose corn syrup, a sweetener often used in soda, has yielded mixed results in terms of its health costs and benefits.

The chemistry of food is often seen as the realm of food companies and researchers, but as the public demands more information about the contents of what they consume, food chemistry continues to expand in scope.

Molecular Gastronomy. Molecular gastronomy is a modern style of cuisine that emphasizes the chemical transformations that take place during the cooking process. The discipline is new; it was founded in 1992 by two scientists, Hervé This and Nicholas Kurti, and touts itself as part science and part art. Molecular gastronomy is often called culinary alchemy for its surreal juxtapositions that include hot ice cream, spherical ravioli, and olive oil foam.

Hervé This presented his dissertation on molecular gastronomy at the University of Paris in 1996. According to his paper, This identified five goals of the new science. The first goal was to "collect and

Interesting Facts about Food Chemistry

- Crisco was the first vegetable shortening made with hydrogenated oil. It was also one of Procter & Gamble's very first food products, marketed to Jewish housewives at the turn of the century as a kosher food because it could be used with meats.

- J. L. Kraft made the first processed American cheese by shredding discarded cheddar cheese, repasteurizing it, and adding sodium phosphates. Though Americans had been making cheese in factories since the mid-nineteenth century, Kraft became the most popular by far—particularly with the US military, which purchased six million tons in 1921.

- A Nebraska man named Edwin Perkins invented a Fruit Smack beverage concentrate in the early twentieth century. In 1915, Perkins hired a chemist to convert his recipe to a dry mix that later became known as Kool-Aid.

- In 1912, George Washington Carver completed research that showed that peanuts and sweet potatoes reestablish soil fertility in overused fields. The reason, that legumes replace nitrogen in the soil, would not be fully understood until later.

- Though it was a popular vegetable in Italy decades earlier, broccoli was not introduced to the United States until 1928.

- Insulin was sold commercially to diabetics beginning in 1924. The drug allowed those afflicted to eat a wider variety of foods with less risk to their health; it was the first time scientists were able to safely study what foods diabetics could eat. The research led to a better understanding of the metabolic process.

investigate old wives' tales about cooking." The second was to "model and scrutinize existing recipes," and the third was "to introduce new tools, products, and methods to cooking." As a fourth goal, This hoped to "invent new dishes using knowledge from the previous three aims." And finally, his fifth goal was "to use the appeal of food to promote science."

Occupation	Dietitians and nutritionists
Employment 2010	64,400
Projected Employment 2020	77,100
Change in Number (2010–20)	12,700
Percent Change	20%

Bureau of Labor Statistics, 2012

Molecular chefs make use a number of "ingredients" that can be found in a lab, including liquid nitrogen and chemicals like carrageenan (seaweed extract), maltodextrin (a sweet additive made from starch), and xanthan gum (a food-thickening additive).

Impact on Industry

The US Bureau of Labor Statistics projected in 2010 that employment for food chemists and those working in the agricultural and food science field will increase by about 10 percent from 2010 to 2020. About 33,500 agricultural and food scientists were employed in the United States in 2010. Most professionals in food science, about 35 percent, work in food manufacturing, followed by scientific research and development services (13 percent) and schools and private companies (8 percent). Food chemistry jobs often require a PhD and there is little on-the-job training in terms of basic principles.

Food Manufacturing Companies. Most food chemists and food scientists work for a food manufacturing company that produces a food product. In this setting, food chemists work with raw agricultural materials as well as direct-to-consumer products. Chemists fill jobs that span from the inception of a product in the lab to its realization on the line, where chemists perform routine tests on the finished product to ensure that they meet quality standards. (However, industry downsizing has led to many research and laboratory jobs being transferred to ingredient supply companies.) Food chemists perform inspections to ensure processing safety, and sometimes develop and test new ingredients also deemed safe for use.

Ingredient Supply Companies. Others working in food chemistry work for ingredient supply companies. These companies supply food processing companies with the ingredients necessary to make their products. Ingredients include many key components of processed foods, including flavors, thickening agents, and stabilizers. (Flavor chemists, or flavorists, are responsible for engineering artificial and natural flavors in foods and consumables from ice cream to pharmaceutical products.) In the lab, researchers create and test prototypes, combining and extracting different components of food products to address the rheological and packaging concerns of the larger food manufacturers.

Other Industries. Some food chemists work for pharmaceutical companies as flavorists or biotechnologists, developing new products. The manufacture of food and drugs are very similar and often utilize the same types of equipment. There is also a growing movement toward "nutraceuticals"—food products designed with additional health benefits—and the merging of these two fields to develop new products.

Other food chemists pursue careers in agriculture. For example, food chemists are working to find new sources of fuel such as ethanol, which comes from corn.

Government Agencies. The United States Food and Drug Administration (FDA) is always recruiting food chemists to perform a variety of tasks. The FDA requires chemists to review new drug applications, as well as propose labels for an ultimate recommendation of approval or nonapproval. In the lab, food chemists are researching dietary supplements for humans and the effects of drugs and agricultural chemicals on cattle and other domestic livestock. Other FDA jobs require a significant amount of field work in which food chemists visit plants and facilities to inspect equipment and methods.

Occupation	Food scientists and technologists
Employment 2010	13,900
Projected Employment 2020	15,000
Change in Number (2010–20)	1,100
Percent Change	8%

Bureau of Labor Statistics, 2012

In 2011, President Barack Obama signed the Food Safety Modernization Act (FSMA). The legislation, which focuses the government's regulatory aims on prevention, is considered the most significant food safety legislation in seventy years. One result of the new measure is that the FDA has hired more workers to oversee inspections.

Academic Research and Teaching. Food chemists working in academia research methods and processes that are later applied to business practices in the private sector. A good example can be seen in Purdue University professor Phillip Nelson, who developed important advancements in aseptic processing. Basic academic research in food chemistry includes aspects of nutrition, food quality, and equipment engineering, as well as improving the health of animals and soil quality. Organizations like the United States Department of Agriculture (USDA) and the National Institutes of Health (NIH) give grants to fund such research.

Social Context and Future Perspectives

The growth of the food industry and industries producing food products has been exponential over the course of the last century. Science as it relates to food became a fully fledged field of study only sixty years ago—though, as stated in the above descriptions, research pertaining to food and food chemistry was being conducted long before that.

Much like Pasteur, whose observations of fermentation and subsequent invention of pasteurization changed the way scientists and consumers understood food and disease, innovations in the food industry today are rapidly being applied to the pharmaceutical industry and even to the development of biofuel. Food chemistry of the twenty-first century is no longer limited to the logistics of manufacturing sliced bread. Food chemistry today is applying new principles and technology to feed developing nations and to ensure that industrialized ones are practicing safe methods of food production. The latter is not an easy task in a world where food is often consumed for its convenience rather than its nutritional value. Food chemists must ensure that all food products—from fast-food hamburgers to pesticide-free vegetables—are safe for all consumers.

Proponents of food fortification—first practiced in the United States during World War II and now in places like rural China and Vietnam—understand that food not only affects health and productivity, but can also make consumers sick. As we move into the next phase of a growing field, the food chemists of the future are regarded by many as part of the solution to an ailing world.

Further Reading

Belitz, Hans-Dieter, Werner Grosch, and Peter Schieberle. *Food Chemistry*. 4th rev. ed. Munich: Springer, 2009. Print. Consists entirely of figures describing the components of food chemistry. Long considered the definitive textbook and reference in the field.

Coultate, Tom P. *Food: The Chemistry of Its Components*. 5th ed. Cambridge: RSC Paperbacks, 2009. Print. Examines the chemical components of food both large (like lipids) and small (like pigments). Also features special topics, an updated breakdown of legislative changes in the field, and extensive bibliography.

Seiber, James N., ed. *Journal of Agricultural and Food Chemistry*. 1952–present. Scholarly Journal. Published out of the University of California, Davis, this journal prints original and current research. Topics of papers include food- and agriculture-related chemistry and biochemistry, as well as fields including nutrition, biofuel, and food safety.

United States Food and Drug Administration. United States Department of Health and Human Services, 13 Apr. 2012. Web. 8 July 2012. Provides a comprehensive look at all industries pertaining to food chemistry and concise explanations of regulations and public health policy. Updated frequently with everything from articles on food preservation during extreme weather to the government's policies on biotechnology.

Welch, R. W., and P. C. Mitchell. "Food Processing: A Century of Change." *British Medical Bulletin* 56.1 (2000): 1–17. Print. Offers an in-depth look at food processing over the past century. Includes tables with eras and corresponding developments in food science and food chemistry.

About the Author: Molly Hagan, BFA, is a freelance journalist and writer for *Current Biography* magazine. She has written the biographies of well-known economists, physicists, climatologists, and mathematicians, among many others. She conducted interviews for an in-depth profile of neuroscientist and pioneering researcher Dr. Daniela Schiller of Mount Sinai Hospital in New York.

Food Technologist or Nutritionist

Earnings (Yearly Average): $53,250 per year

Employment and Outlook: Faster than average growth

O*NET-SOC Code: 19-1012.00

Related Career Cluster(s): Agriculture, Food & Natural Resources; Health Science; Business, Management & Administration

Scope of Work

Nutritionists investigate and apply science to the understanding of health and nutrition for the benefit of others. Often, they manage food services in hospitals, schools, and similar institutions, while also conducting research and promoting sound eating habits. Some of the most common areas of specialization within the field of food technology and nutrition include clinical, pediatric, administrative, and consultant nutrition.

A nutritionist can help to restructure a patient's eating and exercise habits to minimize the effects of diet-related conditions such as heart disease, high cholesterol, diabetes, hiatus hernia, and ulcers. For healthy patients, counselors might provide guidance directed at minimizing the risk of cancer, obesity, or high blood pressure, or they might help target individual problems such as food allergies. Counselors may even provide specific artificial nutritional guidance to patients unable to consume food normally.

Over the last three decades, increased interest in fitness and nutrition has caused an increase in job opportunities in fields such as food manufacturing, advertising, and marketing. In such positions, nutritionists might present information to clients in the form of literature for distribution, while also reporting on the nutritional content of certain recipes and recommending amounts of dietary fiber or vitamin supplements to be taken.

> ## Transferable Skills
>
> - Interpersonal/Social Skills – Motivating others
> - Interpersonal/Social Skills – Teaching others (SCANS Work-place Competency—Interpersonal)
> - Interpersonal/Social Skills – Being able to work independently
> - Research & Planning Skills – Identifying problems
> - Research & Planning Skills – Determining alternatives
> - Research & Planning Skills – Analyzing information
> - Technical Skills – Using technology to process information (SCANS Workplace Competency—Information)
> - Technical Skills – Working with data or numbers

Education and Coursework

To become a nutritionist, one must acquire at least a bachelor's degree. However, high school students interested in preparing themselves for a potential career in nutrition should make sure to include courses in biology, chemistry, health, mathematics, and communication in their schedules. At a collegiate level, students can major in dietetics or even food systems service management. In these majors, students can expect to receive instruction in courses related to foods, nutrition, chemistry and biochemistry, biology and microbiology, anatomy, physiology, and institution management. Aspiring nutritionists and food technologists are also encouraged to study aspects of business, statistics, psychology, sociology, and economics as well. In 2008, the American Dietetic Association (ADA), which oversees the Commission on Accreditation for Dietetics Education, approved 279 bachelor's degree programs and 18 master's degree programs in the United States.

Through graduate programs, students can pursue more specific fields of study, including molecular nutrition or animal nutrition. Graduate programs in nutrition often culminate in a PhD in nutrition, but they often vary widely in specialization and emphasis. The graduate program at Hunter College in New York City, for instance, focuses on urban public health and also offers a dietician internship.

The University of North Carolina at Chapel Hill offers a postdoctoral training program in cancer health. Other popular courses of study include nutrition for athletes, nutritional programs for schools and communities, and health care regulations.

Career Enhancement and Training

While some states only require certification or registration for aspiring nutritionists and dieticians, a majority of states require both national and state licensure. The most common way to become licensed is to earn the Registered Dietitian (RD) credential, awarded by the Academy of Nutrition and Dietetics. The certification process is fairly comprehensive and involves the completion of an internship in nutrition counseling or food service management under the supervision of a registered dietitian. This is followed by a national exam administered by the ADA and an ongoing schedule of courses or professional seminars every five years to remain up to date on advances in nutrition research.

Another group of nutritionists are employed as medical doctors. To reach this position in the field, aspiring candidates should pursue postgraduate training in nutrition and network with other expert clinicians. It is also helpful to join nutritionist organizations such as the American Society of Clinical Nutrition and to pursue accreditation from the American Board of Nutrition.

Top-tier nutritionists with years of experience may move up to positions as associate director, assistant director, director of a dietetic department, or another management role. Those workers may procure advanced degrees or experience in allied health, human resources, or healthcare administration. Others may seek self-employment or advance to sales positions as representatives for equipment, pharmaceutical, or food manufacturers.

Daily Tasks and Technology

For clinical nutritionists employed at hospitals, clinics, and prisons, daily work revolves around close client contact. Much of clinical nutritionists' work involves consultations with health care professionals, after which they plan and implement nutritional programs for individuals. Each program is unique. After an initial screening, the nutritionist might start by presenting the client with a trial diet and exercise regimen to sample for a few weeks. In the interim, the nutritionist is available to answer questions that may arise, before conducting a follow-up interview and pressing for any necessary revisions. They may also provide guidance in shopping, reading labels, and preparing meals.

At the management level, nutritionists and food technologists do similar work but on a larger scale, overseeing meal planning and preparation for large groups. In addition, they may hire and train food service workers, while also creating a budget to buy and maintain food supplies and equipment. Further tasks performed by managing nutritionists include enforcing sanitation regulations and preparing reports. Community nutritionists counsel groups at clubs, agencies, and health maintenance organizations (HMOs). Working with families, they structure nutritional plans, provide instruction for shopping visits, and create individual manuals for proper food preparation.

Nutritionists work with a number of tools, including calorimeters, which measure the calories in different kinds of foods; glucose monitors, which test blood sugar; and skinfold calipers, which estimate body fat by measuring the thickness of a skinfold. They also use analytical and medical software.

Earnings and Employment Outlook

According to the Bureau of Labor Statistics (BLS), nutritionists' salaries range from $33,330 to $75,480 with a median of $53,250 in 2010. According to other sources, recent graduates in the nutrition field earned between $31,998 and $55,228 per year in 2011. The level of one's base pay can depend on a number of circumstances, such as employer, level of certification, and geographic location.

As reported by the BLS, in 2010 the majority of nutritionists held jobs at hospitals, collecting an average yearly salary of $54,290 in 2010. Those working at nursing care facilities earned a comparable if slightly lower yearly salary. Dietitians employed by outpatient care centers brought in more, at an average of $56,180.

Nutritionists hired into the corporate sector typically earn greater starting salaries than those who work in the public sector. The highest salaries come from scientific and technical consulting services,

A Conversation with Sally Rush

Job Title: Senior Vice President with Seiberling Associates, Inc.

What was your career path?

- High school cooking teacher introduced me to her roommate that was a food scientist with Stouffers.
- Food Science undergraduate, Ohio State University (OSU) in Columbus, OH
- Internship between junior and senior year in quality control department at General Mills. I realized I liked the engineering aspects of the quality work more than the food chemistry work. When I started my senior year at OSU, I began taking engineering free electives and more math classes to prepare for a graduate program in food process engineering.
- 1982: BS in Food Science; started graduate school for Food Process Engineering at OSU
- 1982-1984: Awarded Seiberling Fellowship for Food Process Engineering
- Summer 1983: Internship at Seiberling Associates, Inc. (SAI), an engineering firm that specializes in clean and sterile process engineering for the food and pharmaceutical industry.
- June 1984: Graduated with a MS in Food Process Engineering. Started as process engineer at SAI.

What are three pieces of advice you would offer someone interested in your profession?

1. Be flexible and prepared to invest time into your career in food technology, paying forward for the future. Please keep in mind that this profession involves engineering and production support on a 24-hour basis, often at your clients' facilities around the world; this is not a 9-to-5 desk job.
2. This job requires good communication skills in both the written and verbal format. A good idea or solution to

an engineering problem will not serve anyone well if it cannot be effectively communicated to clients and co-workers.

3. Strive to be technically sound and a nice person while doing your job. It does not matter how brilliant and driven you are if you are difficult to get along with on a project team—a bad attitude, sharp words, or hostile actions under stressful situations will block transfer of information and delay a projects progress.

What paths for career advancement are available to you?

My career path can lead to executive vice president, then perhaps president and CEO. My career history at SAI is below:

2009 to Present	Senior Vice President (Beloit, WI)
2001 – 2009	Vice President (Roscoe, IL/Beloit, WI)
1993 - 2001	Associate (Roscoe, IL)
1991 - 1993	Manager, Process Design (Roscoe, IL)
1989 - 1991	Project Manager (Roscoe, IL)
1986 - 1989	Process Engineer (Dublin, OH)
1984 - 1986	Process Engineer (Roscoe, IL)

which hire an average of ninety workers with a yearly average salary of $75,450 as of May 2010, according to the BLS. Also in the top tier is the federal executive branch, which employed 1,830 nutritionists at an average wage of $69,610 in 2010. As far as geographic region relates to income, California and New York reportedly offer starting wages above the national average, while Maryland offers nutritionists the highest yearly salary, an average of $77,010.

Growing interest in health and wellness, an increase in the aging population, and new research on the significance of diet in preventing illness all contribute to the mounting need for nutritionists in the United States. According to the US Department of Labor and the BLS, employment of nutritionists should rise faster than the average for all occupations through 2020.

Related Occupations

- **Public Health Researchers**: In the public sector, a public health researcher works to construct advocacy programs around topics such as nutrition and disease prevention. In the private sector, they conduct experiments and oversee clinical trials.

- **Health Educators:** Health educators promote wellness through education. Many work in health care facilities, universities, and public health departments. Others lead public health campaigns on topics such as aging, nutrition, and weight loss.

- **Food Scientists:** Food scientists use chemistry and other sciences to study the fundamental principles of food. They examine nutritional content and develop new methods of selecting, preserving, processing, packaging, and distributing foods.

- **Home Health Aides:** Home health aides help people who are disabled, chronically ill, or cognitively impaired to accomplish daily tasks such as bathing, shopping for groceries, and preparing meals.

- **Food Service Managers:** Food service managers handle the daily operations of businesses and institutions that prepare and serve food and beverages to customers, clients, or patients.

Future Applications

The trend toward good nutrition and fitness continues to intensify in both public and private sectors. Corporations involved in the production, processing, and marketing of food products have an increased sense of competition with regard to meeting evolving nutritional standards. This commitment will increase the need for nutritionists and dietary specialists to fill a number of positions. Changing standards in the last decade alone have led to increased customer awareness. Consumers are willing to seek out healthy foods more than ever before, whether for weight loss, disease management and prevention, or general fitness.

On the public end, the federal government has renewed its commitment to strong nutritional standards in the name of preventative health care. In 2012, the US government released new standards for school meals across the country. In an aim to limit calories, lower sodium levels, and present students with a greater variety of fruits and vegetables, these new standards will raise the bar on student nutrition for the first time in fifteen years. These changes will affect 32 million students across the country.

With this renewed interest and strong commitment from the US Department of Agriculture as well as corporations, the role of the nutritionist should transform and intensify over the next decade, increasing the need for workers in the field.

Molly Hagan

More Information

Academy of Nutrition and Dietetics
120 South Riverside Plaza, Ste. 2000
Chicago, IL 60606-6995
http://www.eatright.org

American Clinical Board of Nutrition
6855 Browntown Rd.
Front Royal, VA 22630
http://www.acbn.org

International & American Associations of Clinical Nutritionists
(IAACN)
15280 Addison Road, Ste. 130
Addison, TX 75001
http://www.iaacn.org

Nutrition.gov
National Agricultural Library
Food and Nutrition Information Center
Nutrition.gov Staff
10301 Baltimore Avenue
Beltsville, MD 20705-2351
http://www.nutrition.gov

Forensic Science

FIELDS OF STUDY

Chemistry; biology; biochemistry; mathematics; microbiology; physics.

DEFINITION

Forensic science is commonly defined as the application of science to legal matters. Although forensic science incorporates numerous disciplines, ranging from accounting to psychology, in the traditional sense, forensic science refers to the scientific analysis of evidence collected at crime scenes, which is also known as "criminalistics." Pattern evidence, such as fingerprints, bullets, and tool marks, is often compared visually, and chemical evidence (such as illicit drugs) and biological evidence (such as DNA, blood, and bodily fluids) are analyzed and compared using scientific instruments.

Basic Principles

Forensic science is the application of scientific principles to the analysis of numerous types of evidence, most commonly evidence collected at a crime scene. Crime scene investigators, usually police officers, collect evidence at the scene of a crime and submit it to a crime laboratory for analysis by forensic scientists.

Crime laboratories contain different sections, each of which specializes in a particular type of analysis, such as controlled substances, DNA, firearms and tool marks, latent prints, questioned documents, toxicology, and trace evidence. The type of analysis conducted depends on the type of evidence as well as the circumstances of the crime. A single piece of evidence may be analyzed in more than one section. For example, a firearm may be analyzed in the latent prints and DNA sections, as well as the firearms and tool marks section.

Following analysis, forensic scientists may be summoned to present their findings in a court of law. Forensic scientists present their analysis and interpretation of the evidence before a judge and jury, who are charged with determining the guilt or innocence of the defendant. The unbiased, accurate analysis presented by the forensic scientist is an integral part of the criminal proceedings.

Core Concepts

Forensic science incorporates numerous subdisciplines, but the most common types of analysis conducted by crime laboratories are the analysis of illicit drugs, biological evidence, latent prints, firearms, footprints, tire marks, tool marks, and trace evidence. Latent prints, footprints, tire marks, and tool marks are considered pattern evidence. The patterns of an unknown sample (usually from the crime scene) and a known sample are visually compared to find similarities between the two. Samples can also be analyzed, either chemically or biologically, with scientific instruments. Some of the more common methods of testing are infrared spectroscopy, ultraviolet/visible microspectrophotometry, gas chromatography-mass spectrometry, and electrophoresis.

Infrared Spectroscopy. In infrared spectroscopy, the chemical structure of a sample is determined based on how the sample interacts with infrared radiation. Chemical bonds can absorb infrared radiation of a specific energy, which causes the bond to vibrate. Additionally, each bond can vibrate in different ways. Therefore, when infrared radiation is introduced, chemical bonds within the sample absorb different energies, and the results are shown in the form of an infrared spectrum. The spectrum is essentially a graph of radiation transmitted versus wave number, which is related to the energy of the radiation. Additionally, transmission can be mathematically converted to absorbance such that the spectrum can be displayed as absorbance versus wave number. The infrared spectrum of a sample displays numerous absorptions, each corresponding to a particular type of chemical bond and a particular type of vibration. The infrared spectrum of a sample is unique to that sample, and therefore, this technique can be used to definitively identify compounds.

Ultraviolet/Visible Microspectrophotometry. Infrared spectroscopy and ultraviolet/visible microspectrophotometry are both based on the principle of the interaction of radiation with a sample. However, ultraviolet/visible microspectrophotometry is typically used to compare the dye or pigment composition of samples. The technique is used to determine the color of a sample and identify subtle differences in color that cannot be seen with the naked eye.

A microspectrophotometer consists of a microscope with a spectrometer attached, which allows the analysis of microscopic pieces of evidence. The sample is viewed under the microscope, and ultraviolet and/or visible radiation is introduced. Depending on the chemical structure of the sample, wavelengths of light will be absorbed, reflected, or transmitted. The transmitted light is collected in the spectrophotometer, and the intensity of each wavelength is measured. Results are displayed in the form of a spectrum that is a graph of transmittance (or absorbance) versus wavelength. Subtle differences in color between two samples are observed as differences in wavelengths of light transmitted or absorbed in the corresponding spectra. Such differences are caused by differences in chemical composition between the two samples, and therefore, comparison of the resulting spectra can be used to determine if the two samples are similar in color.

Gas Chromatography–Mass Spectrometry. In any chromatography technique, sample mixtures are separated based on differences in interaction between a mobile phase and a stationary phase. In gas chromatography (GC), the mobile phase is a gas, and the stationary phase is a liquid coated on the inner walls of a very thin column. Liquid samples are typically introduced into the system and carried, in the mobile phase, through the stationary phase. Sample components that have a stronger attraction for the stationary phase spend longer in that phase, and components with less attraction spend less time in that phase and move more quickly through the system. The time it takes for sample components to travel through the system and reach the detector is known as the retention time.

In gas chromatography–mass spectrometry (GC-MS), the detector is the mass spectrometer, which contains three major components: the ion source, the mass analyzer, and the detector. On emerging from the GC column, sample components enter the ion source, where each component is first ionized. The resulting ion is known as the molecular ion. This ion is unstable because of its high energy, so it breaks down, or fragments, into smaller ions. Molecular ions and fragment ions then enter the mass analyzer, where the ions are separated according to their mass-to-charge ratio. The separated ions enter the detector, where the number of ions of each mass-to-charge ratio is counted. Results are displayed in the form of a mass spectrum, which is a graph of intensity versus the mass-to-charge ratio. Because molecules break down, or fragment, in a predictable manner, the mass spectrum can be used to determine the structure of the original sample component. Furthermore, because the fragmentation pattern is unique to a molecule, the mass spectrum can be used to definitively identify the component.

On analyzing a sample by GC-MS, two pieces of information are obtained. First, from gas chromatography, a chromatogram is obtained, which is a graph of detector response versus retention time. Each separated component in the sample mixture is shown as a peak on the chromatogram. Components that take longer to reach the detector have greater attraction for the stationary phase and have longer retention times. Additionally, for each separated component, the mass spectrum is also obtained, which can be used to definitively identify the component.

Electrophoresis. Although electrophoresis is also used to separate sample mixtures, the technique is not considered a chromatographic technique because no mobile phase is involved. Instead, sample mixtures are separated based on differences in migration under the influence of an applied electrical potential. Therefore, electrophoresis is used for the analysis of samples that have an electric charge.

Although there are different types of electrophoresis, capillary electrophoresis is most commonly used for DNA profiling purposes. In this technique, a capillary column is filled with a polymer, and the ends of the column are immersed in reservoirs containing a buffer solution. The reservoirs also contain electrodes to allow the application of the electric potential. The sample is introduced to one end of the column, and the sample components move through the column under the influence of the applied potential. Separation occurs based on differences in the migration rate of the components through the column, which depends on size and charge. Separated components pass through a detector at the other end of the column, producing an electropherogram.

The electropherogram shows the migration time of the separated components. Smaller components move more quickly, reaching the detector before larger components and have shorter migration times.

Applications Past and Present

The major role of the forensic scientist is to analyze submitted evidence for the purposes of characterization and identification. For example, a blue fiber collected from the scene may be submitted to the trace evidence section, where forensic scientists characterize the fiber (for example, by its dimensions, color, cross-sectional shape) and then identify the type of fiber (for example, nylon, polyester, acrylic). Furthermore, when a known sample is available (such as fibers from the suspect's clothing), forensic scientists compare it with the unknown sample (collected from the crime scene) to determine if the two most likely originated from a common source. This process of characterization, identification, and comparison requires multiple stages of analysis, ranging from visual examination to instrumental analysis.

Infrared Spectroscopy. The technique of infrared spectroscopy is commonly used in the controlled substance and the trace evidence sections of the crime laboratory. This technique can identify illicit drugs present in unknown samples, the type of fiber found at a crime scene or on a person, the polymer present in a paint chip, or the organic compounds present in explosive residues. The evidence is prepared for analysis in several ways, depending on the type of sample.

Solid samples of illicit drugs can be mixed with potassium bromide and pressed into a pellet, which is then placed in the spectrometer. Infrared radiation is passed through the sample, which will absorb at characteristic energies depending on its chemical structure. The transmitted radiation is collected and the infrared spectrum is generated. Because potassium bromide does not absorb infrared radiation, the subsequent infrared spectrum shows only contributions from any drug present in the sample.

For opaque samples, such as fibers or paint chips, attenuated total reflectance–infrared (ATR-IR) spectroscopy is more commonly used. The sample is positioned over a crystal, and pressure is applied to ensure good contact between the sample and crystal. Infrared radiation

Interesting Facts about Forensic Science

- Forensic entomology involves the study of insects that invade a body after death to determine the time that has elapsed since the person's death.
- The saliva on a discarded cigarette contains enough DNA to identify the person who smoked it.
- The first use of fingerprint evidence to solve a criminal case was recorded in Argentina in 1892. Police official Juan Vucetich used a bloody fingerprint found at the crime scene to prove that two boys were murdered by their own mother.
- "Forensic" comes from the Latin *forensis*, which means public, or "of the forum." The forum was a public square in ancient Roman cities where, among other things, criminal cases were tried. In modern times, forensic science is defined as science relating to the law.
- In 1981, a German publishing company purchased what were thought to be Adolf Hitler's diaries. However, forensic document examiners proved that the diaries were fake, based on the presence of a paper-whitening agent that was not used in paper manufacturing until at least 1954.
- Marie Lafarge was the first person to be found guilty of murder based on toxicology evidence. Although she poisoned her husband with arsenic, initial testing did not find any arsenic in his body. However, when French scientist Mathieu Joseph Bonaventure Orfila repeated the tests, he found arsenic in the man's body and proved that the initial testing was inaccurate.
- In 1995, O. J. Simpson was cleared of murdering his wife, Nicole Brown, and her friend Ronald Goldman, despite DNA evidence identifying blood at the crime scene as belonging to the former football player. Furthermore, DNA from Simpson, Brown, and Goldman was found in a leather glove found at the scene.

is passed through the crystal, and because of the close contact, the radiation penetrates a small depth into the sample. Certain energies are absorbed depending on the chemical bonds within the sample, resulting in the characteristic spectrum of the sample.

The infrared spectrum of the questioned sample can be compared to a database containing infrared spectra for known standards (drugs, fibers, paints, and so on) to identify the unknown sample. However, care must be taken when comparing a spectrum to spectra in a database. Although the spectrum of a given compound is unique, it can vary slightly depending on the instrument used to analyze the sample and standard. Rather than relying on a database search, it is often preferable to analyze the unknown sample and known standards on the same day, using the same instrument, to allow for a direct comparison of spectra.

Although samples can be rapidly analyzed using infrared spectroscopy, the technique works best for relatively pure samples. If impurities are present in the sample and they also absorb infrared radiation, the resulting spectrum contains contributions from both the sample and the impurities. This can complicate interpretation of the spectrum and subsequent identification of the sample.

Microspectrophotometry. The comparison and analysis of colored samples is often undertaken using microspectrophotometry. This technique is used in the trace evidence and questioned documents sections to compare the dye or pigment composition of fibers, paints, and inks.

Methods for sample preparation vary depending on the type of sample to be analyzed. Fibers are flattened and mounted on a microscope slide with a drop of immersion oil. Paint samples require more involved preparation, particularly for transmission spectra. The paint chip must be cut into a section so thin that light can be transmitted through it. Spectra of inks can be obtained directly if the paper is sufficiently thin to allow transmission. Otherwise, the ink must be removed from the document. This can be done by removing a small sample of the paper containing the ink and immersing the paper in a solvent to extract the ink. The resulting ink solution is placed on a microscope slide, and the solvent is allowed to evaporate, leaving a residue of ink for analysis. However, this is a destructive procedure because the document is damaged in removing the sample. Alternatively, a piece of clear tape can be placed on an area of the document that contains the ink. When the tape is lifted off, particles of ink adhere to the tape. These particles can be removed from the tape and transferred to a microscope slide for analysis. The document is minimally damaged using this procedure.

Although microspectrophotometry offers a rapid means to investigate the dye or pigment composition of certain samples, no extensive spectral databases are readily available. Therefore, the technique is more useful when known samples are available and the color of the unknown and known samples can be compared directly, based on spectral interpretation.

Gas Chromatography–Mass Spectrometry. As with infrared spectroscopy, gas chromatography–mass spectrometry is commonly used in the controlled substances and trace evidence sections, as well as in the toxicology section, for the determination of drugs and poisons in body fluids.

GC-MS is advantageous over infrared spectroscopy in that samples containing impurities can still be identified because of the separation abilities of gas chromatography. For example, gas chromatography analysis of a drug mixture containing methamphetamine and caffeine separates the two components. In the resulting chromatogram, two peaks are observed: one for methamphetamine and one for caffeine. The mass spectrum of each peak is also obtained, which can be used to definitively identify each component.

In most cases, samples must be in liquid form for GC-MS analysis. This is achieved by adding a suitable solvent to the sample and analyzing the resulting solution. For body fluid or tissue samples, a solid phase extraction or liquid-liquid extraction is necessary to isolate any drugs and poisons from additional components present in the fluids or tissues.

Solid samples can be analyzed using pyrolysis GC-MS. In this case, a pyrolysis unit is attached to the gas chromatography inlet. Solid samples (for example, paint chips or fiber fragments) are placed in a small quartz tube and introduced into the pyrolysis unit, which rapidly heats the sample to a very high temperature. The sample is broken down and vaporized in the pyrolysis unit, and then carried in the flow of carrier gas onto the gas chromatography column, where the sample components are separated.

Before analyzing the sample, it is important to demonstrate that the GC-MS system is free from contamination. This is usually done by injecting a volume of the solvent used to prepare the sample. If the solvent and instrument are not contaminated, the resulting chromatogram should show no peaks. For pyrolysis GC, the empty quartz tube is analyzed to demonstrate that there is no contamination in the tube or instrument.

Because the mass spectrum rather than the retention time is unique to a sample component, the spectrum of an unknown sample is compared to a suitable database of spectra. However, there may be slight differences between the database spectrum and the spectrum obtained for the unknown sample, depending on the instrument used to collect the spectra. It is often preferable to prepare and analyze a known standard in the same way as the unknown sample and then compare the corresponding mass spectra.

Electrophoresis. DNA profiling makes the most use of electrophoresis. Typically, blood, semen, saliva, or another body fluid from the crime scene is used to generate a DNA profile, which is compared with profiles generated from known samples. If known samples are not available, the generated DNA profile can be compared to a database of profiles. The Federal Bureau of Investigation (FBI) maintains a database of DNA profiles submitted by crime laboratories across the United States. This database, the combined DNA index system (CODIS), contains profiles from crime scenes, convicted criminals, and missing persons.

Modern DNA profiling is based on the characterization of short tandem repeats (STRs) that are regions (loci) on the chromosome that repeat at least twice within the DNA. For profiling, the number of repeats at each location on the chromosome is determined. To do this, the DNA is first amplified via the polymerase chain reaction (PCR), in which the double-stranded DNA is split into two single strands and a mixture of enzymes and primers are used to replicate specific STR regions of the DNA. In the United States, STRs at thirteen loci are typically considered. The reaction is repeated many times, generating exact copies of the STRs. Because of this amplification procedure, profiles can be obtained from very small samples of DNA.

The STRs are analyzed using electrophoresis, most commonly capillary electrophoresis, which allows rapid and automated analysis. The STR mixture is separated based on differences in migration rate through the capillary column, which is related to the size of the STR. The resulting electropherogram displays a series of peaks that correspond to the STRs at each loci. Additionally, for each STR, there are two variants, one inherited from the mother and one from the father; therefore, the electropherogram actually shows a pair of peaks at each loci. A match in the number of STRs for both variants at all loci is considered strong evidence that the unknown and known samples originate from the same person. Because DNA is unique to an individual, this is one type of evidence that is considered individualizing rather than class evidence.

Impact on Industry

Forensic science aims to determine identifying or individualizing characteristics to link people, places, and objects. As the field of forensic science evolves, newly developed technologies and instrumentation allow evidence to be analyzed and compared in an increasingly rapid, objective, and reliable manner. Additionally, with advances in technology making the analysis of crime scene evidence more exact, courts of law are relying on forensic scientists much more often to analyze and present their findings in civil and criminal cases.

Forensic scientists held about 13,000 jobs nationally in 2010. Employment of forensic scientists is expected to grow about as fast as the average for all occupations through the year 2020, which means employment is projected to increase 10 to 19 percent.

Government Agencies and Military. Many federal agencies, such as the FBI, the Drug Enforcement Administration (DEA), and the Bureau of Alcohol, Tobacco, Firearms, and Explosives (ATF), employ forensic scientists. All are overseen by the US Department of Justice, and all have forensic science laboratories. These laboratories offer analytical services to local and state law enforcement agencies and conduct research to develop new analytical tools and technologies to advance forensic science.

Within the US Department of the Treasury, the Treasury Inspector General for Tax Administration operates a forensic science laboratory that principally analyzes suspected counterfeit documents, using fingerprint and handwriting analyses, along with digital image enhancement procedures. The US Postal Inspection Service operates a forensic science laboratory with the role of analyzing evidence from postal-related crimes. This laboratory mainly conducts fingerprint, document, and chemical analyses, along with digital image enhancement.

The US Fish and Wildlife Forensics Laboratory is operated through the Department of the Interior and is the only laboratory worldwide that focuses solely on crimes against wildlife. Laboratory expertise in genetic and chemical analysis, as well as firearms, trace evidence, latent prints, and pathology is used to analyze wildlife evidence to identify species and determine cause of death.

Forensic scientists have also been employed in the military. During the Iraq War, certain engineering battalions were trained in forensic science to help better determine the whereabouts and activities of enemy combatants and insurgents.

Federal Funding. The National Institute of Justice (NIJ) is the largest funding agency for forensic science within the United States. The agency funds research that improves methods for the collection, analysis, and interpretation of forensic evidence. Funds for research, development, and evaluation go to projects that improve the analytical tools and technologies available to forensic scientists, from developing new methods for the comparison of evidence to developing new analytical instrumentation for forensic analyses. Forensic laboratory enhancement funds are for projects that improve sample throughput in laboratories, enabling evidence to be analyzed in a timely manner. The agency also awards research fellowships to individuals to conduct specific research that will improve or enhance existing practices in forensic science. In 2009, the institute awarded a total of $284 million.

In addition, the majority of forensic science laboratories in the United States are funded by the local government, the state, or the federal government. These laboratories offer a variety of services to their customers, who are typically police departments and other law enforcement agencies. The actual services offered vary depending on the size of the laboratory and the geographical area that it covers. Typical services include analysis of illicit drugs, body fluids (often for DNA), fingerprints, firearms, tool marks, and trace evidence. Within any state, there may be only one laboratory that offers all of these services, with a number of smaller laboratories throughout the state offering two or three services.

Private Laboratories. A number of private forensic science laboratories (such as paternity testing or sport testing laboratories) operate throughout the United States. The majority of these laboratories offer expertise in one or two areas (for example, analysis of illicit drugs and trace evidence) rather than a full range of

Occupation	Forensic science technicians
Employment 2010	13,000
Projected Employment 2020	15,400
Change in Number (2010–20)	2,400
Percent Change	19%

Bureau of Labor Statistics, 2012

services. The vast majority of these laboratories focus on DNA analysis, particularly paternity testing. Because these laboratories are privately funded, their services are offered to the general public and are not limited to law enforcement agencies.

Academic Research and Teaching. As of 2012, there were thirty-eight forensic science programs accredited by the American Academy of Forensic Sciences (AAFS) Forensic Science Education Programs Accreditation Commission (FEPAC). In most cases, the degree obtained is a master of science in forensic science with a concentration in a specific discipline, for example, forensic biology, forensic chemistry, or forensic toxicology.

Social Context and Future Prospects

Forensic science is a truly dynamic field, constantly seeking further improvements and advancements in its analytical methodologies. Although great advances have been made in forensic science, many more have yet to be achieved. In 2009, the National Research Council published *Strengthening Forensic Science in the United States: A Path Forward*, a report on forensic science in the United States. The report highlighted several deficiencies in the field and recommended improving education, training, and certification for forensic scientists as well as developing standardized procedures and protocols for evidence analysis and reporting. Additionally, the report recommended research into the reliability and validity of many of the procedures used for evidence analysis. The report concluded that more research is necessary, not only to improve existing practices but also to develop new technologies that can be implemented in forensic science laboratories. It called for the development of a national institute of forensic science that would have many objectives, including the development of standards for certification for forensic scientists and accreditation of forensic laboratories, along with improving education and research in the field.

Further Reading

Bertino, Anthony J., and Patricia N. Bertino. *Forensic Science: Fundamentals and Investigations*. Mason, OH: South-Western Cengage Learning, 2009. Examines the tests and techniques used for the scientific analysis of various evidence types, including hairs and fibers, DNA, handwriting, and soil.

Brettell, Thomas A., John M. Butler, and José R. Almirall. "Forensic Science." *Analytical Chemistry* 79.12 (2007): 4365–4384. A review of forensic science applications used in common disciplines.

Embar-Seddon, Ayn, and Allan D. Pass, eds. *Forensic Science*. 3 vols. Pasadena: Salem, 2008. Extensive coverage of forensics, including historical events, famous cases, and types of investigations, evidence, and equipment.

Houck, Max M., and Jay A. Siegel. *Fundamentals of Forensic Science*. 2d ed. Burlington, MA: Academic, 2010. An introduction to forensic science and common techniques used for the analysis of physical, biological, and chemical evidence.

James, Stuart H., and Jon J. Nordby, eds. *Forensic Science: An Introduction to the Scientific and Investigative Techniques*. 3d ed. Boca Raton, FL: CRC, 2009. Discusses mass spectrometry techniques in relation to forensic applications, including forensic toxicology, controlled substance identification, and DNA analysis.

Kobilinsky, Lawrence, Thomas F. Liotti, and Jamel Oeser-Sweat. *DNA: Forensic and Legal Applications*. Hoboken, NJ: Wiley-Interscience, 2005. Presents an overview of DNA analysis, including the historical perspective, scientific principles, and laboratory procedures.

Rudin, Norah, and Keith Inman. *An Introduction to Forensic DNA Analysis*. 2d ed. Boca Raton, FL: CRC, 2002. Contains an overview of DNA analysis, beginning with its history and examining the principles on which it is based.

Saferstein, Richard. *Criminalistics: An Introduction to Forensic Science*. 10th ed. Upper Saddle River, NJ: Prentice Hall, 2011. Provides an introduction to forensic science, detailing the techniques to analyze physical, biological, and chemical evidence.

About the Author: Ruth Waddell Smith, PhD, obtained her doctorate in forensic and analytical chemistry from the University of Strathclyde (Glasgow, Scotland) in 2003. After completing a postdoctoral fellowship at Los Alamos National Laboratories in New Mexico, she moved to Michigan State University, where she became an assistant professor of forensic chemistry. She teaches graduate-level forensic chemistry classes and conducts research, applying novel analytical methodologies for the analysis of forensic evidence. She has published more than fifteen peer-reviewed articles in forensic science and analytical chemistry journals and regularly presents her research at national conferences.

Forensic Scientist

Earnings (Yearly Average): $51,570

Employment and Outlook: Average growth

O*NET-SOC code: 19-4092.00

Related Career Cluster(s): Law, Public Safety, Corrections & Security; Government & Public Administration; Science, Technology, Engineering & Mathematics

Scope of Work

Forensic scientists perform a wide range of tasks at crime scenes and in the laboratory. If a case goes to trial, forensic scientists are often called upon to give testimony. Throughout their work, forensic scientists collaborate with many other law enforcement professionals. In a more managerial capacity, they may supervise a laboratory or groups of other forensic scientists. Many of them will work for the government at either a local level (a police department) or a federal level (the Federal Bureau of Investigation). Other possibilities include teaching or consulting.

Forensic scientists do not always work in police departments; sometimes they are employed at agencies such as the US Fish and

Wildlife Service, where forensic science is used to fight crimes against wildlife. Scientists with botany or entomology specializations may also be employed as forensic scientists.

Education and Coursework

Requirements for becoming a forensic scientist vary, depending upon the specific duties of the position or upon the location of the law enforcement agency at which the scientist is employed. For instance, working in a large city with a high volume of crime may require a higher level of education, whereas a rural area may require less expertise and education, due to the comparative rarity of criminal cases. A forensic scientist is usually classified as a civilian employee and is not required to attend police academy training.

At the high school level, a strong background in the sciences is the best preparation for a future as a forensic scientist. This includes instruction in biology, chemistry, mathematics, and physics. It is also important to develop confidence in writing and public speaking—forensic scientists must compose coherent, detailed reports and present evidence in court. Aspiring forensic scientists will benefit from joining speech or debate teams at their school or in their community to hone their verbal skills.

To supplement academic offerings in high school, it is also advisable to become involved with local law enforcement agencies. Many police departments offer community or youth programs where civilians can familiarize themselves with the structure and facilities of the police department and learn about the duties involved in the various jobs on the force.

While joining the police force does not require a college degree, working in forensic science requires a minimum of an associate's degree. In most cases, a bachelor's degree is the acceptable educational entry level. Some universities offer a degree in forensic science, but at many institutions only more traditional majors in the sciences are possible. The FBI recruits students with chemistry, biology, or physics degrees to be forensic examiners. Regardless of what branch of government aspiring forensic scientists hope to work in, a strong

---

Transferable Skills

- Communication Skills – Reporting information
- Interpersonal/Social Skills – Working as a member of a team (SCANS Workplace Competency – Interpersonal)
- Research & Planning Skills – Gathering information
- Research & Planning Skills – Determining essential information
- Research & Planning Skills – Analyzing information
- Organization & Management Skills – Paying attention to and handling details
- Technical Skills – Using technology to process information (SCANS Workplace Competency – Information)
- Technical Skills – Performing scientific, mathematical, and technical work

---

foundation in one of these disciplines is essential. Courses in mathematics are also important.

To supplement a college education, college students, graduates, or postdoctoral students may also intern at some of the FBI's regional offices or in its Washington, DC, headquarters, or at a local police department. It is possible to receive academic credit for these internships. The FBI also occasionally offers paid internships through the FBI Honors Internship Program.

Postgraduate study is not necessary for most forensic science positions, but it may be required for related and more specialized occupations, such as coroner.

Career Enhancement and Training

Many law enforcement agencies require applicants to take the National Police Officer Selection Test or a civil service exam, depending upon how forensic scientists are classified in their agencies. For instance, a large institution such as the Los Angeles Police Department classifies forensic scientists as civilians, but at smaller agencies, regular officers may perform some crime scene processing. Once hired, forensic scientists will often have to pass proficiency exams formulated by the employer. Employees may expand their scope of knowledge by training in additional areas, such as ballistics.

For those just starting out on a career track, it may be advantageous to apply to a leadership development program such as the one run by the Presidential Management Fellows (PMF) Program. The FBI, for instance, participates in this program, which provides mentoring, networking, and intensive training in a particular field. Presidential Management Fellows working with the FBI are given top secret clearance and the possibility of permanent employment when the fellowship is completed. Entry into police departments or the FBI requires background checks and generally a psychological evaluation.

Forensic science is a profession that is expanding and changing every day. Belonging to professional organizations is a way of keeping up with new technologies and methods, while also networking with others in the field. Organizations like the American Academy of Forensic Sciences, the National Center for Forensic Science, and the Forensic Sciences Foundation hold meetings, sponsor classes, and provide opportunities for professional development and publication.

Daily Tasks and Technology

The size of the law enforcement agency may greatly affect the daily tasks of the forensic scientist it employs. Larger agencies, such as the LAPD, hire criminalists, chemists, fingerprint experts, and firearms specialists. A smaller agency may hire a generalist who can perform a number of different jobs, or they may outsource specific tasks such as DNA analysis.

The daily work of a forensic scientist may involve being present at crime scenes, which can sometimes be unpleasant. Forensic scientists take photographs, collect evidence (including weapons and bodily fluids), dust for fingerprints, and make sketches. Their work continues at the laboratory, where they classify, catalog, and assess the collected evidence. They may also analyze blood or other samples relevant to the crime before writing up their findings in a report. Throughout this process, every step must be documented to maintain a clear record of everyone who has interacted with the evidence.

Communication skills are a necessity. Forensic scientists must work with experts in other fields to decipher the evidence, and they are often called upon to give testimony in court cases, which means preparing findings and communicating them in an understandable way to a jury and to lawyers.

Technology used by forensic scientists varies based on their area of expertise and the size of the agency for which they work. Forensic scientists often work with microscopes, DNA analysis equipment and software, biological evidence kits, different types of cameras, laboratory information management systems (LIMS) software, Combined DNA Index System (CODIS), and the National Crime Information Center (NCIC) database, as well as more common computer programs for word processing and image editing. Exposure to chemicals and toxic substances may be a part of some forensic scientists' job, and protective gear may be required in such cases.

Earnings and Employment Outlook

The outlook for jobs in this field is optimistic due to the growing frequency with which DNA and other types of evidence are now used in court. However, recent cuts to federal and state budgets, as well as a rising interest in the field, mean there is significant competition for jobs.

There are, however, opportunities in places other than local law enforcement agencies and the FBI. Forensic scientists are also employed by the US Fish and Wildlife Bureau, the military, private companies and labs, and insurance agencies. Forensic scientists with a certain level of experience and expertise may also choose to hire themselves out as consultants or teach at colleges and universities.

The outlook for jobs in this field is optimistic due to the growing frequency with which DNA and other types of evidence are now used in court. However, recent cuts to federal and state budgets, as well as a rising interest in the field, mean that there is significant competition for jobs.

A Conversation with Ruth Smith

Job Title: Associate Professor, Forensic Chemistry

What was your career path?

- Bachelor of Science in Forensic and Analytical Chemistry, University of Strathclyde, Glasgow, UK (1999)
- PhD in Forensic and Analytical Chemistry, University of Strathclyde, Glasgow, UK (2003)
- Postdoctoral researcher, Los Alamos National Laboratory, Los Alamos, NM (2003-2005)
- Assistant Professor, Forensic Science Program, Michigan State University, East Lansing, MI (2005-2011)
- Associate Professor, Forensic Science Program, Michigan State University, East Lansing, MI (2011-present)

What are three pieces of advice you would offer someone interested in your profession?

1. Take full advantage of opportunities presented to you.
2. Make things happen—don't sit back and wait.
3. Keep an open mind—sometimes research takes you down a path that you never imagined (but ends up being much more fun).

What paths for career advancement are available to you?

There are many opportunities available in a university setting. Most people begin as an assistant professor and it typically takes six years to be promoted to associate professor. After that, the nest advancement would be promotion to full professor, which again takes approximately six years. Depending on the individual, there are opportunities not only to advance your research but also to become more involved in the administrative side of the university. This may be by serving on various committees both within your department and within the university or by taking administrative roles within the university.

Earnings vary based on some factors common to all professions: geographical location, level of experience, and level of education. Within the realm of forensic science, salary will vary based upon specialization and the size of the company or agency.

Forensic scientists can increase their earning potential by acquiring additional certifications from places like the American College of Forensic Examiners International or local universities. In addition, scientists with advanced or specialized degrees may be able to procure higher salaries. Forensic dentists or forensic anthropologists, for instance, possess particular skills and thus may occasionally have the advantage over generalized forensic scientists when seeking employment.

Related Occupations

- **Biochemists and Biophysicists:** Biochemists and biophysicists work primarily in the laboratory, analyzing DNA and other substances or performing experiments to show the effects of drugs and other chemicals on the body.

- **Medical Scientists:** Medical scientists research diseases and their treatment, analyze biological materials for toxins or signs of illness, and work with other health professionals to ensure the safety of drugs or to develop health-related programs and standards.

- **Coroners:** Coroners work in close association with the police, removing bodies from crime scenes, investigating the causes of suspicious death by performing autopsies and biological analysis, and reviewing medical history or other documents associated with the deceased.

- **Fire Investigators:** Fire investigators collect and analyze evidence from locations where fires have occurred to determine the cause of the fire. They also interview witnesses, work with law enforcement, arrest suspected arsonists, and provide testimony in court cases involving arson.

Future Applications

Forensic science is a growing field due to the demand for DNA and other types of trace evidence in court proceedings. This type of analysis is becoming increasingly important in new areas of law enforcement, such as initiatives against poaching and animal trafficking.

The DNA and evidence backlog in criminal cases is immense. In recognition of the need for more DNA and other evidence processing, the federal government has established grants to update and improve crime laboratories and to assist local law enforcement agencies with processing and cataloging DNA samples for the national Combined DNA Index System (CODIS) database. There is also funding available through the recently implemented Federal Forensic DNA Backlog Reduction Program.

The science of fighting crime constantly calls for the application of new skills and new technologies. For instance, entomologists may be employed to interpret insect evidence, or palynologists (pollen and spore specialists) may be consulted to provide information about locations based upon plant evidence found on the victim or at the scene. While forensic science is generally considered to be more of a physical science, various branches of law enforcement and industry also rely upon forensic specialists in computer science to fight cyber crime and to combat fraud. Therefore, it is very likely that the profession will continue to grow and evolve with changing technology.

J. D. Ho, MFA

More Information

American Academy of Forensic Sciences
410 North 21st Street
Colorado Springs, CO 80904
www.aafs.org

American Chemical Society
1155 Sixteenth Street, NW
Washington, DC 20036
http://acs.org

American College of Forensic Examiners International (ACFEI)
2750 East Sunshine Street
Springfield, MO 65804
www.acfei.com

National Center for Forensic Science
12354 Research Parkway
Orlando, Florida 32826
http://ncfs.ucf.edu/index.html

US Fish & Wildlife Service
National Forensics Laboratory
1490 East Main Street
Ashland, OR 97520-1310
www.lab.fws.gov/

Geochemistry

FIELDS OF STUDY

Geology; chemistry; earth sciences; biology; mathematics; computer sciences; mineralogy; petrology; geochemistry; geophysics; geomorphology; structural geology; engineering geology; sedimentology; stratigraphy; paleontology; physical geology; soil science; oceanography; atmospheric sciences; planetary sciences; hydrology; climatology; meteorology; inorganic chemistry; analytical chemistry; organic chemistry; physical chemistry; chemical thermodynamics; marine chemistry; spectroscopy.

DEFINITION

Geochemistry concerns itself with the distribution of chemical elements and their isotopes in the geospheres of earth. Geochemistry examines the geological processes and their cycles which led to this ongoing distribution from the formation of the solar system to the present and the future of earth. Geochemistry also studies rocks, minerals, soil, water, the atmosphere, and the biosphere. Geochemistry contributes to humanity's discovery and exploitation of natural resources (from ores to hydrocarbons), the determination of suitable areas for agricultural production, and the mitigation of humanity's effect on the environment, including conventional and nuclear waste management. Geochemists also contribute to climate studies.

Basic Principles

In the nineteenth century, geochemistry was conceptualized as a science that used chemistry to examine issues in geology. Swiss German chemist Christian Friedrich Schönbein coined the term "geochemistry" in 1836 and, soon after, the first textbooks in the field were published in Germany. A pioneer of geochemistry was American scientist Frank Clarke. Leading a United States Geological Survey (USGS) group in the early twentieth century, Clarke published the final edition of his geochemical data in 1924. The 1950s saw the building of a solid foundation of the discipline through the influential works of three European geochemists: Finnish geochemists Kalervo Ranka-ma and Thure Sahama, and Austrian Norwegian geochemist Victor Moritz Goldschmidt. Goldschmidt died in 1947 before his influential textbook came out, in 1954. In his honor, the American Geochemical Society hosts the annual international Goldschmidt Conference bring-ing together scientists in the field.

In the early twenty-first century there are two major directions in geochemistry. One effort examines the formation of the earth and the distribution of chemical elements throughout geological times. This should lead toward understanding of how geological features are formed and precisely determining the age of existing geological formations. A key goal is to develop theories leading toward an ex-trapolation of these processes into the future. This field links up with planetary sciences, seeking connections between the geochemistry of the earth and that of other bodies in the solar system.

The second emphasis in geochemistry analyzes the current distri-bution of chemical elements and their isotopes in the geospheres of the earth. The practical applications are in natural resource discovery and exploitation, agricultural optimization, environmental protection, waste management, and engineering solutions.

Core Concepts

Geochemistry is interested in the original distribution of chemical ele-ments on Earth. For this reason, the field also studies the formation of the solar system. Once the earth formed, there began a constant, ongo-ing process of changing the chemical composition of the planet based on chemical and distribution processes. For geochemists, it is impor-tant to learn about the history of these processes and develop methods to determine the age of particular rock and soil samples to place them in geologic time. Finally, geochemistry is concerned with understand-ing where chemical and distribution processes may lead in the future, determining the fate of the planet.

Origin of the Universe and Solar System. To explain the distribution of the chemical elements on Earth, geochemists must study the past. They start their inquiry with the calculated origin of the universe—the big bang, some 14 billion years ago—when all of its matter and energy was created. As the first stars formed, nuclear fusion of their core elements of hydrogen and helium moved them along a path of development leading to the creation of the chemical elements through nucleosynthesis; these elements then spread through the cosmos. Once the solar system formed out of a contracting molecular cloud of interstellar dust, the sun and planets appeared. For this point, geochemists look at the initial distribution of elements on Earth. They are aided in this endeavor by the study of the chemical composition of meteorites that have crashed on Earth. Old objects from the early days of the solar system, these meteorites preserve a record of the distribution of elements during those times. To look back into time, geochemists have also analyzed samples of lunar rock brought back by the Apollo missions to the moon; they have also remotely analyzed Martian rocks. These extraterrestrial rocks have not weathered as their counterparts on Earth have and therefore have preserved their earlier composition. The field of these studies is also called cosmochemistry.

Geospheres. Geochemists distinguish between the different geospheres of the earth. There is the core, knowledge of which comes from geophysical calculations and comparison with suitable meteorites. The earth's core is very dense, with a solid inner and liquid outer core. The mantle of the earth, the largest geosphere, is analyzed in its reaction with the crust of the earth, which geochemists can observe both on the bottom of the oceans (as oceanic crust) and on dry land (as continental crust). The crust and the top portion of the mantle are defined as the lithosphere. Analysis of the biosphere relies on biochemistry to understand the chemical processes leading to the creation of a habitable area for humanity and other life. The hydrosphere of the earth—primarily made up of its oceans and seas—is subject to geochemical analysis as well. Finally, analysis of the atmosphere examines the composition of the outermost geosphere of the earth, its development, and its future changes.

Inorganic Chemistry. Geochemistry relies heavily on inorganic chemistry, including crystal chemistry, to determine the chemical composition of rocks and minerals found on earth. Inorganic chemistry provides geochemists with the theoretical and analytical tools to determine how the electronic structure of the atoms of a particular element influences its actual properties. The periodic table of elements is utilized to classify the chemical elements found on earth and to group them according to their characteristics.

Thermodynamics. The three laws of thermodynamics are crucial in geochemistry, because they allow analysis of the chemical reactions taking place on the earth over geologic time. Thermodynamics provide geochemists with a theoretical foundation to model how the chemical composition of the earth changed over time as heat influenced the distribution of chemical elements and the formation of new rock compounds.

Geochemical Processes. The understanding and analysis of geochemical processes is a key concept in geochemistry. Of particular relevance are the reactions of acids and bases, salts and their ions, as well as oxidation-reduction reactions. Classification of clay minerals is done according to the processes leading to their creation. Key geochemical processes are weathering and diagenesis, the latter referring to the change of sedimentary material during the process of becoming a sedimentary rock formation. The analysis of geochemical processes yields an understanding of the transport of elements moving them from one site to another over time.

Isotope Chemistry. Geochemists study both stable and radioactive isotopes of the elements. Elements have isotopes if they exist as separate atoms that have the same number of protons, but a different number of neutrons. This gives each isotope a different mass number made up from its protons and neutrons. Elements can have both stable and radioactive isotopes, as is the case with carbon. The decay of radioactive isotopes generates heat, and its measurement by geochemists is used to date events during geological time. This is done to learn more about the origin of igneous rocks, formed from magma and lava, and the chemical composition of the lithosphere. Isotope fractionation—or the separation of isotopes during chemical processes—is analyzed to date rocks and fossils and to provide a measurable record of past climate changes and ocean temperatures.

Biogeochemistry. This subdiscipline of geochemistry was developed by Russian geochemist Vladimir Vernadsky, who introduced the idea in his 1926 book *The Biosphere* (translated into English in 1986). Biogeochemistry works on the premise that, since its appearance, life has significantly shaped the geological features on earth. Of particular contemporary interest are the study and modeling of chemical element cycles such as that of carbon and nitrogen that affect life on earth. Biogeochemistry is highly interdisciplinary, combining scientific research in many fields to develop its models for life's impact on the biosphere.

Applications Past and Present

Mining. The principles of geochemistry were applied first to mining in order to analyze the chemical composition of ores centuries before geochemistry developed in its modern form. Two German Renaissance scientists, Georgius Agricola and Lazarus Ercker, were the first to describe what can be recognized as being methods for chemical analysis of different ores. In 1556, one year after his death, Agricola's *De re metallica* (*On the Nature of Metals*, 1912) appeared. Ercker published his *Beschreibung der allerfürnemsten Mineralischen Erzt und Bergwerksarten* (*Treatise on Ores and Assaying*, 1951) in 1580. However, it was not until American chemist Frank Clarke published *The Data of Geochemistry* in 1908 that the principles of geochemistry were used in their modern scientific form. Clarke used geochemistry to analyze ore deposits he encountered during his work as chief chemist of the USGS, begun in 1883 and ending in 1925. His successors at the USGS developed the basis of contemporary geochemical prospecting by 1947.

Contemporary geochemists work in two capacities for the mining industry. First, as mineral exploration geologists, they bring their knowledge to prospecting for new ore deposits. They survey and take soil and rock samples from a prospective field, also looking for chemical anomalies in their samples that hint at an ore deposit. Second, as mine production geologists, they are responsible for providing the scientific and technical information for mining and processing mineral deposits efficiently. This includes consideration of economic, safety, and environmental aspects.

Interesting Facts about Geochemistry

- Through radiometric dating of crashed meteorites, which are the oldest accessible rocks that have retained their original shape, geochemists have calculated that the earth is about 4.54 billion years old.

- Geochemical analysis of the distribution of the chemical elements on the earth has determined that, because of the relative abundance of metallic elements, the sun is actually a Population I star. This means the sun was created in part out of the remnants of a nearby star, which exploded as a supernova before the solar system was formed.

- Because of the Apollo missions, geochemists have been able to analyze the composition of lunar rocks brought back to earth from the moon.

- Geochemists were instrumental in proving the existence of lead poisoning in the environment and in humans due to human use of lead in products, particularly after the Industrial Revolution. As a result, lead exposure has been minimized by lowering permissible amount of lead in such products as paint and by banning the use of lead as a gasoline additive.

- It is only through the chemical processes of weathering, which turns solid rocks into sediment and soil, that the earth has become habitable for life.

Petroleum Geochemistry. Petroleum geochemistry has been used to discover new oil fields since some time after the beginning of the oil age in the mid-nineteenth century. Using some of the principles and techniques from mineral prospecting, petroleum geochemistry has specialized in the quest to find new oil and natural gas deposits. Because of the immense value of a successful oil deposit discovery, petroleum geochemists are among the best-paid geochemists.

When supporting prospecting for oil deposits, petroleum geochemists seek to identify source rocks where hydrocarbons like oil and natural gas have formed from organic matter. Next, as geochemistry is concerned with tracking the distribution of chemical elements on the earth, their techniques and methods can be used to analyze possible paths and distribution of hydrocarbons from the original source rock. Observed findings of hydrocarbons on the surface or in water—getting there through seepage or leaks, for example—are analyzed to be tracked back to locate new deposits. Petroleum geochemists rely on standard geochemical methods such as isotope chemistry, and use tools like gas chromatography and mass spectronomy to analyze source rocks and hydrocarbon traces.

Radiometric Dating. In 1905, British chemist and physicist Ernest Rutherford applied the principles of radioactivity—discovered in 1896 by French physicist Henri Becquerel and his PhD students Marie and Pierre Curie—to find the age of rock samples. Because radioactive isotopes of an element decay at a steady rate to form isotopes of another element, measuring and comparing the amount of the so-called parent element with amount of the daughter element in a rock or mineral sample enables the determination of its geological age. This is possible because of the exceptional length of the half-life of some radioactive isotopes, lasting billions of years. For example, the decay of uranium-238 (U-283) into lead (Pb-206) has a half-life of 4.5 billion years, almost that of the contemporary estimate of the earth's overall age. Thus, comparison of the measured relationship between uranium-238 and lead-206 in a rock sample can date its origin accurately in geological time.

In 1913, British geologist Arthur Holmes was the first to use radiometric dating of rock samples to calculate the age of earth. His publication *The Age of the Earth* (1913) arrived at an age of 1.6 billion years. This shocked those in the scientific community who believed that the earth was much younger, even though Holmes's figure was still about 3 billion years short of earth's true age. By the early twenty-first century, radiometric dating had been firmly established as a geochemical method for calculating the exact periods of the earth's geological time scale. Because of its relatively short half-life of 5,730 years, the decay of the carbon-14 isotope into nitrogen-14 isotopes is used in radiocarbon dating for determining the age of archeological objects and more recent rock and soil samples.

Geochemical Modeling. Understanding geochemical processes has led to geochemical modeling. This is done to analyze the effects of chemical reactions behind geochemical cycles, and to model the cycles that have affected geological development and life on planet. Of particular interest has been geochemical modeling of geochemical cycles that directly affect humanity, such as the cycle of surface, ground, and atmospheric water. Modeling the mixing and dilution of chemical elements during geological processes—work undertaken to account for the chemical composition of the resulting binary mixtures—and assessing the relative abundance of elements ultimately seeks to develop a better understanding of the earth's future development.

American geochemists Robert Garrels and Charles Christ applied geochemical modeling to studies in aqueous geochemistry, related to the chemical study of the world's waters. They published their results in *Solutions, Minerals and Equilibria* (1965). While their study relied on a physical equilibrium status, contemporary geochemical modeling also examines nonequilibrium states. Of particular concern is reactive transport modeling in porous media, which simulates how chemical reactions influence the transport of a fluid medium like magma through the planetary crust.

Climate Change Studies. Geochemical analysis of the chemical composition of the atmosphere and the chemical reactions that occur there has found a major application in geochemistry's contribution to the study of climate change, and in particular human-caused (anthropogenic) climate change. In the 1970s, geochemists and other scientists found that the ozone layer protecting the surface of the earth from the sun's ultraviolet radiation was diminishing. Normally, ultraviolet radiation breaks up the molecular bond of the oxygen molecule to form ozone in the stratosphere, ten to fifty kilometers (six to thirty miles) above the earth. There, equilibrium of ozone creation and destruction existed. However, when people began to release chlorofluorocarbons and bromofluorocarbons—used for aerosols and refrigeration—into the atmosphere, the materials traveled into the stratosphere. There, fluorocarbons triggered chemical reactions destroying ozone molecules.

In reaction to these scientific findings, the United States, Canada, and Norway became the first countries to ban production of fluorocarbon-based aerosols in 1978. After discovery of the ozone hole over Antarctica in 1985—a discovery to which geochemists contributed—

the Montreal Protocol of 1987 phased out production of all fluoro-carbon products by 1996. This international agreement was amended over time to phase out other ozone destroying compounds, by 2010 for some and 2030 for others. By 2006, there was clear scientific evidence that the ozone layer was recovering, a process expected to be completed in 2050.

The geochemical study of global warming contributes to another key current issue. Beginning with an article in the American journal *Science* on August 8, 1975, awareness has risen that the increased release of so-called greenhouse gases into the atmosphere causes global warming. The issue has been contentious, as most greenhouse gases, particularly carbon dioxide, are created by human industrial activity, and limiting the emission of greenhouse gases thus has significant economic cost. Nevertheless, there has arisen international concern that the increasing greenhouse gases in the earth's atmosphere will lead to an increased atmospheric absorption of infrared radiation emitted by rock and soil on earth, leading to a rise in the earth's temperature. This rise could cause droughts as well as floods, particularly if the ocean levels were to rise due to the melting of polar ice caps. In response, international agreements to limit greenhouse gases were concluded. The United Nations Framework Convention on Climate Change was signed on May 9, 1992, and became effective on March 21, 1994. Out of it, the Kyoto Protocol arose, an international agreement to lower greenhouse gas emissions. Even though the Kyoto Protocol was signed on December 11, 1997, and became effective on February 16, 2005, the United States still had not ratified the agreement as of 2012. Canada formally withdrew from it on December 12, 2011.

Soil Studies. Geochemistry has contributed to soil studies, in particular the analysis of soil formation and the distribution and transport of chemical elements in soil. Geochemists have participated in soil surveys mapping and classifying the different soils of a region and their possible uses in agriculture. Russian geologist Vasily Dokuchaev has been commonly credited with establishing soil science through his influential 1883 publication on Russian soils. In the twentieth century, geochemists added to soil science through research in soil biochemistry and soil mineralogy. With humanity's need for food growing, cultivating and managing soil with the goal of optimizing agricultural production has been a key concern, to which geochemical research has contributed. The issue of understanding and mitigating human-caused soil degradation through pollution and contamination has also incorporated geochemical research.

Management of Conventional and Nuclear Waste. Geochemists contribute to both conventional and nuclear waste management. Geochemical expertise is needed in designing new landfill deposits with mitigation of groundwater and soil pollution. For nuclear waste, geochemists help to identify the most stable geological formations for final storage. They contribute geochemical expertise to the study of the processes in the rocks around existing and planned nuclear waste repositories and model rock evolution over geological time, as nuclear waste decays very slowly.

Engineering. Geochemistry is applied to develop engineering solutions, particularly in geologically unstable regions. Knowledge of the geochemistry of a proposed engineering site supports design of customized solutions. Geochemists have increasingly worked in cooperation with engineers and architects.

Impact on Industry

Worldwide, geochemists typically work in academic settings or for national or international research agencies, or otherwise are either directly employed in the industry, particularly the oil and gas and mining industry, or offer their expertise as provider of professional, scientific and technical services. In the United States, geochemists number among the 33,800 geoscientists employed in 2010, a figure that excludes hydrologists and geographers.

United States federal research funding for the geosciences has been of significant importance to the work and employment of geochemists. Federal funding is distributed not only to federal agencies, but also to universities and colleges, private research centers, nonprofit organizations, and even industrial firms. In the geosciences, the dollar amount of federal funding for the geosciences increased from 1970 to 2004 but dropped between 2004 and 2012. In 2007, it amounted

Occupation	Geoscientists
Employment 2010	33,800
Projected Employment 2020	40,900
Change in Number (2010–20)	7,100
Percent Change	21%

Bureau of Labor Statistics, 2012

to about $3.2 billion. However, the percentage of federal research funding that is allocated to the geosciences declined from 11 percent in 1996 to 6 percent in 2007.

Government Agencies. The USGS is one of the most important United States government agencies to employ geochemists on its staff of about 8,500 people. Atmospheric geochemists work for the agency's National Climate Change and Wildlife Science Center, supporting the development of climate and land-use forecasts. At the USGS Astrogeology Research Program, geochemists contribute to the planning of exploration missions to the bodies of the solar system; they also research the formation and evolution of the solar system and analyze data gained from remote sensing and image processing. Similarly, geochemists work with the National Aeronautics and Space Administration (NASA) on questions involving missions to study the chemical composition of the solar system's planets, moons, asteroids, and dwarf planets. The Oak Ridge National Laboratory in Tennessee also employs geochemists, particularly in the field of aqueous geochemistry. All in all, federal agencies employed 2,800 geoscientists in 2010, among them the geochemists.

Military. Geochemistry has contributed to successful prospecting for uranium—an element needed for the manufacture of nuclear weapons. Geochemists have supported climate studies for the aftereffects of a nuclear war, in particular the issue of a nuclear winter caused by the accumulation of soot in the stratosphere from the burning of destroyed cities.

University Research and Teaching. Geochemists are widely employed by universities and colleges, where they engage in academic research and postsecondary education. They are part of the 2,100 geoscientists in academia. Geochemists at universities pursue a variety of research topics and address some fundamental questions in gaining more knowledge of both the chemical composition of the earth and other planets and moons, as well as the chemical cycles of the geospheres. Geochemists teach their subject to the next generation of scientists, stressing an interdisciplinary approach.

Occupation	Environmental scientists and specialists
Employment 2010	89,400
Projected Employment 2020	106,100
Change in Number (2010–20)	16,700
Percent Change	19%

*Bureau of Labor Statistics, 2012

Petroleum and Mining Industries. Geochemists contribute significantly to the value created in the petroleum and mining industry. This is done especially in the field of exploration, but also as mine production geologists. Overall, the geosciences component of the share of these industries in the United States' gross domestic product has been estimated by the American Geosciences Institute to have almost doubled in the early twenty-first century, from $27.3 billion in 2002 to $57.4 billion in 2008.

Social Context and Future Prospects

Geochemistry supports humanity's quest for knowledge about the origin of its planet and the solar system, the chemical composition of its habitat, and possible further developments of the earth. In its practical applications, geochemistry also contributes to exploration and the efficient use of natural resources—particularly oil, natural gas, and mineral ores—and a sustainable use of the planet's water and soil. These varied fields should provide geochemists with ample opportunities for further research and industry employment.

For geochemists, both the United States Bureau of Labor Statistics (BLS) and the American Geoscience Institute indicate strong, above average future employment growth. These employment prospects also came with good salary expectations for geochemists. The best-paid jobs are in petroleum geochemistry, averaging a median salary of $122,000 in 2011. However, in this field, the AGI saw the least job growth by 2018. There were plenty of other areas in geochemistry with strong estimated job growth, though, particularly for professional, technical, and scientific advisors and in waste management.

Further Reading

Albarède, Francis. *Geochemistry: An Introduction.*2nd ed. Cambridge: Cambridge UP, 2009. Print. Focuses on inorganic chemistry and the presentation of the chemistry, physics, and mathematics involved in geochemistry. Discusses the earth's geospheres, as well as biogeochemistry and environmental geochemistry.

Faure, Gunter. *Principles and Applications of Geochemistry.* 2nd ed. Upper Saddle River: Prentice, 1998. Print. Introduced the science and its applications with chapter summaries and test problems for studying the material.

Li, Yuan-Hui. *A Compendium of Geochemistry.* Princeton: Princeton UP, 2000. Print. Begins with structure of chemical elements, moves to solar nebula as source of terrestrial elements, and includes discussion of chemical composition of igneous and sedimentary rocks and earth's oceans; concludes with the biosphere.

Misra, Kula. *Introduction to Geochemistry: Principles and Applications.* Chichester: Wiley, 2012. Print. Written for readers at advanced undergraduate and graduate levels and includes sections on: crystal chemistry dealing with atomic structure of elements, chemical reactions focusing on thermodynamics, isotope chemistry related to dating rocks and minerals, and earth supersystem discussing the geospheres.

Walther, John. *Essentials of Geochemistry.* 2nd ed. Sudbury: Jones, 2009. Print. Emphasizes thermodynamics and the concept of chemical equilibrium; offers good presentation and discussion of basic principles and key concerns of geochemistry.

About the Author: R. C. Lutz, PhD, is an instructor of business English at an international consulting company. His students include professionals in science and engineering, particularly in the chemical, process, oil and gas, and petrochemical industry, but not limited to these fields. He is the author of survey and encyclopedia articles in the applied sciences, among other subjects. After obtaining his MA and PhD in English literature from the University of California at Santa Barbara, he worked for a few years in academia before moving to a consulting company. He has worked across the globe in the United States, the Sultanate of Oman, the United Arab Emirates, Turkey, and Romania.

Geochemist 🖋

Earnings (Yearly Average): $84,470 (Bureau of Labor Statistics, 2011)

Employment and Outlook: Faster than average growth (Bureau of Labor Statistics, 2010)

O*NET-SOC Code: 19-2042.00

Related Career Clusters: Agriculture, Food & Natural Resources; Government & Public Administration; Manufacturing

Scope of Work

Geochemists analyze the composition of the earth as well as the chemical processes leading to and influencing the distribution of elements in the earth's core and crust. They have traditionally supported geological surveys and analyzed the chemical composition of the earth's water, soil, sediments, and rocks. Geochemists also contribute to climate studies, including study of the effects of human behavior on the earth's climate.

Geochemists work in a wide range of industries and specialized fields, including ore mining, exploration and exploitation of natural resources, and agriculture. Some geochemists work in waste management, analyzing the effects of waste on groundwater or supporting geological disposal of nuclear waste. They may also serve as architectural and engineering advisors. Those working in the field of petroleum geochemistry, a branch of petroleum geology, support the oil and gas industry by locating and analyzing deposits.

Education and Coursework

A high school student interested in pursuing a career in geochemistry should take classes in geology and other earth sciences, chemistry, and physics. Courses in mathematics and computer science as well as English and communication are also useful. Many students may

---

Transferable Skills

- Communication Skills – Negotiating with others (SCANS Workplace Competency – Interpersonal)
- Communication Skills – Reporting information
- Interpersonal/Social Skills – Cooperating with others
- Interpersonal/Social Skills – Working as a member of a team (SCANS Workplace Competency – Interpersonal)
- Research & Planning Skills – Gathering information
- Research & Planning Skills – Solving problems (SCANS Thinking Skills)
- Technical Skills – Using technology to process information (SCANS Workplace Competency – Information)
- Work Environment Skills – Traveling

---

benefit from participation in extracurricular activities related to geology, such as mineralogy clubs or excursions to interesting geological formations.

A bachelor's degree is the minimum educational requirement for a career in geochemistry. An undergraduate student should work toward a sound education in geology, taking courses in physical and structural geology, petrology, mineralogy, sedimentology, geochemistry, geophysics, geobiology, and economic geology. In addition, students should take courses in organic and physical chemistry as well as physics, mathematics, computer science, and engineering. A student may obtain practical experience through an internship, during which he or she may work as a geological assistant or technician under the supervision of experienced professionals. Although a bachelor's degree in the geosciences is preferred by many employers, a degree in chemistry, physics, or even mathematics or computer science, when supplemented with significant coursework in geology, may also provide a suitable educational foundation for a geochemist.

To advance in the field, a geochemist may be required to obtain a graduate degree. When choosing a master's degree program, a student should determine his or her preferred area of specialization and choose a program with strengths in that area. Indicators of academic strengths are research areas and publications of a program's faculty members as well as the theses of prior graduates and their job placements. Students interested in working in a particular field, such as waste management, mining, or engineering services, should choose a program with faculty active in research in that field. When pursuing a PhD, a student must typically choose a particular area of expertise and write a thesis based on original research in geochemistry under the guidance of a faculty advisor. A PhD is usually required for those seeking to teach geochemistry at the postsecondary level.

Career Enhancement and Training

Some states require that a geochemist obtain a license before he or she can work as a registered geologist (RG). Requirements for becoming a registered geologist vary considerably from state to state. Typically, a geochemist must amass some years of work experience under a registered geologist before applying and must also pass an exam. After becoming a registered geologist, a geochemist must typically renew his or her license for a nominal fee, often annually. Some states require geochemists to complete continuing education courses as a condition of renewal.

Membership in professional organizations such as the Geochemical Society is highly recommended for geochemists. The Geochemical Society coorganizes the annual international Goldschmidt Conference, publishes the online newsletter *Geochemical News*, and copublishes the magazine *Elements*. In addition to hosting various events, the society provides members with reduced-price subscriptions to various scholarly journals and access to job listings in the field. The organization is a member of the American Geosciences Institute (AGI), a professional association representing more than forty member societies and more than 250,000 geoscientists.

Networking through participation in professional conferences, attendance at special lectures, and use of online media is often essential, as it helps geochemists remain aware of advances and new research in geochemistry and the related fields. As many geochemists work on field excursion teams composed of scientists from a variety

A Conversation with Brian Hagopian

Job Title: Chemist and Consultant

What was your career path?

My career started in chemical research with a biotech company, where I quickly determined that research was not a permanent career path for me. I took on additional responsibilities (purchasing) and saw all the perks that sales people got (company car, nice clothes, etc.), so I decided to move toward sales and marketing, first becoming a technical support specialist in the plastics industry, then moving to a technical sales position with an instrumentation company, both of which had me traveling all over the country, which was fun for awhile, but got old quickly and wasn't something I wanted to do permanently. Looking for a more "local" sales job, I took a position selling filtration and water purification equipment. This was my first position where I had a base salary and received "commission" based on my sales performance. With a metric system like this, I received regular feedback, was able to do some critical self-analysis and correction, and flourished. After seven years in this position, I outgrew the company and struck out on my own, incorporating as a brand new company, which was formed in 1989—one of the worst times to start a new business. The new water purification company, Fluid Solutions, required long hours and was a financial struggle for about three to four years until there was a large enough customer base to ensure the success of the business. After fifteen years in the business, and with twenty-five employees and about $5 million in annual revenues, the business was sold to another company, and I continued to work in the business for another ten years, recently retiring and starting an independent consulting business in the same field.

What are three pieces of advice you would offer someone interested in your profession?

1. Set goals for yourself. It may be scary to think about it, but how old do you want to be when you retire? How much money will you need to retire? How can you get

there? Start with a twenty-year (or thirty or forty) plan, determine where you will need to be at the halfway point, the quarter way point, five years out, two-and-a-half years out, and one year out. Then break it into smaller increments, eventually coming up with "what do I need to do this week (or month) to move toward my goals"—and start doing it. It's okay for the plan, goals, etc., to change every year or two; in fact, it's normal. The key is to have a goal, with metrics, deadlines, etc., to motivate you.

2. Get involved by volunteering. Ideally, find a professional society in your industry of choice, join, and attend meetings. Try to find a group that "feels right" or will help promote your objectives. Volunteer your time freely, and for the greater good of the group, and your efforts will come back to reward you fivefold. If you come across as transparent and lack depth of commitment, those around you will notice and you will not be successful.

3. When you choose to do something, go all the way. Don't partially commit—go for it and go "all in." If you are "out there" and dedicated, people will notice and you will receive future "payback" because you were involved. And don't be afraid to take chances, or to make the wrong decision. It's how we all learn. Leave your ego at the door and learn to critically evaluate yourself and your actions objectively. You will become stronger for it.

What paths for career advancement are available to you?

I created most of my own career paths, changing jobs quickly in my first five years out of college as I became exposed to various industries and positions, and not being completely satisfied with any of them. Chemistry provided an excellent technical background where you have more options as far as fields to enter. Ultimately, if you're smart and energetic, you have control over your career path.

of disciplines, basic awareness of related sciences is advantageous. Networking may also prove beneficial for geoscientists seeking to advance in the field or enter a new industry.

Daily Tasks and Technology

Geochemists typically work in the field, a laboratory, an office, or a classroom. During field excursions, they generally work as part of a team made up of geoscientists and other scientists. In the field, they may be responsible for collecting rock, soil, water, or atmospheric samples and observing and documenting geological features. Locations can be remote, ranging from tropical jungles to Antarctica, and working in the field requires a certain level of physical stamina.

After obtaining samples, geochemists may examine the samples in a laboratory. Analysis of their findings is done in a computer-supported environment and often requires geochemists to design models and theories explaining the significance of their data. Some geochemists focus on analyzing data provided by colleagues, including planetary scientists. Geochemists are often expected to present their results in academic papers or at industry conferences.

Geochemists use both traditional and very advanced tools. When in the field, they may use tools such as hammers, chisels, and augers to collect rock samples; however, they may also use ground-penetrating radar and sonar equipment and other technology. In the laboratory, geochemists rely on a wide array of spectroscopy and gas chromatography applications and instruments to analyze the chemical composition of samples. Neutron activation analysis may be performed to determine the composition of sample materials. Geochemists may also perform mathematical modeling when developing theories to explain chemical distribution processes. Their work may rely greatly on analytical and scientific software, computer-aided design programs, and graphics, photo imaging, and map creation software.

Earnings and Employment Outlook

Demand for geochemists, as for all geoscientists, is expected to experience faster than average growth between 2010 and 2020. The US Bureau of Labor Statistics estimates employment growth of 21 percent in the geosciences during this period, while the AGI expects a 23-percent increase in employment of geoscientists between 2008 and 2018. The AGI also revealed that by 2011, more than half of all geoscientists employed were within fifteen years of retirement, and there were more than twice as many geoscientists between the ages of fifty-one and fifty-five as there were between the ages of thirty-one and thirty-five. As the geoscience community continues to age and large numbers of scientists retire, it is likely that there will be significant demand for geochemists to fill the open positions. Job growth is expected to vary based on industry, with the professional, scientific, and technical services industry projected to experience the highest growth. Salaries for geochemists also vary greatly, with the petroleum industry offering the highest average annual wages. In general, geoscientists typically earn more on average than chemists and biologists and less than physicists, and average salaries have increased relatively steadily despite fluctuations in the US economy.

Demand for geochemists, as for all geoscientists, is expected to experience faster than average growth between 2010 and 2020.

Related Occupations

- **Geologists:** Geologists study the formation, history, shape, and composition of the earth, analyzing geological features such as rock formations and natural phenomena such as plate tectonics.

- **Petroleum Geologists:** Petroleum geologists use geoscientific procedures to locate oil and gas deposits for extraction and use as fuel.

- **Geophysicists:** Geophysicists study the physical properties of areas such as the earth's magnetic field.

- **Seismologists:** Seismologists specialize in the study of earthquakes and their effects, including tsunamis.

- **Engineering Geologists:** Engineering geologists combine geology with civil and environmental engineering, taking the composition and properties of the earth into account when planning projects.

Future Applications

Geochemists will see much demand for their work as human activities increasingly affect the natural environment. As nonrenewable natural resources are used up, the discovery and extraction of additional resources will require the input of geoscientists in a variety of disciplines. Of particular relevance to geochemists is the petroleum industry, which will likely rely on increasingly sophisticated scientific methods of exploration and production.

The increasing public and governmental interest in remediating humanity's effects on the environment is also expected to create new employment opportunities for geochemists. According to the AGI, demand for geochemists working in waste management is expected to increase by more than 30 percent by 2016. Such scientists may work in a variety of industries, including mining, petroleum production, and atmospheric and space science.

R. C. Lutz, PhD

More Information

American Association of Petroleum Geologists
PO Box 979
Tulsa, OK 74101
www.aapg.org

American Geosciences Institute
4220 King Street
Alexandria, VA 22302
www.agiweb.org

Geochemical Society
1 Brookings Drive, CB 1169
St. Louis, MO 63130
www.geochemsoc.org

Green Chemistry

Physics; chemistry; biology; engineering; mathematics; computer science; physical chemistry; quantum mechanics; statistical mechanics; computational chemistry; biophysics; classical mechanics; analytical chemistry; calculus; differential equations; linear algebra; statistics; numerical analysis; advanced statistics; chemical kinetics; thermodynamics; economics; toxicology; nanotechnology; biotechnology; catalysis; environmental policy; systems/industrial engineering; chemical engineering.

DEFINITION

Green chemistry is a relatively new field focused on finding new, more environmentally friendly approaches to chemical reactions or techniques. Green chemists strive to design more efficient ways to utilize resources, reducing the use of nonrenewable resources and decreasing waste. Green chemistry also involves reducing the use of products that are harmful to human health and the environment, for example, the replacement of a carcinogenic chemical with a safer alternative. This emerging field is of growing importance as society increasingly searches for ways to balance environmental stewardship with the quality-of-life benefits of advanced technology.

Basic Principles

The foundations for green chemistry were laid in the 1970s, which were characterized by an unprecedented push for increased environmental awareness and protection. However, it was not until the early 1990s that the field of green chemistry truly came into being. Paul Anastas—known as the father of green chemistry—coined the term while working as a chemist at the United States Environmental Protection Agency (EPA). Anastas and John C. Warner later developed the Twelve Principles of Green Chemistry, which define the field and continue to be used as a basis for green chemistry initiatives. Today, green chemistry is a thriving field; universities are establishing green chemistry academic programs, and corporations are placing increasing emphasis on green chemistry as they strive to increase the efficiency of their manufacturing processes and comply with increasingly stringent regulations in the United States and abroad concerning acceptable pollution levels. Finally, green chemists are also highly employable in such government agencies as the EPA as researchers and consultants.

Although the terms "green" and "environmental" are used interchangeably in many contexts, green chemistry and environmental chemistry are different fields. As described above, green chemistry is about reengineering chemical processes to minimize harm to people and the environment; in contrast, environmental chemistry is the study of chemistry pertaining to the environment. The latter would include studying the iron cycles in a lake or the variations in organic content in soil with depth. Using climate change as an example, an environmental chemist would seek to better understand the reactions occurring in the atmosphere that are depleting the ozone layer, whereas a green chemist would invent a new method for the large-scale manufacturing of plastics that minimizes the release of toxic gas.

Core Concepts

Green chemists rely on a combination of chemistry and cost-benefit analysis to improve the environmental friendliness of chemical processes. Concepts from both of these fields that are especially relevant to green chemistry are introduced below.

Life-Cycle Analysis. The most critical (and often overlooked) aspect of analyzing greenness, be it the greenness of a process or a product, is to consider its "cradle-to-grave" impact, also known as life-cycle analysis. For example, consider the issue of plastic bags. Legislation is being introduced in various cities, states, and countries to eliminate their use or penalize their users. At first glance, this approach might seem unquestionably green—replacing plastic bags with paper or reusable bags would reduce litter. However, a thorough life-cycle analysis paints a different picture. Instead of only considering the item disposal, life-cycle analysis considers the greenness of the material, the manufacturing of the product, its distribution, use, and disposal in quantitative terms whenever possible. In this case, the manufacturing of plastic bags creates 70 percent fewer emissions than that of paper bags or compostable reusable bags, demonstrating the complexities of this issue. Furthermore, nine out of every ten people reuse plastic bags; a plastic bag ban in Ireland increased the sale of trash bags by 400 percent. Life-cycle analysis is a fundamental tool used by green chemists when making decisions about how to best minimize environmental impact.

Atom Efficiency. Atom efficiency is a key concept in green chemistry. In simple terms, atom efficiency refers to the degree to which the different compounds that go into a synthesis come out in the product rather than as waste. Atoms are the basis of this measurement because chemical reactions involve rearranging the chemical bonds between atoms, making atoms the conserved quantity. Higher atom efficiencies indicate reactions with less waste.

Catalysis. Much of green chemistry entails the use of catalysts, substances that speed up a reaction but are either unaltered or regenerated over its course. Thus, a simplified expression of a catalyzed reaction is reactants + catalyst products + catalyst. Because catalysts are renewable by definition, they embody the very spirit of green chemistry. Though some catalysts are quite toxic, an efficiently designed catalysis reaction requires a very small amount of toxic catalyst, which is often more environmentally friendly than the use (and subsequent discarding) of a large quantity of a less toxic substance. Although catalysts are regenerated in the primary chemical reaction, they tend to become unusable over time due to reaction with their environment. In addition to searching for new catalysts, research in this area includes extending a catalyst's lifetime and increasing its surface area, improving its efficiency.

Solvents. A solvent is the substance that provides a favorable environment for the chemicals of interest. For example, water is the solvent in saltwater; it provides the salt with an environment in which it can dissolve. Water is a common solvent and is biologically benign. However, many other common solvents are quite toxic, such as chloroform. Solvents are generally used in large volumes, especially in large-scale chemical manufacturing, and then discarded. In addition to being toxic to the environment, hazardous solvents are also a danger to the people exposed to them: researchers, employees at chemical manufacturing plants, and end users. A thriving area of green chemistry entails finding ways to synthesize a given product using mild solvents (e.g., replacing chloroform with water) and using less solvent overall.

Renewable Materials. In addition to finding ways to use renewable resources, such as wood or solar energy, instead of nonrenewables, such as coal, green chemists also look for ways to utilize industrial and agricultural waste when possible. For example, the inorganic silicates formed from the ashes of biomass combustion can be used as a nontoxic fire-retardant binder. Starch is a common agricultural byproduct with many applications, including in carpet adhesive. Starch occurs naturally in potatoes, corn, rice, and wheat, among other staple foods, and can be obtained as waste from food processing.

Twelve Principles of Green Chemistry. The foundation of this field, set down by Paul Anastas, consists of twelve principles for reducing harm to the environment and human health. A complete description of these principles exceeds the scope of this work, and the reader is encouraged to consult the Further Reading for additional information. The basis of the principles can be divided into two elements: reduce, reuse, and recycle (the three Rs) and safety.

Of the three Rs, Anastas's principles are heavily focused on "reduce." For example, the first principle reads, "It is better to prevent waste than to treat or clean up waste after it is formed," emphasizing the reduction of waste, and many of the other principles focus on streamlining reactions in terms of minimizing the use of energy and materials that do not end up in the final product. Examples of "reuse" are found in the seventh and ninth principles, which encourage the use of renewable resources and catalysts, respectively. "Recycle" is not heavily emphasized in the principles, as the disposal of the product is somewhat outside the realm of green chemistry, which tends to focus on the creation of the product instead.

Regarding safety, these principles advocate for the use of materials that minimize toxicity and the risk for explosions, fire, etc. The third

---

Interesting Facts about Green Chemistry

- The eighty-eight winners of the Presidential Green Chemistry Challenge from 1995 to 2012 have saved 21 billion gallons of water, eliminated 7.9 billion pounds of carbon dioxide emissions, and reduced the use of 825 million pounds of hazardous chemicals annually. These figures do not include the contributions of the nearly fifteen hundred entrants that did not win.

- The 2005 Nobel Prize in Chemistry was awarded to Yves Chauvin, Robert Grubbs, and Richard Schrock for their work in the field of metathesis. Metathesis reactions are generally more efficient, simpler, and more environmentally friendly than conventional reactions.

- Starch, a waste product from many food processing practices, has applications in papermaking, clothing starching, corrugated boards, wallpaper adhesive, packing peanuts, and yarn making. Starch is contained in rice, potatoes, and wheat, which are staple foods around the world.

- Although the source of colony collapse disorder (CCD), which is decimating the honeybee population and endangering agriculture worldwide, is unclear, hazardous pesticides are the leading candidates. If this is the case, it will represent one of the most convincing, publicly accessible arguments for the immediate need for greener chemistry practices.

- Coconut husks can be used to manufacture car parts. Not only is this use of a waste product environmentally friendly, but it also adds value to coconuts, improving the economies of areas containing coconut farms.

principle states, "Wherever practicable, synthetic methodologies should be designed to use and generate substances that possess little or no toxicity to human health and the environment," and the twelfth principle reads, "Substances . . . used in a chemical process should be chosen to minimize potential for chemical accidents, including releases, explosions, and fires." Furthermore, the tenth principle suggests that products be designed such that whatever they break down into is also nontoxic.

Applications Past and Present

Energy. Green chemistry is fundamental in developing renewable energy to the point where it will completely replace oil, coal, and natural gas. Green chemistry is involved in optimizing solar cells, ensuring that they capture as much energy from the sun as possible, and creating solar cells in interesting forms, such as bendable films and nearly transparent window films. In terms of biomass, green chemistry is used to identify the best biomass feedstock, conversion technique, and processing parameters. After energy is captured, it must be stored until use. To this end, green chemists are devising green storage devices, such as a catalyst that can use the captured energy to split water into hydrogen and oxygen, which are stored separately. When the energy is needed, the hydrogen and oxygen are recombined, releasing energy.

Plastics. Plastics are everywhere: furniture, electronics, safety equipment, toys, storage, cars, and clothing, just to name some everyday examples. Plastics are also integral to medicine, manufacturing, and food processing. The ubiquity of these materials, their often-hazardous syntheses, and the health and environmental risks posed by their degradation make them strong candidates for green chemistry research. Efforts are underway to make biodegradable plastics using organic catalysts, to reduce the use of hazardous compounds in the manufacturing of polyurethane, and to design syntheses that produce plastic from biological sources. In addition to lessening the environmental damage caused by the production of plastics, green chemistry also aims to identify and circumvent health hazards posed by long-term exposure to plastics. For example, bisphenol A (BPA) made the news when its abilities to mimic estrogen came to light. BPA is used to produce certain types of plastic used in food storage; it can remain in the finished product and leak into food. After public pressure, many companies have removed BPA from their products. However, its replacement, bisphenol B, may be just as dangerous. Green chemistry efforts are underway to assess these hazards and find suitable replacements.

Wastewater Treatment. Water pollution has many sources: the chlorine added to water to reduce waterborne disease; sewage; and industrial waste, to name a few. Chlorine is particularly harmful; it reacts with other compounds to form carcinogens, which are then consumed by humans and by plants and animals that are later consumed by humans. Green chemistry can be used to remove some of this pollution, especially when applied before discharge. Many of the traditional treatment processes generate large amounts of toxic waste due to their use of hazardous chemicals to remove water contaminants. Green approaches to this issue focus on the use of microbes, less toxic chemicals, and chemicals that degrade rapidly into nontoxic components.

Agriculture. One of the biggest challenges in modern agriculture is pest control. The acres of well-maintained, fertilized, homogenous fields of crops are perfect feeding grounds for pests, and the plentiful food source and lack of predators leads to unprecedentedly large pest populations. The application of pesticides to combat these infestations poses a human health risk and an environmental hazard in terms of runoff and drift (wind-induced dispersion of sprayed pesticides). Furthermore, any given pesticide is usually only of limited application—insects quickly adapt to pesticides, rendering them useless after a certain amount of use. Scientists attempting to remedy this situation rely heavily on green chemistry and green chemical engineering. An example of the successful application of green chemistry in this field is Dow AgroSciences's development of spinosad, an insecticide that is produced by the decay of an organism, is effective in low doses, and degrades in sunlight quickly enough that it doesn't linger in the environment.

Pharmaceuticals. In addition to designing new drugs, pharmaceutical companies have much to gain from devising more efficient syntheses. As the patent expired on 4-isobutylacetophenone, which is used to produce the painkiller ibuprofen, its makers were motivated to find a new, less wasteful and toxic synthesis. The original synthesis produced large amounts of aluminum-contaminated wastewater and acidic gases and required cyanide and elemental phosphorus, which are extremely toxic. This process required six steps, and less than 40 percent of the atoms that were used as reactants ended up in the products (the rest being waste). At first glance, the newly devised synthesis sounds more toxic: it uses hydrofluoric acid, which is extremely dangerous and can cause death even when spilled on relatively small patches of skin. However, this synthesis uses hydrofluoric acid as a catalyst, meaning that it is recovered and repeatedly reused. Thus, considering the overall danger to humans and the environment, the new synthetic procedure is a dramatic improvement upon the original. In addition, the new synthesis requires only three steps and 80 percent of the atoms used as reactants are in the final products, a near-doubling of the efficiency of resource use.

Cosmetics and Personal Care Products. The cosmetics industry, which has long relied on petroleum products to produce moisturizers and cleansers, switched to palm oils in response to increasing economic pressure. Although this change satisfies the principle of using renewables whenever possible, the increase use of palm oils has led to various ecologically harmful practices, such as deforestation to create fields for palm crops and the carbon dioxide generation that accompanies modern agricultural practices. To overcome these issues, scientists have been studying ways to produce the key components of cosmetics in more environmentally friendly ways. For example, the paraffins found in lipstick wax may be able to be obtained from waste wheat straw, and enzymes may be able to create esters, which are used keep mixtures of oily and watery substances, such as lotions, from separating. From a health perspective, increased understanding of the dangers of certain compounds found in pesticides, health products, and food packaging has led to their removal. Until recently, some formulations of Johnson & Johnson's baby shampoo contained formaldehyde, a known carcinogen. The applications of green chemistry in this area serve to both increase the sustainability of manufacturing practices and decrease health risks.

Impact on Industry

As the field of green chemistry is still relatively new, there are few published statistics regarding current or future job prospects. According to the United States Bureau of Labor Statistics, the job growth from 2010 to 2020 for similar careers (e.g., chemist, chemical engineer) is expected to be approximately 5 percent. However, it could be argued that the demand for green chemists will grow fairly rapidly compared to that for other chemists as the global economic crisis and increased environmental regulation motivates improvements in efficiency and pollution reduction.

Occupation	Chemists
Employment 2010	82,200
Projected Employment 2020	85,400
Change in Number (2010–20)	3,200
Percent Change	4%

Bureau of Labor Statistics, 2012

Government Agencies. In all levels of government, green chemists work as researchers and consultants. On the national level, the EPA has a designated green chemistry program in addition to related offices, such as the Office of Pesticide Programs, the Office of Pollution Prevention and Toxics, and the Office of Research and Development. State governments also have similar agencies under the names Environmental Protection Agency, Department of Environmental Conservation, Department of Environmental Quality, and Department of Natural Resources, among others. These agencies address issues ranging from indoor air quality to lead contamination to oil spill cleanup. Government organizations at all levels play a crucial role in motivating green chemistry research and setting and enforcing regulations regarding acceptable exposure limits, waste treatment, and safe practices.

Military. The military has two very good reasons to prioritize green chemistry. First, the Department of Defense is the largest consumer of energy in the United States. Second, the military is highly aware of the security risk posed by reliance on foreign oil. The Army has launched a competition to encourage bases to adopt net-zero energy programs, whereas the Navy has vowed to have half its bases operating at net-zero energy use by 2020. Additional efforts include the movement to run all Navy ships on biofuel by 2016 and the widespread installation of solar panels. These changes would not be possible without green chemistry, which continues to reduce the financial tradeoffs of switching to net-zero energy use or emissions through such research efforts as reducing the cost and improving the efficiency of solar panels and finding ways to reuse waste to produce new materials or provide energy. As green chemistry continues to advance, it will become increasingly feasible and rewarding for both public and private enterprises to "go green."

University Research and Teaching. The number of green chemistry programs offered at American universities has been steadily increasing. Major programs include the University of York's Green Chemistry Centre of Excellence in the United Kingdom, the Center for Green Chemistry and Green Engineering at Yale and the Department of Chemistry at the University of Oregon. As the demand for green chemistry grows, the number of institutions offering designated programs will also grow. Academic institutions have been some of the earliest adopters of green chemistry research due to stipulations that require most grant applicants to elaborate upon how their research contributes to society. Many academic researchers have found green chemistry to be an excellent combination of basic science and research with clear humanitarian motivations.

Industry—Chemical Manufacturers. The use of green chemistry has intrinsic economic advantages for chemical manufacturers: Properly applied, green chemistry reduces costs by utilizing more efficient processes and reducing waste, which must be properly treated and disposed of, often at great expense. Chemical manufacturers and similar industries contribute large amounts of ground-level ozone and high global warming potential gases (namely, hydrofluorocarbons, perfluorocarbons, and sulfur hexafluoride) and will need to find alternative production processes to keep up with increasingly stringent environmental regulations. Furthermore, in terms of human health, green chemistry reduces the exposure of workers to potentially harmful chemical solvents and dangerous reaction conditions. It is not unusual for a synthesis to require high temperatures and pressures or known carcinogens.

Industry—Other. Many businesses have been able to leverage their green practices to improve public opinion of their brand. For example, Starbucks coffee company boasts about its environmental initiatives, ranging from expanded recycling programs to use of green building materials to forest conservation. The McDonald's fast-food chain also touts its collaboration with such agencies as Conservation International and Greenpeace. Many companies have made green chemistry the foundation of their business plan. Lush and The Body Shop are two examples of cosmetics companies that market their all of their products as being environmentally friendly and minimally toxic due to their utilization of various forms of green chemistry.

Occupation	Chemical technicians
Employment 2010	61,000
Projected Employment 2020	65,100
Change in Number (2010–20)	4,100
Percent Change	7%

Bureau of Labor Statistics, 2012

Social Context and Future Prospects

Interest in green chemistry is growing as society at large becomes more concerned with pollution and its long-term effects on our health. As evidenced by climate change and dwindling natural resources, many current lifestyles and industrial practices are unsustainable. In addition, people are becoming more aware of the negative effects of long-term exposure to some now-common synthetic materials, such as certain types of plastic. Although the benefits gained by the use of these materials may still outweigh the negative health effects, consumer pressure gives companies that can devise alternatives to these materials a marketplace advantage.

Green chemistry also has interesting economic ramifications for the producers of renewable resources. For example, the use of coconut husks in car parts would increase the price of coconut husks (currently considered waste), benefiting farmers in the equatorial regions in which they are grown. Furthermore, the reappropriation of waste into industrial feedstock also lessens the issue of how to dispose of this waste. In the example of coconut husks, Ghanaian farmers have traditionally disposed of coconut husks in a large pile. However, the coconut husks pose a health hazard in that they collect water, creating a breeding ground for mosquitoes, the transmitters of malaria to humans. Many other countries suffer from overflowing landfills, making waste reduction vital.

The long-term goal of green chemistry has been best expressed by its founder, Paul Anastas: "We'll know that green chemistry is successful when the term 'green chemistry' disappears because it's simply the way we do chemistry." Ideally, the principles of green chemistry will become seamlessly embedded in the design of new chemical processes. However, even if green chemistry becomes absorbed into chemistry at large, there will always be a need for researchers and consultants who specialize in assessing and improving the environmental friendliness of chemical reactions and products.

Further Reading

Anastas, Paul T., and John C. Warner. *Green Chemistry: Theory and Practice*. New York: Oxford UP, 2000. Print. A high-level textbook, written by the founders of green chemistry, that serves as the fundamental text for the field, introducing the major concepts and strategies of green chemistry.

"Green Chemistry." *US Environmental Protection Agency*. US Environmental Protection Agency, 18 June 2012. Web. 25 Oct. 2012. Provides an overview of the field and the EPA's green chemistry efforts, including sponsoring the Presidential Green Chemistry Challenge.

"Green Chemistry at a Glance." *American Chemical Society*. American Chemical Society, 2012. Web. 25 Oct. 2012. Includes information on the American Chemical Society's Green Institute, educational materials, and the latest green chemistry news.

Jacobs, Jeremy P. "'Green Chemistry' Guru Charting New Course for EPA Science." *New York Times*. New York Times, 20 June 2011. Web. 25 Oct. 2012. Outlines Anastas's dual role as scientist and bureaucrat, as well as his past and present contributions to the field.

Lancaster, Mike. *Green Chemistry: An Introductory Text*. Cambridge: RSC, 2010. Print. An overview of green chemistry that discusses the green technology industry, as well as research, alternative energy, renewable resources, and waste.

Matlack, Albert. *Introduction to Green Chemistry*. 2nd ed. New York: CRC, 2010. A thorough text on green chemistry that discusses some of the lesser-known areas of green chemistry, such as the environmental effects of population, feedstock, biofuel, and electronic waste.

About the Author: Cassandra Newell, BA, graduated from Colby College with a bachelor's degree in chemistry and Russian and attended graduate school at MIT, completing two and half years of work toward a PhD in physical chemistry before leaving to pursue other interests. Cassandra worked as a research assistant at both institutions, studying such topics as molecular recognition, guest-host chemistry, terahertz and acoustic spectroscopy, proton and electron transfer in chemical systems, and the physicochemical properties of a novel water-splitting catalyst with important renewable energy implications.

Analytical Chemist

> **Earnings (Yearly Average)**: $69,790 (Bureau of Labor Statistics, 2010)
>
> **Employment and Outlook**: Slower than average (Bureau of Labor Statistics, 2010)
>
> **O*NET-SOC Code**: 19-2031.00
>
> **Related Career Clusters**: Agriculture, Corrections & Security; Education & Training; Food & Natural Resources; Health Science; Law, Public Safety, Manufacturing

Scope of Work

The work of an analytical chemist, as the name indicates, is the analysis of material identities, quantities, and properties through the application of the principles of chemistry. This is essential for a number of practices and in many different contexts. In industrial applications, in which materials and specific compounds are produced, analytical chemists carry out procedures to determine that the materials being used and produced are the correct materials and of the correct purity for the specified standards. Analytical procedures are used to monitor the progress of chemical processes in order to control the rate at which they occur. In medical and biological fields, analytical chemists carry out procedures to determine and monitor the amounts of specific biochemical materials that are present in samples obtained from living systems, whether of human, animal, or plant origin. Forensic analysis, including DNA matching, is an invaluable tool in the investigation of criminal activities. Because all matter is chemical in nature, analytical chemists provide services in many fields, such as geology, art history, and archeology.

Education and Coursework

As a profession, analytical chemistry is a highly specialized branch of chemistry. At the same time, the methods and technologies of analytical chemistry are essential tools in the normal work of all branches of the chemical sciences. The value of those methods and technologies lies in a thorough comprehension of the underlying chemical and physical principles on which they are based. This therefore requires that the individual has the appropriate training for the work that will be carried out. Understanding of the fundamental principles is acquired through the corresponding course of study, which will vary according to position. This requires as a minimum the completion of a bachelor's degree with specialization in physical and analytical chemistry, and including general, organic, and inorganic chemistry, as well as biochemistry theory. However, for the majority of analytical chemistry positions, a bachelor's degree will not be sufficient; for analytical positions demanding the highest levels of accountability and accuracy, such as forensics laboratories and medical research facilities, a master's or doctorate is required. In the undergraduate degree program, individuals study the basic scientific principles that apply to that particular field of application. For example, in a program geared to routine biochemical analysis in an analytical service laboratory, the program includes training in basic chemistry, physics, and mathematics, reaction kinetics, and the routine analytical methods relevant to biochemical systems. For the more advanced master's and PhD degrees, however, the training will be much more extensive and theory-based, including such subject matter as pharmacology, radioisotope processes, detailed chemical and biochemical reaction mechanisms, a broader range of highly specialized and powerful analytical techniques, and with the normal requirement of completing a thesis project of original research. As with other career options, it is

---

Transferable Skills

- Organization & Management Skills – Managing equipment/materials (SCANS Workplace Competency – Resources)
- Technical Skills – Performing scientific, mathematical, and technical work
- Research & Planning Skills – Analyzing information
- Research & Planning Skills – Solving problems (SCANS Thinking Skills)
- Communication Skills – Reporting information
- Interpersonal/Social Skills – Working as a member of a team (SCANS Workplace Competency – Interpersonal)
- Work Environment Skills – Working in a laboratory setting

---

possible to acquire an idea of what a career in analytical chemistry might be like by observing analytical chemists at work first-hand, by arrangement with local hospitals, colleges, and universities, or through private industries. Any of these may provide the opportunity to observe the work that is carried out in their facilities, on a limited basis. Others may provide internships or volunteer opportunities. There are also a number of organizations whose purpose is to support the work of chemistry-based professions, including analytical chemistry, and several peer-reviewed journals in which the new work of analytical chemists is reported.

Career Enhancement and Training

In many cases, an individual working in an analytical service laboratory is required to hold certification from an accrediting organization as a requirement of the position. For example, a medical laboratory technician working in the analytical service department of a hospital typically must maintain certification credentials issued by the relevant society of laboratory technicians that sets the standards of performance that must be maintained by its members. In the United States, each state has its own regulatory body for this function. Through the appropriate society, as well as through numerous colleges and universities, ongoing training is available for its members, and is typically a requirement of membership in order to maintain currency with new standards and technologies as they become available. In other positions that require an advanced degree with a specialty in analytical methods, additional certifications are not required, but the individual is nonetheless expected to maintain currency of knowledge through additional training and continuous learning opportunities provided through training seminars presented by various industries and vendors of analytical devices, through attendance of workshops at professional conferences, and special postgraduate courses provided by colleges and universities. Networking is an important aspect of this ongoing education, since it provides the opportunity for individuals working in different locations to learn from each other's experiences, although the confidential nature of much of the material of analysis, especially in medical and forensic applications, can be an issue.

Daily Tasks and Technology

The typical day of an analytical chemist depends very much on the nature of the environment in which he or she works. For most, the day consists of preparing samples for analysis, keeping the appropriate records of the analytical procedures and results, and maintaining the equipment that is used. The technology of analytical chemistry is by far the most important aspect of an individual's daily tasks, and a great many different devices and techniques have been devised.

Regardless of the nature of the chemistry-based science in which analysis is being performed, the sole purpose of each and every device is the measurement of some very specific chemical or physical property. In the vast majority of cases, the property being measured is the quantity of a specific material that is present in a sample. Analytical chemists test water samples to determine the amount of dissolved materials that they contain, ranging from naturally occurring metallic salts such as iron and calcium to any of the various compounds considered to be pollutants, such as volatile organic compounds (VOCs), polychlorinated biphenyls (PCBs), and any of the hundreds of different pesticides and fertilizing materials that are used each day throughout the country. Analytical chemists in medical service laboratories routinely test blood, serum, and tissue samples for the amount of materials such as cholesterol, proteins, potassium, calcium, sodium, and other chemical and biochemical components that are present.

In forensics laboratories and chemical research facilities, analytical chemists use sophisticated devices such as high performance liquid chromatography, Fourier transform infrared spectrometers, mass spectrometers, nuclear magnetic resonance spectrometers, ultraviolet-visible spectrophotometers, and many other devices to determine the molecular structure and absolute identity of specific compounds that have been recovered from crime scenes. The materials of interest may be biological or chemical in nature, and range from DNA to simple dust. The important feature is the unique identity of the material, characterized through precise and strictly defined measurements.

Analysis is also an essential tool of quality control programs and process monitoring, especially in food sciences, pharmaceutical preparation, and the innumerable formulations used in industrial production processes.

Earnings and Employment Outlook

Automated analytical devices have replaced many of the positions that have traditionally employed analytical chemists, especially those in which the analyses are both routine and repetitive according to set procedures. An automated device can carry out literally hundreds of analyses per day, something that once required the work of several analytical chemists. The unfortunate aspect of this trend is that employment opportunities for analytical chemists have decreased in traditional areas, although new opportunities have arisen in other areas. Thus, the outlook for this career is that it will experience slower growth than the expected average. Because analytical chemistry is a more specialized field, it tends to command higher rates of pay. According to national salary survey data on the website *Payscale*, the average salary for analytical chemists ranged from $36,090 to $78,466 as of October 1, 2012. The US Bureau of Labor Statistics reported the median pay for analytical chemists in 2010 was $69,790 per year, or $33.55 per hour for full-time employment. This compares very favorably with other career options such as chemical technician, and this trend is not likely to change significantly given the vital importance of analytical chemistry in many fields. A bachelor's degree is considered the minimum credential for an entry-level analytical chemist position, although an associate's degree in a specific area of application, as mentioned above, is the minimum for the most basic positions in the corresponding area of application.

Related Occupations

- **Environmental Scientist:** Environmental scientists use analytical chemistry methods and techniques to determine the environmental presence of materials and the effects of human activities.

- **Agricultural and Food Scientist:** Agricultural and food scientists conduct chemical analysis of foodstuffs and the agricultural processes by which they are produced in order to help protect the safety of the world's food supply and to enhance the productivity of agricultural operations.

- **Biochemist or Biophysicist:** Biochemists and biophysicists use the methodologies of analytical chemistry in medical laboratories to study the chemical and physical principles of biological systems.

- **Geoscientist:** Geoscientists use analytical chemistry methods and techniques in the geological sciences to study and elucidate the chemical processes at work within the planet. They may also work in fields such as in archaeology.

- **Project Managers and Quality Control Specialists:** Analytical chemists are well suited to project management and other management positions, and are essential to quality control processes in many fields of application.

Future Applications

Analytical chemistry is bound to maintain its central and important role in the chemistry-based sciences as new methods and technologies arise. The introduction of more effective digital electronic devices, for example, will provide greater sensitivity in analytical procedures, and

A Conversation with Scott Shearer

Job Title: Vice President, Global Quality

What was your career path?

After receiving a Bachelor of Science (BS) degree in chemistry and a PhD in analytical chemistry, I spent five years as a bench chemist at a pharmaceutical company. I moved to a new company and began to have managerial responsibilities in an analytical chemistry lab. The responsibilities continued to increase and included quality control activities. At my next company I had responsibility for both quality assurance and quality control (or simply Quality). My responsibilities continued to increase to where I am today.

What are three pieces of advice you would offer someone interested in your profession?

1. A BS degree in a technical science field (chemistry, biology, pharmaceutical science, etc.) is very helpful.
2. Attention to detail is very important.
3. Ability to read and understand government regulations (e.g., 21 CFR Part 211) is critical.

What paths for career advancement are available to you?

Currently, I am at the top level of my field. The only advancement left would be to higher levels of VP (i.e., Senior VP, Executive VP).

perhaps produce entirely new methodologies for those procedures. In medical sciences, the growing population and the drive to achieve complete understanding of biological processes ensures that the demand for corresponding analytical chemistry-based procedures will also continue to grow apace. Similarly, environmental concerns are placing increasing pressure on analytical chemists to use and develop the science in order to achieve solutions to environmental problems. For example, analytical chemistry is essential for monitoring the

conditions arising from the many and various environmental disasters, large and small, that occur throughout the world, from possible
groundwater contamination to major disasters such as oil spills or the
radioactive contamination resulting from the 2011 tsunami that struck
Japan. Geochemistry is also a growing area of analytical chemistry, as
nations seek to find environmentally better and more effective means
of extracting and processing petroleum resources, and to replace those
resources with renewable resources of biological origin. Every aspect
of every science that deals with the chemical interactions of materials therefore requires the services of analytical chemists, and although
growth of the profession in general is expected to be relatively slow in
terms of employment opportunities, specific branches of the science
can be expected to grow at more rapid rates, and someone considering
a career in this field would be well advised to research specific growth
areas in order to identify the greatest opportunities.

Richard M. Renneboog, MS

More Information

American Academy of Forensic Sciences
410 N Twenty-First Street
Colorado Springs, CO 80904
www.aafs.org

American Chemical Society
1155 Sixteenth Street NW
Washington, DC 20036
www.acs.org

US Department of Labor
Division of Occupational Employment Statistics
PSB Suite 2135
2 Massachusetts Avenue NE
Washington, DC 20212-0001

Materials Science

FIELDS OF STUDY

Chemistry; physics; physical chemistry; spectroscopy; optics; photonics; quantum mechanics; statistical mechanics; electromagnetism; condensed-matter physics; fluid mechanics; solid-state physics; biophysics; biochemistry; plasma physics; classical mechanics; electronics; engineering; mechanical engineering; mathematics; calculus; differential equations; linear algebra; statistics; computational material design; computer science; materials chemistry; analytical chemistry; thermodynamics.

DEFINITION

Materials science examines the structure and properties of materials in order to create materials with useful and novel properties. To this end, materials scientists use principles from chemistry, physics, various subfields of engineering, and applied mathematics. Depending on the material being studied and its intended applications, other fields, such as biology or even planetary science, may be relevant. Materials science has applications in every imaginable industry in which synthetic materials are used and is responsible for countless innovations, among them lighter and stronger automotive parts, bacteria-resistant medical supplies, superior toothpastes, and plastic bags that keep fruit fresher. The key element that distinguishes materials science is the field's focus on the means of creating or developing materials rather than the basic science of the underlying principles.

Basic Principles

The advent of materials science occurred when humans first began to create tools and built structures. Its importance is exemplified by the fact that many time periods, including the Bronze Age, the Iron Age, and the Silicon Age, are named for the materials that contributed greatly to human development during those periods. Similarly, the Industrial Revolution, while not named for a specific material, refers to a period of significant development in the means of creating materials and incorporating them into devices. For much of history, knowledge of what would now be considered materials science was passed from parent to child, leading to the use of terms such as "smith" and "carpenter" as family names in addition to job titles. Later, apprenticeship became the dominant form of education, eventually evolving into the higher education system of the twenty-first century. Materials science is a common major or academic department at larger or more science-oriented colleges and universities, and the fields of chemistry, physics, biology, and engineering also encompass elements of the science.

Materials science and materials engineering often overlap; however, science and engineering are distinct fields. Scientists attempt to understand phenomena, whereas engineers seek to apply scientific knowledge to problems. Although these definitions are not mutually exclusive, scientists and engineers approach their work differently: A scientist might design a device as a proof of concept, whereas an engineer would experiment with different designs to optimize the performance of a given device. Thus, materials scientists are primarily concerned with understanding why materials behave as they do and using that knowledge to devise new materials, while materials engineers focus on optimizing the application of these concepts and materials for particular uses.

Core Concepts

Metals. Metals, as materials, are composed of metallic elements that exist as positively charged ions embedded in a sea of electrons, known as "delocalized electrons" because they are not tightly bound to their source atoms. These bonds contrast with covalent and ionic bonds, in which electrons are localized between their source atom and the bonded atom. Metals conduct electricity and heat well. Metal materials may be pure metals or alloys, which are mixtures of metals. Brass (composed of copper and zinc) and bronze (copper and tin) are examples of alloys.

Ceramics. Ceramics are solids that are held together by covalent or ionic bonds. Because the nature (strength, length, orientation) of these bonds depends on the identity of the constituent compounds, the properties of these materials vary much more dramatically than those of metals. Ceramics may be semiconductors (conductors of electricity at high temperatures) or superconductors (perfect conductors of electricity) or may be piezoelectric (the application of pressure influences its mechanical properties and vice versa) and pyroelectric (the application of heat influences its mechanical properties and vice versa).

Semiconductors. Semiconductors, the basis for electronics, conduct electricity at high temperatures. The conductivity of these materials can be fine-tuned through a process called "doping," which is the intentional introduction of a given impurity into an otherwise perfectly ordered material. This introduced material has a different number of electrons than the host material, which affects how readily electricity flows through the material. Doping produces either n-type or p-type semiconductors, depending on whether the impurity has more or fewer electrons than the host atoms, respectively.

Polymers. Polymers are solids composed of chains of repeating units, or monomers. For example, silk is composed of repeating units of fifty-nine amino acids, and polyethylene is composed of ethylene monomers. The properties of polymers can vary dramatically: Silk is a polymer, but amber and rubber are as well. This variation can be ascribed to the fact that both the identity of the monomer and its microstructure (how it is organized into a chain) determine how a polymer behaves. Examples of different microstructures include chains with branches, comb polymers (many shorter chains descending from a central chain, forming a comb shape), and star polymers (numerous polymers all extending from the same central point, forming a star shape). Polymers also differ in chain length.

Plastics. Plastics are polymers that retain whatever shape they are formed into, whereas nonplastic polymers, such as rubber, return to their original shape after the deforming force is removed. This property is known as plasticity. Plastics may also contain additives used as fillers or to fine-tune their properties. Like all polymers, plastics come in a wide variety of types, as defined by the constituent monomers and microstructure, and these types have different properties. Plastics are also categorized by how they respond to heating: Thermoplastics maintain their chemical structures when melted, while thermosetting plastics do not. Thus, thermoplastics can be molded repeatedly, whereas thermosets can only be molded once.

Composites. Composite materials contain numerous components with substantially different chemical and physical properties that retain these individual properties when combined. One example of a composite is concrete, which is composed of cement and an aggregate, such as sand or gravel. When combined to form concrete, neither the cement nor the aggregate undergoes physical or chemical changes.

Biomaterials. Biomaterials are materials with biological applications and biological materials that can serve other uses. In the former case, materials are designed to be incorporated into living things and must therefore exhibit biocompatibility, which refers to a material's ability to be accepted by a biological system, without toxicity in the original material or any of the degradation products that might be produced by exposure to physiological conditions. In the latter case, biological materials are altered to serve human needs, such as when wood is pressurized to create a building material that is much more resistant to decay and deformation than the original material.

Nanomaterials. Nanomaterials are materials on the nanoscale, that is, on the order of nanometers, or 10^{-9} meters. These materials are particularly interesting because the properties of nanoscale components are at times dictated by quantum mechanics rather than classical (Newtonian) mechanics. An example of nanomaterials is quantum dots, which are semiconductor particles with diameters of 2 to 10 nanometers. The color that these particles emit can be adjusted by changing their size, with smaller particles emitting colors toward the blue end of the spectrum and larger particles emitting colors toward the red end of the spectrum.

Applications Past and Present

Medicine. The applications of materials science in medicine range from new drug delivery systems to improved prostheses and artificial organs. The discovery of new materials for use in medical equipment has led to improvements in durability, cost, and practicality.

For example, dental fillings were made of gold for centuries. More recently, ceramic materials were used as cheaper alternatives, with the added advantage of being less noticeable due to their subtler, off-white color. However, ceramic fillings eventually degrade. To address this issue, researchers are working to develop new filling materials that are cheap, strong, biocompatible, and stable. One candidate material is titanium, which can be implanted into the jawbone itself in a biocompatible fashion. Materials science has similarly been key to the development of scaffolding used to grow tissue artificially. When tissues are grown in the laboratory, they require scaffolding for support, much like a vine requires a trellis. Materials scientists work to create biocompatible, effective scaffolding for this purpose.

Transportation. Materials scientists are responsible for scientific advancements that affect nearly every category of vehicle. The materials in the framework of these vehicles must be both lightweight for fuel efficiency and strong for safety. Furthermore, a wide range of materials is needed to produce everything from flame-retardant upholstery to heat-resistant engine parts. One example of a promising category of material for use in automobiles and other engine-propelled vehicles is piezoelectric ceramics, which are ceramics that respond to physical deformation with an electrical response and electrical stimulation with a physical deformation. Lead zirconate titanate is an example of a piezoelectric ceramic. In cars, piezoelectrics are used as passive sensors (for instance, in accelerometers or airbag impact sensors) and generators (spark plugs) due to their ability to convert movement or impact into electricity. They also function as active sensors (such as fuel level sensors) and actuators (such as those used to position mirrors) thanks to their ability to respond to electricity mechanically.

Electronics. The electronics industry was born of the development of new materials that gave humans great control over the flow of electrons and the ability to create circuits, allowing scientists to build devices to serve their needs. One of the most important classes of materials in the electronics industry is semiconductors. Silicon is an example of a semiconductor, and its prevalence in electronics has given rise to terms such as "Silicon Valley" and "the silicon revolution." The purity

---

Interesting Facts about Materials Science

- The strongest known synthetic material is graphene, a one-atom-thick sheet of carbon atoms that is two hundred times stronger than steel.

- Spider silk is one of the strongest naturally occurring materials and remains the subject of much study. The strength of spiderwebs is complemented by their unique stretching properties. Spiderwebs first soften and then harden during stretching, and this behavior is dependent on the direction and force of the stretching.

- The densest known synthetic material is ultradense deuterium, pending further experimental verification. This material, which is composed of deuterium atoms (hydrogen with an extra neutron) packed extremely closely, would be denser than the core of the sun, weighing 140 kilograms (about 300 pounds) per cubic centimeter.

- Among the lightest synthetic materials is aerogel, an analog of gel in which the liquid component is replaced by a gas, producing a smoky solid.

- Impurities can dramatically affect the behavior of a material. For example, water does not conduct electricity in its pure form. However, most water is an excellent conductor of electricity due to the presence of minerals and other impurities.

---

of silicon in electronics applications is crucial; one area of continuing research focuses on the development of better methods for creating thin films of pure silicon based on an understanding of its structure and properties.

Food and Drink. Packaging is crucial to keeping food fresh, especially considering how far most food must travel to reach the consumer's home. Containers for food such as produce must typically be transparent, allowing the buyer to check the contents for damage, and maintain the optimal levels of water vapor, oxygen, and carbon dioxide to maintain freshness and discourage rot or drying. For any food or drink container, it is crucial that the material not degrade or leach into the product, as such materials can harm human health. For example, bisphenol A (BPA) is present in some plastics but can disrupt the endocrine system when ingested. Studies suggest that BPA is present in most people in detectable quantities, which has raised particular concerns about pregnant women and the potential effects of fetal exposure to BPA. Companies have begun to phase out the use of BPA in food packaging both voluntarily and in response to new regulations. In response to such concerns, materials scientists are working to develop better materials and methods for packaging foodstuffs.

Energy. Materials science plays an important role in the attempt to meet ever-increasing energy demands across the globe as supplies of nonrenewable energy sources dwindle. For example, research into fuel cells, which turn fuel into electricity by means of a chemical reaction, relies on materials science to devise better anode, cathode, and electrolyte materials to improve the efficiency of these cells and best accommodate the specific fuels being used. Similarly, materials scientists are continually striving to create more efficient, sturdier, and more versatile photovoltaic systems, which convert solar energy into electricity, as well as to determine the materials that will create the cleanest, most efficient biofuels.

Sensors. Sensors are used in a wide range of fields to detect specific targets, which may include tumors, pollutants in wastewater, or physical imperfections in a crucial device component. Ideally, a sensor responds with high selectivity and specificity, meaning that it responds nearly every time it encounters the target and rarely responds to anything other than the target. The advantage of a sensor is that it responds to something that is difficult to detect, such as the presence of a contaminant in parts-per-million concentrations, in a way that is much easier to detect, such as by emitting light or changing color. One sensor design involves the use of self-assembled monolayers (that is, single layers of a material) on gold, glass, or another substrate to detect biologically relevant molecules. The binding of the target molecule improves the fluorescence of the self-assembled monolayer, and this change can be easily detected.

Impact on Industry

According to the US Bureau of Labor Statistics, employment of chemists and materials scientists, which the organization groups into a single category, is expected to increase by 4 percent between 2010 and 2020. This growth rate is slower than the average for all occupations. However, this grouping overlooks some of the differences between and among materials science and chemistry careers. Indeed, the employment outlook for materials scientists is likely to be significantly better than that for many other scientists due to the direct applicability of materials science to products and the wide range of applications requiring improved materials. Employment opportunities in materials science are and will continue to be primarily in industry. The United States, the member nations of the European Union, and China contain particularly large numbers of materials scientists due to their strong economic positions and large manufacturing bases.

Government Agencies. Materials scientists hold research positions in numerous national laboratories and work as consultants in many federal and state government agencies that involve the creation or implementation of new technology, such as the Environmental Protection Agency. An agency of particular relevance for materials scientists is the National Science Foundation's Division of Materials Research. This entity is not a research group per se; rather, it provides funding for research projects, keeps interested parties abreast of developments in the field, hosts materials science events, and recognizes outstanding developments in the field. It is also a good resource for materials scientists seeking employment, offering a listing of relevant vacancies and networking events.

Military. Materials science is vital to the creation of new vehicles, armor, and weapons. The US Army Research Laboratory has a division devoted to materials science, which focuses on several different areas of research: mechanical behavior of materials, synthesis and processing of materials, physical properties of materials, and materials design. These groups investigate such topics as the synthesis of materials under extreme pressures, time restraints, and temperatures and the ways in which materials respond to extreme stress, such as that caused by a bullet.

University Research and Teaching. An increasing number of universities are creating dedicated materials science departments; however, materials scientists can find work in a wide variety of departments, including chemistry, physics, biology, and engineering departments as well as the more highly specialized departments found at larger research universities. The practicality and employment outlook of the field make it a very attractive field for students seeking job and financial security.

Occupation	Chemical technicians
Employment 2010	61,000
Projected Employment 2020	65,100
Change in Number (2010–20)	4,100
Percent Change	7%

Bureau of Labor Statistics, 2012

In addition to professors, many universities hire researchers and support staff knowledgeable about materials science to accelerate progress.

Electronics Industry. The electronics industry would not exist without the developments made in materials science. Advances in this field are largely possible due to the introduction of improved or entirely new materials. Thus, this industry relies heavily on materials scientists and is one of the primary employers of professionals in the field.

Petroleum and Energy Industries. Petroleum- and energy-related industries are key employers of materials scientists. Researchers in these industries may study the properties of sediment containing fossil fuel in order to inform extraction techniques or work to create superior plastics from petroleum. The field of renewable energies is also ripe with materials science opportunities; for instance, scientists may design more efficient solar cell materials, materials that use algae to convert carbon dioxide into oxygen, or novel biofuels.

Other Industries. Most of the industries that create tangible products use materials developed by materials scientists. The personal care industry uses materials science to design better toothbrushes, while the construction industry uses materials science to design better building materials. The manufacturing industry relies heavily on materials science to develop better ways of manufacturing products. Other relevant industries include the textile industry, in which scientists may work to produce stronger or more climate-appropriate clothing, and the food and drink industry, in which researchers may develop new materials in which to package and transport foods.

Social Context and Future Prospects

Materials science will likely continue to contribute to significant advances in industry and science as a whole and particularly in the medical field. For example, much of the work in the fields of cancer detection and treatment involves the creation of biocompatible materials that can target tumors, such as tumor-targeting quantum dots that fluoresce after reaching their targets. Other materials are being designed to deliver chemotherapy drugs directly to tumors, minimizing the damage done to healthy cells and allowing the patient to maintain better overall health during the treatment. As these technologies mature, the identification and treatment of cancer will become more successful and less invasive. On a broader scale, materials science offers potential treatments for a wide range of human ailments, promising to improve the overall quality of life.

Occupation	Materials scientists
Employment 2010	8,700
Projected Employment 2020	9,600
Change in Number (2010–20)	900
Percent Change	10%

Bureau of Labor Statistics, 2012

Another prominent example of the social significance of materials science is its relevance in addressing climate change. As the negative effects of human activity on the environment become increasingly clear, pressure is mounting to find more economical and efficient ways to use natural resources. To this end, materials science has sought to find ways to reduce dependence on nonrenewable resources and reuse "waste" material in an economically viable fashion. For example, a key area of research in materials science is the improvement of solar cells. Future solar cells will be more efficient, more versatile, and less expensive to make. Another popular research area is the use of waste material as a substitute for freshly generated material in various production and manufacturing processes. For example, materials scientists seek to incorporate agricultural waste, such as coconut husks and palm fronds, into new materials and use waste materials to generate energy to offset the energy consumed by processing raw agricultural products.

Further Reading

Gordon, J. E. *The New Science of Strong Materials; or, Why You Don't Fall Through the Floor.* Princeton: Princeton UP, 2006. Print. Conveys why materials science is integral to the development of new technology and explains the basic scientific principles that define the properties of many common materials.

Hosford, William F. *Materials Science.* New York: Cambridge UP, 2007. Print. Provides an overview of the key concepts and principles of materials science, serving as a comprehensive introduction to the field.

Hummel, Rolf E. *Understanding Materials Science: History, Properties, Applications.* 2nd ed. New York: Springer, 2004. Print. Discusses the mechanical and electrical properties of materials and analyzes some of the anthropological, social, and economic implications of materials development.

Irene, Eugene A. *Electronic Materials Science.* Hoboken: Wiley, 2005. Print. Surveys the applications of materials science to electronics, one of the field's key areas of research.

"Materials Science." *ACS.* American Chemical Society, n.d. Web. 10 Sept. 2012. Provides an authoritative description of what materials science is, what materials scientists do, and the job prospects in the field.

About the Author: Cassandra Newell graduated from Colby College with a bachelor's degree in chemistry and Russian language and literature and attended MIT, completing two and a half years of work toward a PhD in physical chemistry before leaving to pursue other interests. She worked as a research assistant at both institutions, studying such topics as molecular recognition, guest-host chemistry, terahertz and acoustic spectroscopy, proton/electron transfer in chemical systems, and the physicochemical properties of a novel water-splitting catalyst with important renewable energy implications. Since leaving academia, she has pursued projects pertaining to science communication, such as editing scientific manuscripts and writing about science for nonspecialists.

Materials Chemist

Earnings (Yearly Average): $69,760 (Bureau of Labor Statistics, 2012)

Employment and Outlook: Slower than average growth (Bureau of Labor Statistics, 2012)

O*NET-SOC Code: 19-2031.00

Related Career Clusters: Agriculture, Food & Natural Resources; Architecture & Construction; Manufacturing

---

Scope of Work

Materials chemists work to understand the relationship between the atomic and molecular structures of materials and the physical properties of those materials, ultimately seeking to improve the performance of existing materials as well as develop new materials. Production processes are a significant aspect of materials chemistry, as these determine the physical structure of a material at the atomic level. Materials chemists may also study how materials change internally as the result of their everyday performance. All such structures and phenomena must be describable within the framework of modern atomic theory. Materials chemists work in a wide variety of industries, particularly in research and materials management. Others use their knowledge to teach materials science in academic and industrial engineering programs. Ongoing research and development in materials chemistry and materials science in general is essential to a great many fields, especially with regard to electronics and computer technology.

Education and Coursework

A career in materials chemistry typically requires significant specialized education. A bachelor's degree is the minimum requirement for materials science positions, and a master's degree or doctorate in a specific area of expertise is generally preferred. Materials chemists

---

Transferable Skills

- Writing concisely (SCANS Basic Skill)
- Working as a member of a team (SCANS Workplace Competency – Interpersonal)
- Using technology to process information (SCANS Workplace Competency – Information)
- Understanding which technology is appropriate for a task (SCANS Workplace Competency – Technology)
- Applying the technology to a task (SCANS Workplace Competency – Technology)
- Performing scientific, mathematical and technical work
- Working with machines, tools or other objects
- Working with data or numbers

---

must have a solid background in mathematics, chemistry, physics, engineering, and technology as well as administration and management practices. They must also be versed in communications and writing, as they may need to present their findings verbally or in writing to employers, government organizations, or peers.

The specific educational path an aspiring materials chemist takes depends a great deal on the type of materials that are of interest. A metallurgist, for example, would not be required to study the same areas that a polymer specialist, electronic materials specialist, or biomaterials specialist would be required to study. It is therefore very important to decide on an area of specialization before beginning advanced studies, as this will play a large part in determining which institution and program of study to attend. Advanced degree programs focus on academic training in specific areas of chemistry, which may include synthetic organic chemistry, advanced bioorganic chemistry, organometallic chemistry, and colloid chemistry. In addition, a student seeking an advanced degree must typically carry out an original research project and write a thesis.

It is possible for interested students to gain some experience in materials chemistry before committing to the years of study necessary to complete an advanced degree in an area of specialization. One way is to undertake a short-term training program through a private training facility or community college. For example, a short training program in advanced composite materials can provide a broad working knowledge of those materials and their properties sufficient to encourage further study and may also qualify the individual to seek employment in that field if further study is not desired. Organizations such as the American Chemical Society and the Institute of Materials, Minerals and Mining also provide numerous educational resources for potential and practicing materials chemists.

Career Enhancement and Training

Materials chemists are not generally required to hold licenses or certifications in order to work in the field. In some cases, however, a specific certification is required by federal regulations. For example, a materials chemist with an advanced degree in polymer science or advanced composites would still be required by regulations to maintain a government-recognized certification in order to work in aircraft maintenance with advanced composites. Because the field of materials chemistry changes as new materials and applications are developed, materials chemists must remain up to date on developments and changes that take place in their particular fields of expertise. Many institutions therefore offer postgraduate or extension-learning opportunities to allow individuals to upgrade their knowledge.

Conferences and seminars provide a means of both learning about advancements in the field and developing a professional network with others working in similar fields. Networking is an essential aspect of careers in dynamically changing fields such as materials chemistry. It is important to use such a network both to acquire new knowledge and to identify new opportunities for research, employment, or education.

Daily Tasks and Technology

Materials chemists perform a variety of functions in their daily work. Practical work is carried out in laboratories to test processes and methods by which specific materials are made or to examine the internal structures of materials and their responses to various applied forces such as tension, compression, and shear. Another significant aspect of laboratory work is quality testing of materials and components made from them in order to ensure that they meet specified performance requirements and remain within required tolerances. In some industries, a materials chemist may oversee and carry out a single essential process and ensure that the product of that process meets standards of composition and quality. Materials chemists are typically required to prepare reports and communicate with different clients and associates on a regular basis.

In research-oriented roles, materials chemists may use a variety of analytical methods to examine the microscopic internal structures and physical properties of materials and relate those to material strengths and weaknesses. Materials chemists filling administrative roles may plan the testing and maintenance of material supplies, meet with customers in order to determine needs and the most appropriate materials to use, and interact with suppliers to obtain materials that meet the specific requirements of a particular application. In a teaching environment, materials chemists instruct others in the detailed science of materials and material strengths.

The technology applicable to the practice of materials chemistry is as varied as the materials studied, as different materials and processes call for specialized test methods. Typical analytical devices such as spectrometers and other measuring devices are used routinely for study of material compositions. Other measuring devices are used to determine such properties as electrical resistance and material hardness. In the most advanced research applications, devices such as the atomic force microscope are used to prepare and study specific material combinations on the nanoscale.

Earnings and Employment Outlook

Overall employment growth within the field of materials chemistry is expected to be somewhat slower than average. However, this should not be taken to mean that all specialized areas within the field will exhibit the same behavior. The field is subject to dynamic change, such that the development of a single new material, process, or application can spur rapid and significant growth in that area. There are several areas that promise to experience rapid growth within the overall field of materials science. One such area is biomaterials, as scientists seek to develop new materials that can interact with or replace organic materials such as living bone, skin, and other tissues. Other growing areas of research include the development of fuels from renewable resources and the creation of advanced materials, particularly composites, for applications in aerospace and transportation technologies. Perhaps the most significant area of growth is the field of electronic materials, as electronic technology approaches the limits of the capabilities of present materials. As demand for materials chemists in these fields grows, it can be expected that wage standards will also increase until the supply of qualified persons exceeds the demand for their services, after which the wage standard will likely decrease somewhat. Unlike other fields, however, materials chemistry offers significant opportunities for the development of residual incomes from patents for both materials and processes.

Overall employment growth within the field of materials chemistry is expected to be somewhat slower than average.

Related Occupations

- **Chemical Engineers:** Chemical engineers focus on the application of chemistry to industrial processes and may produce or design materials or systems.

- **Polymer Chemists:** Polymer chemists work within the broader field of materials chemistry, focusing exclusively on the properties of polymeric materials.

- **Biochemists:** Biochemists examine the properties of living things, such as plants or animals, and study their composition and biochemical processes.

A Conversation with Nina S. Lewin

Job Title: Attorney

What was your career path?

I graduated with a degree in chemistry from Colgate University and went on to work in the plastics and coating industry, first as a technical support person and then as a sales engineer. My science background was a key to my success and to my ability to give clients a value-added approach to selling what the companies had to offer. I then went on to start a business with my husband, another chemist, in the high-purity water industry. Our philosophy of being proficient in the scientific field we were working in gave our clients confidence in our abilities to work with them to solve their technical problems, not just sell them a product. Now I am a criminal defense attorney. My scientific background is sometimes a hindrance (I am not the storyteller many of my colleagues are) and often a help (I understand the science and limitations behind DNA, breathalyzer machines, fingerprinting, etc.). The logical and scientific approach to problem solving is an advantage for me.

What are three pieces of advice you would offer someone interested in your profession?

1. Stick with the sciences—the method of thinking will benefit you in any subsequent field you enter.
2. Make sure you like working in the lab or find an ancillary job that requires an understanding of the science without the daily hands-on component.
3. You can usually learn anything else well when you have done well in the sciences.

What paths for career advancement are available to you?

Once you have a science degree, I think you can do anything else you want to! I went on to law school twenty-five years after I got my chemistry degree. Your science degree will open many doors.

- **Quality Control Analysts:** Quality control analysts ensure that the materials used by scientists in many fields meet specific standards of quality and composition.

- **Materials Managers:** Materials managers supervise the use and storage of specialized materials in order to maintain their usability and to protect the safety of others.

Future Applications

Materials chemists will likely continue to play a crucial role in the development of key materials and processes, and their importance to technological development as a whole should not be underestimated. The entire electronic revolution came about as the result of a single experiment that demonstrated the feasibility of the transistor. The original device was a crude conglomeration of components that occupied a space roughly equivalent to the palm of one's hand, based on theoretical principles of materials chemistry that predicted how the device should work. By the early twenty-first century, literally millions of functional transistors were routinely formed on silicon chips in an area the size of a fingernail. Using materials that are in development, scientists seek to allow for the storage of one terabyte of data, or more, in an area of one square centimeter. Studies being carried out by materials chemists using atomic force microscope technology are pointing the way to the production of transistors on the atomic and molecular scale. The chemistry of graphene and carbon nanotubes in particular promises to revolutionize not only electronics but also materials science in general, as new applications for these materials are found in areas ranging from biomaterials to advanced electronics.

Richard M. Renneboog, MS

More Information

American Chemical Society
1155 16th Street NW
Washington, DC 20036
www.acs.org

Materials Chemistry Thematic Research Group
McGill University
801 Sherbrooke Street West
Montreal, Quebec, Canada H3A 2K6
www.chemistry.mcgill.ca/index.php

Society of Plastics Engineers
13 Church Hill Road
Newtown, CT 06470
www.4spe.org

Medicinal Chemistry

FIELDS OF STUDY

Chemistry; organic chemistry; inorganic chemistry; biochemistry; pharmacology; synthetic organic chemistry; biology; natural products chemistry; kinetics; mathematics; physics; analytical chemistry.

DEFINITION

Medicinal chemistry is the application of chemistry to the identification, synthesis, and preparation of pharmaceutical and medicinal compounds. Medicinal compounds come from a variety of sources and ideally serve a single purpose in their application as pharmaceuticals. The basic science of pharmaceutical materials is organic chemistry, which is utilized in the analysis and identification of biologically active materials, the preparation of those materials and their derivatives, and determination of their modes of function within biological systems. Synthetic organic chemistry is a very broad field of study and application and is the means by which chemical compounds are prepared in usable quantities.

Basic Principles

Medicinal chemistry is predicated on the fact that all life depends on a complex combination of chemical and biochemical processes. Within each process, each specific chemical material performs a specific function. Of course, the same material may be involved in several different processes, so there is also a great deal of overlap between systems. The interplay between all of the systems results in the individual living being, from the smallest and simplest of protozoa to the most complex and largest of animals and plants. The failure of a particular biological or biochemical system to function normally or the invasion and infection of the living being by other organisms can produce various states of illness in the individual; these resulting illnesses often requiring treatment with medicinal materials that will correct the biochemical problem or eliminate the invasive organisms. Medicinal chemistry generally refers to the identification and preparation of medicinal materials, based on the mode of action in which they are to be employed. This includes the preparation of both entirely synthetic compounds as well as compounds from natural sources, based on the principles of organic chemistry and biochemistry. This is very much a two-way process, as medical practitioners and researchers work to identify the nature and causes of medical and other errant conditions affecting people, animals, and plants. This knowledge initiates the research in medicinal chemistry to find and create the pharmaceuticals needed for the treatment of those conditions.

Core Concepts

The essential sciences of medicinal chemistry are synthetic organic chemistry, biochemistry, bioorganic chemistry, and biology, with analytical procedures being the most used and useful tool.

Synthetic Organic Chemistry. Synthetic organic chemistry is the branch of organic chemistry that deals with the theory and methodology of synthesizing specific molecules by controlled reactions of other molecules and compounds. It is founded on an in-depth understanding of the ways in which various functional groups within organic molecules can react with other materials and chemical agents. This is affected by the electronic structure of the particular compounds and functional groups, as well as by physical restrictions arising from the three-dimensional shapes of the reacting molecules. Much of the work of synthetic organic chemists involves finding ways around those restrictions in order to carry out a synthetic reaction that will yield a desired product having the correct molecular geometry. A great number of traditional and modern medicines have been obtained from natural plant and animal sources, and an untold number of such compounds are yet to be discovered. The natural products chemist—using the principles of organic and analytical chemistry—works to identify new compounds from plant and animal sources. It then falls to the synthetic organic chemist to find means of preparing those same compounds artificially so that the natural source need not be destroyed for harvesting of a compound. This is especially important when an identified material is available only in very small quantities, as was the case with the anticancer compound Taxol, obtained from the Pacific yew tree.

Bioorganic Chemistry. Bioorganic chemistry is also founded on the same functional group chemistry, but is concerned only with the limited number of functional groups that are involved in biochemical compounds and interactions. These are the materials of protein and tissue structures, energy transfer, ion transport, hormones, regulators, and the multitude of other known and unknown chemical components of living systems. It is estimated that there are more than one hundred thousand different chemical compounds involved in the various biochemical cycles that compose a living system, each behaving according to the fundamental principles of chemistry to perform a single role in the overall system. Bioorganic chemists work to identify the individual components of each system—some of which are present in mere picogram quantities—and to understand how each component attains, and is affected by, its unique three-dimensional structure. Proteins, for example, are composed of numerous amino acids in polymeric chains, linked together through the peptide bond structure in which the carboxylic acid function of one amino acid unit is bonded to the amine function of another amino acid unit. Since each amino acid contains both a carboxylic acid function and an amine function, the resulting protein is essentially a linear polyamide. However, due to the geometry of the amino acid groups and the electronic nature of the substituent groups attached to them, proteins acquire a complex three-dimensional shape that is determined by the identities of their component amino acids. Within the overall structure of the protein molecules are local regions that have a specific three-dimensional shape and electronic environment that enables them to interact only with molecules and parts of molecules that have a complementary shape and electronic structure. These materials, typically called enzymes, are responsible for carrying out essentially all biochemical reactions within the living system; each has a very specific function within that system. Understanding and identifying those functions is an essential component of medicinal chemistry, as the interactions of these materials with pharmaceutical compounds are essential to whether or not the pharmaceutical compound is effective.

Biochemistry. Biochemistry is the more general science of the chemical nature of living systems and includes the specialist field of bioorganic chemistry. Whereas bioorganic chemistry is concerned only with the reactions and interactions of organic molecules within living systems, biochemistry has the broader context that incorporates minerals and inorganic salts, gas exchange, ion transport mechanisms, energy transfer thermodynamics, cell structures, and kinetics of processes occurring in and between cells in an organism. There is, of course, a great deal of overlap between biochemistry and bioorganic chemistry; the extensive nature of the science of biochemistry has also led to other areas of specialization within that field. Biochemists study the chemical and physical principles behind the processes that occur within living systems, such as genetics, cell division, and cell structure formation. The ultimate goal of biochemical research is to know and define all of the various processes so that a complete understanding of living systems can be obtained, which in turn would allow an equal understanding of how living systems can fail and what to do for them medicinally when they do fail.

Biology. Biologists work to identify the various organic and physical systems within living organisms, the focus being on the macroscopic scale rather than the chemical scale. In the context of medicine this is in order to understand the reasons and manners in which those systems can malfunction so that they can be repaired through the use of the appropriate medicines and medical treatments.

Analytical Procedures. In all areas related to medicinal chemistry, analytical procedures are essential to the undertaking. In the operation of research that is chemical in nature, practitioners utilize the range of analytical devices and techniques typical of chemistry in general. This is especially true in the isolation and identification of new compounds isolated from natural sources. Such analysis allows the researcher to determine the molecular structure of the material, which is absolutely essential for any synthetic approach to preparing the material in quantity by artificial means. In medical practice, spectrometers and other analytical measuring devices are often utilized to determine the quantities of specific biochemical compounds present in living systems; this is a means to monitor the functioning of specific medicinal compounds. In the biological aspect of the field other devices, such as microscopes, are used to examine in detail the pathology of tissues that are affected by various conditions and the medicinal compounds developed for testing.

Applications Past and Present

Basis in Traditional Medicine. Every aspect of medicinal chemistry derives from the starting point of native herbal lore and the use of specific plant materials for the treatment of specific ailments. In many cultures this is a refined and well-respected art, if not an exact science. With the growth of workable chemical theories—still long before the development of the modern atomic theory and its ability to define molecular structures—scientists of the day began to isolate and identify various chemical principles from natural sources and to associate them with medicinal uses. One of the oldest of these was salicin, an anti-inflammatory agent isolated by the German chemists from the bark of the white willow tree. Today, this material is known as salicylic acid, the fundamental component of its acetylated derivative (aspirin, acetylsalicylic acid, or ASA). Due to its uncomplicated molecular structure, chemists of that time were able to prepare industrial quantities of this material using the empirical knowledge of synthetic chemistry that was available to them. Prior to this, medicinal compounds were obtained solely through extraction from their natural sources, and it was long believed that only living or organic systems could produce the materials that were extracted from them.

Early Organic Chemistry. This belief was disproven when, in 1828, a German chemist by the name of Friedrich Wöhler was able to synthesize urea, a naturally occurring organic material, from entirely nonorganic starting materials. The discoveries related to salicin and urea mark the beginning of modern medicinal chemistry. The science received its greatest boost, however, with the development of modern atomic theory, with its ability to describe molecular structures, reaction mechanisms, molecular geometries, and reaction energetics.

Interesting Facts about Medicinal Chemistry

- In the mid-1800s, the French chemist Louis Pasteur discovered that tartaric acid exists in two forms that are identical to each other, except that their molecular structures are mirror images. Such compounds are called "enantiomers." Ensuring that the molecular structure about an enantiomeric center in a molecule is correct is the most difficult challenge in synthetic organic chemistry.

- Before German chemist Friedrich Wöhler produced the organic compound urea from entirely inorganic materials in 1828, it was believed that compounds from biological sources could not be produced artificially.

- Medicinal chemistry is founded on the science of synthetic organic chemistry, in which chemists seek to produce artificially—or synthesize—compounds having specific molecular structures through sequences of controlled reactions.

- Bioorganic chemistry is the study of the manner in which organic chemical reactions are carried out in the essentially inorganic, water-based medium of living systems.

- Organic materials were originally thought of as being vital for life, and «vitalists» believed organic materials could not be produced from inorganic materials. Inorganic materials were correspondingly thought of as not being vital for life. Science has long since demonstrated that both organic and inorganic materials are necessary for the health of living systems.

- The antitumor drug known as paclitaxel, otherwise known as Taxol, is produced by the Pacific yew tree only in small amounts. Harvesting sufficient material for testing almost led to the extinction of the Pacific yew tree, but medicinal chemists were able to prevent this by successfully synthesizing Taxol in the laboratory.

Perhaps the most important aspect of organic chemistry to be developed, in regard to medicinal compounds, was French chemist Louis Pasteur's discovery of the property of chemical enantiomorphism—the ability to have mirror image forms—before turning his attention to the fermentation process and bacteriology. This is the property wherein a single compound can exist in two forms in which the corresponding molecular structures are identical in every way, except that one is the mirror image of the other. Such compounds also have identical physical and chemical properties, and are differentiated from each other only by their effect on plane-polarized light. When passed through a sample of each form, one will rotate the plane of the polarized light in the clockwise direction (to the right, or dextrorotatory), while the other will rotate the plane of the polarized light by the same amount in the counterclockwise direction (to the left, or levorotatory). It is a curious fact that all known biochemical systems use the levorotatory isomers exclusively and are unable to use the dextrorotatory isomers. Since all of the amino acids used in the formation of proteins are "optically active" in the levorotatory sense, this feature has had an enormous role in the development of living systems through evolutionary processes and in determining the overall shape of protein molecules and other biochemicals; it is also a vitally important aspect of the successful synthesis of all medicinal compounds.

Two Branches of Medicinal Chemistry. Partly because of the early relationship of organic chemistry to biological systems, the work of synthetic chemists has fallen into two basic camps with regard to medicinal chemistry. The first is the isolation and identification of compounds from natural sources, or natural products chemistry. This branch entails a heavy component of analysis following the recovery of a previously unknown material from a plant or animal source that may have been experiencing stress or a specific set of environmental conditions. Analysis is carried out to determine the exact molecular weight of the compound and to fully characterize its chemical and physical properties. This is achieved through various methodologies: Infrared spectrometric analysis is used to determine the types of functional groups that are present in the molecule; spectrometric analysis in the ultraviolet and visible range provides information about the nature of the bonds between atoms in the molecule. Nuclear magnetic resonance (NMR) spectrometry—based on different base nuclei, chiefly proton and carbon-13—is used to identify the bonding, three-dimensional orientations and positions of hydrogen and carbon atoms, respectively, within the molecular structure. Mass spectrometry is used to determine the exact molecular mass of the compound, as well as to provide structural information from the fragmentation patterns that are observed, although NMR is by far the more powerful technique for obtaining structural information. Numerous other properties can also be tested, but these methods are the primary analytical techniques. These methods are also routinely applied in monitoring the progress of reactions and determining their effectiveness.

The second branch, which is also the primary focus of medicinal chemistry, is synthetic organic chemistry. In this discipline, the chemist draws upon the wealth of documented knowledge about various reactions and the conditions under which they are carried out. This provides the basic steps for the synthesis of specific compounds, as the synthetic chemist can be assured of what to expect when the same or very similar reactions are carried out in the same way. On numerous occasions, however, a reaction procedure will not work, or is unsuitable for other reasons, and new synthetic methods must be sought. Research in synthetic methods is an extensive field of synthetic organic chemistry in its own right. Generally, the goal of synthetic methods research is to find a means of producing a specific molecule or part of a molecule cleanly and efficiently (without undesirable side products) or to prove the viability of a previously untried material in carrying out a specific type of reaction.

Medicinal Chemistry Research. As medicinal chemistry is inextricably linked to biochemistry and biology—and the ultimate end of pharmaceutical materials is to function in harmony within living systems so as to ameliorate or cure a pathological condition—the range of materials involved in medicinal chemistry is greatly extended. In the twenty-first century a great deal of research is carried out in the field of molecular cell biology, in which the interactions of various compounds with the materials of genetics and cell structures is the focus. Here as well, a great deal of analysis and testing is carried out, employing several methodologies that are relevant to chemistry in general and some that are unique to biological systems. Electrophoretic separations of biological components, particularly of DNA and other proteins, is one of the most generally applicable techniques and provides a unique characterization for biological compounds. Technological advances beyond the electron microscope also play a role in biological analysis, though they are limited to surface analysis at the atomic level. Such devices as the scanning tunneling microscope and the atomic force microscope now make it possible for researchers to examine cell structures such as viruses and molecular structures such as DNA more closely than has ever been possible. They also enable the manipulation of individual atoms, allowing distinct atomic-scale structures to be constructed and tested.

Impact on Industry

Government Agencies. Medicinal chemistry is a highly regulated field, because the end result is the production of pharmaceutical materials that will be used by people. It is therefore imperative that all precautions be taken to safeguard people against ineffective drugs and the harmful side effects of useful ones. It would not be good, for example, to release a drug for general use that cures headaches but causes kidney failure as a side effect. Potential new drugs are thus required to undergo a great deal of testing and verification before they will be added to the national pharmacopeia and released for use. This requirement increases the cost of developing new drugs and medicinal materials. The testing and verification stage is also the point at which the various fields and branches involved in the science of medicinal chemistry come together. The National Institutes of Health (NIH) and the Centers for Disease Control (CDC) are the principal watchdog organizations in the United States, and collaborate extensively with their counterparts in other countries, such as Health Canada. The Environmental Protection Agency (EPA) also has a vested interest in medicinal chemistry, since the production processes for pharmaceuticals carry a significant risk of industrial pollution and the waste products of pharmaceutical consumption typically are introduced into the environment through wastewater, sewage, and physical disposal.

Military. Military interests in medicinal chemistry are narrower than they are for general consumption because they focus primarily on the amelioration of situations that may be encountered by military personnel. Medicinal chemistry in the military context—not including research that would also benefit the general public—can be traced back to World War I and the development of counteractives for gas and chemical warfare. Such materials as mustard gas and lewisite demanded the development of specific pharmaceutical materials that would counteract the effects of those materials in anyone who had been exposed. In the late twentieth and early twenty-first centuries, the

Occupation	Medical scientists
Employment 2010	100,000
Projected Employment 2020	136,400
Change in Number (2010–20)	36,400
Percent Change	36%

Bureau of Labor Statistics, 2012

threats posed by nerve gases and by biological agents used in warfare and acts of terrorism are taken very seriously—especially with the appearance of new viruses and the resurgence of viruses and diseases once thought to have been entirely defeated by medical science. Evolution is a dynamic process that continually changes the playing field as viruses and bacteria mutate and become resistant to existing pharmaceuticals.

Medicinal chemistry in the military context inevitably has negative outcomes as well as beneficial goals. It is an unavoidable fact that, in searching for materials that will have positive effects, researchers discover materials that can have potential as weapons and will be deadly if misused. The defensive value of this knowledge should not be underestimated: It is important to understand the threat of materials that can be used as weapons so that effective measures can be developed to prevent the damage they may cause if used aggressively.

University Research and Teaching. Medicinal chemistry is one of the most rapidly growing fields of science and application, and as such demands the services of qualified teachers and researchers. Very few of these positions are available to anyone with less than a PhD, although a master's degree is acceptable in some cases. Essentially all research conducted in universities is funded through grants, often in collaboration with pharmaceutical companies and their research departments. Given the scope of medicinal chemistry, it should not be surprising that research and teaching in universities involves many different departments and their faculties, with members from various departments often forming a collaborative research group spanning many areas of expertise.

Social Context and Future Prospects

Medicinal chemistry holds a unique place in applied science, not so much because of what it does, but for the potential of its side effects. The ultimate goal of medicinal chemistry is the production of pharmaceutical compounds and materials that will save the lives of people, animals, and even plants. One obvious outcome of this is that the human population will increase at a faster rate than it would otherwise, placing ever greater pressure on the natural resources and wild areas of the planet. At the same time, however, the ability to synthesize pharmaceutical compounds obtained from those same natural sources actually works to alleviate the pressure placed on them through harvesting of those compounds, thus helping to preserve the natural resources. It is an odd balancing act, and no other science holds a similar place in human society.

There are a great many social hurdles that are encountered by medicinal chemistry as a science, not the least of which are its roles in the controversial science of stem cells and litigation arising from the side effects of various pharmaceuticals. Regulations governing the release of new pharmaceuticals will likely become even more restrictive over time, which will in turn increase

Occupation	Medical and clinical laboratory technologists and technicians
Employment 2010	330,600
Projected Employment 2020	373,500
Change in Number (2010–20)	42,900
Percent Change	13%

*Bureau of Labor Statistics, 2012

the costs of pharmaceuticals in general. This alone would ensure that synthetic organic chemists will always have a valuable role to play in the development of syntheses that are effective at producing complex compounds at the lowest possible cost.

Further Reading

Alessio, Enzo. *Bioinorganic Medicinal Chemistry*. Weinheim: Wiley, 2011. Print. Presents a sound introduction to the concepts of bioinorganic chemistry, including radiopharmaceuticals. Also discusses the functions of physiology dependent not only on organic chemistry, but on numerous inorganic materials that are also essential components of biological systems.

Corey, E. J., Barbara Czako, and Laszlo Kurti. *Molecules and Medicine*. Hoboken: Wiley, 2012. Print. An illustrated book for a general readership discussing the chemistry behind numerous commonly encountered pharmaceutical compounds.

Dewick, Paul M. *Medicinal Natural Products: A Biosynthetic Approach*. Chichester: Wiley, 2009. Print. Provides a thorough introduction to the biochemical pathways and mechanisms by which various classes of compounds, including various hydrocarbons, alkaloids, peptides, proteins, and carbohydrates, are manufactured in plants and other living organisms.

Foye, William O., and Thomas L. Lemke. *Foye's Principles of Medicinal Chemistry*. 6th ed. Baltimore: Lippincott, 2008. Print. Written for advanced students, pharmacists, and practitioners of medicinal chemistry. Approaches the subject in great detail, using case studies and an emphasis on patient-focused pharmaceutical care.

Thomas, Gareth. *Medicinal Chemistry: An Introduction*. 2nd ed. Hoboken: Wiley, 2011. Print. Provides a thorough introduction to the science of medicinal chemistry without assuming prior knowledge in any area from basic principles through advanced combinatorics and pharmacokinetics.

About the Author: Richard M. Renneboog holds a master's degree in synthetic organic chemistry from the University of Western Ontario. He subsequently spent a number of years working in the Department of Chemistry at University of Alberta attempting to synthesize non-protein analogs for the active site of an enzyme. He currently works independently as a technical consultant and writer in Canada.

Oncologist

Earnings (Yearly Average): $166,400 (Bureau of Labor Statistics, 2012)

Employment and Outlook: Faster than average growth (Bureau of Labor Statistics, 2012)

O*NET-SOC Code: 29-1069.00 **Related Career Cluster(s):** Education & Training; Health Science; Human Services

Scope of Work

An oncologist is a physician trained in the study, management, or treatment of neoplastic diseases (cancers). Most oncologists are further trained in subspecialties of the profession, which can include surgical oncologists, trained in the removal of solid tumors; radiation oncologists, trained in the use of radiotherapy for treatment of cancers; and oncologists who specialize in the treatment of cancers with chemotherapeutic agents. Not all neoplastic disease involves solid tumors, and some oncologists often specialize in certain types of cancers. For example, leukemia and lymphomas represent cancers of blood forming cells; oncologists specializing in these areas are generally trained as hematologists. Some oncologists may specialize in brain tumors, referring patients with other forms of cancers to a different oncologist.

Oncologists may also specialize in the type of patient with which they deal, such as pediatric oncologists, who treat cancer in children or young adults.

Education and Coursework

Since an oncologist is trained as a physician, education in the medical field is a requirement. Students begin by earning a bachelor's degree. The undergraduate program should include courses in general biology as well as in both inorganic and organic chemistry, mathematics, and physics. Courses in biochemistry, microbiology, and immunology

---

Transferable Skills

- Interpersonal/Social Skills – Providing support to others
- Research & Planning Skills – Identifying problems
- Research & Planning Skills – Determining alternatives
- Research & Planning Skills – Gathering information
- Research & Planning Skills – Defining needs
- Organization & Management Skills – Handling challenging situations
- Technical Skills – Applying the technology to a task (SCANS Workplace Competency – Technology)
- Technical Skills – Performing scientific, mathematical, and technical work

---

(while not required) will prove particularly helpful in any future medical school program.

Grades are important for admittance to any professional school, but are not the only determining factor for acceptance. Work experience in the field, as well as faculty or instructor recommendations, play significant roles in acceptance to a medical school. Students should develop as much work experience as possible; this may include serving as a volunteer or carrying out an internship while working with physicians or in medical facilities such as hospitals. As undergraduates, students should also take advantage of any opportunity to work directly with science faculty, including carrying out undergraduate research where available.

A master's degree is unnecessary for acceptance to medical school. Some schools have an MD/PhD program for students who wish to emphasize research rather than a general medical practice, but for the student interested primarily in diagnosis or treatment of cancer— an oncologist—the standard medical program is sufficient. Medical school training usually involves a four-year program, culminating with an internship and residency, preferably providing experience in dealing with cancer patients.

The specialty in oncology requires several years further training beyond medical school, providing practical experience in the field of oncology. In order to be certified as an oncologist by the American Board of Internal Medicine—one of several such boards that oversee the practice of medicine—the physician must pass both written and oral examinations on the subject.

Most oncologists will train in specific areas of oncology, with emphasis in surgery being among the most rigorous of such programs. Surgical oncology requires up to five years of a residency program followed by several years of a fellowship. The field of surgical oncology is overseen by the Society of Surgical Oncology. Other programs include medical oncology, with emphasis on chemotherapeutic treatments, and radiation oncology.

Career Enhancement and Training

A physician planning on specializing in oncology must first become certified in internal medicine, a process overseen by the American Board of Internal Medicine (ABIM). ABIM certification requires a three-year residency program terminating with an examination. Once the physician is certified in internal medicine an additional fellowship program is required: a two-year training program in oncology followed by an examination. Periodic reexamination is required to maintain certification.

If the physician wishes to specialize in specific areas of oncology—such as radiation or pediatric oncology—additional certification is necessary. Specialization in radiation oncology requires a four-year residency following an internship in internal medicine. Certification is contingent upon passing an examination administered through the American Board of Radiology.

Several professional societies exist, the largest being the American College of Physicians, an umbrella organization that oversees most major medical specialties. The American Society of Clinical Oncology (ASCO) provides updates of relevant information as well as access to clinical tools. ASCO places a particular emphasis on the physician-patient dynamic, and many of its publications address this area. The American Association for Cancer Research provides access to those interested in the research area rather than that of clinical practice. The society publishes numerous professional journals as well as supporting professional conferences with emphasis on the latest findings on the subject.

Daily Tasks and Technology

The first interaction between the cancer patient and a physician may involve either the routine examination consisting of the general physical or results of preliminary tests, or concerns about physical changes such as presence of a lump, physical symptoms, or unusual bruising or bleeding. At this stage the physician is likely a general practitioner rather than a specialist. The physician will likely recommend a biopsy or other further testing, which can include computed tomography (CT) scans or magnetic resonance imaging (MRI) if the tumor is internal.

If tests for cancer are positive, the patient will be referred to a specialist, an oncologist trained in that particular specialty—breast, lung, or colon cancers for example. The oncologist is likely associated with either a private or a university hospital. Once the examination is completed and the type and extent of the cancer is confirmed, the oncologist will determine the best procedures to be followed.

In most situations a team, rather than any single individual, is involved in treating the disease. If the tumor is solid and localized, a surgeon or surgical oncologist will determine the optimal means of removing the tumor.

Following removal of the tumor, the surgical team—which now may include a medical oncologist if chemotherapy is necessary, or radiation oncologist if that is the course to follow—will make further recommendations for additional treatment. Depending upon the site of the tumor and the likelihood that is has metastasized (spread), the team will recommend either radiation treatment or a course of chemotherapy. Radiation therapy, carried out by a technician trained in the process, will take place in the hospital. The program of chemotherapy, the length of which is dependent upon the type and extent of cancer, may take place in the form of an outpatient. Follow-up examinations and monitoring of patient health will continue until the disease has been resolved; the prognosis is dependent on numerous factors, including the type of cancer, metastasis, and the response of the disease to treatment.

A Conversation with Brian M. Cali

Job Title: Founder and Senior Vice President, Preclinical Research and Development, Ironwood Pharmaceuticals

What was your career path?

As a junior in high school, I was given the opportunity to conduct research in a summer science program at Roswell Park Cancer Institute. From that point on, I was hooked on scientific research. In fact, I was sure I wanted to be a professor at a research university...until I was exposed to the biotechnology industry as a postdoctoral fellow at the Whitehead Institute. The idea of translating science into products that benefit patients was very exciting. And so I became involved in the founding of a biotechnology company (Microbia, now called Ironwood) with three other postdoctoral fellows from the Whitehead. Fifteen years later, we are still on this wonderful adventure of discovering, developing, and commercializing new medicines!

What are three pieces of advice?

1. Follow the heart. People are happiest, work hardest, and ultimately most successful (in all definitions of the word) when they pursue careers that ignite their passion. Do not do make career choices because they seem more logical, lucrative, or "safer." Career choices that are at least a little scary offer the greatest chance for personal growth, and open up possibility for serendipity—which leads to my next point...

2. Whatever the "plan," be ready to ditch the plan. Early in my scientific training, I didn't know that biotechnology and entrepreneurship were viable options for someone with my training. And yet, as I was exposed to new ideas and opportunities, I found a very engaging career path that had nothing to do with my original plan to become a professor. This theme is one I hear over and over again from people who have found exciting careers—they had no idea when they set out that they would ever be doing what they do (so happily) today.

3. Work with great colleagues who share your passion. People who are excellent at what they do push you, indirectly and directly, to be better. They also support you and encourage you. If you find yourself in a situation in which your workplace is not providing this kind of challenge and sustenance (assuming you don't work alone), start looking for something new ASAP.

What paths for career advancement are available to you?

I currently oversee research and early development for our company. Over the years I have gained experience leading drug discovery and clinical development projects, working closely with (and learning from) colleagues in a wide variety of disciplines and in a variety of therapeutic areas. I continue to learn about both the science in these areas and the process of growing an organization in a way such that it remains cutting-edge scientifically and competitive as a business.

Earnings and Employment Outlook

Despite misrepresentations of the increasing incidence of cancer—with the exception of those cancers that are smoking-related—most cancers are chronic diseases of older persons. As the population ages, the incidence of certain cancers will also increase. Consequently, oncology as a field and the employment outlook for trained oncologists will continue to be highly positive.

Salary levels will likely increase as well, subject to several interrelated factors. The issue of health and medical care in the United States will likely continue to generate controversy in the upcoming decade, with possible implications related to salaries affected by Medicare and Medicaid programs being part of that equation. Other factors will also have an impact on average salaries. Oncologists working in the private sector—private practice or employment in hospitals associated with universities—will likely continue to earn more than those in the public domain. The location of the practice will also have an effect on salary levels. Oncologists working in larger cities or in states located on the coasts will encounter higher costs of living, with increased salary compensation as a result. Improved technology, however, continues to provide access to medical information even for physicians living in smaller cities or towns, often locations for newer medical facilities. Average salaries in these areas, including the Midwest, where cost of living is lower, will also be lower.

Related Occupations

- **Hematologist:** Hematologists are specialists in diseases of the blood, which can include leukemia and lymphomas.

- **Pathologist:** Pathologists are physicians trained in the diagnosis of diseases, with emphasis on characteristics of cells and tissues.

- **Radiation Therapist:** Radiation therapists, while not necessarily physicians, may specialize in radiation therapy of tumors, working as part of a team in treatment of some forms of cancer.

- **Oncology Nurse:** Trained in a nursing program, oncology nurses address the day-to-day treatment and monitoring of cancer patients.

- **Geneticist:** Geneticists are trained in the study of the underlying genetics of diseases such as cancer, and may also provide counseling or advice in dealing with genetic predisposition to the disease.

- **Radiochemist:** Radiochemists specialize in use of radiotherapy in diagnosis (cancer imaging) or treatment of disease.

- **Molecular Biologist:** Usually a PhD rather than a physician, a molecular biologist may choose to study the underlying causes of cell abnormalities.

Future Applications

Among the most significant advances in the field of oncology is the understanding that, while cancer does not represent a single disease, the underlying causes of most forms of cancer have their origins in the molecular disruption of cell regulation. These discoveries have had two immediate impacts on the field: first, the possibility of genetic screening to identify persons at greatest risk for development of the disease, and second, the application of personalized medicine aimed at the specific sites or cellular pathways disrupted in the patient.

For these reasons, the fields of molecular biology (the study of changes within the cell at the molecular level) and genetics (the study and application of genetic factors that may place the person at increased risk for cancer), as well as improved counseling on the subject, will become increasingly important.

In the past an oncologist had few options in dealing with the disease: Surgery to remove a solid tumor, directed radiation against the cancer, or chemotherapy and its attendant side effects. During the 1990s the first of the anticancer drugs directed at specific pathways became available. In the future it is likely the team that treats the patient will include, in addition to the oncologist, other members who can provide recommendations for specific treatments directed solely against the tumor while leaving normal cells and tissues unharmed.

Richard Adler, PhD

More Information

American Association for Cancer Research
615 Chestnut Street, 17th Floor,
Philadelphia, PA 19106-4404
http://www.aacr.org/

American Board of Internal Medicine
10 Walnut Street, Suite 1700,
Philadelphia, PA 19106
http://www.abim.org/

American Board of Radiology
5441 E. Williams Circle
Tucson, AZ 85711-7412
http://www.theabr.org/

American Society of Clinical Oncology
2318 Mill Road, Suite 800
Alexandria, VA 22314
http://www.asco.org/

Society of Surgical Oncology
85 W. Algonquin Road, Suite 550
Arlington Heights, IL 60005
http://www.surgonc.org/

Nuclear Chemistry

FIELDS OF STUDY

Physics; chemistry; physical chemistry/chemical physics; quantum mechanics; statistical mechanics; electromagnetism; nuclear and particle physics; computational chemistry; computational physics; theoretical particle physics; classical mechanics; mathematics; calculus; differential equations; linear algebra; statistics; numerical analysis; computer science; programming; radioactivity; biology; biochemistry; biophysics; nuclear magnetic resonance spectroscopy; magnetic resonance imaging.

DEFINITION

Of the three subatomic particles (protons, electrons, and neutrons), much of chemistry is concerned with electrons, which are responsible for the chemical bonds that join atoms into molecules. In contrast, nuclear chemistry is the study of the chemistry of nuclei—the protons and neutrons that form the dense core of atoms. More specifically, nuclear chemistry can include the following: the chemistry of atoms with high atomic numbers, in which the nucleus is larger and therefore plays a greater role; the chemical relevance of the basic properties of nuclei; the chemistry of large systems that owe their behavior to nuclear phenomena; and the use of scientific and medical techniques based on nuclei.

Basic Principles

The field of nuclear chemistry emerged largely from the work of Marie Curie, a physicist and chemist and the winner of two Nobel Prizes. Curie discovered radioactivity toward the end of the nineteenth century, during her studies of radium, polonium, and other radioactive elements. The first use of radiation in medicine also dates to this time period. The second major event in nuclear chemistry was the development of quantum mechanics, which provides a physical model for describing how nuclei and other very small particles behave. World War II saw the deployment of the first atomic bombs, which were developed by applying nuclear chemistry to release large amounts of energy from very little matter. The first nuclear reactor was used to generate electricity in 1951, and the first application of magnetic resonance imaging occurred shortly thereafter. Given its youth relative to other fields—organic chemistry or materials science, for example—nuclear chemistry has already come a long way and permanently changed the course of medicine, science, and human history.

The word *nuclear* has negative connotations due to its association with atomic weaponry and the devastation caused by the Three Mile Island, Chernobyl, and Fukushima nuclear meltdowns. In fact, a technique known to chemists and physicists as nuclear magnetic resonance (NMR) is called magnetic resonance imaging (MRI) when used as a procedure in the medical field to avoid the implication that it involves exposure to nuclear radiation, which can cause radiation sickness and cancer. The word *nuclear* in NMR actually refers to what is being studied: the nuclei of atoms in the body. By measuring the differences in how nuclei respond to a magnetic field, scientists and medical specialists can produce an image of the scanned area that differentiates between and among organs, tissues, and bones. *Nuclear* is a broad term, referring to phenomena in which atomic nuclei play a predominant role.

Core Concepts

Nuclei in Atoms. Atoms are composed of electrons, protons, and neutrons; nuclei contain the latter two in a very small, very dense core at the center of an atom. The number of protons and neutrons in the atom determines the element and isotope of the atom, respectively. For example, an atom with a single proton is a hydrogen atom, one with thirty-seven protons is rubidium, and one with ninety-two protons is uranium. The isotope of a given element is determined by the number of neutrons in the nucleus. Generally, the most stable form of each element is that in which the number of neutrons is equal to the number of protons, but some other arrangements can also be quite stable. For example, the element carbon usually refers to carbon-12, with the numeral indicating the sum of the number of protons and neutrons. However, carbon-13 is another stable form of carbon, and carbon-14 is quite well known due to its use in carbon dating. Because carbon-14 decays into nitrogen-14 with a known half-life (the amount of time it takes for half of a given quantity to decay) of approximately 5,700 years, comparing the prevalence of carbon-14 in biological material (a fossil, for example) with the amount of nitrogen-14 yields the age of the biological material.

Radioactivity. Some isotopes are unstable, meaning that they have too much energy and will eventually release some of the excess energy. The identity of the final, more stable nucleus (the daughter nucleus) depends on the way in which this excess energy is released. In alpha decay, unstable atoms emit a particle comprising two protons and two neutrons—that is, a helium nucleus. Thus, the daughter nucleus is actually a different element from the parent nucleus; for example, uranium can undergo alpha decay into thorium. In beta decay, the parent nucleus emits an electron and another subatomic particle called an electron antineutrino. Whereas alpha decay decreases the atomic number by two, beta decay actually increases it by one. Thus, uranium could undergo beta decay to neptunium. The third and final of the main decay mechanisms is gamma decay, in which the parent nucleus releases high-energy photons. In this process, the daughter nucleus is the same as the parent, because no nuclear matter is lost or gained. Depending on the context, discussions of radioactivity can focus on the change in the parent nucleus (in a physics context) or the radiation emitted (in medical and health contexts).

Quantum Mechanics. Nuclei are small; the diameter of a single nucleus is on the order of 2 to 15 femtometers, tens and hundreds of times smaller than the diameters of an atom. Whereas our everyday world is described adequately by classical, or Newtonian, mechanics, phenomena on this small of a scale are best described by quantum mechanics, a field that was developed in the early twentieth century. The world of quantum mechanics is a strange one: the difference between particles and waves disappears, and everything becomes probabilistic rather than deterministic, meaning that a researcher can compute the *probability* that a particle is at a given location at a given time but can never actually pin down exactly where it is. These results and more follow from the discovery that energy (in addition to other quantities) only exists in discrete units, called *quanta*. That is, a particle can have 1 quantum of energy, 2 quanta of energy, and so forth, but it cannot have 1.2 quanta of energy. This principle completely revolutionized the understanding of physics, thanks to work by many famous scientists, such as Albert Einstein, Niels Bohr, and Erwin Schrödinger.

Nuclear Spin. In addition to being a crucial concept for understanding nuclear chemistry, spin is also a good example of a purely quantum-mechanical concept with no analogue in the Newtonian world. Despite its name, the spin of a particle has nothing to do with actual rotation, but this fact was only discovered after the name had caught on. For most purposes, spin can be imagined as the rotation of a particle without sacrificing accuracy; readers interested in learning more about spin should consider further study of quantum mechanics and particle physics. Imagining nuclei as spinning tops capable of spinning in different directions, where those directions correspond to different spin numbers, is sufficient for this overview.

Nuclear Magnetic Resonance Spectroscopy. NMR spectroscopy is a technique used by scientists to elucidate the structures of molecules. A magnetic field is used to align the nuclear spins (the spinning tops described above) in one direction. Radio waves are then used to knock the spinning tops out of alignment, and the time it takes for the spins to realign is recorded. This realignment time varies based on each nucleus's local environment. After some calculations, scientists can determine which atoms are bonded to one another, how they are bonded (for example, with a single bond or a double bond), and the exact distance between them. This information can then be used to identify the overall structure of the molecule being studied.

Magnetic Resonance Imaging. MRI operates in the same fashion as NMR spectroscopy but is applied to medical imaging rather than identification of molecular structure. Instead of focusing on the responses of each individual atom, MRI looks at relatively large areas, identifying trends in how nuclei in the body respond to the magnetic field and radio waves. This information can be used to differentiate between organs, tissues, fluids, and bone, providing doctors with a useful image of a person's internal anatomy without harming the patient.

Interesting Facts about Nuclear Chemistry

- Nuclear testing has released a measurable amount of tritium, an isotope of hydrogen with three neutrons, into the oceans. Although the release of radioactive material has many negative consequences, it has also been unexpectedly useful. Scientists have been able to track the rate at which water circulates in the ocean by using the half-life of tritium (12.5 years) and measuring the concentrations of tritium at different depths and locations in the ocean.

- Nuclear magnetic resonance (NMR) spectrometry generally uses magnetic field strengths of approximately 12 teslas (T), which is close to the attractive force required to levitate a frog (16 T). In comparison, a refrigerator magnet has a magnetic field strength of approximately 0.005 T.

- The very strong magnetic fields used in NMR and magnetic resonance imaging (MRI) instruments are produced by superconducting electromagnets. To achieve superconductivity, the electromagnet must be cooled to four degrees Celsius above absolute zero—the coldest temperature possible—using liquid helium.

- The atomic bombs used to bomb Nagasaki and Hiroshima in World War II were only three meters long and weighed just four tons, but they released energy equivalent to twenty thousand tons of TNT.

- The United States has approximately five thousand nuclear weapons, half of which are ready for immediate deployment. However, much of this nuclear stockpile is quite literally rusting, and many of the weapons are so old that the original designers have passed away, taking with them information about how to fix these weapons.

- Different types of radiation require different types of protection. For example, alpha particles, which are helium nuclei emitted from radioactive materials, can be blocked by paper or clothing. In contrast, beta radiation can be blocked by aluminum foil, whereas gamma radiation requires several feet of lead for shielding.

Applications Past and Present

Research. NMR spectroscopy allows chemists, physicists, and biologists to determine the structure of, and therefore identity, an unknown compound. Chemists and biologists might use NMR to identify a newly synthesized compound or the conformation of a protein, whereas physicists might use the information about the strength of a chemical bond and the spin of the nuclei to draw conclusions about the physical behavior of the electrons and nuclei. Electron paramagnetic resonance (EPR) spectroscopy is the analogous technique for electrons rather than nuclei. However, because few compounds have electron configurations with a net spin—in most cases, the spins cancel one another out—it is a much less common technique, used primarily to study free radicals and some magnetic compounds.

Medicine—Magnetic Resonance Imaging. MRI is a popular imaging technique due to its ability to provide information about structures in the body that is difficult to obtain using other techniques while being essentially harmless. An MRI can be used to detect swelling, inflammation, tumors, blockages, organ damage, or fluid leakages. It can also help to diagnosis nervous-system problems, such as Alzheimer's disease, dementia, or multiple sclerosis. Most negative effects experienced during or after an MRI are due to interactions between the strong magnetic field used for imaging and any metal that might be imbedded in the patient, such as iron present in some tattoos. Before recommending an MRI, doctors determine whether the patient has a pacemaker, metal joint, or anything else that might cause discomfort or injury in a high magnetic field.

Medicine—Radiation Therapy. Cancer is caused by tumorous cells—cells that duplicate and grow without restraint, forming tumors. One method of treating cancer is to kill these cells by subjecting them to radiation. Radiation can be applied externally, using instruments that send high-energy x-rays through the tumorous region of the body, or internally, by having the patient ingest radioactive materials that release radiation as they decay inside the body. The efficacy of radiation therapy lies in applying the radiation such that maximum damage is done to cancerous cells and minimum damage is done to healthy cells.

Nuclear Power. One of the well-known applications of nuclear chemistry is in nuclear power. Nuclear energy is generated by using the energy released by large, less stable nuclei, such as those of the element uranium, as they break into smaller, more stable nuclei. This energy is then used to heat water into steam, which in turn drives a turbine and generates electricity. Nuclear power has the advantages of being independent of imported energy sources (like oil) and generally being a more environmentally friendly process: it generates little waste and involves far less carbon emission than burning fossil fuels. However, malfunctions can cause nuclear meltdowns, releasing radiation into the area surrounding the nuclear power plant and harming residents and the environment. The incidents at Three Mile Island (1979, United States), Chernobyl (1986, Soviet Union), and Fukushima (2011, Japan) are good examples of the dangers of nuclear power. Because the material used to generate nuclear power is the same as that used to produce nuclear weapons, nuclear power also has political implications for countries that are not thought to currently possess nuclear weapons.

Nuclear Weapons. Nuclear weapons rely on the massive amount of energy stored in atomic nuclei. The sudden release of this energy not only inflicts enormous damage from the initial bombing but also releases radiation that lingers in the environment, causing deaths due to radiation poisoning in the short term and cancer in the long term. The first and, to date, only use of nuclear weapons was in the World War II bombing of Hiroshima and Nagasaki in Japan, but nuclear-weapon stockpiles exist in at least eight different countries, with the United States and Russia having almost twenty thousand warheads between them. A variety of nuclear weapons exists, and research into improvements in their design is ongoing.

Impact on Industry

According to the United States Bureau of Labor Statistics (BLS), chemists can expect a 4 percent growth in employment between 2010 and 2020, which is low compared to the 14 percent national average across all careers. In contrast, nuclear technicians—that is, technicians who assist nuclear scientists—can expect a 14 percent growth over the same period based on expected increases in the demand for nuclear power. Combining these reports, the job growth for nuclear chemists is likely to be closer to the average growth rate than the number for all chemists suggests.

Government Agencies. Nuclear chemistry falls within the domains of several federal agencies, including the Department of Energy (DOE) and the National Institute for Standards and Technology (NIST). Naturally, the DOE is interested in nuclear chemistry for its applications in nuclear energy; however, its research has also implications for medicine, other areas of chemistry, and even land-mine detection. NIST is most interested in nuclear analytical chemistry, or the application of nuclear chemistry to identifying chemical compounds and determining their concentration in a sample of interest. Nuclear chemists can find jobs in these agencies, among others, as researchers and consultants.

Occupation	Chemists
Employment 2010	82,200
Projected Employment 2020	85,400
Change in Number (2010–20)	3,200
Percent Change	4%

Bureau of Labor Statistics, 2012

Military. The military's use of nuclear weaponry ensures the need for nuclear scientists, engineers, and technicians now and in the future. In addition to developing new nuclear-weapon technology, the military must maintain its current supply, performing maintenance and decommissioning weapons as necessary, as well as develop ways to protect against and treat radiation poisoning. The military also makes use of nuclear energy; for instance, nuclear submarines use nuclear reactors for power, which has the advantages of supplying a greater amount of power and, because nuclear reactions do not consume oxygen, unlike combustion does, requiring fewer trips to the surface to exchange air.

Academic Research and Teaching. From a teaching perspective, nuclear chemists will always be an integral part of university chemistry departments because of the importance of NMR imaging in identifying synthesis products. However, research in nuclear chemistry at the university level has slowed, and many of the active research topics require very strong magnets, which are quite expensive and beyond the budget of some programs. Depending on their specific research interests, nuclear chemists can also find work in physics departments, as the fields of nuclear chemistry and nuclear physics overlap in many areas. Anyone seeking a career in academia should carefully consider the particulars of university positions, as there are generally

Occupation	Nuclear technicians
Employment 2010	7,100
Projected Employment 2020	8,100
Change in Number (2010–20)	1,000
Percent Change	14%

Bureau of Labor Statistics, 2012

far more applicants than available postgraduate and professorial positions. The intense competition means that academics usually work long hours with relatively low pay.

Health Care. Nuclear chemistry has revolutionized medicine in terms of both imaging and treatment. The employment outlook is good for nuclear chemists and other nuclear scientists in industries that provide health services or develop instrumentation and techniques for MRI and radiation treatment. Topics of research include developing ways to lower the cost of MRIs and using solid-state NMR spectroscopy to determine the structures of biomolecules such as proteins, which are too large and complex to study using conventional techniques. In addition to researchers, these industries hire consultants, salespeople, and medical professionals specializing in nuclear chemistry.

Energy. Traditional energy sources—namely, fossil fuels—are becoming increasingly unviable due to issues of cost, scarcity, and environmental damage. Of the various alternative energy sources, nuclear chemistry is currently the most practical in terms of replacing fossil fuels altogether. However, concerns about the health and environmental tolls of nuclear power have prevented its large-scale application in the United States; existing plants are being closed down, and new plants are not being constructed. Depending on the progress made in solar, wind, and biomass energy and how rapidly the demand for alternative energy increases, the future role of nuclear energy could be quite substantial.

Social Context and Future Prospects

Over the last century, nuclear chemistry has had a profound effect on many areas of science and technology that are still being developed today. NMR has revolutionized how chemists identify molecules, and MRI is one of the most useful medical-imaging techniques. Radiation treatment has greatly improved cancer prognoses. Additionally, a better understanding of the health effects of radiation has helped scientists understand the relationship between sun exposure and skin cancer. Nuclear power is an important energy source for many countries, and nuclear weaponry has changed the global political landscape. The wide-reaching applications of the field ensure that nuclear chemistry will continue to be an important area of study for many years to come.

Due to its breadth, the future of nuclear chemistry and nuclear science is quite promising. The aging American nuclear arsenal will need to be addressed soon; if a policy of complete nuclear disarmament were adopted, which is unlikely, disassembling and disposing of existent nuclear stockpiles would be a long, difficult project. In the more likely event of continued nuclear armament, research will be ongoing to develop better nuclear weaponry. Nuclear power faces a similar scenario; some people would like to see the use of nuclear power completely halted, but it is likely to continue to play a strong role in energy production worldwide as we search for alternatives to fossil fuels.

The prospects for the application of nuclear chemistry in medicine are even better. Magnetic resonance imaging is and will continue to be a key imaging technique; further research will include cost-reduction efforts to reduce the number of patients who must undergo potentially harmful procedures, such as x-rays, due to the prohibitive cost of an MRI. Concerning radiation therapy, future research will focus on minimizing the damage done to normal cells while maximizing the damage done to cancerous cells. For example, the development of ways to make internal radiation therapy treatments more specific to tumorous cells would reduce the negative side effects of the procedure, which would improve quality of life and the overall survival rate.

Further Reading

Ferguson, Charles D. *Nuclear Energy: What Everyone Needs to Know.* New York: Oxford UP, 2011. Print. An overview of nuclear energy, written after the meltdown of the Fukushima power plant. Addresses the science behind nuclear energy and the environmental and political issues surrounding it.

Goldsmith, Barbara. *Obsessive Genius: The Inner World of Marie Curie.* New York: Norton, 2005. Print. Examines the personal and professional life of twentieth-century chemist Marie Curie. Also discusses the history and culture of nuclear chemistry.

Loveland, Walter D., David J. Morrissey, and Glenn T. Seaborg. *Modern Nuclear Chemistry.* Hoboken: Wiley, 2001. Print. Provides an exhaustive review of nuclear chemistry, from core concepts to cutting-edge applications. Includes an overview of the relevant quantum mechanics.

"Nuclear Physics (NP)." *US Department of Energy: Office of Science.* USA.gov, 7 Aug. 2012. Web. 3 Oct. 2012. Provides an overview of the role of nuclear science in alternative energies.

Siracusa, Joseph M. *Nuclear Weapons: A Very Short Introduction.* Oxford: Oxford UP, 2008. Print. Summarizes the history of nuclear weaponry, the political evolution of weapons policy in the United States and abroad, and future ramifications of nuclear proliferation.

About the Author: Cassandra Newell graduated from Colby College with a bachelor's degree in chemistry and Russian language and literature. She then attended the Massachusetts Institute of Technology, completing 2.5 years of work toward a PhD in physical chemistry before leaving to pursue other interests. She worked as a research assistant at both institutions, studying such topics as molecular recognition, guest-host chemistry, computational chemistry, terahertz spectroscopy, acoustic spectroscopy, and proton/electron transfer in chemical systems. She also has experience as a teaching assistant and tutor in the fields of spectroscopy and quantum mechanics. Since leaving academia, she has pursued projects pertaining to science communication, such as editing scientific manuscripts and writing about science for nonspecialists.

Radiochemist 🖋

Earnings (Yearly Median): $69,790 (Bureau of Labor Statistics, 2012)

Employment and Outlook: Slower than average growth (Bureau of Labor Statistics, 2012)

O*NET-SOC Code: 19-4051.02

Related Career Clusters: Manufacturing; Health Science; Transportation, Distribution & Logistics

Scope of Work

Radiochemistry is a scientific discipline in which radioactive isotopes are used to study the properties of chemical processes. Radiochemists use the naturally occurring energy of radioactive decay as a tool of measurement, manipulation, and analysis. Radiochemists might be tasked with radioactively labeling DNA for research or developing a strategy to contain and clean up nuclear waste. Medical applications of radiochemistry are prevalent and varied, ranging from diagnosing and fighting cancer to pharmaceutical development and medical imaging. As with most scientists, radiochemists can work in both the field and the laboratory. Occupation in academic research is common, but the versatility of radiochemistry means employment in a wide breadth of professions is possible.

Education and Coursework

Students considering a career in radiochemistry should have a strong educational foundation in mathematics and multiple scientific fields. At the high-school level, advanced-placement courses in chemistry and physics should be partnered with writing and communication instruction that gives students the necessary skills to express ideas clearly and concisely. High-school coursework should prepare students for study at a four-year undergraduate science program.

> **Transferable Skills**
>
> - Communication Skills – Reporting information
> - Research & Planning Skills – Gathering information
> - Research & Planning Skills – Analyzing information
> - Technical Skills – Using technology to process information (SCANS Workplace Competency – Information)
> - Work Environment Skills – Working in a laboratory setting
> - Technical Skills – Performing scientific, mathematical and technical work

Typically, entry-level radiochemists hold a bachelor's degree in chemistry, but specializing in other scientific disciplines could also prepare students for careers in the field. In the course of research, radiochemists must compose detailed papers presenting their findings. Therefore, a college-level understanding of scientific writing and communication is necessary, beyond lab work and core curriculum.

Most radiochemists obtain master's and doctorate degrees that might help them break into a particular industry. For example, a postgraduate stint in medical school, followed by residency at a hospital or clinic, is recommended for students hoping to work in radiochemical medicine. Similarly, a research fellowship at a university or private laboratory is a crucial step for those seeking radiochemistry careers in academia. Both provide hands-on training in the field that will prove crucial in demonstrating qualification for permanent employment.

Career Enhancement and Training

A radiochemistry license is typically not required for either research or private laboratory positions, but certification by the American Board of Nuclear Medicine and the American Board of Radiology is necessary for employment in the medical field. Licenses are issued upon the passing of a skills-assessment examination following the completion of a residency program accredited by the Accreditation Council for Graduate Medical Education.

A variety of grants are available for radiochemists who require funding for research or additional training. The US Department of Energy (DOE), for example, provides support for research dealing in radiochemical imaging of dynamic biological processes. The DOE grant program seeks to develop analytical techniques for use in the study of potential biofuels.

Daily Tasks and Technology

Because radiochemistry deals in the most basic constructs of nature, products of radiochemical research have potentially limitless application. Radiation is everywhere, and scientists are only beginning to discover the true reach of its utility. Therefore, a "typical" job description for radiochemists is difficult to pin down. A large portion of radiochemists are employed in academic research. These chemists conduct lab experiments and studies, the results of which can be used to develop industry-specific radiochemical tools and processes.

Radiochemists who work in the medical field might spend time developing pharmaceuticals that manipulate the diagnostic, cancer-fighting properties of decaying isotopes. For example, radioactive iodine was one of the earliest radiochemical pharmaceuticals, and it is still the primary tool for detecting and treating thyroid disease. Additionally, some medical-imaging techniques rely on radiochemists to develop nuclear tracers that, when ingested by patients, can be detected with gamma scanners, allowing doctors to construct images of internal functions from the emitted radiation.

Radiochemists working in nuclear power plants are tasked with monitoring the safety and quality of the power-generating process. They play an important role in detecting and controlling radiation leakage, ensuring healthy, manageable levels of exposure for plant employees. Radiochemists also play an important role in the postgeneration stages of the nuclear-power process. Once radioactive fuel is spent, it must be disposed of, and radiochemists determine the best way to do so. Radioactive waste can remain dangerous for literally thousands of years. Thus, radiochemists must determine how to store and contain hazardous emissions by analyzing decay rates and penetration levels to develop techniques for environmentally sound and effective disposal.

Earnings and Employment Outlook

Exact salaries for radio and nuclear chemists vary with location, employer, and level of experience. According to the US Bureau of Labor Statistics (BLS), those working as chemists make anywhere between $38,000 and $116,000, with a median pay of $69,790. According to the National Association of Colleges and Employers (NACE), an entry-level chemist with an applicable bachelor's degree is likely to be offered a salary of $40,000. Expected salary for first-year radiochemists with a master's degree, according to NACE, is $44,700, and those entering the field with a doctorate are expected to be offered an annual salary of $59,700.

Employment of chemists is expected to increase by 4 percent between 2010 and 2020, according to the BLS. This is slower than the average growth for all occupations. Jobs for chemists in the manufacturing sector, such as pharmaceuticals and chemical products, are expected to decline as companies attempt to control costs by partnering with research institutes and universities to do work normally performed by in-house, salaried chemists. However, chemists are still vital in assessing the environment impact of different manufacturing and industrial processes. Radiochemists in particular should see a rise in jobs researching and controlling the environmental effects of nuclear waste from power plants, medical equipment, or various industrial processes.

Employment of chemists is expected to increase by 4 percent between 2010 and 2020, according to the BLS. This is slower than the average growth for all occupations.

As scientists uncover more about the mechanisms of the subatomic world, radiochemists will become of greater and greater utility. Radiochemists have particular sets of skills that align well with current scientific trends, pointing to good prospects for future and continued employment. Nuclear power plants continue to show promise as one of the cleanest, most efficient options of energy creation available, and radiation-based medical procedures are becoming more common every day. Despite these promising prospects, the number of students pursuing careers in radiochemistry has decreased significantly over the past decade, leaving open the jobs of soon-to-retire radiochemists, according to the National Academy of Sciences.

Related Occupations

- **Hazardous Waste Management Chemists:** Hazardous waste management chemists identify pollutants in the environment and develop chemical strategies for combating them.

- **Nuclear Engineers:** Nuclear engineers study and apply subatomic physics, using the fission and fusion of atomic nuclei to various ends.

- **Nuclear Medicine Technologists:** Nuclear medicine technologists work primarily with medical imaging machines, administering radioactive drugs and monitoring patients during procedures.

- **Chemical Systems Operators:** Chemical systems operators monitor and manage the chemical processes and machinery used in manufacturing and other industrial applications.

Future Applications

As the push for clean energy and green living continues, radiochemists are likely to see a boom in environment-focused positions. According to the BLS, the chemical-manufacturing industry continues to hire radiochemists to develop technologies to reduce pollution and improve efficiency. Demand for radiochemists in the nuclear-energy field will increase as nuclear power plants become more prevalent and money is invested in advancing nuclear systems. The continued buildup of radioactive waste will necessitate more research into waste-disposal strategies, in which radiochemists play a crucial part. Radiochemists will also be integral in the shift from fossil fuels to biofuels and other alternative forms of energy.

More Information

American Board of Nuclear Medicine
4555 Forest Park Boulevard, Suite 119
St. Louis, MO 63108
www.abnm.org

Pacific Northwest National Laboratory
Radiochemical Science and Engineering Group
902 Battelle Boulevard
Richland, WA 99352
http://radiochemscieng.pnnl.gov

Radiochemistry Society
PO Box 3091
Richland, WA 99354
www.radiochemistry.org

Royal Society of Chemistry Radiochemistry Group
Thomas Graham House
Science Park, Milton Road
Cambridge CB4 0WF
UK
www.rsc.org

Petrochemistry

FIELDS OF STUDY

Chemistry; geology; mathematics; materials science; analytical chemistry; organic chemistry; polymer chemistry; physical chemistry; inorganic chemistry; materials chemistry; biochemistry; flow chemistry; chemical engineering; synthetic chemistry; geochemistry; nanotechnology; petrology; mineralogy.

DEFINITION

Petrochemistry concerns itself with the production of petrochemicals and their intermediaries, which are used in the chemical industry in a diverse variety of products and applications. The traditional sources of petrochemicals are petroleum (crude oil) and natural gas. Contemporary petrochemicals include inorganic chemicals such as ammonia and even pure sulfur, gained from crude-oil refining processes and natural-gas processing. Additional petrochemicals are derived from synthesis gas.

Petrochemistry occupies an intermediary position between the petroleum or oil-and-gas industry and the manufacture of end products in the chemical industry. Petrochemical plants are generally integrated at petroleum refineries, from where they derive their primary feedstock, or built in close proximity to them.

Basic Principles

In the early twentieth century, chemists realized that they could manufacture chemicals from the byproducts of crude-oil refining. In 1857, the world's first commercial oil refinery was commissioned in Romania, and the oil age began in earnest with the 1859 success of American Edwin Drake's oil drilling in Pennsylvania. In 1872, the first petrochemical was manufactured. It was carbon black, gained from partial combustion of natural gas in the air, and was used as ink and pigment.

With the inventions of the gasoline and diesel engines, in 1876 and 1892, and the automobile in 1885, petroleum refineries focused on the manufacture of engine fuels from crude oil. Since 1913, thermal cracking of crude oil increased gasoline and diesel yields, leading to an increase of very light hydrocarbons. Chemists soon took advantage of this new source from refineries to replace the manufacture of these chemicals from coal or chalk. Butadiene, unwanted at refineries, was used to manufacture synthetic rubber following a process invented in 1909 in Germany. After World War II, the rise of the plastics industry created an exploding market for petrochemicals as their feedstock. By 2012, basic, specialty, and pharmaceutical chemicals created from petrochemicals had increased their value. This trend was reinforced by use of petrochemicals in nanotechnology.

Contemporary petrochemicals derive from core primary sources. Aromatics are extracted from the naphtha stream after they undergo catalytic reforming at a refinery. Olefins, or unsaturated hydrocarbons, are manufactured by cracking hydrocarbon molecules with more carbon atoms into lighter molecules with fewer carbon atoms. This is done at refinery units or at designated plants, such as an ethylene cracker operating apart from the refinery processes of manufacturing hydrocarbon fuels. Paraffins, or saturated hydrocarbons, are typically sourced from refinery processes. Natural gas is an important source of petrochemicals, including ammonia. Because of this source, ammonia is considered a petrochemical even though it lacks a carbon atom. The same is true for sulfur, a byproduct of desulfurization of gasoline and diesel at refineries.

Core Concepts

Petrochemical production is closely linked to petroleum refining and natural-gas processing, as these are the sources of its raw materials and products. In consequence, petrochemistry relies on some key refining processes that can be adjusted to yield more petrochemicals instead of fuel and fuel additives if so desired. The vast majority of petrochemicals serve as raw materials for the chemical industry to create end products from them.

Steam Cracking. Steam cracking is the primary mode of producing the two most common petrochemicals, ethylene (ethene) and propylene (propene). The term *cracking* refers to the process of using heat to break up larger hydrocarbon molecules into smaller ones. Steam cracking is a form of thermal cracking, which was invented independently in Russia in 1891 and in the United States in 1908. In steam cracking, a stream of hydrocarbons in either gas or liquid form is mixed with steam and sent into the furnace of the steam cracker. Temperatures inside the furnace range from about 760 to 840 degrees Celsius (1,400 to 1,544 degrees Fahrenheit), but the hydrocarbons stay in the furnace for only 0.3 to 0.8 seconds. They are cooled down, or quenched, immediately after leaving the furnace to stop further reactions and to extract the desired cracked petrochemical products.

The hydrocarbon mix for the steam cracker can come from a variety of sources. A straightforward, stand-alone ethylene cracker would get most of its hydrocarbon feedstock in the form of ethane, a component of natural gas. Steam crackers can also be fed with hydrocarbons in the form of straight-run naphtha or gas oil from the distillation towers of an oil refinery. In this case, the share of propylene and precursors of butadiene as well as aromatics is increased, and multiple quenching and distillation processes are needed to extract the desired petrochemical products.

Catalytic Reforming; Aromatics Extraction and Separation. The majority of the petrochemicals known as aromatics are a byproduct of the catalytic reforming of straight-run heavy naphtha streams at a petroleum refinery. The process of catalytic reforming was invented by American chemist Vladimir Haensel for the Universal Oil Products company, which put the process into commercial operations in 1949. Catalytic reforming is done to increase the octane number of the resulting raffinate (material from which a component has been removed), which is blended into gasoline to improve its quality. Catalytic reforming can be used to produce aromatics, but not every refinery does so. Sometimes, aromatics extraction from the raffinate is done at a different refinery.

To extract the aromatics—benzene, toluene, and xylenes—a solvent is added to the raffinate leaving the catalytic reformer. This solvent binds only the aromatics, which can then be separated from the rest of the raffinate in an extraction tower at the refinery. Next, the solvent is removed from the aromatics in an extraction-stripper column. Here, steam strips the aromatics off the solvent, which leaves the unit at the bottom while aromatics depart from the top. The aromatics are typically washed with water of any remaining impurities before being sent to a gas-fractionating plant. At the plant, benzene and toluene are separated by distillation. Separating the remaining aromatics presents a technological challenge because their boiling points are very close; thus, a system of super-distillation and crystallization is used. Meta-xylene and para-xylene are separated either by being chilled into crystal form, using their separate solidification points, or through a molecular sieve adsorbent designed to adsorb only para-xylene molecules.

Vapor-Phase Adsorption. Normal paraffins, which are saturated hydrocarbons, are typically extracted from refinery product streams vaporized into the gaseous stage. The hydrocarbon feedstock is sent across a bed of molecular sieves that adsorb the paraffin molecules. In a complementary unit, ammonia is sent across the filled molecular sieves, and the paraffin molecules are desorbed and leave the unit separate from the ammonia.

Synthesis—Ammonia. Industrially, ammonia is manufactured through the reaction of nitrogen with hydrogen, which comes from a hydrocarbon source. The most common hydrogen source is methane, the biggest component of natural gas. Hydrogen can also come from refinery gases, from steam reforming of naphtha refinery streams, or from partial oxidation of very-long-chained hydrocarbon molecules forming residues at a refinery. Because of this connection to hydrocarbons, ammonia can be considered a petrochemical.

Desulfurization. Desulfurization of gasoline and diesel has been mandated in developed countries, including the United States and the European Union, for environmental reasons. As a result, refineries have modernized their units so that gasoline and diesel are treated with hydrogen to extract sulfur in the form of hydrogen sulfide. In a subsequent sulfur-recovery unit using the Claus process, invented in 1883, sulfur is extracted in elementary form.

Oxidation, Nitration, Halogenation, Hydroxylation. Raw petrochemicals are subjected to a series of chemical reactions that add other atoms to their molecules. This is done to create intermediary products from the petrochemicals for further use by the chemical industry. Ethylene is primarily oxidized to form ethylene oxide of great purity. Ethane and propane are nitrated, adding nitrogen dioxide to their molecules, to create nitromethane and nitroethane, as well as 1- and 2-nitropropane. These products are used as solvents or feedstock for further synthesis processes. Similar processes subject petrochemicals to the addition of chlorine in halogenation and of alcohols in hydroxylation reactions.

Applications Past and Present

Petrochemicals and their intermediaries provide the raw materials for a vast array of products created by the chemical industry that have become essential elements of contemporary life. The production of plastics, synthetic rubber, synthetic fibers and fiberglass, polycarbonates, solvents, adhesives, detergents, herbicides, pesticides, and pharmaceuticals all begins with petrochemicals.

Applications for petrochemicals have risen dramatically since the manufacture of the first petrochemical, carbon black, in 1872. In the 1920s, chemists discovered that petrochemicals could serve as a more economical source of hydrocarbons than coal. Butadiene from refinery steam crackers became an important element of synthetic rubber in both North America and Germany. One of the first plastics, Bakelite, began using phenol for its phenol resins, which ultimately derived from benzene extracted after catalytic reforming at refineries after 1949. In general, petrochemical applications rose together with the plastics industry in the second half of the twentieth century, with further innovative applications developed since. To look at contemporary applications, it is useful to order these by the primary petrochemical from which they derive.

From Ethylene. Ethylene (chemical name ethene) is one of the most widely used petrochemicals. In its raw form, it acts as a ripening agent for fruits and plants, but this use is dwarfed by the applications derived from the chemical processing of ethylene. When ethylene is polymerized under pressure and with a catalyst, it forms polyethylene, which is the most common plastic. It is used for packaging, plastic foils, and plastic bottles, as well as for injection molding parts and household plastic items.

Oxidation of ethylene delivers ethylene oxide, which is further processed, particularly into ethylene glycol. About half of ethylene glycol is used as antifreeze for engines; the other half is processed to form polyesters, among them polyethylene terephthalate, abbreviated as PET. PET is used for synthetic fibers and plastic bottles. (PET does not contain polyethylene; the prefix *poly* refers to the compound itself.) Washing powders, paints, and dyes are also made on the basis of ethylene oxide.

Chlorination of ethylene creates ethylene dichloride (also known as 1,2-dichlorethane), which is a feedstock in the manufacture of PVC (polyvinylchloride), a plastic widely used in the construction industry for piping, for clothing and toys, or as a rubber substitute.

Ethanol can be produced by hydrating ethylene. Made this way, ethanol is used for solvents or as an intermediary for pharmaceuticals. This ethanol has a different petrochemical origin compared to the bioethanol used as a gasoline additive.

Combining the two petrochemicals of ethylene and benzene delivers ethylbenzene. This is used to manufacture styrene, from which the plastic polystyrene is created.

From Propylene. Propylene is processed to manufacture chemicals with a wide variety of applications. It is commonly oxidized to form propylene oxide. Propylene oxide can be used as an intermediary for polyol, out of which polyurethanes are made. Polyurethanes provide flexible and hard foams, seals, adhesives, fibers, and garden hoses. Propylene oxide leads to the manufacture of propylene glycol, an engine coolant also used to deice aircraft.

Propylene is polymerized to manufacture acrylonitrile, which is then used to make acrylic fibers that can replace wool in clothing. Another application is the thermoplastic acrylonitrile butadiene styrene (ABS). ABS is used for its impact resistance and toughness, for example in luggage manufacture or for car components.

Propylene is oxidized to form acrylic acid. Acrylic acid leads to acrylic polymers, which are widely used to create transparent and elastic plastics, among them the trademark product Plexiglas. Other products include paints, elastomers, strong adhesives, or flocculants for waste water treatment.

Epxoy resins are created in a series of chemical manufacturing steps that begin with propylene. Hydrated propylene forms isopropyl alcohol, commonly known as rubbing alcohol.

From Butadiene. Butadiene is a component of the so-called C4 cut of petrochemicals with four carbon atoms in their molecule. Its primary use is as part of synthetic rubbers, of which there are many different kinds and which accounted for about two-thirds of global rubber production in 2012. 1,3-butadiene is used directly in the styrene-butadiene rubbers. It is also processed further to form isoprene and chloroprene synthetic rubbers. One important use of synthetic rubber is in the manufacture of car tires, where it is favored because of its compatibility with petroleum products, such as oil or fuel, that may leak from the car or be present on the road. In hot climates, tires made from synthetic rubber endure better than those made from natural rubber.

From Benzene. Benzene is an aromatic prime petrochemical from which many products are created through multiple processing steps. It is also combined with ethylene to form ethylbenzene for plastics production. Alkylation of benzene with propylene in the presence of a zeolite-based catalyst creates cumene (chemical name isopropylbenzene). Cumene is then turned into cumene hydroperoxide, which is the feedstock for the industrial synthesis of phenol and acetone. Phenol is used to manufacture plastics like Bakelite, synthetic fibers like nylon, epoxies for coatings and adhesives, detergents, pharmaceuticals, and herbicides. A special phenol compound, bisphenol A, is used to manufacture polycarbonates, which are used to make hard but lightweight plastic shells, such as in mobile telephones or for the touch screens of smart phones. Acetone is used either directly as a thinner, including in nail polish remover, or as a solvent.

When benzene is made to react with hydrogen, it forms cyclohexane. Cyclohexane is used to produce adipic acid and caprolactam, both raw materials for the production of nylon.

Nitration of benzene leads to nitrobenzene, which is hydrated to form aniline. From this, after another intermediary step, polyurethanes are produced. Alkylation of benzene creates the material for a variety of detergents. Historically, the pesticide DDT was made from

---

Interesting Facts about Petrochemistry

- Carbon fiber is used in many racing and high-end cars because it combines low weight with great strength. Its full name, carbon fiber–reinforced polymer, identifies its connection to polymers derived from petrochemicals, such as epoxy and polyester.
- Methanol is used to make industrial ethanol undrinkable so that it cannot be consumed recreationally while remaining exempt from liquor taxes.
- Superglue (cyanoacrylate) is a powerful adhesive manufactured from petrochemicals. Dissolving and removing it requires acetone, which is another petrochemicals-based product.
- Smart phones and computer tablets could not work without their touch-sensitive screens being made with small films of polycarbonate, an innovative plastic derived from petrochemicals.
- Ancient Egyptians used ethylene released from slashed figs to hasten their ripening. Ethylene is a natural plant hormone.
- The aromatic petrochemical toluene was at one time used to strip cocaine from coca leaves for Coca-Cola's secret formula. The company has not revealed if this still occurs.
- Petrochemicals are used in the manufacture of pharmaceuticals, which causes them to enter the human body. Aspirin uses cumene, an aromatic by-product from a refinery's catalytic reformer for gasoline blends.

---

chlorobenzene. Because of its vast environmental damage, DDT has been generally phased out of use. Benzene itself is carcinogenic; this limits its direct applications, such as its use as an octane booster in fuel.

From Toluene. Toluene is a petrochemical directly used as powerful solvent for paints, glues, ink, and lacquers, as well as in paint thinner. It is also used to generate carbon nanotubes in a solution. Commonly, toluene is nitrated twice with nitric acid to form toluene diisocyanate, which is used to manufacture polyurethanes in an alternative to the polyurethane-production process via propylene.

Toluene is used in the manufacture of explosives like TNT (trinitrotoluene). It is also an ingredient of jet and racing fuel, added to boost octane.

Some toluene is dealkylated to form benzene. Toluene, like benzene, can be used in the production of nylon. For this, toluene is partially oxidized to form benzoic acid, which can then be used to create caprolactam, a precursor to the synthesis of nylon.

From Xylol. Para-xylene, which is a petrochemical with a particularly challenging extraction process, is almost exclusively used to manufacture terephthalic acid and dimethyl terephthalate. Both substances are used in the production of PET bottles and polyester yarns and fibers.

Ortho-xylene is used to manufacture terephthalic anhydride. This chemical is used as plasticizer for plastics, increasing their fluidity and ability to be molded. It is commonly used for PVC pipes to increase their plasticity.

Meta-xylene does not have many uses and is often converted to either para- or ortho-xylene. Mixtures of all three of these xylene isomers are typically referred to as xylol. Xylol is used as solvent, as varnish or paint thinner.

From Synthesis Gases. The two most important products created from synthesis gases are methanol and ammonia. Methanol is used as solvent, fuel, and antifreeze. From methanol, formaldehyde is produced via catalytic oxidation. Formaldehyde is used to make inexpensive and durable furniture by bonding wood veneer with plastic laminate. Methanol is part of the chemical processes that lead to the production of PET bottles, through its role in creating acetic acid. Methanol has become important for biodiesel through production of methyl esters for this alternative fuel. The controversial fuel additive MTBE (methyl tertiary butyl ether) is also based on methanol. Because of concerns over groundwater contamination with MTBE, its use was banned in California in 2004, and other states have followed suit.

Ammonia is used to manufacture fertilizers. Ammonia-based fertilizers have been of great importance as providers of nitrogen to agricultural crops to enhance their production. Ammonia is also used to manufacture explosives, via nitric acid, and to create intermediary products for the pharmaceutical industry.

From Sulfur. Desulfurization of gasoline and diesel has, in effect, turned sulfur into a petrochemical. Virtually all sulfur produced has been extracted from crude oil–based fuels, in which sulfur is an unwanted ingredient. Sulfur is converted into sulfuric acid in two alternative processes using oxygen and water. Sulfuric acid is used in the chemical manufacture of fertilizers, such as superphosphates and ammonium sulfates. It is also used for detergents, resins, and pharmaceuticals. Some sulfuric acid is used to manufacture catalysts for the petroleum industry. This use returns sulfur atoms to the location of their previous extraction.

Impact on Industry

Historically, the petrochemical industry has been concentrated in North America and Western Europe. In the United States, this occurred because of the country's rich deposits of crude oil and natural gas and the strong development of both refineries and the chemical industry, which created production capacities to serve both the domestic and the international market. In Western Europe, the petrochemical industry grew because of technical know-how and a sophisticated refinery and chemical-industry base serving the demand of highly industrialized nations. However, since the late twentieth century, there has been a marked shift of the petrochemical industry, either to source countries in the Middle East or to Asia, where the market for products made from petrochemicals and their intermediaries has risen tremendously. Historically, Japan has enjoyed a strong and highly developed petrochemical industry, and new petrochemical plants have been built at world-scale level in countries such as China, Thailand, and Singapore. As a result, the petrochemical industry in the United States has slowed its expansion.

However, the American petrochemical industry is still of significant value. In 2010, the value of petrochemicals manufactured in the United States was $67.7 trillion, according to the United States Census Bureau. This represents a significant recovery from 2009, when the value was $43.5 trillion. A comparison shows that the petrochemical industry is highly cyclical and dependent on the development of the price of crude oil; in 2010, crude-oil prices rose significantly and there was some economic recovery, so the value of petrochemicals rose strongly.

Occupation	Geological and petroleum technicians
Employment 2010	14,400
Projected Employment 2020	16,500
Change in Number (2010–20)	2,100
Percent Change	15%

*Bureau of Labor Statistics, 2012

For persons interested in a career as a petrochemist, the chances for employment in the domestic petrochemical industry are challenging. The United States Bureau of Labor Statistics (BLS) forecasts a drop of 12.6 percent in US employment of chemists by the petroleum industry from 2010 to 2020. Reasons include the industry shift abroad and the consolidation of the petrochemical industry. Academic employment of petrochemists and chemists is expected to grow by 15.6 percent in the same decade, although this is very dependent on the level of federal funding for research and development, a decline in which would affect the number of faculty positions sustainable in the field. However, there are good international job prospects for petrochemists, particularly in Asia and the Middle East.

Government Agencies. In the United States, government agencies such as the Environmental Protection Agency (EPA) seek to ensure that the use of petrochemicals is safe for the environment. The Occupational Safety and Health Administration (OSHA) oversees and ensures that for every petrochemical substance and petrochemical intermediaries, as for all chemicals and chemical compounds, a material-safety data sheet is created and maintained. It is designated primarily to inform workers of potential hazards when handling the product.

In countries with a nationalized or semi-nationalized oil, gas, and petrochemical industry, such as Saudi Arabia, the government acts as owner of companies producing petrochemicals. In 2012, Saudi

Arabia's SABIC (Saudi Basic Industry Corporation) was 70 percent owned by the government; only citizens of the Cooperation Council for the Arab States of the Gulf (GCC) were allowed to own the other 30 percent.

Military. Before and during World War II, synthetic rubber produced from petrochemical feedstock, especially 1,3-butadiene, was considered of strategic importance for the war efforts of both the Axis powers and the United States. Germany pioneered the production of synthetic rubber before and during the war when it was cut off from natural rubber sources. When Japan conquered Southeast Asia and its rubber plantations in early 1942, the United States launched a concentrated effort to make up for the loss of this natural source with the production of synthetic rubber. It took the intervention of then-Senator Harry Truman to persuade Standard Oil of New Jersey to yield German synthetic rubber patents, which it had gained in peacetime cooperation with Germany's IG Farben company, to the American war effort. During Operation Pointblank in September 1944, German synthetic-rubber plants were attacked by Anglo-American bombers.

Occupation	Petroleum engineers
Employment 2010	30,200
Projected Employment 2020	35,300
Change in Number (2010–20)	5,100
Percent Change	17%

*Bureau of Labor Statistics, 2012

Academic Research and Teaching. Increasingly, and following the trend for all chemists, petrochemists earn a PhD in a specific field of chemistry or a related science before entering the American workforce. Traditionally, a majority of petrochemists have gone to work in the petrochemical, petroleum, or chemical industry. With the contracting of the domestic job market in these industries, the percentage of petrochemists and chemists dropped from 66.5 percent in 1995 to 52.7 percent in 2010, according to a 2010 census by the American Chemical Society. Historically, a number of petrochemical inventions were made by petrochemists and chemists working in the industry, instead of in academia. With 32.1 percent of chemists, including petrochemists, employed in academia in 2010, this trend may be reversing.

Major Corporations. Despite industry contraction in the United States, 8,632 people were employed in the manufacture of petrochemicals in 2010, down from 9,167 in 2009. Yet their total 2010 payroll of $871.5 million, of which $518 million was for direct wages, was almost unchanged from 2009. Since the petrochemical industry is a process industry dependent on economies of scale, there are relatively few large petrochemical companies, all of which are active in the petroleum and chemical industries as well.

The major petrochemical companies incorporated in the United States are Exxon Mobil Chemical, Dow Chemical, DuPont, and Chevron Phillips Chemical. Large international petrochemical companies include for example Germany's BASF, Saudi Arabia's SABIC, the United Kingdom's INEOS, and Japan's Sumitomo Chemical.

Social Context and Future Prospects

The shape of contemporary life would be vastly different without the products derived from petrochemicals and their intermediaries. The quest to find more lightweight-yet-sturdy, elastic-yet-tough, clear, and scratch-resistant synthetic materials has culminated in such innovative products as polycarbonate films for smart-phone touch screens and crash helmets for motorcyclists. The packaging and bottling industries have been revolutionized by plastics from petrochemicals, as have the fiber and textile industries by polyester yarns. New paints, adhesives, and solvents support production of ever-more-useful end products.

The dramatic development of petrochemicals since the 1950s has made exploitation of natural hydrocarbon resources such as crude oil and natural gas vastly more efficient. A contemporary refinery gives off very little of its production as unwanted and unusable byproducts. The value creation of raw hydrocarbons is actually much greater for petrochemicals than for fuels.

Grave social problems have been created by the extraction of hydrocarbons without concern for the people living at the extraction sources. A negative example is the plight of the Ogoni people of Nigeria, whose land has been massively degraded by oil extraction without any local benefits. To keep more of the value created from petrochemicals in their own countries, oil-rich nations of the Middle East have built up their own petrochemical industries, as in Saudi Arabia, or have ambitious plans to do so, as does the United Arab Emirates.

There are many research-and-development efforts in the field of petrochemicals to find new applications and improve existing processes. However, as the petrochemical industry has consolidated in the United States and is not expected to expand, a future petrochemist may consider an international career in the industry more rewarding than facing a challenging job market at home. Scientific work at universities is very dependent on public funding of research and thus is linked to domestic budget policies.

Further Reading

Burdick, Donald L., and William L. Leffler. *Petrochemicals in Nontechnical Language.* 4th ed. Tulsa: PennWell, 2010. Print. Comprehensive coverage of the subject that focuses on chemical properties of petrochemical molecules, written to be as accessible as possible. Figures for illustration.

Galambos, Louis, Takashi Hikino, and Vera Zamagni, eds. *The Global Chemical Industry in the Age of the Petrochemical Revolution.* Cambridge: Cambridge UP, 2007. Print. Series of essays examining the changes petrochemicals brought to the chemical industry after World War II. Includes case studies of several countries and the effect on major players in the chemical industry.

Gary, James H., Glenn E. Handwerk, and Mark J. Kaiser, eds. *Petroleum Refining: Technology and Economics.* 5th ed. Boca Raton: CRC, 2007. Print. Focuses on the production of aromatics, unsaturates, and saturates in chapter 15, "Petrochemical Feedstocks." Diagrams, tables.

Matar, Sami, and Lewis F. Hatch. *Chemistry of Petrochemical Processes.* 2nd ed. Boston: Gulf Professional, 2001. Print. Useful survey of the chemical processes involved in the creation of petrochemicals from raw materials of crude oil, natural gas, and unconventional hydrocarbon sources. Focuses on different petrochemicals and their production.

Speight, James G. *The Chemistry and Technology of Petroleum.* 4th ed. Boca Raton: CRC, 2007. Print. Covers petrochemicals in chapter 23 in an accessible and clearly understandable fashion. General discussion followed by description of chemical processes for petrochemicals. Tables and figures.

Wells, G. Margaret. *Handbook of Petrochemicals and Processes.* 2nd ed. Aldershot: Gower, 1999. Print. Comprehensive presentation of a wide variety of petrochemicals; describes production processes for each. Identifies international classifications, applications, and major producers. Figures and tables.

About the Author: R. C. Lutz, PhD, is an instructor of business English at an international consulting company. His students include professionals in science and engineering, particularly in the chemical, process, oil and gas, and petrochemical industries, but not limited to these fields. He is the author of survey and encyclopedia articles in the applied sciences, among other subjects. After obtaining his MA and PhD in English literature from the University of California at Santa Barbara, he worked for a few years in academia before moving to a consulting company. He has worked in the United States, the Sultanate of Oman, the United Arab Emirates, Turkey, and Romania.

Petrochemist 🍃

Earnings (Yearly Median): $69,760 (Bureau of Labor Statistics, 2012)

Employment and Outlook: Slower than average growth (Bureau of Labor Statistics, 2012)

O*NET-SOC Code: 19-2031.00

Related Career Cluster(s): Manufacturing; Agriculture, Food & Natural Resources; Education & Training

Scope of Work

Petrochemists are concerned with the production of bulk petrochemicals and their intermediaries. Petrochemicals are defined by their derivation from hydrocarbon sources, namely crude oil, natural gas, or liquefied petroleum. Some petrochemicals, such as ammonia, are inorganic, meaning they are not carbon-based, but they are still derived from the processing of hydrocarbons. Petrochemists work primarily in the oil and gas industry, particularly in connection with refineries and stand-alone petrochemical plants such as ethylene crackers, or in academia.

Petrochemists seek to optimize production of the most desirable petrochemicals and to research new applications for petrochemicals. Because petrochemicals are the basic feedstock for polymers—that is, plastics and synthetic fibers—and for the majority of specialty chemicals, their production is of great commercial importance. Petrochemists work closely with chemical engineers to design processes maximizing the output of desired petrochemicals. In academia and industry, petrochemists look for innovative ways to create petrochemicals and to find new applications for them.

Education and Coursework

Work as a petrochemist requires at least a bachelor of science degree. In high school, students interested in a career in petrochemistry should take many science classes, and at the highest levels offered. Students should also take laboratory classes. Solid skills in mathematics, computer science, English, and communications should be acquired. Mineralogy and geology classes, if offered at the high-school level, are good opportunities to learn more about the most common basis of petrochemicals, oil and gas.

Undergraduate students should pursue a bachelor of science degree in chemistry while also gaining a broad general education in the sciences. In chemistry, students should take core classes in analytical, organic, inorganic, physical, and materials chemistry. A course in polymer chemistry, such as one focusing on organic chemistry of polymers, should definitely be taken. Because petrochemists in the industry often work in teams with other scientists, students should take courses in physics, geology, and biology. A practical understanding of mathematics and computer science should be acquired, too. Some knowledge of engineering is helpful to understand the work of chemical and petroleum engineers. The same is true for materials science, biochemistry, and synthetic chemistry. Taking general-education classes in economics is good preparation for a job in the industry.

Most chemistry jobs in the United States require more education than a bachelor's degree. According to the 2010 census of the American Chemical Society (ACS), as of 2010, only 17.7 percent of all chemists had a bachelor's degree only, down from 24.3 percent in

---

Transferable Skills

- Interpersonal/Social Skills – Working as a member of a team (SCANS Workplace Competency–Interpersonal)
- Research & Planning Skills – Solving problems (SCANS Thinking Skills)
- Organization & Management Skills – Making decisions (SCANS Thinking Skills)
- Technical Skills – Using technology to process information (SCANS Workplace Competency – Information)
- Work Environment Skills – Working in a laboratory setting
- Work Environment Skills – Working in a fast-paced environment

---

1990. For graduate studies, students should look for universities with strong reputations in chemistry and specializations in petrochemistry. At the graduate level, students should deepen their studies of organic and polymer chemistry and also take advanced courses in petrochemistry. From 1990 to 2010, the percentage of chemists with master's of science degrees in chemistry was stable at about 17 percent.

The majority of petrochemists, like other chemists, earn a doctorate degree. The ACS states that from 1990 to 2010, the percentage of chemists with PhDs has risen from 58.5 to 64.4. This trend has been reinforced by the employment shift from industry to academia, where a PhD is generally required. A PhD thesis in petrochemistry has to present original research in the field. Doctoral students should work closely with their faculty advisers to find a subject tailored to personal research strengths and interests.

Career Enhancement and Training

Typically, petrochemists do not require a special license to perform their work. Many petrochemists join the American Chemical Association or become members of the American Petroleum Institute. Conferences and seminars organized by both professional associations, as well as many other academic or industry-sponsored conferences, provide ideal platforms for petrochemists to network and keep abreast of opportunities for employment and professional development.

After graduating from school, petrochemists traditionally must choose whether to work for the petrochemical industry or stay in academia. Some also become government employees, typically in research positions.

In industry, petrochemists' careers are focused on developing profitable petrochemical applications and process solutions and performing laboratory work with the goal of creating economic value. Here, work experience and performance is the key to professional success. According to the ACS, in the petrochemical industry, median salaries for those with a BS degree double with fifteen to nineteen years of work experience. However, this trend will depend on the overall economic shape of the petrochemical industry and the professional success of the individual.

In government positions, the ACS found, petrochemists, like other chemists, tended to see their median salary double after about ten to fourteen years of experience. The leveling of salaries could set in after twenty-five years of experience.

Academia emphasizes publication of original research work. Here, the traditional career ladder should lead to tenure and full professorship. Academic salaries, which are lower than those for industry and government positions, double fifteen to nineteen years after one obtains an undergraduate degree.

Daily Tasks and Technology

Most petrochemists spend considerable time in laboratories, where they typically work within teams of scientists. The type of laboratory work depends on the employment sector. In the petrochemical industry, emphasis is on both analyzing currently produced petrochemicals and designing experiments leading to improved yield, better quality, and more economical production. Here, petrochemists also perform laboratory experiments to test new applications and their economic viability. In government agencies, laboratory work can focus on determining the environmental safety of petrochemicals and examining the possible health and environmental hazards. In academia, laboratory work emphasizes original research as well as a widening of the knowledge of petrochemical characteristics and the discovery of new compounds and applications, initially regardless of economic considerations.

Industry petrochemists may visit the sites of petrochemical production (such as aromatics extraction plants at a refinery), observe processes there, and take samples back to their laboratory. Increasingly, they rely on computer modeling to optimize or innovate petrochemical production. They may also be required to present their findings at managerial meetings of their company.

In academia, faculty petrochemists interact with their undergraduate and graduate students through teaching and by performing experiments. Academic petrochemists spend some time pursuing government grants supporting their research teams.

Petrochemists employ the full range of contemporary laboratory and computer equipment in the sciences. Of particular importance are centrifuges, pumps, lasers, spectrometers, and titration and distillation equipment. Standard chemical tools such as Erlenmeyer flasks and test tubes are used in conjunction with highly sophisticated scientific computer software.

Earnings and Employment Outlook

The US Bureau of Labor Statistics (BLS) expects employment for chemists, including petrochemists, to grow by just 4 percent from 2010 to 2020, a much slower rate than average. The reasons for this are complex. A key factor is that the petrochemical industry, traditionally based in the United States and western Europe, is moving its plants to Asia and the Middle East.

There is employment growth for petrochemists in academia, with a projected 15.6 percent job increase for all chemists from 2010 to 2020. A 10.9 percent job growth is forecast for petrochemists and other chemists who provide professional, scientific, and technical services.

However, BLS predicts a 12.6 percent decline in employment of chemists by the petroleum industry from 2010 to 2020. In chemical manufacturing, BLS predicts a contraction of employment of chemists from 26,000 people in 2010 to 24,600 in 2020. Basic chemical-manufacturing jobs are expected to decline 15.1 percent. In synthetics, to which petrochemistry delivers feed stocks, chemists' jobs are expected to decline by 7.1 percent. Hardest hit will be agricultural chemical manufacturing; jobs for chemists in that field are expected to decline by 22.2 percent. In pharmaceutical manufacturing, the job outlook is stable.

The US Bureau of Labor Statistics (BLS) expects employment for chemists, including petrochemists, to grow by just 4 percent from 2010 to 2020, a much slower rate than average.

Median salaries for petrochemists are lowest in academia. The 2010 ACS census presents salary figures that exceed those of BLS. For all chemists, the ACS sees a median 2010 salary of $89,000. Chemists in the industry earned a median salary of $100,000, those in government positions $94,200, and those in academia $68,000. Traditionally, petrochemists have been among the most highly paid chemists in the chemical industry.

Related Occupations

- **Chemical Engineers:** Chemical engineers design production processes for chemicals, including petrochemicals. They are highly valued because chemistry is a process industry and intelligent engineering solutions can make a substantial economic difference.

- **Petroleum Engineers:** Petroleum engineers develop engineering solutions to extract oil and natural gas from new or mature deposits. They are among the most highly paid science professionals.

- **Petroleum Geologists:** Petroleum geologists utilize their knowledge of geology to aid in the exploration of new deposits of oil and natural gas.

A Conversation with Richard Renneboog

Job Title: Technical Consultant and Writer
(MSc in Synthetic Organic Chemistry)

What was your career path?

My career path consisted of obtaining a postgraduate degree in organic chemistry, augmented by an associate degree in electronics engineering technology. These provide a broad technical knowledge base and well-developed research skills that support consultative work and technical writing. They also enable ongoing opportunity for continuous learning, an essential tool in this kind of career.

What are three pieces of advice you would offer someone interested in your profession?

First, realize that the nature of work and career is changing at an ever increasing rate, and that there is little likelihood that your career will go as planned. New opportunities and needs arise. Therefore, be as flexible as possible in building your academic background while focusing on your area of interest. Second, as much as is humanly possible take every opportunity for continuing education in any topic that interests you and not just in your area of specialization. The interconnectedness of your knowledge base is surprising, even though topics seem totally unrelated. Third, strive to succeed at what you do, but do not be afraid of unsuccessful endeavors, because they too are learning experiences that can lead you to other opportunities and successes.

What paths for career advancement are available to you?

Theoretically, the possibilities for advancement in my career are unlimited. Practically, however, that advancement depends very strictly on the effort I put into the work. As an independent consultant, I don't have corporate programs to support my work, but I do have a great deal more freedom to be successful in areas that would otherwise not be available to me. A career as an independent is not for the faint of heart or

> the ill-prepared, but it is a career path that is becoming more and more valuable because of the flexibility that it provides, and those who are willing to seek out the opportunities can do well.

- **Materials Scientists:** Materials scientists analyze the structure and properties of existing materials to develop new or improved products, often combining materials to form new compounds. They use chemistry and applied physics and contribute to developing nanotechnology.

Future Applications

There has been a strong tendency to increase the value generated from processing hydrocarbons such as oil and gas, which has led to a marked interest in advances in petrochemistry. Nanoscience and nanotechnology have developed rapidly in the field of petrochemistry, looking for new applications following the production of classic bulk petrochemicals. Nanoscience and nanotechnology provide a rich field for further research and development in both the academic and the industrial sectors.

The petrochemical industry is shifting to a more global base than ever before. Petrochemists should consider non-US-based appointments in the industry. Additionally, the domestic shift in the United States toward academic employment depends on federal funding of research; if this funding should decrease, universities could not sustain their chemistry faculty levels.

Many forecasters calculate there will be a balance between domestic industry cutback and the need to research new petrochemical applications. Most have no doubt that the coming decades will see great innovations in petrochemistry. This would continue the development of significant new applications, a trend similar to that in the field of polycarbonates.

R. C. Lutz, PhD

More Information

American Chemical Society
1155 Sixteenth Street NW
Washington, DC 20036
portal.acs.org

American Fuel and Petrochemical Manufacturers
1667 K Street NW, Suite 700
Washington, DC 20006
www.afpm.org

American Petroleum Institute
1220 L Street NW
Washington, DC 20005-4070
www.api.org

European Petrochemical Association
Avenue de Tervueren 270 Tervurenlaan
1150 Brussels
Belgium
www.epca.eu

Pharmacology

FIELDS OF STUDY

Chemistry; biology; biochemistry; physiology; microbiology; pathology; anatomy; genetics; mathematics; physics.

DEFINITION

Pharmacology is the study of how drugs and other chemical compounds act in a living organism. The field of pharmacology examines the basic chemical properties, biological effects, therapeutic value, and potential toxicity of drugs. Scientists who study pharmacology are involved in medicine, nursing, pharmacy, dentistry, and veterinary medicine. They develop new drugs, improve the safety of existing drugs or chemicals, and prevent and treat countless diseases. Pharmacology is a highly integrated field, applying basic principles of chemistry, biology, and physics to the safe and effective use of drugs and chemical compounds in living systems.

Basic Principles

Pharmacology is the study of how drugs and chemical compounds affect living processes. Pharmacology is closely related to biochemistry and physiology in terms of substantive knowledge and experimental techniques. Pharmacology is also closely related to chemistry and physics because it relies on a basic understanding of the fundamental chemical and physical properties of drugs, as well as of living organisms. Pharmacology also involves mathematics for quantification of its basic principles. Pharmacology is not an autonomous field of study but unifies the study of chemicals and living organisms and the interactions between them, and uses the knowledge and techniques of several other science disciplines for its foundation.

Pharmacology can be broadly divided into four categories: pharmacodynamics and pharmacokinetics, toxicology, pharmacotherapy, and pharmacy. Pharmacodynamics and pharmacokinetics examine the biological effect produced by a drug, as well as how the drug gets to the site of action and the fate of the drug in the body. They also evaluate the safety and effectiveness of drugs. Toxicology analyzes the toxic or harmful effects of drugs and chemical compounds and the mechanisms and conditions by which they occur. It also focuses on the signs, symptoms, and treatments for poisoning. Toxicology studies not only therapeutic agents but also the harmful effects of chemicals in manufacturing, food, water, and the atmosphere. It is instrumental in defining the legal relationship between accidental or intentional chemical exposure and the subsequent harmful effects.

Pharmacy is closely related to pharmacology, but it is a clinical, patient-focused discipline responsible for the safe preparation and dispensing of therapeutic agents. The application of drugs for the prevention or treatment of disease is called pharmacotherapy. Pharmacists work closely with physicians and other health care providers and use their knowledge of drugs and drug preparations to optimize pharmacotherapy.

Core Concepts

Drug-Receptor Interactions. The foundation of pharmacology lies in the understanding of how drugs interact with their target receptors. Though only a few basic types of drug-receptor interactions exist, the molecular details vary widely among different classes of drugs and receptors. Additionally, classifying drugs by their mechanism of action simplifies pharmacology, because this basic knowledge of how a drug works translates to predictable actions in cells, tissues, and organs, and explains how a drug mediates its therapeutic and adverse effects. Without basic fundamentals of chemistry, biology, physics, and physiology, the simple interaction between drug and receptor could not be expanded to its broad physiological context.

The technology used in the study of drug-receptor interactions includes in vivo and in vitro experiments, as well as modern computer software for mathematical and statistical modeling. Such software systems allow researchers to create models of drug compounds and receptors, simulate the interaction between drugs and receptors, predict the bioavailability of drugs, and re-create physiological environments in which a drug can be absorbed and distributed. Molecular modeling of drugs can also predict drug metabolism and drug interactions, although the clinical and therapeutic relevance of such activity is difficult to ascertain from a computer-generated model.

The study of drug-receptor interactions encompasses biopharmaceutics, which evaluates the relationships among the chemical and physical properties of a drug, the dosage form of the drug, the route of administration, and the biological effect. The Biopharmaceutics Classification System (BCS) is a research tool that provides a framework for making decisions in the early stages of drug development. The BCS provides solubility and permeability information for known compounds to predict the actions and reactions of a new drug in the body.

Liquid Chromatography. Chemical assays are important in the initial analysis of drug products and metabolites. Assays may be performed on a variety of substances or on samples from a variety of species, including humans, rats, and primates. Samples may be obtained from the liver, the drug's target organ, or blood or another body fluid. Liquid chromatography is often used to identify and quantify drug molecules or metabolites based on size, charge, or polarity. A small volume of the sample to be tested is placed into a liquid (mobile phase) that is pushed through a column (stationary phase) by a pump. The sample interacts with the material in the column—usually saturated carbon chains—and a detection device captures the activity of the sample as it leaves the stationary phase. Every compound has a characteristic time that it stays in the stationary phase, called retention time; therefore, this retention time can be used to identify a compound.

Several types of detection devices may be used at the end of a liquid chromatography column. Ultraviolet and fluorescence spectroscopies detect the ability of organic compounds to absorb light in the electromagnetic spectrum. Each compound absorbs light characteristically, allowing for the identification of organic compounds, including drug products and metabolites.

Positron Emission Tomography. Positron emission tomography (PET) scans are used to evaluate the pharmacokinetics of drug products. Highly sensitive and specific, they are often used in drug development. PET scans allow modeling of drugs in the blood and tissues and yield measurements of receptor density on a target tissue. They are also used to study drug distribution throughout the body and drug metabolism. A PET scan is a specialized type of nuclear imaging that produces three-dimensional pictures of the processes of the body. To conduct a PET scan, a radioactive substance is tagged to a drug molecule and introduced into the body. The scanner detects the gamma rays emitted by the radioactive tag throughout the body over time. A computer then collects the images and reconstructs the body, allowing visualization of the target molecule within the body over a period of time.

Clinical Trials. After a drug is developed and its pharmacokinetic and pharmacodynamic properties are characterized, it is taken through several phases of clinical testing to determine the actual response achieved in patients. Clinical trials are necessary to determine the safe and appropriate doses for patient populations and uncover drug interactions or safety issues that may not be apparent during drug development phases. Patients are administered test drugs under highly regulated conditions.

Applications Past and Present

Pharmacology is a highly integrated and interdisciplinary field that is divided into specialized applications. However, many of these divisions overlap, and pharmacologists collaborate with scientists in other fields to perfect the safe and effective use of drugs and other chemicals. Pharmacology principles may be applied to a variety of disease states, as well as individual and community health and environmental applications.

Clinical Pharmacology and Therapeutics. Clinical pharmacology and therapeutics are related areas that study the effects of the pharmacokinetics and pharmacodynamics of a drug in humans. Clinical pharmacology applies the knowledge of how drugs work to how they can affect disease processes. It also examines how a disease process may alter the action of drugs in the body. Pharmacogenomics is a new field within clinical pharmacology that examines how individual genetic variations and genome components alter drug pharmacokinetics and pharmacodynamics.

Closely related to clinical pharmacology, therapeutics encompasses the use of drugs to treat, prevent, or cure a disease. Therapeutic applications of pharmacology are necessary to optimize drug effectiveness and safety and prevent medication errors. Clinical pharmacology and therapeutics are also essential to the design and management of clinical trials.

Behavioral Pharmacology. Behavioral pharmacology studies the effects that drugs have on behavior. This specialized field of pharmacology covers topics including the molecular foundation of drug activity on neurotransmitters and the therapeutic and clinical ramifications of drugs on behaviors. Behavioral pharmacology also encompasses the evaluation and treatment of substance abuse and addiction disorders.

Cardiovascular Pharmacology. Cardiovascular pharmacology examines the effects of drugs on the heart and vascular system, as well as on other body mechanisms that regulate cardiovascular functions. Cardiovascular pharmacology includes all aspects of pharmacology, from the understanding of the mechanism of action of cardiovascular drugs to the use of drugs in clinical and therapeutic settings.

Endocrine Pharmacology. Endocrine pharmacology studies drugs that are hormones or hormone derivatives and drugs that alter the function of hormones. Endocrine pharmacology is concerned with the use of drugs to treat or prevent diseases of metabolic origin.

Neuropharmacology. Neuropharmacology investigates drugs that affect the central and peripheral nervous system, including the brain, spinal cord, and nerves. Neuropharmacologists may analyze the causes of disease or define brain activity to apply pharmacologic principles to the treatment or prevention of nervous system disorders, addiction and abuse disorders, behavioral disorders, and psychological disorders. Neuropharmacology also applies to the understanding and use of anesthesia.

Biochemical and Cellular Pharmacology. Biochemical and cellular pharmacology works at the smallest level of drug action. This field integrates biochemistry, physiology, and cell biology to understand how drugs influence the chemical actions of a cell.

Chemotherapy. Chemotherapy is the application of pharmacological principles to the treatment of microbial infections and cancer. Advances in chemotherapy make it possible to administer a drug to kill or inhibit the growth of a tumor or infecting organism without significantly impairing the normal function of the host body.

Drug Discovery and Legal Aspects. The field of drug discovery and development and regulatory affairs encompasses discovery and validation of new drugs or chemical products, molecular modeling, clinical testing, drug regulation, and the legal and economic aspects of drug use.

Drug Metabolism and Disposition. Drug metabolism and disposition studies the pharmacokinetics and enzymatic metabolism of drugs. This field encompasses the identification of drug metabolites, the regulation of drug metabolism, the relationship between the structure and function of drugs and metabolites, and the classification of drug-metabolizing enzymes.

Molecular Pharmacology. Molecular pharmacology studies the chemical and physical properties of drugs to define how they interact with receptors at the molecular level. This field is deeply rooted in mathematical techniques and molecular biology. Molecular pharmacology deals with all classes of drugs and all types of receptors at the cellular and subcellular level.

Toxicology. Toxicology studies the adverse effects of drugs or other chemicals. This includes not only therapeutic drugs but also household, environmental, and industrial chemicals that may pose a hazard to people or other organisms. Toxicology applies the principles of pharmacokinetics and pharmacodynamics to the design and interpretation of drug safety studies. The principles of pharmacology and toxicology may also be applied to forensics to aid in the medical and legal identification and interpretation of drugs or toxic substances.

Veterinary Pharmacology. Veterinary pharmacology applies the principles of pharmacology to drugs and disease states of animals.

Interesting Facts about Pharmacology

- One of the world's oldest medical documents, the Ebers papyrus, which dates to around 1550 BCE, details how Egyptians prepared and used more than seven hundred drugs and medicinal concoctions, some of which are still used.
- Spanish physician and chemist Mateu Orfila, sometimes called the father of toxicology, published the first comprehensive text on forensic toxicology in 1813; his work emphasized the need for identification and quality assurance in the pharmaceutical, clinical, environmental, and industrial fields.
- Between 1923 and 2000, sixteen pharmacologists received the Nobel Prize in Physiology or Medicine.
- Paul Ehrlich is credited with originating modern chemotherapy, as he is the first scientist who used synthetic compounds to combat infectious diseases; he was awarded the Nobel Prize in Physiology or Medicine in 1908 for outlining the principles involved in using chemicals to destroy cells.
- During World War II, the United States accelerated a wartime program to investigate antimalaria drugs, thereby providing a boost to pharmacology research.
- Only one out of every five drugs in clinical trial receive FDA approval and are eventually marketed.

Systems and Integrative Pharmacology. The study of systems and integrative pharmacology involves drug action and toxicity in the whole animal. Closely related to therapeutics and clinical pharmacology, this specialty examines the big picture of drug action to optimize and individualize drug therapy.

Impact on Industry

The pharmacology industry involves university researchers, pharmaceutical and health care corporations, and government agencies, and a pharmacology education prepares students for work in pharmacology research, toxicology, and biotechnology. Pharmacologists develop new drugs in the pharmaceutical industry, perform basic or applied research at academic institutions, conduct clinical research to establish the effectiveness of drugs in humans, prepare legal and regulatory documents for drug product registration, and work in drug information or pharmaceutical sales. Pharmacologists may work in a research laboratory, a hospital, a university, a pharmaceutical company, or other health care business.

Although it is impossible to estimate the economic impact of the science of pharmacology, the closely related pharmaceutical and medications industry, which is deeply rooted in the principles of pharmacology, had global revenues of $643 billion in 2006. The industries related to pharmacology are highly integrated, with significant collaboration and overlap among academic institutions, industries, medical institutions, and government agencies. Many large pharmaceutical companies are headquartered in the United States, but others are in Europe and Asia.

There were approximately 275,000 pharmacists employed nationally in 2010. About two-thirds worked in retail and community pharmacies, and around another one-fourth worked in hospitals. About one-fourth worked part-time. Employment of pharmacists is expected to grow faster than the average for all occupations through the year 2020, which means employment is projected to increase 20 to 28 percent. This is due to the increased pharmaceutical needs of a larger and older population and greater use of medications. Other factors causing job growth are scientific advances that will make more drug products available, new developments in genome research and medication distribution systems, more sophisticated consumers seeking more information about drugs and coverage of prescription drugs by a greater number of health insurance plans.

Industry and Business. The pharmaceutical and medications manufacturing industry is the largest end user of pharmacology. The industry designs, develops, manufactures, distributes, and markets prescription and over-the-counter medications and health care products. Although most new drugs receive research and clinical input from academia, the majority of drug development and testing is completed by the pharmaceutical industry. The Pharmaceutical Research and Manufacturers of

America represents the pharmaceutical and biotechnology companies that are involved in producing safe and effective medications.

Government Agencies and Military. The discovery, manufacture, and prescription of drugs has economic and political consequences. In the United States, the Food and Drug Administration (FDA) regulates the manufacture, sale, and administration of drug products to ensure safety and effectiveness for the consumer. The FDA imposes strict regulations on the management of clinical trials and requires extensive applications and regulatory filings for each new drug product to be developed or marketed in the United States.

In 2004, the FDA launched the Critical Path Initiative to transform the way that FDA-regulated products are developed, evaluated, manufactured, and used. The initiative affects the design of trials, surveillance of postmarketing safety, and training of scientists and researchers in drug discovery and development. It also encourages the use of new technologies and discoveries to improve drug design. In 2010, the FDA expanded the initiative to include advances in personalized medicine, defenses against drug-resistant bacteria, and the availability of drugs to combat tropical diseases. The initiative's efforts are intended to meet the ongoing public health needs of the United States and the rest of the world.

The United States Pharmacopeia (USP) is a nongovernmental organization that sets public standards for prescription and over-the-counter medicines, health care products, food ingredients, and dietary supplements. The USP dictates the quality, strength, purity, and consistency of these products if they are sold in the United States. The United States Pharmacopeia–National Formulary (USP-NF) presents standards for all drug products, dietary supplements, and excipients. It also sets forth standards for packing, labeling, and storing drug products, as well as detailed information regarding testing quality and assurance measurements.

The military has about 540 pharmacists and 2,650 pharmacy technicians. Newly commissioned pharmacists are assigned to military hospitals or clinics, where they manage daily operations. Positions for pharmacists in the Coast Guard are filled by US Public Health Service officers. In time, pharmacists plan and direct pharmacy or other health programs.

Occupation	Pharmacist
Employment 2010	274,900
Projected Employment 2020	344,600
Change in Number (2010–20)	69,700
Percent Change	25%

Bureau of Labor Statistics, 2012

Academic Research and Teaching. The pharmacology industry and profession relies on universities and the academic sector to train pharmacologists in basic science, the principles of pharmacology, and laboratory and experimental techniques. Universities offer expert educators and essential learning experiences in core pharmacology curriculum. Academic pharmacology researchers are often involved in partnerships with companies in the pharmaceutical or health care industries in which they provide input or research for new drug development or conduct or evaluate clinical trials.

The Association of Medical School Pharmacology Chairs (AM-SPC), which brings together pharmacologists from medical schools throughout North America, works to promote pharmacology as a discipline within graduate and medical school curriculums. The association endorses basic science research, research funding, partnerships with industry, and faculty development to improve pharmacology research and training of students.

Emory University in Atlanta, Georgia, was ranked the premier university in the world for pharmacology and toxicology research. Many students within the program are members of the Georgia Biomedical Partnership, a professional group representing scientists and executives within the pharmaceutical and biotechnology sectors, highlighting the collaboration between academia and industry.

Pharmacology is generally not offered as an undergraduate degree by most universities. Therefore, most people first obtain an undergraduate degree in a basic science such as biochemistry or physiology, where the majority of academic positions related to pharmacology reside. As of 2012, there were nine clinical pharmacology training programs accredited with the American Board of Clinical Pharmacology (ABCP), and nine additional programs registered with the ABCP.

Social Context and Future Prospects

The advances in science and medicine during the twentieth century stimulated advances in pharmacology that continue into the next century. Throughout the ages, drugs and medicinal products have

Occupation	Pharmacy technicians
Employment 2010	334,400
Projected Employment 2020	442,700
Change in Number (2010–20)	108,300
Percent Change	32%

Bureau of Labor Statistics, 2012

been used to create safer, healthier, more productive lives. The world's population is growing and aging, and the understanding of disease states is more advanced than ever before. Pharmacologists are in high demand as the requirement for safe and effective new drugs remains strong in the short- and long-term future.

Better medicines are needed globally, and pharmacology is poised to deliver the necessary researchers, educators, clinical and therapeutic practitioners, and experts in drug evaluation, safety, use, and regulation. Pharmacologists of the future will work with epidemiologists, public health scientists, economists, and social scientists to drive innovation and clinical application of drug products.

Pharmacology is critical to the pharmaceutical and health care industries and has a major impact on individual and public health. It optimizes the understanding and use of existing drugs and chemicals, discovers and evaluates new drugs, and defines the variability in toxic and therapeutic responses to drugs. In the future, pharmacologists may be able to use the principles of genomics and genetics to individualize drug therapy. This could lead to the use of drugs that target one specific protein or receptor to guarantee a clinical response, while erasing the possibility of unwanted adverse effects.

Further Reading

Bertomeu-Sánchez, José Ramón, and Agustí Nieto-Galan, eds. *Chemistry, Medicine, and Crime: Mateu J. B. Orfila (1787–1853) and His Times*. Sagamore Beach, MA: Science History, 2006. A collection of essays that present an overview of the life and work of Orfila and his contributions to pharmacology and toxicology.

Katzung, Bertram, Susan Masters, and Anthony Trevor, eds. *Basic and Clinical Pharmacology*. 11th ed. New York: McGraw-Hill, 2009. A comprehensive textbook that includes more than three hundred full-color illustrations, drug comparison charts, and case studies outlining the clinical applications of pharmacology.

Rubin, Ronald P. "A Brief History of Great Discoveries in Pharmacology: In Celebration of the Centennial Anniversary of the Founding of the American Society of Pharmacology and Experimental Therapeutics." *Pharmacological Reviews* 59.4 (2007): 289–359. An overview of the great scientists and pharmacology discoveries of the nineteenth and twentieth centuries.

Vallance, Patrick, and Trevor G. Smart. "The Future of Pharmacology." *British Journal of Pharmacology* 147 (January 2006): S304–307. A perspective on the future of pharmacology as an integrative science, as well as discussions of the important divisions within the field.

Walsh, Carol T., and Rochelle D. Schwartz-Bloom. *Levine's Pharmacology: Drug Actions and Reactions*. 7th ed. Abingson, England: Taylor & Francis, 2005. Outlines the history of pharmacology, general principles, and individual factors that influence drug action.

About the Author: Jennifer L. Gibson, BS, PharmD, earned her undergraduate degree in biochemistry from Clemson University, with a research emphasis in enzyme structure and function. She worked in the field of genomics and DNA sequencing and was part of the team that completed the International Rice Genome 10 Sequencing Project. She earned her doctor of pharmacy degree from the Virginia Commonwealth University School of Pharmacy. She has clinical practice expertise as a pharmacist in a hospital setting. Additionally, she is a medical communicator with experience in researching and preparing scientific publications for international journals and creating medical education resources and presentations.

Pharmacist

Earnings (Yearly Median): $113,390 (Bureau of Labor Statistics, 2012)

Employment Outlook: Faster than average growth (Bureau of Labor Statistics, 2012)

O*NET-SOC Code: 29-1051.00

Related Career Clusters: Agriculture, Food & Natural Resources; Business, Management & Administration; Health Science

Scope of Work

Pharmacists typically distribute medications to patients and advise them on proper use to ensure that those medications are taken safely. Clinical pharmacists often work in hospitals, educating health-care professionals about the correct dosages and side effects of various prescription medicines. Sometimes they work directly with patients, providing instructions and guidance. They also oversee more technical aspects of handling medications, such as labeling and packaging, to make sure that the drugs are dispensed according to government regulations. Other clinical pharmacists work in an educational capacity, both in schools and in the larger health-care community. Consultant pharmacists serve as advisers for insurance companies and health-care facilities and may monitor patients' prescriptions.

Education and Coursework

A doctor of pharmacy (PharmD) degree is the minimum educational requirement for a career in the field. Some PharmD programs require a bachelor's degree for acceptance, but many will accept students who complete a two-year preprofessional track that features courses in biology, physics, anatomy, physiology, and pharmaceutical practices. For most programs, acceptance also depends on completion of the Pharmacy College Admissions Test (PCAT). As many employers

---

Transferable skills

- Communication Skills – Speaking effectively (SCANS Basic Skill)
- Interpersonal/Social Skills – Counseling others
- Research and Planning Skills – Identifying problems
- Organization and Management Skills – Paying attention to and handling details
- Organization and Management Skills – Making decisions (SCANS Thinking Skill)
- Technical Skills – Performing scientific, mathematical and technical work
- Technical Skills – Working with your hands

---

typically prefer to hire graduates of accredited programs, students interested in entering the field should focus on applying to programs that are accredited by the Accreditation Council for Pharmacy Education.

PharmD programs are usually completed in four years, although some institutions offer three-year programs. Candidates complete courses in pharmacology, medical ethics, law, and health management, along with coursework focusing on medical dosages and patient consultations. Courses on prescription-drug abuse and a pharmacist's role in preventing it have become more common as awareness of such issues has increased. During the second half of the program, candidates participate in Advanced Pharmacy Practice Experiences (APPEs) that give them supervised practical experience in different areas of pharmacy. Individuals seeking to obtain advanced pharmacy positions must typically complete a residency of one to two years that may involve research. Overall, an individual should leave a pharmacy program with leadership and communication skills as well as a foundation in hard science and medical training.

Career Enhancement and Training

After successfully completing a PharmD program, a pharmacist must complete two tests to obtain a license to work in the field. The first test is the North American Pharmacist Licensure Examination (NAPLEX), which covers pharmacotherapy and the dispensing of medications and tests one's ability to provide accurate health-care information to patients. The second is the Multistate Pharmacy Jurisprudence Examination (MPJE). This exam tests students on federal and state licensure requirements and regulatory law. Both exams are administered by the National Association of Boards of Pharmacy, a professional organization that also provides various educational and networking resources to practicing pharmacists.

Pharmacists typically begin their careers in positions focused on dispensing drugs and advice to patients. Over time, they may move on to supervisory or administrative positions or to particular areas of specialization. The Board of Pharmaceutical Specialties certifies pharmacists in areas such as nutrition support pharmacy, psychiatric pharmacy, and ambulatory care pharmacy. The Commission for Certification in Geriatric Pharmacy and the American Board of Applied Toxicology also offer specialized certifications.

Daily Tasks and Technology

As pharmacists work in a variety of areas, their responsibilities vary greatly. A pharmacist working in a drugstore is primarily responsible for filling prescriptions. This involves inspecting the prescription to determine whether the prescribed drug will negatively interact with the patient's other medications or conditions, offering information on how and when to take the medication, and providing guidance regarding potential side effects. For many medications, pharmacists provide standard dosages issued by pharmaceutical companies. In some cases, however, pharmacists must mix or otherwise modify drugs themselves, typically with the assistance of pharmacy technicians. In addition to interacting with patients and technicians, pharmacists must also communicate with health-insurance companies and keep insurance records. When a pharmacist owns or manages his or her place of employment, the necessary record keeping extends to managing inventory and keeping track of other information related to the business.

Large employers and insurance companies employ some pharmacists to provide medication therapy management, which may include holding face-to-face sessions with patients, tracking cholesterol or blood glucose levels, or advising customers on diet and exercise. For clinical pharmacists employed by hospitals, providing this kind of direct patient care is a primary responsibility. Clinical pharmacists may accompany doctors on their rounds, advising them on medications and monitoring the health of the patients. Consultant pharmacists provide efficiency advice to health-care facilities or insurance providers.

Earnings and Employment Outlook

According the United States Bureau of Labor Statistics, employment of pharmacists is expected to increase by 25 percent between 2010 and 2020. This growth can be attributed to scientific advancements, increased insurance coverage, an aging population, and an expected increase in the number of medications consumed by the average person. In addition, pharmacists are well paid, earning a median annual wage that is significantly higher than the median for many other occupations.

According the United States Bureau of Labor Statistics, employment of pharmacists is expected to increase by 25 percent between 2010 and 2020.

Perhaps due to increased drug consumption, pharmacists are increasingly being hired to work in locations such as physician's offices and nursing homes. Mail-order pharmacies also provide employment opportunities for pharmacists, despite controversy within the health-care industry regarding the level of patient care and guidance provided by such businesses. As such pharmacies are often more affordable for patients and insurance companies and allow older patients and patients with limited mobility to receive medications quickly and easily, they will likely continue to provide opportunities for pharmacists to put their skills and training to use.

Related Occupations

- **Biochemists:** Biochemists apply chemistry and biology to research in the medical field.

- **Medical Scientists:** Medical scientists conduct research to improve human health and health care and prevent and treat disease.

- **Pharmacy Technicians:** Pharmacy technicians assist licensed pharmacists by filling, labeling, and packaging prescriptions, as well as completing other service tasks in a hospital or retail pharmacy.

- **Physicians and Surgeons:** Physicians and surgeons diagnose and treat patients who are ill or injured and often specialize in particular areas of medicine.

- **Registered Nurses:** Registered nurses work directly with patients and their families to administer treatments and otherwise provide care and support.

Future Applications

Changes in health-care practices across the United States are affecting how many pharmacists are doing business. Increased use of mail-order and Internet pharmacies has caused many pharmacists to take positions at such companies rather than at independent or chain pharmacies. As competition for retail pharmacy jobs has increased, many pharmacists have chosen to specialize in areas such as nuclear and military pharmacy, while others have sought clinical pharmacy positions at hospitals and care centers.

As the number of elderly Americans increases and care becomes more complex, many pharmacists are also seeking special accreditation in geriatric pharmacy. This allows them to seek employment in nursing homes, where they work in-house to manage the care of long-term patients and ensure that treatments do not overlap or cause detrimental interactions. As health care becomes increasingly tied to politics and public policy, jobs are also opening up in the public and private sectors. Health-insurance companies are hiring pharmacists

A Conversation with Ginny Hoffman

Job Title: Pharmacist

What was your career path?

After graduating as a pharmacist, I worked for ten years providing pharmacy services (drugs, drug advice, analysis of drug levels in the blood) in a hospital setting. I then worked in an independent retail pharmacy for a short while following a move to a new town. I took many years off to raise my family and then eased back into the pharmacy world through volunteer situations (medical missions to Honduras, local free clinic for the working poor), and now work part-time in an independent retail pharmacy.

What are three pieces of advice you would offer someone interested in your profession?

1. Your drug knowledge will NEVER be up to date and you can never stop learning and studying.
2. For most pharmacists, you must be able to concentrate well through constant distractions and interruptions.
3. Most pharmacists are on their feet all day long. This may seem minor, but it takes its toll very quickly for some people.

What paths for career advancement are available to you?

There are opportunities to advance—as a district manager or in research settings—but advancement generally takes you away from actual pharmacy work. The great majority of pharmacists prefer to work in traditional retail or hospital settings. The work changes and is always challenging, but a new pharmacist and one with thirty years of experience will generally work side-by-side with similar duties and a fairly similar paycheck. The entry level pay is great, but thirty years later, the pay will not have advanced much other than cost of living/inflation adjustments.

to grapple with ways to prevent costly inefficiencies, increasing the number of available administrative positions. As the US government works to reform the health-care industry and ensure that all Americans will be able to receive necessary care, pharmacists will be needed at all levels to assist in implementing reforms and caring for newly insured individuals.

Molly Hagan

More Information

American Association of Colleges of Pharmacy
1727 King Street
Alexandria, VA 22314
www.aacp.org

American Pharmacist Association
2215 Constitution Avenue NW
Washington, DC 20037
www.pharmacist.com

American Society of Health-System Pharmacists
7272 Wisconsin Avenue
Bethesda, MD 20814
www.ashp.org

Polymer Chemistry

FIELDS OF STUDY

Chemistry; organic chemistry; inorganic chemistry; biochemistry; polymer chemistry; mathematics; physics; analytical chemistry; biochemistry.

DEFINITION

Polymer chemistry is the branch of organic chemistry concerned with polymerization and the materials formed by polymerization. In a polymerization reaction, a large number of small molecules become chemically bonded together to form a much larger molecule. Polymer chemists work to produce new polymers with specific properties, to blend and compound existing polymer formulations for improved applicability, and to design the processes by which bulk quantities of specific polymers can be produced on an industrial scale. Polymer chemistry also includes the study and development of adhesives, rubbers, detergents, paints, and materials used for repair and insulation. A significant aspect of polymer chemistry relates to the now-ubiquitous presence of highly stable synthetic polymers in the environment. Polymer chemistry is therefore perhaps the most diverse field of industrial chemistry, due to the large number of compounds involved and the extent to which polymers are distributed throughout modern life.

Basic Principles

The essential science of polymer chemistry is organic chemistry, specifically the chemistry of polymerization reactions. In polymerization, a large number of small molecules become chemically bonded to each other to form a single large molecule, which may have a structure that is either linear or three-dimensional. As this applies generally, there are a large number of mineral forms based on silicon. However, the vast majority of polymers are based on carbon, with its innate ability to form stable extended chains. While silicon, being of the same periodic group as carbon, is capable of forming extended chain structures, carbon is unique among the elements in the number and variety of molecular structures that it can form. Thus, polymers are found not just in synthetic materials such as plastic and rubber but also in nature, as biopolymers such as cellulose and protein.

The key feature of polymerization reactions is that small molecules that may or may not be identical bond to each other in specific ways. In polyethylene and cellulose, for example, the polymer molecules are formed when individual molecules of ethylene and glucose, respectively, join together in a linear fashion. Each monomeric molecule has a single location at which the next molecule can be added to the chain. When more than one such site exists in the monomer, however, chains can become interconnected in a three-dimensional network rather than as a linear structure. It is thus entirely possible for a massive quantity of a suitable monomer to eventually become a single molecule through a polymerization reaction, although the likelihood of this happening is exceedingly small. In a typical polymerization reaction, many thousands of individual polymeric chains are forming at the same time independently of each other and are terminated when an unfavorable addition occurs or when an impurity is encountered that interrupts the chain-lengthening process.

Core Concepts

Addition Polymers. Addition polymers are the most common form of polymeric materials, the most readily recognizable one being polyethylene. In the formation of an addition polymer, a quantity of simple small molecules join up in a head-to-tail manner according to the nature of the site of addition. By controlling conditions, it is, for example, possible to produce an entire series of "linear alkane" molecules from ethylene: butane, hexane, octane, decane, and so on through chain lengths consisting of thousands of ethylene units. The ultimate molecular weights of such addition polymers are always multiples of the molecular weight of the starting monomer, or monomers when combinations of different monomeric materials are used in the formulation.

Condensation Polymers. Condensation polymers are similar to addition polymers in that monomeric units add together in a linear fashion.

They differ, however, in that two different reaction sites, or functional groups, are normally required in the monomers used. The term *condensation* here refers to the structure of the linkages between monomer units in the polymeric molecule. In each one, it is as though the components of a small molecule such as water or hydrogen chloride have condensed together out of the parent functional groups. The ultimate molecular weights of condensation polymers are the combined weights of the monomers minus the corresponding amounts of condensation products, according to the formulation being used.

Cross-Linked Polymers. When more than one reactive site or functional group that can undergo an addition or condensation reaction is available in the same molecule, the resulting polymer molecules do not form linearly. Instead, each site can take part in a different polymerization chain reaction, and in this way, multiple polymer chains can become linked together in a very large three-dimensional molecular structure. The bonds between parallel polymerization chains are called *cross-links*. A complex system of polymeric materials that is of great importance in modern technological applications is the so-called epoxy resins, based on monomers in which the functional site is the epoxide group. Polymerization of these compounds occurs when the epoxide ring structure breaks open and adds to another in a chain reaction.

Copolymers. Copolymers are variations of the basic types of polymers. Their molecular structures depend on the formulation being used rather than the type of reaction that takes place. A copolymer would be formed when a combination of ethylene and propylene is used instead of just one of the two. The polymeric combination is normally indicated by a fractional subscript for each component. The copolymers provide the most common way of varying the physical properties of the resulting products, and the possible variations are essentially infinite.

Catalysis. Many polymers are produced using a catalyst to mediate the reaction process. A catalyst is a compound or material that speeds up a chemical reaction by reducing the energy barriers that reacting components must overcome, while the catalyst itself is not changed in the reaction. Catalysts normally function by forming a complex with the monomers, bringing them directly into the proper orientation for the reaction to occur between them. In the production of polyethylene, for example, the catalyst material joins with units of ethylene without forming a chemical bond to those units. They can then easily form a bond between themselves, during which process the active end of the growing chain is released from the catalyst, which can then add another ethylene unit to undergo further reaction. Eventually, the long polymeric chain is released completely from the catalyst, which can then be recovered unchanged from its initial form.

Reaction Conditions. Most polymers are produced on an industrial scale, requiring the utilization of great amounts of energy. Accordingly, many processes are carried out in the gas phase, as this is the state of matter that is easiest to manipulate in large quantities. This also facilitates the separation of product materials from the gaseous process stream. Reactions can also be carried out in liquid-phase conditions. In other cases, components of the polymer in liquid form are combined in place and allowed to react, producing the polymeric material in its final shape. This is the method typically used in molding operations such as those used for the manufacture of modern aircraft components from advanced composite materials.

Biopolymers. Biopolymers are polymeric materials that are produced by living organisms. In plants, the most abundant biopolymers are celluloses, starches, and lignins. Celluloses and starches are produced by the polymerization of glucose molecules that are the product of photosynthesis. Lignins are hard structural materials produced by other biochemical pathways in plant metabolism. In animals, a wide variety of biopolymers are produced, including numerous proteins and structural materials such as collagen and DNA. These are the products of enzyme-mediated condensation reactions with combinations of simple amino acids, bases, and sugars.

Fiber and Matrix Applications. A very significant field of polymer chemistry focuses on the development of new polymers and polymerizing formulations to be formed into fibers and matrix materials for advanced composite materials. These may be produced from biopolymers, as is the case with carbon fiber produced from cotton, or from synthetic polymers, as is the case with the polyamide material known as Kevlar. These and other fibers of mineral origin are encased in a matrix of cross-linked polymer resin, creating structures of low weight and extremely high strength. A great deal of chemical awareness is required for their development, since the fiber and resin materials must be chemically inert with respect to each other and to other materials with which they come into contact.

Applications Past and Present

Explosives and Propellants. While explosives and propellants are a minor aspect of polymer chemistry, they have nevertheless played a significant role in the history of the field. The first successful synthetic polymer, nitrocellulose, falls into this category. An effective method of its synthesis was discovered accidentally by the Swiss German chemist Christian Friedrich Schönbein in 1846. Because it burned rapidly and with almost no smoke, nitrocellulose was quickly identified as a desirable alternative to the highly smoky black powder used in the production of gunpowder. Nitrocellulose thus became known as "gun cotton," and a furious competition ensued among European nations seeking synthetic methods for producing it that would circumvent Schönbein's patents. Since that time, a number of other explosives and propellants, such as Cordite, have been developed, all of them based on nitrocellulose.

Fibers and Fabrics. Other researchers quickly developed other uses for nitrocellulose, as well as additional methods of modifying cellulose to produce other plastics. The first and most commercially successful of these variations on nitrocellulose became the material known as celluloid, which as the first fully formable plastic became the foundation of the film industry and a plethora of objects that could be produced en masse with the new material. A further refinement of processes based on cellulose is the viscose process, by which cellulose is modified into cellulose xanthate and then recovered. The process, developed in order to find a method of creating artificial silk, produced the fine-fiber materials known as rayon and its many variants.

Interesting Facts about Polymer Chemistry

- Christian Friedrich Schönbein accidentally discovered an effective method of synthesizing nitrocellulose in 1846 when he used his wife's cotton apron to wipe up a spilled mixture of nitric and sulfuric acids, then hung it by a hot stove to dry. The apron ignited and burned so quickly that it disappeared in a wisp of smoke.
- In the mid-1860s, elephant ivory from Ceylon (now Sri Lanka), used to make billiard balls, became so rare and expensive that a reward of $10,000 in gold was offered to anyone who could produce an effective substitute. This became the first application of the polymer known as celluloid.
- Nylon, a polyamide invented in 1935 by Wallace Carothers, is impervious to water and does not burn, rot, or break down over time. Projects are presently under way to mine various old landfill sites for the nylon that they contain.
- Linear polymers form as single long molecules through individual chain reactions. Three-dimensional polymers form when a network of chain reactions combines to produce a single molecule. In principle, the contents of a tanker truck full of an appropriate material could polymerize into a single molecule.
- Advanced composite materials used in the manufacture of modern airplanes, boats, automobiles, and other machines combine the strength of multiple layers of fibers with the resilience and rigidity of three-dimensional polymers. The fibers may be organic polymeric material, such as Kevlar and carbon fiber, or mineral polymers, such as glass, metal, and basalt.
- The largest known molecule of a naturally occurring biopolymer is the DNA molecule.

A great many other synthetic polymers have been developed for use in fiber and fabric production. Each particular polymer has its own unique characteristics and physical properties that make it useful. One of the most common fabric polymers is nylon, of which there are innumerable variants. Nylon is a polyamide, meaning that the repeating units of its molecular structure are connected by amide bond systems. Nylon is another material originally developed as a substitute for the natural biopolymer silk; it has since found use in many other fabric applications in clothing, sheet goods, tents, boat sails, and others.

The variety of diamine and diacid molecular structures that are known lends itself to the development of a tremendous variety of polyamide materials. One of the most resilient of these is the material known as Kevlar. The material, like the more ordinary nylons, can be formed into fibers that have an exceptionally high tensile strength due to the intertwining of the polymer molecules in the material, rather like so many coil springs that have become muddled together. The fibers thus have the ability to dissipate a great deal of energy along their length when impacted perpendicularly by a blunt object such as a bullet.

Fibers produced from polymers are essential in the assembly of advanced composite materials. Carbon fiber, in particular, is extremely valuable in this application. Carbon fiber is typically produced by one of two methods. One method involves the carbonization of pitch, a viscous residue obtained from coal tar. The other, which involves the carbonization of cellulose fibers usually obtained from cotton, is the more common method of the two. Cellulose is a carbohydrate material in which each carbon atom in the material is bonded to the components of a water molecule. In the carbonization process, these are driven off as water molecules, leaving the bare carbon skeleton intact. The result is carbon fibers that are extremely versatile and become immensely strong when encased and compressed in a resin matrix. Polymeric fibers used in such applications are limited in number due to the basic restriction that the fiber material must be chemically inert with respect to the matrix material. With the exceptions of carbon fibers and Kevlar fibers, the vast majority of advanced composite materials incorporate fibers of mineral origin. This does not preclude the importance of carbon and Kevlar fiber, however. Carbon-fiber advanced composites are the material of choice for the construction of high-performance devices such as modern jet aircraft and are constantly being researched for adaptation to other roles. Kevlar fiber holds something of a companion position and is used often in the production of advanced composite structures designed to withstand impact, such as blast doors and safety seats in aircraft and other military equipment.

Matrix Materials. The other component of an advanced composite material is the matrix within which the fiber structure is bound. These are typically epoxy-based resins that polymerize in place with heating, called thermosetting resins. As the polymerization occurs, the liquid resin becomes hard and extremely stable. Further heating does not soften the material, but above a certain temperature the material begins to break down and decompose chemically. In contrast, a thermoplastic resin is solid below its glass-transition temperature but becomes progressively softer and eventually liquid as the temperature increases. Both types of resins are used in advanced composite structures, according to the conditions that the final product will be required to withstand. In the production phase, the fiber and matrix combination is typically consolidated under reduced pressure, using the even distribution of atmospheric pressure as the external applied force.

Thermoplastics. The most useful feature of polymers, without question, has been their ability to be molded into any desired shape. This is a unique ability of thermoplastic materials, which become liquid when heated and then solidify on cooling. Typically, a solid polymer feedstock is heated to its liquid form and then formed into a desired shape under pressure, the shape being retained when the material cools below its glass-transition temperature. The addition of other components to the formulation can change a hard, brittle plastic into a resilient, even soft, malleable material. A variety of techniques and methods has been developed for manufacturing objects from fresh and recovered plastics. These include primarily injection molding for three-dimensional objects and blow molding for sheet-like objects such as plastic bags and bottles. In the former, liquefied polymeric material completely fills the interior cavity of a mold, while in the latter, a bubble of the material is literally blown outward to coat the inside of the mold. Injection-molded objects may then be further modified by standard machining practices, while blow-molded pieces are produced as the final product without further modification.

Foams. Cross-linked polymers that form three-dimensional molecular networks typically expand to fill space as the gaseous by-products of polymerization exert pressure internally. This feature also allows those materials to be used to produce objects of a particular shape or materials that fulfill a specific purpose. Foam rubber typically is not actual rubber but a resilient type of three-dimensional polymer foam. Similarly, Styrofoam is composed of small granules of polystyrene that have been expanded as an entrained solvent is driven off with heating. When the correct amount of such materials is allowed to expand within a mold, an object with the corresponding shape is produced. Foams are noted for their insulating properties, and the application of liquid components by spraying onto the interior surfaces of walls is commonly used to produce urethane foam insulation.

Impact on Industry

Government Agencies. Quite apart from the everyday objects used in the operations of government agencies and organizations, polymer chemistry plays an extremely important role in the development and construction of specialized equipment and machines. This is especially true of agencies involved with aerospace applications. One of the most significant aspects of air and space transport, for example, is the combination of high strength and low weight. The remote manipulator arm, also known as the Canadarm, that was used extensively for the manipulation of materials in space during the National Aeronautics and Space Administration's (NASA) Space Shuttle program was constructed from carbon-fiber-based advanced composite materials. Designers and manufacturers of modern aircraft also make extensive use of advanced composite construction, all of which must meet stringent regulatory control standards overseen by federal agencies. Government regulatory bodies also monitor the environmental impact of polymers and polymer chemistry, determining and establishing exposure limits to environmental contaminants from the production side of the polymer industry and resolving the problem of disposal for polymer products that have reached the end of their useful life.

Military. Military applications of polymers and polymer chemistry have a long history, extending back to the use of cellophane as a lens material in gas masks during World War I and the replacement of black powder by nitrocellulose "gun cotton" before that. Food, ammunition, and other supplies have long been shipped overseas protected from moisture by polymer wrapping materials such as Saran wrap. In the military as well, the many and various items of everyday

Occupation	Chemical engineers
Employment 2010	30,200
Projected Employment 2020	32,000
Change in Number (2010–20)	1,800
Percent Change	6%

Bureau of Labor Statistics, 2012

life that are the products of polymer chemistry are vitally important, primarily due to ease of production, sturdiness, waterproof capabilities, imperviousness to decomposition, and weight-strength considerations. The standard gear of a soldier includes water canteens, eating utensils, survival goods, and clothing made of synthetic polymer fabrics. Sidearms and standard-issue rifles utilize stocks, grips, and other parts made from polymeric materials rather than wood. Various ammunition types, particularly nonlethal and crowd-control rounds, depend on the incorporation of plastic components in their structure. Military aircraft are almost exclusively constructed using advanced composite materials, allowing superior structural stability, flexibility of design, and resistance to radar detection. Given that military aircraft such as fighter jets must withstand atmospheric temperature variations ranging from ground-level desert heat to extreme cold at high altitude over a matter of about two minutes or less, structural and dimensional stability of the aircraft's components are vitally important, and a great deal of research and development has been expended in obtaining polymeric materials that perform as they must. Seacraft are no less important, and although their stability depends on their great mass, the use of polymers and plastics is becoming increasingly important in their operation and maintenance.

Academic Research and Teaching. Polymer chemistry has become a specialized branch of the chemical sciences, requiring an advanced knowledge of organic chemistry as a minimum qualification. University-level research and teaching in the field requires a minimum of a doctoral degree, although there are very rare exceptions to this rule. A less academically qualified individual who has made an exceptional career in the polymer industry may also be able to obtain a university

Occupation	Materials scientists
Employment 2010	8,700
Projected Employment 2020	9,600
Change in Number (2010–20)	900
Percent Change	10%

Bureau of Labor Statistics, 2012

teaching post based on his or her specific experience in the field. Little actual research and development in polymer chemistry is actually carried out, however, and most polymer research is geared toward the adaptation of existing polymers to specific applications, such as catalytic substrates, separation media, and the like. The obvious exception to this is in a specialized branch of chemical engineering in which effective production models and methods for efficient synthesis of industrial quantities of materials are actively researched and materials are assessed for use in specific real-world applications. An excellent example of the latter is the use of advanced composite materials such as preimpregnated carbon-fiber fabrics in the maintenance and augmentation of wood and concrete constructions and the fabrication of structures, such as bridges, that have previously been constructed from traditional building materials.

Social Context and Future Prospects

It is impossible to think of the modern world without polymers and plastics. Some have described the twentieth century as the "plastic century," beginning with the commercialization of naturally occurring biopolymers. These fairly humble beginnings rapidly evolved into the modern polymer and plastics industry that touches every aspect of twenty-first-century life, from the most advanced plastics used in modern technology in developed nations to the crude footwear made in Africa from discarded plastic soda bottles to the "plastic dump" where errant plastic items collect in the middle of the northern Pacific Ocean.

As an industry, polymer chemistry has an indefinite future. Relatively little work is focused on the development of new polymers, except for very specific applications. Rather, the majority of the work of polymer chemists is in developing new and better formulations for existing polymers and determining the best ways to recover and utilize plastics that have been discarded after their original use. Presently, the focus on polymer chemistry is centered on the development of green technologies that will have a considerably smaller environmental impact than their predecessors. Polymer chemists will therefore be developing polymerization processes that use less toxic and less polluting materials, many of which will demand the complete restructuring or replacement of existing processing facilities. They will also be intent on the development of safely biodegradable polymers, many of which will incorporate cellulose and other biopolymers rather than stable synthetic polymers derived from petroleum. Another significant aspect of polymer chemistry that will become increasingly important is its use in advanced composite materials, used in modern aircraft almost to the exclusion of all other materials, as well as in an increasing number of other applications demanding high strength and low weight.

Further Reading

Bahadur, P. and N. V. Sastry. *Principles of Polymer Science*. 2nd ed. Middlesex: Alpha Sci., 2005. Print. A text and reference book written for undergraduate and graduate students in chemistry, chemical engineering and materials science; presents basic and advanced aspects of polymer science, including natural, inorganic, and specialty polymers.

Davis, Fred J. *Polymer Chemistry: A Practical Approach*. New York: Oxford UP, 2004. Print. A more advanced text for chemists already working in the field or who are new to the field of polymer chemistry, containing detailed descriptions of synthetic methodology and preparations for a wide range of polymers, with regard to their application in the development of new materials.

Fenichell, Stephen. *Plastic: The Making of a Synthetic Century*. New York: Harper, 1996. Print. Delivers a thorough look at the history and development of the plastics industry, discussing many of the issues that have arisen through the ubiquity of polymers in the modern world.

Peacock, Andrew J., and Allison R. Calhoun. *Polymer Chemistry: Properties and Applications*. Cincinnati: Hanser, 2006. Print. Uses specific examples and case studies to illustrate the principles of polymer science. Written for undergraduates and industry professionals unfamiliar with polymer chemistry.

Sperling, Leslie Howard. *Introduction to Physical Polymer Science*. 4th ed. Hoboken: Wiley, 2006. Print. Includes topics in polymer science such as carbon nanotubes and nanocomposites, DNA and biopolymers, as well as topics such as fire retardancy and tribology.

Teegarden, David M. *Polymer Chemistry: Introduction to an Indispensable Science*. Arlington: Natl. Sci. Teachers Assn., 2004. Print. Provides an introduction to the basic principles and applications of the science of polymer chemistry.

Young, Robert J., and Peter A. Lovell. *Introduction to Polymers*. 3rd ed. Boca Raton: CRC, 2009. Print. Advanced reference book detailing the underlying principles of polymers and their properties, including recently developed synthetic methods for various types of polymers, their behavior and analysis, multicomponent polymer systems, and polymer composites.

About the Author: Richard M. Renneboog, MS, holds degrees in synthetic organic chemistry from the University of Western Ontario in London, Canada, and in electronics engineering technology from Loyalist College in Belleville, Canada. He lives and works as a writer and technical consultant in southwestern Ontario.

Plastics Engineer

Earnings (Yearly Median): $83,120 (Bureau of Labor Statistics, 2012)

Employment and Outlook: Slower than average growth (Bureau of Labor Statistics, 2012)

O*NET-SOC Code: 17-2041.00

Related Career Clusters: Manufacturing; Architecture & Construction; Health Science

Scope of Work

Plastics engineers perform a wide range of jobs related to the design, processing, and application of various plastic products in a number of fields, from the automobile industry to the computer- and toy-manufacturing industries. With a strong background in chemistry and physics, plastics engineers develop new kinds of plastics, or polymers, with individual manufacturers to create products according to their needs. Development is a large part of plastic engineers' jobs, though they also test existing products and look for ways to improve them.

Education and Coursework

The road to a career in plastics engineering begins in high school. Students who are serious about engineering should take advanced classes in math, such as trigonometry and calculus, along with classes in biology, chemistry, and physics. When class is out of session, several universities offer intensive summer programs and internships, which can give some young engineers an edge over their colleagues.

Entry-level jobs require a bachelor's degree, preferably from a specialized program with an emphasis on plastics design and manufacturing. Students in these programs will learn to work with polymer plastics, rubbers, paints, and adhesives. Some programs advance from foundations in mathematics and science to analysis and design. Other programs place engineering courses early in the curriculum so that students can decide whether the discipline is right for them. The engineering courses can include engineering mechanics, systems dynamics, and engineering technologies. Plastics courses can include plastics safety, organic and polymer chemistry, polymeric materials, plastics processing, fluid flow, and plastics mold engineering. An emphasis is placed on laboratory work and engineering design projects that prepare engineers to apply research and theory in the evolving plastics marketplace.

Employers prefer candidates who have attended programs with accreditation from the Accreditation Board for Engineering and Technology (ABET), which requires students to study the natural sciences and advanced mathematics in addition to taking classes in design. A master's degree will provide training in advanced theory and practice.

The degree is typically required of plastics engineers anticipating advancement in their field. Degree candidates might specialize in plastics design, plastics materials, processing, medical plastics design and manufacturing, or elastomeric materials.

Career Enhancement and Training

To be called a professional engineer, one must earn a license. Though requirements for licensure differ from state to state, typical prerequisites begin with a degree from an ABET-accredited university program. One must then complete a pair of comprehensive exams, starting with the Fundamentals of Engineering exam, which lasts eight hours and features 180 multiple-choice questions covering everything from chemistry to ethics, in addition to engineering fundamentals. Degree holders who pass the exam become engineers in training (EITs). Completion of the second exam does not immediately follow the first. EITs must first gain a minimum of four years experience, typically under the supervision of a professional engineer. After fulfilling work-experience requirements, EITs may attempt the second exam, known as the Principles and Practice of Engineering exam, the final step toward becoming licensed professional engineers. Many states require engineers to attend further courses over time in order to keep their licenses.

One way professional plastics engineers can continue to develop is to earn certification in particular areas. This is often the best option for adults already working in plastics who need formal education in their field. Areas of specialization include plastics processing and product design. As technology ushers in changes to the plastics industry, particular certifications can help professional engineers maintain an edge. More knowledge and experience leads to greater independence and autonomy.

Advancement in the field can occur many ways. Many engineers move on to work as technical specialists or engineering managers, overseeing teams of engineers and technicians. The latter is an option for those with an interest in business and administration. Many also pursue opportunities in sales. The in-depth product knowledge gathered over the course of an engineering career can be a vital tool in the marketplace.

Transferable Skills

- Research & Planning Skills – Creating ideas
- Research & Planning Skills – Identifying problems
- Research & Planning Skills – Determining alternatives
- Technical Skills – Using technology to process information (SCANS Workplace Competency – Information)
- Technical Skills – Applying the technology to a task (SCANS Workplace Competency – Technology)
- Technical Skills – Performing scientific, mathematical, and technical work
- Technical Skills – Working with machines, tools, or other objects
- Work Environment Skills – Working in a laboratory setting

Daily Tasks and Technology

Plastics engineers hold a wide variety of jobs based on interest, expertise, and level of experience. Professional engineers working in materials research will determine methods for mixing or intensifying materials. This process involves communicating with a company's business workforce to identify, analyze, and provide technical solutions to development problems. Most jobs in plastics engineering involve some variation on those tasks. They can be broken down and classified into three categories: development, testing, and problem solving.

Development mostly refers to product design, which entails working in labs to determine design and to assess cost, risk, safety, timing, and manufacturing feasibility. Product designers might spend their days creating and modifying engineering drawings while working with teams to generate prototypes for testing. For process engineers, the tasks move beyond developing products into creating and implementing systems for the construction and manufacture of those products. They are also responsible for the design, layout, and sequence of manufacturing processes.

Process engineers are also involved in testing. For example, they are responsible for constructing experiments to evaluate manufacturing processes, after which other engineers test the products to determine their sustainability. Product designers might perform weather, strength, and thermal testing. When these tests provide less than optimal results, engineers must return to the development stage.

Throughout an engineer's day, problem solving is a continuous concern. A standard day of creating and testing products often raises unforeseen issues that must be solved by the engineers. Production planners, for example, consult with factory workers and analyze efficiency records to introduce changes in equipment or labor.

Plastics engineers primarily work within a laboratory setting or in an office, where they utilize computer-aided design (CAD) programs such as PTC Pro/ENGINEER or computer-aided manufacturing (CAM) software for producing models, prototypes, and production parts.

Earnings and Employment Outlook

According to the Bureau of Labor Statistics (BLS), the median pay for a materials engineer was $83,120 in 2010, with the lowest 10 percent earning less than $51,680 and the top 10 percent earning more than $126,800. The highest earners hold positions with the federal government. Geographically, chemical engineers working in Alaska, Delaware, Idaho, and Wisconsin held the advantage in 2009.

Employment for materials engineers is expected to grow 9 percent from 2010 to 2020, which is slower than average for all occupations. The development of new products in traditional fields such as aerospace engineering should continue at a steady pace from 2010 to 2020, while demand should grow in expanding fields, such as nanotechnology and biomedical engineering. As technology continues to change at a rapid rate, companies will look to develop new products and systems to address changing consumer needs in these areas.

Employment for materials engineers is expected to grow 9 percent from 2010 to 2020, which is slower than average for all occupations.

A Conversation with Jeanne Kuhler

Job Title: Lecturer, Ohio State University

What was your career path?

Although I grew up in a very rural area where many of my friends were primarily encouraged to get married early instead of going to college, I was blessed with parents who encouraged me to go to college. It was while working on my bachelor's degree at Indiana University (IU) that I decided to take a chemistry class, which was very intimidating since there were several hundred students in these large introductory chemistry classes at IU, and many of these classmates at IU had gone to large suburban high schools around Indianapolis with very strong high school chemistry classes. Despite my early disadvantages, I found that I loved chemistry enough to study and do well, and was blessed with full scholarships to complete my master's degree in chemistry at Yale University. With the credentials that these degrees provided, I was able to work for major international companies GE Plastics and American Home Products. Later, in order to build on my laboratory and research skills, I completed my PhD. Having a PhD allowed me to have more responsibilities in industrial positions, and also the credentials to teach at the university level, which I currently love, as my students have often continued to inspire me.

What are three pieces of advice?

1. First, I would make sure to develop your ability to learn as soon as you can. To me this means working hard to meet the challenges of coursework of all types, including both mathematical and reading comprehension skills. I think that everyone needs to have the mental foundation early to be able to learn a variety of skills later in life, especially for problem-solving skills. Chemistry is often called the central science, and the heart of all science disciplines is solving current problems and developing new technologies and solutions.

2. Second, I would encourage all students to pursue the subjects that interest them the most. When a person finds a subject fascinating enough to continue to work

hard, even when faced with obstacles, moving forward seems more attainable.

3. Third, I would suggest always being willing to consider new perspectives and learning new skills; many times opportunities will become available when you least expect them.

What paths for career advancement are available to you?

Currently, I work as a full-time faculty member. My current position of lecturer allows me to teach while also allowing me the additional time and flexibility in my schedule to accomplish additional goals that I did not have the freedom to do while working long hours in industrial positions. I've been blessed with two teaching awards during the past few years, and so teaching has been a rewarding career that has allowed me to help make the world a better place by writing recommendation letters to help my students with their career plans, as well as help them to learn chemistry. I also have the opportunity to conduct research without the pressure to constantly obtain research grants for external funding that an assistant professor title at a major research institution such as Ohio State would require. On the other hand, I could pursue the assistant professor position if I would like to do so, and that could lead to the progression to associate professor and full professor. Alternatively, I could continue as lecturer to the rank of senior lecturer, or continue to build on my research and lab instrumentation skills and pursue an industrial chemist position. Many chemists also pursue careers in law, business marketing, production, and technology that have their own career advancement paths.

In the near future, plastics engineers will reshape industrial processes as scientists learn more about the environmental consequences of products and their methods of production. Medical research will create the need for new medical and scientific products. On a fundamental level, materials engineers of all types will be needed to head up research-and-development departments at many of the world's top companies.

Related Occupations

- **Architectural and Engineering Managers:** Architectural and engineering managers develop, implement, and manage projects in architecture and engineering. These jobs include research and problem solving.

- **Biomedical Engineers:** Biomedical engineers investigate problems and create meaningful solutions in the areas of biology and medicine, with the ultimate goal of increasing the quality of patient care.

- **Chemical Engineers:** Chemical engineers use the principles of chemistry to produce research, perform tests, and develop methods for the safe manufacture of chemicals and other products.

- **Mechanical Engineers:** Mechanical engineers design, construct, and analyze mechanical devices such as tools, engines, and machines, including generators, refrigerators, robots, elevators, and conveyer systems.

- **Plastic Machine Workers:** Plastic machine workers set up and run machines that sever, sculpt, and arrange plastic materials. The job can involve adjusting machine settings and speeds, testing finished products, and recording production numbers.

Future Applications

As environmental research pushes engineers to envision and manufacture solutions to current problems, increased demand for sustainable technology is changing the landscape of the plastics field. For example, as solar power becomes more cost effective, it has the potential to draw significantly from the labor of plastics engineers. Plastics could serve as a low-cost replacement for indium tin oxide (ITO), which is used not only in solar panels but also in other more common products. Flat-screen televisions, mobile phones, and other devices with display screens all use the scarce and expensive ITO.

As electronic products become more diverse, the demand for engineers to design and manufacture them will grow. Investment in new and innovative computer-based products is on the rise, and demand for the innovators to deliver on their promise is likely to follow.

Molly Hagan

More Information

American Society for Engineering Education
1818 N Street NW, Suite 600
Washington DC 20036
www.asee.org

National Society of Professional Engineers
1420 King Street
Alexandria, VA 22314
www.nspe.org

Society of Plastics Engineers
13 Church Hill Road
Newtown, CT 06470
www.4spe.org

Technology Student Association
1914 Association Drive
Reston, VA 20191-1540
www.tsaweb.org

Pulp and Paper Chemistry

FIELDS OF STUDY

Chemistry; general chemistry; organic chemistry; chemical engineering; mechanical engineering; bioprocess engineering; microbiology; marketing.

DEFINITION

Pulp chemistry and paper chemistry represent discrete yet dependent fields in the same industry. The pulping procedure utilizes mechanical and chemical processes that convert wood and other natural material into individual fibers. Pulp produced in this manner is then treated with additional chemicals to create paper products that vary based on both the type of pulp utilized and the style of paper desired. Throughout the process, pulp and paper chemists seek to make stronger, more durable, and increasingly environmentally sound products that meet the needs of the modern world.

Basic Principles

Since the emergence of writing, humankind has sought better methods of recording the fruits of literacy, starting with stone, clay, and even papyrus. It was not until the early second century CE that the Chinese created the first paper as it is understood today. The Arab world, in turn, borrowed the concept before transporting it to the European continent. Linen, rather than wood, served as the basis of Western papermaking, a craft that grew dramatically following the fifteenth-century German invention of the printing press. At the time, papermaking was a slow process that produced individual sheets rather than large rolls.

The nineteenth century witnessed the gradual introduction of wood into the pulp and paper process. Utilizing wood made the papermaking process more complex. The introduction of a variety of chemical solutions pioneered by scientists such as Hugh Burgess (who created the soda process of pulping), Benjamin Chew Tilghman (who is credited with the sulfite process), and Carl F. Dahl (credited with the kraft process) all contributed to making wood an effective pulping agent. These chemical advances, in conjunction with Karl Scheele's discovery of the bleaching qualities of chlorine and the invention of the Fourdrinier machine that continuously turns pulp into paper, established the foundation of the modern paper industry.

Broadly, the papermaking process begins with chemical, semi-chemical, or mechanical efforts to separate individual cellulose fibers from the lignin that binds them in wood to create pulp. Once completed, the pulp is washed and, if a lighter color is desired, bleached before being strained and pressed into paper.

Core Concepts

Raw Materials. With any paper product, it is important to consider the parts that constitute the whole. Since the advent of literacy, many items have been used to form paper. Wood, the resource most utilized today, was not employed in the Western world until chemical advances in the nineteenth century made it a suitable pulping agent. Before that, cotton and linen rags typically served as the principal material from which paper pulp was produced. Hundreds of other items were also explored with varying degrees of success. Until the widespread use of wood, however, the growth of the paper industry was constricted by a scarcity of resources and the technological limitations that made paper production a challenge. The four-stage Fourdrinier papermaking machine, coupled with advances in technology utilizing wood for pulp, transformed the paper industry. The prevalence of assorted hard- and softwood trees in North America made the United States one of the world's leading producers of paper products.

Pulp Processing. How wood is processed ultimately determines its later usage. Chemical processing, as the name implies, necessitates adding chemicals to a heated wood mixture that permits the separation of cellulose fibers from the lignin that binds them. In the end, pulp made in this fashion yields a strong paper. When weaker paper is needed, mechanical pulping is ideal. In this method, wood is crushed against a grinder that separates its constituent parts. Semichemical pulping commences with a standard chemical procedure but concludes with mechanical separation of fibers from lignin. This process produces the strength typical of the chemical process, yet affords greater control over the fibers during the paper-production stage.

Kraft Process. In the United States, approximately 80 percent of the chemical pulp produced comes from the kraft process, owing in part to its use of an alkaline procedure that is considered by some to be less environmentally destructive than earlier sulfite-based techniques. This method places wood chips in a water-based chemical mixture of sodium sulfide and sodium hydroxide that is exposed to high heat and pressure. This "white liquor" separates the lignin from the fibers before a washing process extracts the chemicals from the pulp. The pulp is further washed and bleached before it is converted to paper. The white liquor that remains is diluted with the wash water, forming "black liquor"—a combination of the waste water, pulping chemicals, and lignin—which then proceeds through an evaporator, with the remaining concentrate fired in a recovery furnace. Steam resulting from the process is used to fuel the papermaking portion of the procedure. Smelt left in the furnace is mixed with water, creating a "green liquor" that is treated in a caustic bath and converted back to white liquor for reuse.

Pulp Washing and Bleaching. Once pulp is created, it is washed in very hot water to remove the cellulose from the lignin. Should a lighter color be desired, the pulp must then be bleached, since even the most technically advanced pulping processes leave behind some lignin, which darkens the pulp and, by extension, the paper produced from it. Bleaching procedures typically require several steps, from injecting the pulp with the lightening agent to washing with water, before restarting the process until the desired color is reached. Historically, bleaching agents have ranged from chlorine to hydrogen peroxide to sodium hypochlorite. With the pulping process complete, the finished product is, in an integrated mill, transferred to the paper-producing portion of the plant or, in a nonintegrated site, transported to a paper mill, which will then transform the pulp into paper.

Paper Production. At the paper mill, raw pulp is deposited into a head tank, where it is mixed with water to form a slurry often referred to as "white water." By this stage in the operation, the pulp has been treated to maintain proper pH and cut with assorted fillers to suit the standards of the paper being made. This solution is then spread over a screen and pressed in a process that captures the fibers while removing much of the water; industry participants call this the "wet end" of the papermaking process. Heat is then applied to the mixture to facilitate drying and fiber binding. Next, a calender, or series of rollers, presses what remains, joining the fibers together and smoothing the surface area. The continuous operation of modern Fourdrinier machines necessitates a continuous supply of pulp in addition to careful management of the entire process to guarantee paper consistency and quality. The finished product is rolled onto storage wheels from which it will be packaged and marketed.

Applications Past and Present

Early Papermaking. The papermaking craft began in China by a court official named Ts'ai Lun in 105 CE. Chinese craftsmen used cloth scraps, mulberry bark, and other items such as hemp and fishing nets. Raw materials were placed in mud for several weeks, then removed and pounded on a mortar with a pestle. What remained was placed in a tub of water, where a variety of fillers were added until the substance contained inside reached the necessary consistency. It was then framed, drained of water, and heated. After multiple repetitions of the process, paper was formed. From China, the rest of the world would derive their own papermaking processes. By 800 CE, Arabs had introduced papermaking to their land and replaced Chinese plants with linen as the basis of their pulp. Spanish Moors brought papermaking to Europe, where the Italians and the French fast became the principal producers of the commodity. Germany received its first paper mill at the start of the fourteenth century. In the mid-fifteenth century, German goldsmith Johannes Gutenberg invented the printing press. The advent of movable type forever changed the world, bringing with it the rapid dissemination of information and the need for new and improved methods of producing paper.

Despite the ravenous need of the presses, paper production remained a time-consuming, labor-intensive affair that yielded superb-quality paper of limited size. A machine capable of producing larger rolls of paper was clearly needed. In 1798, Louis-Nicolas Robert, a French printer's assistant, fashioned a machine capable of creating sheets of paper over forty feet in length. A cash-strapped Robert sold his patent to Saint-Léger Didot, who in turn enlisted the assistance of the English brothers Sealy and Henry Fourdrinier. By 1804, the Fourdrinier brothers had a fully functioning papermaking machine that, when taken in conjunction with the printing press, helped to create the modern paper industry. The Fourdrinier machine remains the basis of papermaking technology today.

Introduction of Wood. As the need for paper increased and the technology behind papermaking improved, so too did efforts to find new materials from which to form pulp and, ultimately, new types of paper. The nineteenth century would see a revolution in the chemistry of papermaking that would usher in the modern era. Many experimented with materials to replace rags as the basis of paper production. Despite many efforts, most experiments yielded only limited results. A new pulp source was needed that would prove both plentiful and capable of making a wide array of products.

In 1844, Friedrich Gottlob Keller invented a mechanical wood-pulping machine that paved the way for additional experimentation and discovery. Hugh Burgess in 1851 created a chemical pulping process in which wood chips were placed in a caustic chemical soda bath and boiled. Burgess's invention represented a dramatic advance in quality from the paper made by Keller's mechanical process. Several years later, American chemist Benjamin Tilghman broadened the science of papermaking by pioneering the use of sulfites in the pulping process. But German paper-mill worker Carl F. Dahl would introduce perhaps the most influential chemical process of all: sulfate or kraft pulping. What made Dahl's process so revolutionary was that the chemicals used in it could be recycled, and the energy released while pulping helped to fuel papermaking machines. In North America, the kraft process was revolutionary because it worked on all types of wood, including that of the pine tree, which was prolific there. The kraft process made the United States one of the world's leading producers of paper.

Following the remarkable success and widespread applicability of the kraft process, the need emerged for a semichemical process that would more effectively handle the largely unused hardwoods prevalent in North America. This procedure began with an initial chemical bath, briefer and less substantial than in the kraft process, before being followed by mechanical pulping. The new procedure, which emerged in the 1920s, served several purposes, including controlling pulpwood cost inflation and permitting the expansion of the paperboard industry. The latter concern was especially significant, as it fit the packaging needs of a nation that had entered an era of mass production and mass consumption of consumer products. As in the past, the pulp and paper industry answered the needs of a changing nation and world. In this instance, hardwood corrugated board produced by the semichemical pulping process enabled the continued expansion of the American economy.

Coinciding with improvements in the pulping process were more efficient bleaching techniques. As with the pulping process, most of the bleaching performed in the early nineteenth century was done on rag stock. As pulpwood replaced cloth, extant bleaching practices became ineffective. Early twentieth-century changes in bleaching techniques that focused on multistage exposure to whitening agents dramatically improved the process, and shifts in the bleaching agent from chlorine to hydrogen peroxide have made the process less environmentally damaging.

Modern Concerns. As the twentieth century progressed, pulp and paper chemists focused on improving quality and yield while also experimenting with consistency. All the while, their efforts remained guided by the drive to increase company profits. Scientists working in conjunction with mill managers at both the pulp and the paper level helped foster the explosive growth of the business, which became a top-ten manufacturing industry in the United States.

In the second half of the twentieth century, many became more aware of the fragile nature of the earth's ecosystem and noted that human activities were adversely affecting the planet. It was not long before the pulp and paper industry came under scrutiny for its use of a wide assortment of hazardous chemicals and its exploitative

Interesting Facts about Pulp and Paper Chemistry

- The first paper mill in the United States was opened in 1690 near Germantown, Pennsylvania, by William Rittenhouse along a tributary of Wissahickon Creek. Today, Wisconsin holds the title of the largest paper-producing state in the United States.

- During the American Revolution, the Continental Army experienced shortages of all manner of supplies, from food to munitions. Paper in particular was desperately needed, as gunpowder at the time was stored in paper cartridges. Benjamin Franklin opened the doors of his printing press to ensure the necessary paper was found.

- Benjamin Tilghman, the American scientist who created sulfite pulping, is best known for inventing the process of sandblasting.

- About one-third of the material used to make paper in the United States today is scrap material left over from sawmill operations. Forty-two percent of the global industrial wood harvest is used to produce paper products.

- The average American uses approximately 650 pounds of paper each year. Recycling one ton of paper saves approximately seventeen trees. If all of the newspapers produced in the United States were recycled, it is estimated that over 250 million trees would be saved.

relationship with woodlands and forests. Change would once again be forced on the industry.

Today, one of the greatest challenges confronted by pulp and paper chemists is balancing the needs of consumers with the demands of environmentalists. Making the entire industry an efficient custodian of resources has assumed paramount importance, as has improving the quality and productivity of the entire processing procedure. Reducing the environmental impact of the industry must take place in a holistic manner that spans the entire process. Reforestation efforts in cutover timberlands have yielded positive results. Many environmentally conscious paper companies currently replant felled trees in an effort to create a sustainable resource. Gone are the days of clear-cutting followed by abandonment of the region. Scientists are busy designing fast-growing seeds that can replace lost timber at a much faster rate, while many in the industry have committed themselves to less exploitative practices. It is a slow process, but one that clearly represents the next wave in the industry's development.

Once trees are cut, they are sent to the pulping plant, where less environmentally suspect chemicals are used instead of the known carcinogenic agents of the past. Despite growing national and state-level regulation, environmental pollution remains a major concern. Pulp plants dump treated water into local waterways and burn a variety of compounds that emit toxic chemicals into the air. Strange smells, random fish kills, and high cancer rates are often the unfortunate by-products of the paper industry. Minimizing these impacts represents perhaps the greatest challenge confronting the pulp and paper industry. It is a problem that has drawn the attention of environmental groups and even the federal government. The Environmental Protection Agency (EPA) routinely issues critical reports on the processes that produce the nation's paper products.

Aside from environmental concerns, the biggest issue shaping the future of the pulp and paper industry is the computer revolution that began in the second half of the twentieth century. The volume of paper a country produced was once deemed an effective measure of its relative civilization and literacy. Today, an increasing number of individuals from industrialized countries own or have access to computers that make viewing the news and reading books a simple affair accomplished by clicking a few buttons. In the process, how people consume information has changed. Where once the local newspaper afforded a window on the world's happenings, today a person can scan headlines online or receive messages sent directly to their cellular phones alerting them of news items relevant to them. As a result, many newspapers are struggling to compete and increasingly losing their market share to online vendors. The future of the newspaper industry, and to a greater extent the entire paper publishing world, is in peril. Adding to the threats posed to the once-limitless future many once envisioned for the pulp and paper industry is the increased use of plastic in the packaging process. Although not without environmental risks of its own, plastic is often seen as a cheaper alternative to paper.

Some forecasters fear that the pulp and paper business will seek refuge in underdeveloped nations where environmental laws are lax and virgin timber stands abound. Rather than creating a more environmentally sound processing procedure so that they may continue producing in nations such as the United States, many corporations might relocate their operations elsewhere, making environmental exploitation and degradation rather than careful stewardship the standard in the industry, and indeed the only means of staying competitive in the global marketplace. Today the industry offers many opportunities for enterprising pulp and paper chemists whose investigative talents might not only save the environment but also maintain the industry's viability in industrialized nations.

Impact on Industry

Printing and Publishing. Few industries have as much impact on an array of seemingly unrelated fields as that of pulp and paper. Without advances in the production of paper, the widespread dissemination of knowledge in the form of books, newspapers, pamphlets, and broadsides would have been impossible. Improvements in papermaking made widespread literacy possible. Without it, access to the fruits of world civilization would have remained closed to all but the wealthiest denizens in a handful of nations. In recent memory, the pulp and paper industry has been an integral component of the entire publishing world. Newspaper production grew in concert with improvements in the pulping process that made paper production cheaper and thus more readily available. Improvements in book production coincided with new and cheaper sources of paper to make the written word, whether geared to an academic or a general audience, more available than ever before. As universal literacy became the objective of American educators in the later nineteenth century and close to a reality in the twentieth, the pulp and paper industry was there to ensure that it delivered a product at a cost that was not prohibitive.

Advertising, Marketing, and Packaging. The United States, despite the uncertain future created by electronic media, continues its voracious demand for paper products. Americans may be reading news and books in electronic formats, but they remain, as they have been for decades, a consumer culture in which mass consumption of products necessitates elaborate packaging initiatives to help sell commodities. Following the end of the American Civil War, the nation underwent a process of massive industrialization in which advances in mechanization and management coincided with improvements in the existing transportation network. Creation of a national and then a global market made the rise of big business possible. American consumers who were once limited to a small quantity of products soon found themselves inundated with new items, as well as variations on the ones they already knew. With access to so many options, Americans began to buy on an enormous scale. To maintain an edge over competitors, companies hired marketing firms to create better name recognition for their products and thus increase profits. The pulp and paper industry responded to the needs of marketing executives by creating different types of paper products to transform a given marketer's vision into reality. From billboards to print ads to packaging itself, the pulp and paper industry has had a hand in the popularity of a sweeping assortment of products.

Academic and Industrial Research. Industry leaders have long held that the timber business and all of its constituent components are inherently linked with the health of the environment. While the pulp and paper industry once undermined environmental stability, today many of its leaders are working to make things better. From reforestation programs to efforts to reduce the amount of chemicals needed in the pulp and paper processes, the industry has done much to make itself more eco-friendly, at least in North America and portions of Europe. In an age when access to clean water is an ever-present problem, paper manufacturers are searching for ways to recycle the water currently used at their facilities while simultaneously striving to purify that which it sends as runoff into local waterways. University research chemists and scientists employed by the industry itself are always at work to make their processes more efficient and environmentally friendly. As the industry has proven throughout its history, it is the scientific community that has often brought about the latest and most significant advances in the field of paper production. The problems that currently loom on the horizon underscore the ongoing symbiotic relationship between the industry and the scientists who make the production of pulp and paper possible.

Social Context and Future Prospects

Some have posited that American paper production is entering the same period of long-term decline and eventual demise that once befell the steel and textile industries. Wages remain stagnant, and factories that lack the resources to embrace the latest technologies have shut down. In the future, even currently fiscally solvent enterprises could lose their competitive edge as pressure from third-world producers, who face neither the wage nor the environmental concerns of industrialized nations, challenge the industry once dominated by North American interests. Some hope that improvements in technology, plant upgrades, and greater investment will stop the decline.

Interest in greener technology and industrial processes might also increase the solvency of the enterprise in North America at the same time it makes it a better neighbor and employer for those who reside in the shadow of pulp and paper plants. The future remains uncertain, as the ongoing clash between profits and environmental regulations in North America and northern Europe has led many firms to relocate to the more permissive business climates found in places such as Russia and China. Pulp- and paper-industry researchers continue their efforts to make the chemical processes involved in paper production less detrimental to the environment and to the people

Occupation	Chemists and materials scientists
Employment 2010	90,900
Projected Employment 2020	94,900
Change in Number (2010–20)	4,000
Percent Change	4%

Bureau of Labor Statistics, 2012

who live near their plants. These improvements must not only be effective, they must also be reasonably priced. Without the discovery of environmentally safer, more cost-efficient chemical processes, the pulp and paper industry will inevitably find other, less regulated countries in which to do business. Green technology needs to be affordable, or efforts to safeguard the environment will collapse in a wave of outsourcing.

Further Reading

Bajpai, Pratima. *Environmentally Friendly Production of Pulp and Paper*. Hoboken: Wiley, 2010. Print. A work devoted to urging those in the paper industry to adopt more environmentally friendly methods consistent with cleaner production standards.

Biermann, Christopher J. *Handbook of Pulping and Papermaking*. 2nd ed. San Diego: Academic, 1996. Print. A detailed explanation of all phases of the pulp and paper industry. Includes an accessible description of the science behind the process. Color pictures.

Hagiopol, Cornel, and James W. Johnston. *Chemistry of Modern Papermaking*. Boca Raton: CRC, 2011. Print. Explores the many ways chemicals are involved in the paper industry.

Roberts, J. C. *Chemistry of Paper*. Cambridge: Royal Soc. of Chemistry, 1996. Print. Provides insight into the papermaking process from the perspective of the chemists who work in the field.

About the Author: Keith M. Finley, PhD, is an instructor of history at Southeastern Louisiana University and the assistant director of the Center for Southeast Louisiana Studies, where he has worked on several research and film products funded by the EPA and the National Oceanic and Atmospheric Administration (NOAA) that have highlighted the impact of the timber and paper industry in Louisiana.

Wood Chemist

Earnings (Yearly Median): $69,790 (Bureau of Labor Statistics, 2012)

Employment and Outlook: Slower than average growth (Bureau of Labor Statistics, 2012)

O*NET-SOC Code: 19-2031.00

Related Career Clusters: Agriculture, Food & Natural Resources; Architecture & Construction; Education & Training

Scope of Work

Wood is a complex material composed primarily of cellulose and lignin, as well as many other compounds. Its intrinsic structure permits it to be used for many different purposes, ranging from structural materials to renewable sources of various chemical compounds. It is also the source of practically all paper produced in the world. Wood chemists work to determine new or improved methods of utilizing the chemical properties and components of wood in order to manufacture better and stronger wood-based materials, understand the chemical processes by which the various chemical components of wood are produced, determine means by which the chemical components of wood may be broken down and altered to produce other chemicals, and to find ways to control the interactions of wood with other materials such as adhesives, paints, and sealants.

Education and Coursework

Entry-level positions as a wood chemist typically require a bachelor's degree in chemical or industrial engineering or in pulp and paper science. Some employers will accept qualifications in mechanical, electrical, or manufacturing engineering as the minimum requirements. Employers expect entry-level wood chemists to have a minimum grade-point average of 2.8. Therefore, potential wood chemists should expect to study chemistry, physics, biology, and mathematics at the university level. Students of wood chemistry will generally take courses in organic, physical, inorganic, bio-organic, industrial, and analytical chemistry. Because wood is a plant substance, courses in biology and plant sciences are also essential. Some institutions offer specialized programs of study for both the pulp-and-paper and wood-chemistry industries. For more advanced positions involving basic research in the chemistry of wood and wood products, a master's degree

Transferable Skills

- Interpersonal/Social Skills – Working as a member of a team (SCANS Workplace Competency – Interpersonal)
- Research & Planning Skills – Creating ideas
- Research & Planning Skills – Identifying resources
- Research & Planning Skills – Gathering information
- Research & Planning Skills – Analyzing information
- Organization & Management Skills – Managing equipment/materials (SCANS Workplace Competency – Resources)
- Technical Skills – Understanding which technology is appropriate for a task (SCANS Workplace Competency – Technology)
- Technical Skills – Performing scientific, mathematical and technical work

or a PhD will be required, as in almost all other scientific fields. Research positions tend to be grant funded and associated with teaching and research institutions and industrial corporations.

The field of wood chemistry is broad, and it is involved in many different aspects of wood utilization. The subdisciplines of wood chemistry generally include biomass and recycling, wood types, wood products, wood chemistry and properties, wood energy, wood processing, and wood conservation and protection. Given the array of subdisciplines, it should not be surprising that there are institutions and organizations devoted to wood sciences. The mandate of such organizations includes education and training opportunities for those working in the field of wood chemistry and the other wood sciences. Because of the global trade in wood and the indigenous nature of wood species, many of the various organizations have a global presence and serve an international community of wood scientists. Limited opportunities to learn about the nature and habitat of wood do exist through the forestry industry, which relies extensively on knowledge of tree biology.

Career Enhancement and Training

While no specific licensing or certification is required to pursue a career as a wood chemist, it is, nonetheless, a specialized field that demands specific training. The chemical components of wood, and the physical properties of wood derived from those chemical components, are complex and quite unlike the sorts of materials chemists in other fields typically work with. Accordingly, the methodologies and technologies that are used by wood chemists are also quite different. Professional organizations for those who work in the various wood sciences, such as the Wood Technology Society (WTS), focus solely on wood sciences. Such organizations provide a focused set of career enhancement and training resources as well as a central point for professional networking, which can be complicated by the global extent of the wood-sciences field. Wood chemists work in such a specialized field that communication and networking with other wood chemists is typically a long-distance undertaking, and opportunities for direct or on-site collaboration with colleagues in other locations are rare and tend to be costly. Both participation in online forums and attendance at symposia and conferences relevant to the field of wood chemistry are essential means of building and maintaining professional relationships in this field.

Daily Tasks and Technology

The daily tasks of wood chemists depend a great deal on the branch of wood sciences in which they are involved. The vast majority of wood chemists work in the pulp and paper industry, where they maintain the large-scale processing operations of their particular location. The operations range in sequence from the initial treatment of raw wood resources to the final quality-control checks of finished papers. In between are numerous stages of the production process in which chemical processes work to separate wood fibers and break them down into raw cellulose, extract and capture noncellulosic materials, and bleach and physically manipulate the fibers from the process stream. In this capacity, wood chemists are required to provide quality control and work toward improving the overall process.

Another primary area of work for wood chemists is in natural-products research. Wood is the source of a variety of naturally occurring chemical compounds, and a significant aspect of wood chemistry is the recovery and identification of such compounds from within raw wood. Wood chemists working in this area often obtain samples of wood, grind them up, and use various methods to extract the various compounds that they contain. This type of research goes hand in hand with the work of plant scientists who work to determine the biology and genetics of trees and plants, possibly to develop strains that produce greater or lesser amounts of a specific material. This job function is becoming increasingly important as such resources are sought to produce biofuels.

The technology that wood chemists might use differs according to the nature of the work environment. Pulp and paper chemists work in an environment of large industrial machinery designed to manipulate and break down whole trees to produce large quantities of wood-fiber products and paper. Research-and-development chemists work primarily in a typical laboratory environment, using standard laboratory equipment and analytical devices.

Earnings and Employment Outlook

The largest areas of employment growth for wood chemists are in biofuels and biomass recycling. In these fields, a wood chemist with only a bachelor's degree can make a significant contribution, although those with more advanced qualifications will be preferred by employers. The field is expanding globally, and even some oil-exporting nations in the Middle East have instituted biofuel programs, both to stimulate the agricultural sector of their economies and to hedge against the depletion of crude oil reserves.

Biomass conversion of wood-based materials depends on the breakdown of cellulosic material so that the resulting starches and sugars become amenable to the fermentation processes that produce fuel-grade alcohols. Other avenues of biomass conversion include thermal reformation processes and the recovery of natural oil produced as part of the biological processes of living trees and other plants.

There is also increased demand for products from recycled and re-processed paper rather than new paper from raw materials. Improving paper-fiber-reprocessing methodologies is another area of wood chemistry in which growth can be expected. While these specific areas of wood chemistry should experience significant growth, all other areas are likely to experience the relatively slow growth typical of the chemical sciences in general.

Related Occupations

- **Food Scientists:** Food science requires a background in analytical techniques and biochemistry in order to maintain and improve the quality of food materials for both human and animal consumption through the use of wood-sourced materials.

- **Soil and Plant Scientists:** Soil and plant science is the most significant field of green technology, as industrial applications turn increasingly to renewable resources from plants, and it requires understanding of the role played by healthy soils in maintaining these resources.

- **Forestry Scientists:** Forestry scientists set out to understand the ecology of forests and maintain their ongoing health and renewal.

- **Environmental Scientists:** Environmental science is one of the primary fields being impacted by green philosophy; it is closely related to forestry, soil science, and plant science.

- **Pharmaceutical Chemists:** Compounds derived from wood sources are an important aspect of wood chemistry and have increasing applications in pharmaceutical development.

Future Applications

The single largest application of wood as a renewable resource has always been its use as a structural material, and this is not likely to change. The demands placed on the resources from which wood is derived, however, face pressure that increases with population growth and needs. As a product of biological origin, wood is subject to decomposition over time, and developing and discovering methods of prolonging the working lifetime of wood-based structures is expected to be increasingly important. At the same time, forest ecologists and environmentalists recognize that the majority of wood resources' potential is unrealized, yet forests are being eliminated at a faster rate than knowledge about them is growing. Wood chemists will play an important role in both preserving natural forests by actively discovering new and useful wood-sourced compounds and reducing the pressure for the exploitation of wood resources. Perhaps the most important area in which wood chemists will contribute to the long-term viability of forests and wood products in general is the biofuels industry, where they will identify and develop methodologies for the production of combustible fuels such as alcohols and biodiesel from wood-based materials. This is an area of intense research and will soon require the services of a large number of wood chemists.

Richard M. Renneboog, MS

More Information

American Chemical Society
1155 Sixteenth Street NW
Washington, DC 20036
www.acs.org

Wood Technology Society
The Institute of Materials, Minerals and Mining
1 Carlton House Terrace
London SW1Y 5DB
UK
www.iom3.org/content/wood-technology

Toxicology

FIELDS OF STUDY

Analytical chemistry; biochemistry; biology; chemistry; clinical chemistry; environmental science; forensics; mathematics; pharmacology; toxicology; veterinary medicine.

DEFINITION

Toxicology involves the study of toxicants, whether biological, chemical, or physical, and how they affect people, animals, and the environment. Toxicologists determine whether these chemicals are actually or potentially harmful by using their knowledge of chemistry and biology and help develop and implement strategies to eliminate, reduce, or control exposure to those harmful substances.

Basic Principles

Toxicologists study the adverse effects of biological, chemical, or physical agents on living organisms (humans, animals, and plants). Adverse effects can manifest in many forms, ranging from immediate death to subtle changes at a molecular level that do not become known until years later. These effects can also manifest themselves at various levels in the body. For example, some chemical agents affect a certain body organ, others damage a particular type of cell, and even others may interfere with a specific biochemical reaction in the body necessary for life to continue. As medical knowledge has progressed, the understanding of how toxic agents affect the body has grown. A body can be affected on a cellular level by unseen toxins, the damage of which will not be known for many years.

This realization has led to an expansion in the field of toxicology. Toxicologists are now tasked with examining the physical environment to determine whether, how, and at what levels environmental toxins affect humans and other living things. These types of examinations can affect many industries, such as those that emit toxins into the environment and even those that dispose of toxic and hazardous waste and develop agents for biological warfare. Other fields in which toxicology is key is that of animal science (veterinarians who determine treatment for animals who are affected by toxins) and drug development (scientists who determine how certain therapeutic drugs affect the human body and determine safe and effective dosages).

Core Concepts

Toxicology and the study of poisons has a long and interesting history, possibly beginning with early humans, who recognized poisonous plants and animals and used them in the process of killing, whether for food or in war. Writings as early as 1500 BCE depict substances such as hemlock, opium, and certain metals that were used on arrows to kill animals or humans or even as agents in state execution processes. Stories are told of "poison maidens," beautiful young girls who were fed tiny amounts of poison on a daily basis, causing them to become immune to the effects of the poison, until they became poisonous themselves. They were then sent as gifts to rival kings who died when they touched the poisonous girl.

Poisoning as a method of assassination become more popular in the eighth century, when an Arab chemist discovered how to turn arsenic into an odorless, tasteless, nearly undetectable powder. This substance became an easily available murder weapon, and by the Renaissance period, poison rings, knives, letters, and lipstick were in use for those who wished to do away with a political or amorous rival easily and quickly.

Philippus Aureolus Theophrastus Bombastus von Hohenheim (known more commonly as Paracelsus), a sixteenth-century Swiss physician, formulated ideas about poisons and toxicology that are still in use. He carefully studied plant and animal poisons and determined that specific chemical compounds, rather than the plant or animal itself, which was immune to the poison it carried, were responsible for toxicity. He documented how the human body responded to those specific chemical compounds and understood that doses of a particular compound could be beneficial or toxic, depending on the amount given (known as the dose-response relationship). A major concept of toxicology, credited to Paracelsus, is that "all substances are poisons;

there is none which is not a poison. The right dose differentiates a poison and a remedy." Drug companies continue to use this idea, as many drugs, such as warfarin, were developed from substances that caused immediate death. In the case of warfarin, it began as a type of poison for rats that caused their blood to thin, and they would bleed to death. Therapeutic doses of warfarin help stroke victims (or possible victims) to keep from forming blood clots.

French toxicologist Mathieu Joseph Bonaventure Orfila is referred to as "the father of toxicology" and was the first major proponent of forensic toxicology. In the nineteenth century, he prepared a systematic correlation between chemical and biological properties of poisons. He analyzed autopsy materials to show the effects of poisons on specific organs by showing tissue damage and made chemical analysis a routine part of forensic medicine. Orfila is credited as being one of the first to use a microscope to look for blood and semen stains, and he became an expert witness in the sensational murder trials of his time.

Poisoning is still a relatively major cause of death. In the United States, from 2001 to 2004, there were more than 147,000 deaths related to poison; of these 434 were considered homicides, though more may have been murders as it is sometimes difficult to distinguish a poisoning from a natural death or an accident.

Today, toxicologists work in laboratories, performing tests on substances of different types—often human tissue. They must be familiar with and know how to operate highly sophisticated laboratory equipment and understand the functioning of chemical reagents. They must understand and apply highly sophisticated and exact methodologies to determine reliably the presence or absence of a substance in a sample. Each step of every complicated process must be documented to ensure that procedures have been exactly followed, especially in circumstances involving a chain of custody for criminal cases.

Toxicologists must also make informed conclusions about the impact of a certain amount of a specific substance and what effect it would have on a certain individual (based on weight, for example) or what effect a substance would have on a particular environment. These educated opinions are often based on professional, educational, and scientific experience and are sometimes required in court testimony.

Interesting Facts about Toxicology

- Most toxicologists, especially forensic toxicologists, work in labs that are part of law-enforcement agencies. Others work with medical examiners to determine causes of death. Private drug-testing facilities or poison-control centers are another source of employment for these scientists.

- Toxicologists must be mentally strong. They are often exposed to details of horrific crimes and must make judgments about whether a crime was committed.

- A forensic toxicologist is often called on to testify in court as to the effect a certain amount of a substance would have on a particular person. He or she must explain complicated testing methods in language that a jury can understand.

- Some famous victims of poisoning include Socrates (hemlock) and Cleopatra (snakebite). The Emperor Claudius (Tiberius Claudius Drusus Nero Germanicus) was said to have been poisoned by his wife. Some say she served him poison mushrooms. Another story says that he was suspicious of her and would only eat figs he himself had picked from the tree, so she went into the garden and poisoned figs still on the tree.

- In fifteenth-century Italy, Lucrezia Borgia was one of the Borgia family members famous for poisoning rivals. She was said to have worn a ring that contained poison that she poured into drinks of men and women who were threatening to her family and its status.

- Viktor Yushchenko, a popular Ukrainian politician, was said to have been poisoned by government agents after announcing that he would run for president. After a dinner with Ukrainian officials, his face became pockmarked and disfigured. Toxicologists found that he had more than 1,000 times the normal amount of TCDD dioxin in his body.

- Toxicology is a constantly changing field. Successful toxicologists are constantly learning, keeping pace with new chemicals, methodologies, and technologies. A good toxicology candidate is someone who is fascinated by chemicals and the effect they can have on the human body.

Applications Past and Present

Toxicologists can focus their efforts in a variety of areas. Below are a few of the major areas of specialization.

Forensic Toxicology. These scientists usually work as part of a crime-scene team. They perform tests on bodily fluids and tissues to determine whether any drugs or chemicals in the body may have contributed to a crime, such as alcohol, chemicals, drugs (illegal or prescription), gases, metals, or poisons. Alternatively, a forensic toxicologist may work in drug testing, trying to discover evidence of date-rape or performance-enhancing drugs, or in animal-tissue testing for evidence of wildlife crime or environmental contamination, such as chemical spills.

Environmental Toxicology. These professionals focus on the interaction of chemicals on living systems, including how areas and environments are affected by toxic waste or released industrial chemicals. They may also work with workplace exposure to chemicals and metals and understand principles of toxicodynamics.

Medical Toxicology. This type of toxicologist usually works in a laboratory performing tests on bodily fluid and tissue samples to determine whether there are chemicals present. Though their work is similar to that of a forensic toxicologist and may even involve criminal investigations, this type of toxicologist works more with medical cases, such as chemotherapy adjustments or accidental exposures, rather than criminal cases.

Pharmacological Toxicology. Drug companies use toxicologists to help determine the chemical toxicity of drugs under development. These professionals help determine therapeutic levels for drugs and evaluate whether the proposed drugs build up in tissues or are eliminated from the body to determine maximum safe dosages and durations. They may also help determine under what conditions certain drugs should be avoided by monitoring interactions of drugs with other drugs a patient may be taking or other conditions a patient may have. Their knowledge of toxicokinetics can be helpful in these situations. This knowledge also helps determine age-related effects of certain toxic agents, such as whether a drug affects children and the elderly differently than it affects adults.

Impact on Industry

Job Outlook for a Toxicologist. The rapid growth of the biotechnology industry will create the most demand for biological scientists, which includes toxicologists. In addition, more biological scientists and medical scientists will be needed to determine the environmental impact of industry and government actions and to prevent or correct environmental problems. Employment for biological scientists is expected to grow faster than the average for all occupations through the year 2020, which means employment is projected to increase 20 to 28 percent.

Government Agencies and Military. The government remains one of the largest employers of toxicologists in the United States. Toxicologists may find employment with the US Departments of Agriculture, Interior, and Defense, and with the National Institutes of Health. The United States Department of Health and Human Services houses a National Toxicology Program that focuses on shaping public health policy involving any toxicological agents of public concern. Toxicologists who work in this area develop and apply the tools of modern toxicology and molecular biology to evaluate toxicological substances, develop and validate tests to discover these agents, and communicate these tools and tests to public health agencies.

In the military, toxicologists such as forensic toxicologists can work in service-operated laboratories, where they may be responsible for drug testing, developing protective

Occupation	Environmental scientists and specialists
Employment 2010	89,400
Projected Employment 2020	106,100
Change in Number (2010–20)	16,700
Percent Change	19%

*Bureau of Labor Statistics, 2012

gear, analyzing toxic exposure, and conducting and applying research related to biochemical problems and threats.

Industry and Business. Environmental companies, toxic-waste disposal industries, and drug development are just a few of the places that toxicologists prove their worth in industry. In the environmental field, toxicologists help determine whether chemicals released into the environment are likely to harm ecosystems, including animals and humans.

Occupation	Chemists and materials scientists
Employment 2010	90,900
Projected Employment 2020	94,900
Change in Number (2010–20)	4,000
Percent Change	4%

*Bureau of Labor Statistics, 2012

They also test and monitor waste-disposal methods, such as factory effluent or toxic-waste disposal from energy production, that may be harmful to the environment.

Toxicologists are also key to pharmaceutical companies. As new drugs are developed, they monitor the effects on the human body to determine whether the efficacy of the drug outweighs the risks. They may also find work in government laboratories, where they investigate the safety and effectiveness of different types of chemicals. Another industry that employs toxicologists is the veterinary field. These toxicologists work in diagnostic laboratories examining the effects of chemicals on animals. This type of work may also be necessary in the drug-testing field.

University Research and Teaching. Toxicologists are employed by colleges and universities as teachers and researchers. According to a "Job Market Survey" conducted by the Society of Toxicology, approximately 21 percent of toxicologists then surveyed worked in academia, representing the second largest employment sector. Additionally, the Society of Toxicology website lists sixty-seven academic and postdoctoral toxicology programs within the United States.

Social Context and Future Prospects

Toxicologists are necessary in many aspects of environmental industry. They are important in many ecological fields, and some professional societies of toxicologists focus exclusively on this area. For example, the Society of Environmental Toxicology and Chemistry concentrates efforts on the study and analysis of environmental problems. It also focuses on environmental education and the management and regulation of natural resources. Its goal is to find solutions to environmental problems that people can live with on a long-term, everyday basis that support sustainable environments and ecosystems.

As the field of health care expands, toxicologists have opportunities to become more and more involved. New drugs are constantly being developed, and toxicologists are heavily involved with drug testing, both on animals and on humans. Their knowledge of the human body and how chemicals interact with it is crucial in this field.

Further Reading

Evans, G. O., ed. *Animal Clinical Chemistry: A Practical Handbook for Toxicologists and Biomedical Researchers*. 2d ed. Boca Raton, FL: CRC, 2009. Covers pre-analytical and analytical variables along with information on specific-organ toxicity.

Fenton, John Joseph. *Toxicology: A Case-Oriented Approach*. Boca Raton, FL: CRC, 2002. Includes case studies and information about diagnosis, testing, and treatment.

Hayes, A. Wallace, ed. *Principles and Methods of Toxicology*. 5th ed. Boca Raton, FL: CRC, 2008. Discusses principles of absorption, distribution, metabolism, and excretion; helps with understanding and using basic experiments in toxicology.

Klaassen, Curtis D. *Casarett & Doull's Toxicology: The Basic Science of Poisons*. 7th ed. New York: McGraw-Hill, 2008. The "gold standard" of toxicology, includes detailed discussions of concepts, principles, and mechanisms of toxicology.

Nelson, Lewis S., et al. *Goldfrank's Toxicologic Emergencies*. 9th ed. New York: McGraw-Hill, 2011. Includes comprehensive references; begins with general principles and moves to detailed discussions of biochemical principles; discusses various exposures—drugs, plants, metals, household products, as well as occupational and environmental.

Osweiler, Gary D., et al., eds. *Blackwell's Five-Minute Veterinary Consult Clinical Companion: Small Animal Toxicology*. Ames, IA: Wiley-Blackwell, 2011. Overview of toxicology in veterinary practice; includes color photos and tables in an appendix to help with quick differential diagnoses.

Richards, Ira S. *Principles and Practice of Toxicology in Public Health*. Sudbury, MA: Jones, 2008. Introduction to the field of toxicology and its practice in the public-health environment.

Wright, David A., and Pamela Welbourn. *Environmental Toxicology*. Cambridge, England: Cambridge University Press, 2002. Overview of interaction of chemicals and the environment from molecular to ecosystem levels; includes case studies.

About the Author: Marianne M. Madsen, MS, is a research associate in the division of epidemiology at the University of Utah. She also teaches scientific and technical writing for the University of Utah's communication department. She previously worked at the university's department of pathology, stationed at ARUP Laboratories, and for Intermountain Healthcare, a large nonprofit health care system, as a scientific medical writer. Other previous experience includes documenting quality processes as a certified quality manager, functioning as a managing editor of lead trade and technical publications, and acting as project manager for large publication projects.

Toxicologist

Earnings (Yearly Median): $79,230 (Bureau of Labor Statistics, 2012)

Employment and Outlook: Much faster than average growth (Bureau of Labor Statistics, 2012)

O*NET-SOC Code: 19-1021.00

Related Career Clusters: Education & Training; Health Science; Human Services

Scope of Work

Toxicologists monitor the presence of potentially toxic chemicals and study their effects on biological systems such as animals and plants. The specific job carried out by the toxicologist depends upon the place of employment and the function of the employer. Toxicologists employed by public-health departments or agencies may monitor the presence of harmful chemicals in the environment. This may include investigations of possible food or water contamination. If the primary job duties include research, the toxicologist may be involved in carrying out medical studies on the effects of chemicals in humans or animals. This is particularly true in the pharmaceutical industry or similar areas in which companies are actively involved in developing new chemicals or drugs.

Another branch of toxicology is in the area of forensics. These individuals may monitor or measure the presence of chemicals associated with a crime scene. For example, a forensic toxicologist may determine whether or not an individual has been poisoned, or if drugs or alcohol were involved in a fatal accident.

Education and Coursework

Most colleges and universities do not have a program specifically for toxicology. The undergraduate student interested in toxicology as a career generally concentrates in one of the sciences, such as biology, chemistry, or biochemistry; the course work carried out by the student is more critical than the overall program. Students should enroll in as many chemistry courses as are available, particularly laboratory courses in analytical and organic chemistry and biochemistry. Some universities do offer advanced undergraduate courses in toxicology. In addition, students should complete courses in the biological sciences, particularly any that are medically related, as well as mathematics, statistics, and physics. Any experience with instrumentation or analytical software may prove helpful when applying for jobs or professional schools.

Approximately 50 percent of toxicologists have doctoral degrees. A bachelor's degree may allow the individual access to lower, entry-level jobs, but advancement and opportunities for greater responsibilities may be limited. Students enrolled in a graduate program with the goal of an advanced degree may begin to specialize in the area of toxicology in which they are interested. Areas include environmental toxicology, human or clinical toxicology, and forensic toxicology. Course work will include advanced analytical chemistry and biochemistry. Depending upon the laboratory, a master's degree may be sufficient. For

---

> ## Transferable Skills
>
> - Communication Skills – Reporting information
> - Interpersonal/Social Skills – Working as a member of a team (SCANS Workplace Competency – Interpersonal)
> - Research & Planning Skills – Gathering information
> - Research & Planning Skills – Analyzing information
> - Organization & Management Skills – Managing equipment/ materials (SCANS Workplace Competency – Resources)
> - Organization & Management Skills – Organizing information or materials
> - Technical Skills – Performing scientific, mathematical and technical work

example, forensic jobs in toxicology rely more on the practical experience of the individual, and a doctorate degree may not be necessary.

Some students interested in research involving humans—for example, analyzing the genetic effects of toxins—should pursue a medical program, followed by a hospital internship and residency with a specialization in the subject. A master's program takes, on average, approximately two years to complete, while a PhD program may require three to four years. If the student wishes to first obtain a medical degree, an average of four years in medical school will be required. If the goal is a PhD following undergraduate work, it is common to apply directly to a doctoral program rather than spending several years on a master's degree as well.

Career Enhancement and Training

Individuals trained in toxicology are eligible to join the American Academy of Clinical Toxicology. The goals of the organization include clinical training and research into disease and other pathological issues associated with exposure to environmental toxins. Applicants must either possess a doctorate in the biomedical sciences or have a baccalaureate degree and a minimum of five years of experience in the field. The applicant must also have demonstrated competence in the field. Once the application has passed a board of review, the applicant must pass an examination.

Other professional toxicology associations include the American College of Medical Toxicology (ACMT) and the American Board of Veterinary Toxicology. The ACMT consists of physicians whose practices address patients who have been exposed to environmental toxins or who have experienced drug overdoses. While membership is not required for a certified toxicologist, most physicians certified in medical toxicology are members of the ACMT. Application to the society requires prior certification in medical toxicology by the American Board of Emergency Medicine or the American Board of Preventive Medicine.

The American Board of Veterinary Toxicology consists of board-certified veterinarians who monitor or study the effects of environmental toxins on animals. Their work includes monitoring pharmaceutical agents, food additives, radiation, and any other potential hazard to pets and wild animals.

Daily Tasks and Technology

The duties of a toxicologist will vary depending upon whether he or she works primarily in industry, medicine, or academia. Industrial toxicologists work as part of a team that may also include chemists or biochemists, and the specific work carried out depends upon the specific industry. In the pharmaceutical sector, toxicologists may monitor the safety or possible toxic effects of various compounds, utilizing a variety of imaging software or other forms of analyzers to develop three-dimensional images of molecules.

Toxicologists employed by the government may be involved in assessing the toxicity of various chemicals and creating safety profiles that outline safe handling and disposal procedures for various substances. They are also responsible for approving new drugs and medications for the market after first performing rigorous analyses to determine if a substance is both safe and effective. Toxicologists may also work in hospitals or poison-control centers, diagnosing and treating patients who have been exposed to harmful substances or who have overdosed on a medicine or drug.

In the academic field, which includes medical programs as well as undergraduate biology programs, toxicologists may carry out research into the mechanisms of toxic effects in addition to teaching students of biochemistry or biology.

In both industry and academia, research may involve observing the long-term effects of chemicals on humans or animals. In some cases, the effects of a chemical may not be observed for several months or longer, requiring extended periods of observation. If a new chemical is under study, it will likely be rated on a scale of zero (no toxicity) to three (significant toxicity that may be life threatening).

Earnings and Employment Outlook

The earnings and employment levels for toxicologists are expected to rise, according to the United States Bureau of Labor Statistics (BLS), subject to the overall performance of the economy. Persons employed in jobs in the government sector, including those in public-health departments, have experienced significant layoffs as government expenditures are reduced. Industry as well has undergone some contraction, including in areas of basic research. Despite these changes, however, it is expected that employment in the biological sciences, including the field of toxicology, will increase by some 29 percent by 2020; this translates to around 7,700 additional jobs. The BLS also predicts that companies will increase budget allocations in the areas of research and application in the medical area.

It is expected that employment in the biological sciences, including the field of toxicology, will increase by some 29 percent by 2020; this translates to around 7,700 additional jobs.

Salary levels are a function of the highest degree earned by the individual as well as years of experience. Industrial salaries generally exceed those in academia. While the median annual pay for a toxicologist is close to $80,000, a person with a doctorate and significant experience could earn over \$100,000 annually. Entry-level salaries may range between \$35,000 and over \$50,000 for somebody with a doctorate, with the higher salary more likely to be associated with an industrial job.

Related Occupations

- **Environmental Biologists:** Environmental biologists specializing in toxicology study the effects of chemicals in the environment, including contamination in water, food, or air, and the effects of contaminants on human health.

- **Forensic Toxicologists:** Forensic toxicologists frequently work with law-enforcement agencies to identify chemicals that might be associated with a crime or monitor for the presence of illegal drugs.

- **Medical Toxicologists:** Medical toxicologists, almost all of whom have medical degrees, may test for the presence of toxic materials in patients, which can result from drug use or from improper organ function, particularly the liver or kidneys. A medical toxicologist may also be part of a research team studying different methods of monitoring illnesses.

- **Molecular Biologists:** Most often PhD holders, molecular biologists study the molecular changes that occur in a cell in response to various environmental influences. Molecular biologists are generally research scientists.

- **Biochemists:** Biochemists study the chemical properties of living organisms. They may specialize in the study of the chemical changes that take place in biological systems, including as a result of exposure to possible toxins.

Future Applications

The increasing development and use of chemicals, not only in the pharmaceutical and chemical industries directly but also in industries such as agriculture and food service, will create new opportunities for toxicologists. Environmental concerns over air and water contamination

A Conversation with Laura Hagopian
Job Title: Physician

What was your career path?

From my undergraduate degree in chemistry, I went on to medical school and am currently a physician in the Emergency Department.

What are three pieces of advice you would offer someone interested in your profession?

1. Realize that your ultimate career path after a major in chemistry can take various routes; pursue what you are most interested in.
2. Work hard, but also make sure you have time for outside activities.
3. Always work as part of a team.

What paths for career advancement are available to you?

I can continue working in the academic field, provide teaching to students, and perform either basic science or focused medical research.

will also result in an increased role for toxicologists. In recent years, toxicologists have been called on to respond to major environmental disasters, including the containment and remediation efforts following the 2010 *Deepwater Horizon* oil spill in the Gulf of Mexico and the Fukushima Daiichi nuclear meltdown in Japan. Opportunities for toxicologists are not limited to research and development; more than half of all certified toxicologists work as industry consultants.

As industrial technology continues to evolve, along with the ability to synthesize new or modified chemicals, there will be an increased need to monitor or test for any possible toxic side effects. Such rapid development underscores the need for proper risk assessments and safety profiles. Any form of biochemical toxicity must continue to be analyzed and, if possible, the mechanism determined. For this reason, medical or biochemical toxicologists will continue to be in demand.

Current testing of chemicals routinely utilizes animals as test subjects. Besides ethical considerations, the use of animals in testing is expensive and subject to increasingly strict regulations. Future toxicologists will be tasked with developing more efficient models to analyze the possible toxicity of chemical compounds or aftereffects of injuries and diseases as they are metabolized in the body.

Richard Adler, PhD

More Information

American Academy of Clinical Toxicology
6728 Old McLean Village Drive
McLean, VA 22101
www.clintox.org

American Board of Toxicology
PO Box 30054
Raleigh, NC 27622-0054
www.abtox.org

American College of Medical Toxicology
10645 N. Tatum Boulevard, Suite 200-111
Phoenix, AZ 85028
www.acmt.net

Society of Toxicology
1821 Michael Faraday Drive, Suite 300
Reston, VA 20190
www.toxicology.org

Appendixes

General Bibliography

Albarède, Francis. *Geochemistry: An Introduction.* 2nd ed. Cambridge: Cambridge UP, 2009. Print. Focuses on inorganic chemistry and the presentation of the chemistry, physics, and mathematics involved in geochemistry. Discusses the earth's geospheres, as well as biogeochemistry and environmental geochemistry.

Alessio, Enzo. *Bioinorganic Medicinal Chemistry.* Weinheim: Wiley, 2011. Print. Presents a sound introduction to the concepts of bioinorganic chemistry, including radiopharmaceuticals. Also discusses the functions of physiology dependent not only on organic chemistry, but on numerous inorganic materials that are also essential components of biological systems.

Anastas, Paul T., and John C. Warner. *Green Chemistry: Theory and Practice.* New York: Oxford UP, 2000. Print. A high-level textbook, written by the founders of green chemistry, that serves as the fundamental text for the field, introducing the major concepts and strategies of green chemistry.

Askeland, Donald R. *The Science and Engineering of Materials.* New York: Chapman, 1996. Print. Provides a background for many of the chemical-process technologies associated with diverse materials, including polymeric and advanced composite materials.

Bagotsky, Vladimir, ed. *Fundamentals of Electrochemistry.* 2d ed. New York: Wiley-Interscience, 2005. Provides a good introduction to this field for those unfamiliar with it, though later chapters contain material of interest to advanced students.

Bahadur, P. and N. V. Sastry. *Principles of Polymer Science.* 2nd ed. Middlesex: Alpha Sci., 2005. Print. A text and reference book written for undergraduate and graduate students in chemistry, chemical engineering and materials science; presents basic and advanced aspects of polymer science, including natural, inorganic, and specialty polymers.

Baird, Colin, and Michael Cann. *Environmental Chemistry.* 4th ed. New York: Freeman, 2008. A clear and comprehensive survey of the field. Each chapter has further reading suggestions and websites of interest. Index.

Bajpai, Pratima. *Environmentally Friendly Production of Pulp and Paper.* Hoboken: Wiley, 2010. Print. A work devoted to urging those in the paper industry to adopt more environmentally friendly methods consistent with cleaner production standards.

Bard, Allen J., and Larry R. Faulkner. *Electrochemical Methods: Fundamentals and Applications.* 2d ed. Hoboken, NJ: Wiley, 2001. Provides comprehensive treatment of the theory and applications needed to understand this field's fundamentals.

Belitz, Hans-Dieter, Werner Grosch, and Peter Schieberle. *Food Chemistry.* 4th rev. ed. Munich: Springer, 2009. Print. Consists entirely of figures describing the components of food chemistry. Long considered the definitive textbook and reference in the field.

Bertomeu-Sánchez, José Ramón, and Agustí Nieto-Galan, eds. *Chemistry, Medicine, and Crime: Mateu J. B. Orfila (1787–1853) and His Times.* Sagamore Beach, MA: Science History, 2006. A collection of essays that present an overview of the life and work of Orfila and his contributions to pharmacology and toxicology.

Biermann, Christopher J. *Handbook of Pulping and Papermaking.* 2nd ed. San Diego: Academic, 1996. Print. A detailed explanation of all phases of the pulp and paper industry. Includes an accessible description of the science behind the process. Color pictures.

Blackwell, Helen E., and Yunde Zhao. "Chemical Genetic Approaches to Plant Biology." *Plant Physiology* 133.2 (2003): 448–55. Print. Discusses why a chemical-genetics approach would be advantageous in plant biology and addresses some experimentation conducted with the Arabidopsis plant.

Bonetta, Laura. "What Is Chemical Genetics?" *Howard Hughes Medical Institute.* Howard Hughes Medical Inst., n.d. Web. 23 Oct. 2012. Provides a basic introduction to the field of chemical genetics, with links to a number of multimedia features illustrating specific examples of the field.

Brettell, Thomas A., John M. Butler, and José R. Almirall. "Forensic Science." *Analytical Chemistry* 79.12 (2007): 4365–4384. A review of forensic science applications used in common disciplines.

Brock, William H. *The Chemical Tree: A History of Chemistry.* New York: Norton, 2000. Previously published as The Norton History of Chemistry; shows how the development of electrochemistry forms an important part of the story of chemistry; includes an extensive bibliographical essay, notes, and index.

Burdick, Donald L., and William L. Leffler. *Petrochemicals in Nontechnical Language.* 4th ed. Tulsa: PennWell, 2010. Print. Comprehensive coverage of the subject that focuses on chemical properties of petrochemical molecules, written to be as accessible as possible. Figures for illustration.

ChemBank: Initiative for Chemical Genetics. Broad Inst., 2006. Web. 23 Oct. 2012. Collaboration between the NIH and a number of other institutions that has information on numerous small molecules and screens to help researchers who might not otherwise have access to that knowledge.

Cong, Feng, Atwood K. Cheung, and Shih-Min A. Huang. "Chemical Genetics–Based Target Identification in Drug Discovery." *Annual Review of Pharmacology and Toxicology* 52 (2012): 57–78. Print. Explains how the process of chemical genetics is used to approach drug discovery.

Corey, E. J., Barbara Czako, and Laszlo Kurti. *Molecules and Medicine.* Hoboken: Wiley, 2012. Print. An illustrated book for a general readership discussing the chemistry behind numerous commonly encountered pharmaceutical compounds.

Coultate, Tom P. *Food: The Chemistry of Its Components.* 5th ed. Cambridge: RSC Paperbacks, 2009. Print. Examines the chemical components of food both large (like lipids) and small (like pigments). Also features special topics, an updated breakdown of legislative changes in the field, and extensive bibliography.

Davis, Fred J. *Polymer Chemistry: A Practical Approach*. New York: Oxford UP, 2004. Print. A more advanced text for chemists already working in the field or who are new to the field of polymer chemistry, containing detailed descriptions of synthetic methodology and preparations for a wide range of polymers, with regard to their application in the development of new materials.

Dayan, Nava, Lambros Kromidas, and Gaurav Kale. *Formulating, Packaging, and Marketing of Natural Cosmetic Products*. Hoboken: Wiley, 2011. Print. Discusses the shift toward natural beauty products as consumers grow more aware of the potentially toxic substances found in the cosmetics produced by the major firms.

Dessler, Andrew E., and Edward A. Parson. *The Science and Politics of Global Climate Change: A Guide to the Debate*. New York: Cambridge UP, 2010. Print. Introduction to the issue of climate change, including atmospheric chemistry and other atmospheric properties research. Also discusses the potential future of research in the area of climate change.

Dewick, Paul M. *Medicinal Natural Products: A Biosynthetic Approach*. Chichester: Wiley, 2009. Print. Provides a thorough introduction to the biochemical pathways and mechanisms by which various classes of compounds, including various hydrocarbons, alkaloids, peptides, proteins, and carbohydrates, are manufactured in plants and other living organisms.

Dobre, Tanase, and José G. Sanchez Marcano. *Chemical Engineering: Modeling, Simulation, and Similitude*. Weinheim, Germany: Wiley-VCH, 2007. Looks at how computer-aided modeling is used to develop, implement, and improve industrial processes. Covers the entire process, including mathematical modeling, results analysis, and performance evaluation.

Downing, Sarah Jane. *Beauty and Cosmetics, 1550–1950*. Oxford: Shire, 2012. Print. A history of changing ideals of beauty and the cosmetics that were used to achieve it. Includes illustrations and analyses of different eras.

Evans, G. O., ed. *Animal Clinical Chemistry: A Practical Handbook for Toxicologists and Biomedical Researchers*. 2d ed. Boca Raton, FL: CRC, 2009. Covers pre-analytical and analytical variables along with information on specific-organ toxicity.

Faure, Gunter. *Principles and Applications of Geochemistry*. 2nd ed. Upper Saddle River: Prentice, 1998. Print. Introduced the science and its applications with chapter summaries and test problems for studying the material.

Fenichell, Stephen. *Plastic: The Making of a Synthetic Century*. New York: Harper, 1996. Print. Delivers a thorough look at the history and development of the plastics industry, discussing many of the issues that have arisen through the ubiquity of polymers in the modern world.

Fenton, John Joseph. *Toxicology: A Case-Oriented Approach*. Boca Raton, FL: CRC, 2002. Includes case studies and information about diagnosis, testing, and treatment.

Ferguson, Charles D. *Nuclear Energy: What Everyone Needs to Know*. New York: Oxford UP, 2011. Print. An overview of nuclear energy, written after the meltdown of the Fukushima power plant. Addresses the science behind nuclear energy and the environmental and political issues surrounding it.

Ferry, Natalie, ed. *Environmental Impact of Genetically Modified Foods.* Wallingford: CABI, 2009. Print. Comprehensive collection of balanced essays that present and probe varied risks and opportunities of genetically modified food.

Florian, Stefan, et al. "Chemical Genetics: Reshaping Biology through Chemistry." *HFSP Journal* 1.2 (2007): 104–114. Print. Presents a general outline of the relationship between chemical genetics and drug discovery and gives a number of specific examples.

Foye, William O., and Thomas L. Lemke. *Foye's Principles of Medicinal Chemistry.* 6th ed. Baltimore: Lippincott, 2008. Print. Written for advanced students, pharmacists, and practitioners of medicinal chemistry. Approaches the subject in great detail, using case studies and an emphasis on patient-focused pharmaceutical care.

Frederick, John E. *Principles of Atmospheric Science.* Sudbury: Jones, 2008. Print. Introductory text describing the various fields of atmospheric sciences, including atmospheric chemistry, atmospheric physics, and climatology. Describes techniques and research methods utilized in modern climate and atmospheric research.

Fukuda-Parr, Sakiko, ed. *The Gene Revolution: GM Crops and Uneven Development.* London: Earthscan, 2007. Print. Overview of how genetically modified foods affect agricultural development in a variety of sampled countries.

Galambos, Louis, Takashi Hikino, and Vera Zamagni, eds. *The Global Chemical Industry in the Age of the Petrochemical Revolution.* Cambridge: Cambridge UP, 2007. Print. Series of essays examining the changes petrochemicals brought to the chemical industry after World War II. Includes case studies of several countries and the effect on major players in the chemical industry.

Gary, James H., Glenn E. Handwerk, and Mark J. Kaiser, eds. *Petroleum Refining: Technology and Economics.* 5th ed. Boca Raton: CRC, 2007. Print. Focuses on the production of aromatics, unsaturates, and saturates in chapter 15, "Petrochemical Feedstocks." Diagrams, tables.

Gibney, Michael, Ian Macdonald, and Helen Roche. *Nutrition and Metabolism.* 2nd ed. New York: Wiley, 2010. Print. Summarizes both the body's various systems and the roles played by various nutrients in metabolism.

Girard, James E. *Principles of Environmental Chemistry.* Sudbury, MA: Jones, 2010. Emphasizes the chemical principles undergirding environmental issues as well as the social and economic contexts in which they occur. Five appendixes and index.

Goldsmith, Barbara. *Obsessive Genius: The Inner World of Marie Curie.* New York: Norton, 2005. Print. Examines the personal and professional life of twentieth-century chemist Marie Curie. Also discusses the history and culture of nuclear chemistry.

Gordon, J. E. *The New Science of Strong Materials; or, Why You Don't Fall Through the Floor.* Princeton: Princeton UP, 2006. Print. Conveys why materials science is integral to the development of new technology and explains the basic scientific principles that define the properties of many common materials.

Hagiopol, Cornel, and James W. Johnston. *Chemistry of Modern Papermaking.* Boca Raton: CRC, 2011. Print. Explores the many ways chemicals are involved in the paper industry.

Haneklaus, Silvia, ed. *Recent Advances in Agricultural Chemistry*. Brunswick: Bundesforschungsanstalt fuer Landwirtschaft, 2005. Print. Collection of essays, about half in English, on topics ranging from precision farming to new tools such as yield maps of combinable crops.

Hayes, A. Wallace, ed. *Principles and Methods of Toxicology*. 5th ed. Boca Raton, FL: CRC, 2008. Discusses principles of absorption, distribution, metabolism, and excretion; helps with understanding and using basic experiments in toxicology.

Hoffmann, Matthew J. *Ozone Depletion and Climate Change: Constructing a Global Response*. New York: State U of New York P, 2005. Print. Detailed introduction to ozone depletion and various methods used to combat ozone-destroying pollutants in the atmosphere. Contains a historical review of ozone research and modern techniques to study ozone change in the twenty-first century.

Hosford, William F. *Materials Science*. New York: Cambridge UP, 2007. Print. Provides an overview of the key concepts and principles of materials science, serving as a comprehensive introduction to the field.

Houck, Max M., and Jay A. Siegel. *Fundamentals of Forensic Science*. 2d ed. Burlington, MA: Academic, 2010. An introduction to forensic science and common techniques used for the analysis of physical, biological, and chemical evidence.

Howard, Alan G. *Aquatic Environmental Chemistry*. 1998. Reprint. New York: Oxford UP, 2004. Analyzes the chemistry behind freshwater and marine systems. Also includes useful secondary material that contains explanations of unusual terms and advanced chemical and mathematical concepts.

Hummel, Rolf E. *Understanding Materials Science: History, Properties, Applications*. 2nd ed. New York: Springer, 2004. Print. Discusses the mechanical and electrical properties of materials and analyzes some of the anthropological, social, and economic implications of materials development.

Ihde, Aaron J. *The Development of Modern Chemistry*. New York: Dover, 1984. Makes available to general readers a well-organized treatment of chemistry from the eighteenth to the twentieth century, of which electrochemical developments form an essential part. Illustrated, with extensive bibliographical essays on all the chapters; author and subject indexes.

Irene, Eugene A. *Electronic Materials Science*. Hoboken: Wiley, 2005. Print. Surveys the applications of materials science to electronics, one of the field's key areas of research.

Jacob, Daniel B. *Introduction to Atmospheric Chemistry*. Princeton: Princeton UP, 1999. Print. Comprehensive introduction to atmospheric chemistry. Provides detailed information on the essential technologies, techniques, and discoveries within the field, with overviews of environmental issues investigated through atmospheric chemistry research.

James, Stuart H., and Jon J. Nordby, eds. *Forensic Science: An Introduction to the Scientific and Investigative Techniques*. 3d ed. Boca Raton, FL: CRC, 2009. Discusses mass spectrometry techniques in relation to forensic applications, including forensic toxicology, controlled substance identification, and DNA analysis.

Jansen, Lee, and Marc Tischler. *The Big Picture: Medical Biochemistry*. New York: McGraw, 2012. Print. Review of basic biochemistry with emphasis on medical applications. The first portion of the book summarizes organic molecules in the cell, while later chapters address medical issues.

Katzung, Bertram, Susan Masters, and Anthony Trevor, eds. *Basic and Clinical Pharmacology*. 11th ed. New York: McGraw-Hill, 2009. A comprehensive textbook that includes more than three hundred full-color illustrations, drug comparison charts, and case studies outlining the clinical applications of pharmacology.

Klaassen, Curtis D. *Casarett & Doull's Toxicology: The Basic Science of Poisons*. 7th ed. New York: McGraw-Hill, 2008. The "gold standard" of toxicology, includes detailed discussions of concepts, principles, and mechanisms of toxicology.

Kobilinsky, Lawrence, Thomas F. Liotti, and Jamel Oeser-Sweat. *DNA: Forensic and Legal Applications*. Hoboken, NJ: Wiley-Interscience, 2005. Presents an overview of DNA analysis, including the historical perspective, scientific principles, and laboratory procedures.

Lancaster, Mike. *Green Chemistry: An Introductory Text*. Cambridge: RSC, 2010. Print. An overview of green chemistry that discusses the green technology industry, as well as research, alternative energy, renewable resources, and waste.

Li, Yuan-Hui. *A Compendium of Geochemistry*. Princeton: Princeton UP, 2000. Print. Begins with structure of chemical elements, moves to solar nebula as source of terrestrial elements, and includes discussion of chemical composition of igneous and sedimentary rocks and earth's oceans; concludes with the biosphere.

Lide, David R., ed. *CRC Handbook of Chemistry and Physics: A Ready-Reference Book of Chemical and Physical Data*. 90th ed. Boca Raton, FL: CRC, 2009. A vital source of information for designing chemical processes, analyzing results, and estimating costs.

Loveland, Walter D., David J. Morrissey, and Glenn T. Seaborg. *Modern Nuclear Chemistry*. Hoboken: Wiley, 2001. Print. Provides an exhaustive review of nuclear chemistry, from core concepts to cutting-edge applications. Includes an overview of the relevant quantum mechanics.

Malkan, Stacy. *Not Just a Pretty Face: The Ugly Side of the Beauty Industry*. Gabriola: New Society, 2007. Print. Reports on the wide array of potentially deadly chemicals found in makeup and perfumes despite some limited federal oversight.

Manahan, Stanley E. *Environmental Chemistry*. 9th ed. Boca Raton, FL: CRC, 2010. Explores the anthrosphere, industrial ecosystems, geochemistry, and aquatic and atmospheric chemistry. Each chapter has a list of further references and cited literature. Index.

Matar, Sami, and Lewis F. Hatch. *Chemistry of Petrochemical Processes*. 2nd ed. Boston: Gulf Professional, 2001. Print. Useful survey of the chemical processes involved in the creation of petrochemicals from raw materials of crude oil, natural gas, and unconventional hydrocarbon sources. Focuses on different petrochemicals and their production.

Matlack, Albert. *Introduction to Green Chemistry.* 2nd ed. New York: CRC, 2010. A thorough text on green chemistry that discusses some of the lesser-known areas of green chemistry, such as the environmental effects of population, feedstock, biofuel, and electronic waste.

Misra, Kula. *Introduction to Geochemistry: Principles and Applications.* Chichester: Wiley, 2012. Print. Written for readers at advanced undergraduate and graduate levels and includes sections on: crystal chemistry dealing with atomic structure of elements, chemical reactions focusing on thermodynamics, isotope chemistry related to dating rocks and minerals, and earth supersystem discussing the geospheres.

NASA GISS: NASA Goddard Institute for Space Studies. Natl. Aeronautics and Space Admin., n.d. Web. 21 Aug. 2012. Describes a variety of current research programs in the environmental sciences, physics, and atmospheric chemistry. Also contains descriptions of using atmospheric chemistry in the study of climate change and global warming.

Nelson, Lewis S., et al. *Goldfrank's Toxicologic Emergencies.* 9th ed. New York: McGraw-Hill, 2011. Includes comprehensive references; begins with general principles and moves to detailed discussions of biochemical principles; discusses various exposures—drugs, plants, metals, household products, as well as occupational and environmental.

NOAA: National Oceanic and Atmospheric Administration. US Dept. of Commerce, n.d. Web. 21 Aug. 2012. Contains information on a number of research projects investigating atmospheric properties in monitoring weather, pollution, and environmental hazards. Also contains information about research programs supported through the federal funding of NOAA.

O'Connor, Cornelius J., Luca Laraia, and David R. Spring. "Chemical Genetics." *Chemical Society Reviews* 40.8 (2011): 4332–45. Print. Provides an excellent overview of both the field as a whole and a number of detailed specific developments.

Osweiler, Gary D., et al., eds. *Blackwell's Five-Minute Veterinary Consult Clinical Companion: Small Animal Toxicology.* Ames, IA: Wiley-Blackwell, 2011. Overview of toxicology in veterinary practice; includes color photos and tables in an appendix to help with quick differential diagnoses.

Peacock, Andrew J., and Allison R. Calhoun. *Polymer Chemistry: Properties and Applications.* Cincinnati: Hanser, 2006. Print. Uses specific examples and case studies to illustrate the principles of polymer science. Written for undergraduates and industry professionals unfamiliar with polymer chemistry.

Perry, R. H., and D. W. Green, eds. *Perry's Chemical Engineers Handbook.* 8th ed. New York: McGraw-Hill, 2007. First published in 1934, this handbook provides information about the processes, operations, and equipment involved in chemical engineering, as well as chemical and physical data, and conversion factors. More than seven hundred illustrations.

Pointer, Sally. *The Artifice of Beauty: A History and Practical Guide to Perfumes and Cosmetics.* Stroud: Sutton, 2005. Print. Chronicles the historical evolution of the modern cosmetics industry and also offers an important philosophical discussion of who and what defines beauty.

Richards, Ira S. *Principles and Practice of Toxicology in Public Health.* Sudbury, MA: Jones, 2008. Introduction to the field of toxicology and its practice in the public-health environment.

Roberts, J. C. *Chemistry of Paper.* Cambridge: Royal Soc. of Chemistry, 1996. Print. Provides insight into the papermaking process from the perspective of the chemists who work in the field.

Romanowski, Perry, and Randy Shueller. *Beginning Cosmetic Chemistry.* 3rd ed. Carol Stream, IL: Allured, 2009. Print. Provides interested students with insight into what a budding cosmetic chemist can expect if employed in the field.

Rubin, Ronald P. "A Brief History of Great Discoveries in Pharmacology: In Celebration of the Centennial Anniversary of the Founding of the American Society of Pharmacology and Experimental Therapeutics." *Pharmacological Reviews* 59.4 (2007): 289–359. An overview of the great scientists and pharmacology discoveries of the nineteenth and twentieth centuries.

Rudin, Norah, and Keith Inman. *An Introduction to Forensic DNA Analysis.* 2d ed. Boca Raton, FL: CRC, 2002. Contains an overview of DNA analysis, beginning with its history and examining the principles on which it is based.

Saferstein, Richard. *Criminalistics: An Introduction to Forensic Science.* 10th ed. Upper Saddle River, NJ: Prentice Hall, 2011. Provides an introduction to forensic science, detailing the techniques to analyze physical, biological, and chemical evidence.

Schlesinger, Henry. *The Battery: How Portable Power Sparked a Technological Revolution.* New York: HarperCollins, 2010. Provides an entertaining, popular history of the battery, with lessons for readers familiar only with electronic handheld devices.

Schwartz, David, ed. *Medicine Science and Dreams: The Making of Physician-Scientists.* New York: Springer, 2011. Print. Collection of interviews with some dozen professionals, discussing their decisions to enter careers in science. While not all strictly biochemists, the subjects do describe their interests in biochemistry.

Schwedt, Georg. *The Essential Guide to Environmental Chemistry.* 2001. Reprint. New York: Wiley, 2007. Provides a concise overview of the field. Contains many color illustrations and an index.

Siracusa, Joseph M. *Nuclear Weapons: A Very Short Introduction.* Oxford: Oxford UP, 2008. Print. Summarizes the history of nuclear weaponry, the political evolution of weapons policy in the United States and abroad, and future ramifications of nuclear proliferation.

Speight, James G. *The Chemistry and Technology of Petroleum.* 4th ed. Boca Raton: CRC, 2007. Print. Covers petrochemicals in chapter 23 in an accessible and clearly understandable fashion. General discussion followed by description of chemical processes for petrochemicals. Tables and figures.

Sperling, Leslie Howard. *Introduction to Physical Polymer Science.* 4th ed. Hoboken: Wiley, 2006. Print. Includes topics in polymer science such as carbon nanotubes and nanocomposites, DNA and biopolymers, as well as topics such as fire retardancy and tribology.

Spring, David R. "Chemical Genetics to Chemical Genomics: Small Molecules Offer Big Insights." *Chemical Society Reviews* 34.6 (2005): 472–82. Print. Details the specific information that might be gleaned about the workings of proteins by using small molecules to target them.

Strobel, Howard A., and William R. Heineman. *Chemical Instrumentation: A Systematic Approach.* New York: Wiley, 1989. Print. Explores the importance of instrumentation, an essential feature of chemical technology that is fundamental to the control and monitoring of chemical processes in all disciplines, and provides a comprehensive background on the operating principles of numerous instrument types.

Tanford, Charles, and Jacqueline Reynolds. *Nature's Robots: A History of Proteins.* New York: Oxford UP, 2001. Print. Presents stories behind the discovery of proteins and their roles in metabolic reactions. Discusses many of the scientists who laid the framework for biochemistry.

Teegarden, David M. *Polymer Chemistry: Introduction to an Indispensable Science.* Arlington: Natl. Sci. Teachers Assn., 2004. Print. Provides an introduction to the basic principles and applications of the science of polymer chemistry.

Telle, Helmut H., Angel González Ureña, and Robert J. Donovan. *Laser Chemistry: Spectroscopy, Dynamics and Applications.* Hoboken: Wiley, 2007. Print. Introduces concepts on which a solid understanding of femtochemistry may be based, providing a broader context for the science.

Thomas, Gareth. *Medicinal Chemistry: An Introduction.* 2nd ed. Hoboken: Wiley, 2011. Print. Provides a thorough introduction to the science of medicinal chemistry without assuming prior knowledge in any area from basic principles through advanced combinatorics and pharmacokinetics.

Towler, Gavin P., and R. K. Sinnott. *Chemical Engineering Design.* Oxford, England: Butterworth-Heinemann, 2009. Examines how chemical engineers design chemical processes and discusses all the elements and factors involved.

Tymoczko, John, Jeremy Berg, and Lubert Stryer. *Biochemistry: A Short Course.* New York: Freeman, 2010. Print. Abbreviated text for a biochemistry course. In addition to descriptions of biochemical reactions, provides extensive clinical applications of errors that can occur in metabolic functions.

United States Food and Drug Administration. United States Department of Health and Human Services, 13 Apr. 2012. Web. 8 July 2012. Provides a comprehensive look at all industries pertaining to food chemistry and concise explanations of regulations and public health policy. Updated frequently with everything from articles on food preservation during extreme weather to the government's policies on biotechnology.

Vallance, Patrick, and Trevor G. Smart. "The Future of Pharmacology." *British Journal of Pharmacology* 147 (January 2006): S304–307. A perspective on the future of pharmacology as an integrative science, as well as discussions of the important divisions within the field.

Vane, John R., and Regina M. Botting. "The Mechanism of Action of Aspirin." *Thrombosis Research* 110.5 (2003): 255–58. Print. Provides a history and a summary of the workings of aspirin from a researcher involved in many of the key discoveries.

Walsh, Carol T., and Rochelle D. Schwartz-Bloom. *Levine's Pharmacology: Drug Actions and Reactions*. 7th ed. Abingson, England: Taylor & Francis, 2005. Outlines the history of pharmacology, general principles, and individual factors that influence drug action.

Walther, John. *Essentials of Geochemistry*. 2nd ed. Sudbury: Jones, 2009. Print. Emphasizes thermodynamics and the concept of chemical equilibrium; offers good presentation and discussion of basic principles and key concerns of geochemistry.

Welch, R. W., and P. C. Mitchell. "Food Processing: A Century of Change." *British Medical Bulletin* 56.1 (2000): 1–17. Print. Offers an in-depth look at food processing over the past century. Includes tables with eras and corresponding developments in food science and food chemistry.

Wells, G. Margaret. *Handbook of Petrochemicals and Processes*. 2nd ed. Aldershot: Gower, 1999. Print. Comprehensive presentation of a wide variety of petrochemicals; describes production processes for each. Identifies international classifications, applications, and major producers. Figures and tables.

Wright, David A., and Pamela Welbourn. *Environmental Toxicology*. Cambridge, England: Cambridge University Press, 2002. Overview of interaction of chemicals and the environment from molecular to ecosystem levels; includes case studies.

Young, Robert J., and Peter A. Lovell. *Introduction to Polymers*. 3rd ed. Boca Raton: CRC, 2009. Print. Advanced reference book detailing the underlying principles of polymers and their properties, including recently developed synthetic methods for various types of polymers, their behavior and analysis, multicomponent polymer systems, and polymer composites.

Zewail, Ahmed H. "Femtochemistry: Past, Present, and Future." *Pure and Applied Chemistry* 72.12 (2000): 2219–32. Print. Provides an overview of femtochemistry and future research directions and includes several diagrams that help to place femtochemistry in the context of the broader field of chemistry.

Zoski, Cynthia G., ed. *Handbook of Electrochemistry*. Oxford, England: Elsevier, 2007. Surveys most modern research areas of electrochemistry, such as reference electrodes, fuel cells, corrosion control, and other laboratory techniques and practical applications.

Detailed STEM Undergraduate Majors

Computer majors

- Computer and information systems
- Computer programming and data processing
- Computer science
- Information sciences
- Computer administration management and security
- Computer networking and telecommunications

Math majors

- Mathematics
- Applied mathematics
- Statistics and decision science
- Mathematics and computer science

Engineering majors

- General engineering
- Aerospace engineering
- Biological engineering
- Architectural engineering
- Biomedical engineering
- Chemical engineering
- Civil engineering
- Computer engineering
- Electrical engineering
- Engineering mechanics physics and science
- Environmental engineering

- Geological and geophysical engineering
- Industrial and manufacturing engineering
- Materials engineering and materials science
- Mechanical engineering
- Metallurgical engineering
- Mining and mineral engineering
- Naval architecture and marine engineering
- Nuclear engineering
- Petroleum engineering
- Miscellaneous engineering
- Engineering technologies
- Engineering and industrial management
- Electrical engineering technology
- Industrial production technologies
- Mechanical engineering related technologies
- Miscellaneous engineering technologies
- Military technologies

Physical and life science majors

- Animal sciences
- Food science
- Plant science and agronomy
- Soil science
- Environmental science
- Biology
- Biochemical sciences
- Botany
- Molecular biology

- Ecology
- Genetics
- Microbiology
- Pharmacology
- Physiology
- Zoology
- Miscellaneous biology
- Nutrition sciences
- Neuroscience
- Cognitive science and biopsychology
- Physical sciences
- Astronomy and astrophysics
- Atmospheric sciences and meteorology
- Chemistry
- Geology and earth science
- Geosciences
- Oceanography
- Physics
- Nuclear, industrial radiology, and biological technologies

Source: US Department of Commerce, Economics and Statistics Administration

Colleges to Consider

The following resource provides a list of the most highly selective four-year colleges for pursuing and attaining a bachelor's degree in chemistry. This list was built using a college search tool provided by EBSCO Career Guidance System, a staple for guidance counselors and students that offers both a centralized location to work together on career guidance. The list was constructed using the following select criteria:

- **Type of School:** 4 year

- **Average Cost:** Over $30,000

- **Selectivity:** Highly Selective (Minimum requirements: Graduated in top 40 percent of class; B to B+ average; SAT score between 1100–1199 or ACT score between 27–28)

- **Major:** Chemistry, General

Agnes Scott College
Decatur, GA
Enrollment: 871
Tuition (2012-12): $43,476*
agnesscott.edu

Amherst College
Amherst, MA
Enrollment: 1791
Tuition (2012-13): $44,610*
amherst.edu

Barnard College
New York, NY
Enrollment: 2,445
Tuition (2012-13): $41,850
barnard.edu

Bates College
Lewiston, ME
Enrollment: 1,769
Tuition (2011-12): $55,300*
bates.edu

Boston College
Chestnut Hill, MA
Enrollment: 9,088
Tuition (2012-13): $43,140
bc.edu

Bowdoin College
Brunswick, ME
Enrollment: 1,778
Tuition (2012-13): $43,676
bowdoin.edu

*Those undergraduate tuition costs that are comprehensive, and include room and board and possibly other fees.

Brown University
Providence, RI
Enrollment: 6,380
Tuition (2011-12): $41,328
brown.edu

Bryn Mawr College
Bryn Mawr, PA
Enrollment: 1,313
Tuition (2012-13): $41,260
brynmawr.edu

Bucknell University
Lewisburg, PA
Enrollment: 3,554
Tuition (2012-13): $45,132
bucknell.edu

California Institute of Technology
Pasadena, CA
Enrollment: 978
Tuition (2012-13): $38,085
caltech.edu

University of California—Berkley
Berkley, CA
Enrollment 36,142
Tuition (2012-13): $14,985.50
  (residents); $37,863.50
  (nonresidents)
berkeley.edu

Carnegie Mellon University
Pittsburg, PA
Enrollment: 6,281
Tuition (2012-13): $44,880
cmu.edu

Case Western Reserve University
Cleveland, OH
Enrollment: 4,016
Tuition (2012-13): $40,120
case.edu

Claremont McKenna College
Claremont, CA
Enrollment: 1,301
Tuition (2012-13): $43,840
cmc.edu

Colby College
Waterville, ME
Enrollment: 1,815
Tuition (2012-13): $55,700*
colby.edu

Colgate University
Hamilton, NY
Enrollment: 2,947
Tuition (2012-13): $44,330
colgate.edu

Columbia University
New York, NY
Enrollment: 6,027
Tuition (2012-13): $45,028
columbia.edu

Connecticut College
New London, CT
Enrollment: 1,896
Tuition (2012-13): $56,790
conncoll.edu

Cornell University
Ithaca, NY
Enrollment: 14,167
Tuition (2012-13): $43,185
cornell.edu

Dartmouth College
Hanover, NH
Enrollment: 4,194
Tuition (2012-13): $43,782
dartmouth.edu

Davidson College
Davidson, NC
Enrollment: 1,756
Tuition (2012-13): $40,809
davidson.edu

Duke University
Durham, NC
Enrollment: 6,680
Tuition (2012-13): $42,308
duke.edu

Emory University
Atlanta, GA
Enrollment: 5,500
Tuition (2011-12): $40,600
emory.edu

Furman University
Greenville, SC
Enrollment: 2,825
Tuition (2012-13): $41,152
furman.edu

Georgetown University
Washington, DC
Enrollment: 7,590
Tuition (2013): $42,360
georgetown.edu

Grinnell College
Grinnell, IA
Enrollment: 1,692
Tuition (2012-13): $41,004
grinnell.edu

Hamilton College
Clinton, NY
Enrollment: 1,864
Tuition (2012-13): $43,910
hamilton.edu

Harvard College
Cambridge, MA
Enrollment: 6,676
Tuition (2012-13): $54,496*
college.harvard.edu

Harvey Mudd College
Claremont, CA
Enrollment: 777
Tuition (2012-13): $44,159
hmc.edu

Haverford College
Haverford, PA
Enrollment: 1,198
Tuition (2012-13): $43,310
haverford.edu

Hendrix College
Conway, AR
Enrollment: 1,415
Tuition (2012-13): $35,900
hendrix.edu

Lafayette College
Easton, PA
Enrollment: 2,478
Tuition (2012-13): $41,920
lafayette.edu

Lawrence University
Appleton, WI
Enrollment: 1,496
Tuition (2012-13): $39,732
lawrence.edu

Macalester College
St. Paul, MN
Enrollment: 2,005
Tuition (2012-13): $43,472
macalester.edu

Massachusetts Institute of
Technology
Cambridge, MA
Enrollment: 4,384
Tuition (2011-2012): $40,732
mit.edu

Middlebury College
Middlebury, VT
Enrollment: 2,507
Tuition (2012-13): $55,570*
middlebury.edu

New York University
New York, NY
Enrollment: 22,280
Tuition (2012-13): $43,204
nyu.edu

Northwestern University
Evanston, IL
Enrollment: 9,466
Tuition (2012-13): $43,380
northwestern.edu

Oberlin College
Oberlin, OH
Enrollment: 2,959
Tuition (2012-13): $44,512
oberlin.edu

Princeton University
Princeton, NJ
Enrollment: 5,249
Tuition (2012-13): $54,780*
princeton.edu

Reed College
Portland, OR
Enrollment: 6,676
Tuition (2012-13): $44,200
reed.edu

Rensselaer Polytechnic Institute
Troy, NY
Enrollment: 5,322
Tuition (2012-13): $43,350
rpi.edu

Rice University
Houston, TX
Enrollment: 3,708
Tuition (2011-2012): $34,900
rice.edu

Rose-Hulman Institute of
Technology
Terre Haute, IN
Enrollment: 1,895
Tuition (2012-13): $38,313
rose-hulman.edu

Scripps College
Claremont, CA
Enrollment: 966
Tuition (2012-13): $43,406
scrippscollege.edu

Southwestern University
Georgetown, TX
Enrollment: 1,347
Tuition (2012-13): $34,410
southwestern.edu

Stanford University
Stanford, CA
Enrollment: 6,988
Tuition (2012-13): $41,250
stanford.edu

Stevens Institute of Technology
Hoboken, NJ
Enrollment: 2,427
Tuition (2012-13): $41,670
stevens.edu

Swarthmore College
Swarthmore, PA
Enrollment: 1,545
Tuition (2012-13): $42,744
swarthmore.edu

The Johns Hopkins University
Baltimore, MD
Enrollment: 5,066
Tuition (2011-12): $42,280
jhu.edu

The University of Chicago
Chicago, IL
Enrollment: 6,676
Tuition (2012-13): $43,581
uchicago.edu

Trinity University
San Antonio, TX
Enrollment: 2,431
Tuition (2012-13): $46,274*
trinity.edu

Tufts University
Medford, MA
Enrollment: 5,194
Tuition (2012-13): $43,688
tufts.edu

Tulane University
New Orleans, LA
Enrollment: 8,338
Tuition (2012-13): $45,240
tulane.edu

University of Notre Dame
Notre Dame, IN
Enrollment: 6,676
Tuition (2012-13): $42,971
nd.edu

University of Pennsylvania
Philadelphia, PA
Enrollment: 9,779
Tuition (2012-13): $39,088
upenn.edu

University of Richmond
Richmond, VA
Enrollment: 3,000
Tuition (2012-13): $44,210
richmond.edu

University of Rochester
Rochester, NY
Enrollment: 6,676
Tuition (2012-13): $42,890
rochester.edu

University of Southern California
Los Angeles, CA
Enrollment: 17,414
Tuition (2012): $42,162
usc.edu

University of Tulsa
Tulsa, OK
Enrollment: 3,004
Tuition (2012-13): $32,410
utulsa.edu

Vassar College
Poughkeepsie, NY
Enrollment: 2,386
Tuition (2012-13): $45,580
vassar.edu

Wake Forest University
Winston-Salem, NC
Enrollment: 4,775
Tuition (2012-13): $39,190
wfu.edu

Washington and Lee University
Lexington, VA
Enrollment: 1,793
Tuition (2012-13): $42,425
wlu.edu

Washington University in St. Louis
St. Louis, MO
Enrollment: 7,329
Tuition (2012-13): $42,500
wustl.edu

Wellesley College
Wellesley, MA
Enrollment: 2,502
Tuition (2012-13): $41,824
wellesley.edu

Wesleyan University
Middletown, CT
Enrollment: 2,882
Tuition (2012-13): $45,358
wesleyan.edu

Wheaton College
Wheaton, IL
Enrollment: 2,433
Tuition (2012-13): $43,480
wheaton.edu

Whitman College
Walla Walla, WA
Enrollment: 1,598
Tuition (2012-13): $41,790
whitman.edu

Williams College
Williamstown, MA
Enrollment: 2,053
Tuition (2012-13): $44,660
williams.edu

Wofford College
Spartanburg, SC
Enrollment: 1,536
Tuition (2012-13): $34,555
wofford.edu

Worcester Polytechnic Institute
Worcester, MA
Enrollment: 3,849
Tuition (2012-13): $40,790
wpi.edu

Yale University
New Haven, CT
Enrollment: 5,349
Tuition (2012-13): $58,600*
yale.edu

Career Resources Portal

This resource presents some of the more comprehensive career-oriented portals maintained by preeminent and influential societies and organizations representing of chemists, physicists, and other scientists and science-related workers. Selections go beyond those web sites offering a simple job board, and include those portals that offer additional career resources and job-seeking tools.

Note: The following sites were visited by editors in 2012. Because URLs frequently change, the accuracy of these addresses cannot be guaranteed; however, long-standing sites, such as those of national organizations and government agencies, generally maintain links when sites are moved or updated.

American Academy of Forensic Science

www.aafs.org/employment

The employment section of the American Academy of Forensic Science (AAFS) website offers numerous tools for job seekers, as well those seeking employees. The AAFS has a free-to-use system where employers post forensic science-related positions that allow job seekers to search open positions. Other resources on this site include a forum for young forensic scientists, links to other information sites, and videos. The Academy News, which is published bi-monthly, keeps members informed of professional issues, Forensic Sciences Foundation activities, and annual meeting information.

American Association of Petroleum Geologists

www.aapg.org/careers

The AAPG (American Association of Petroleum Geologists) Career Center, available to registered members, supplements the standard functionalities of online job boards. Featured resources include a yearly salary survey for geoscientists and a resource portal for continuing education for those in the field, including online courses, seminars, and conference listings. Also available is information about the AAPG-sponsored Student Expo, which connects potential employees with recruiters.

Members can also receive consultation relative to professional resume writing, social network development, and job-seeking strategies.

American Association of Pharmaceutical Scientists

www.careers.aaps.org

The free Online Career Center maintained by the American Association of Pharmaceutical Scientists (AAPS) offers numerous resources to help connect employers with job seekers in the competitive pharmaceutical sciences industry. Employers are able to post jobs and set up resume agents, while job seekers have the ability to create an account that allows for resume submissions and establishing a job-searching agent. Links to additional resources on the portal include an AAPS-issued salary report and online editions of the AAPS Careers magazine.

American Chemical Society

www.acs.org

The American Chemical Society (ACS) offers a comprehensive careers portal, ACS Careers, on the organization's website. One of the key features of the portal is the jobs database, where employers can post job openings and search resumes, and members can set up a job-seeking account, narrowing their search by such fields as State, Specialization, Organization Type, and Work Function. An online forum offers resources for chemical entrepreneurs, and career consulting can help registered job applicants with a range of job-seeking questions, from interviewing tips to resume building. In addition to consultation and advice, the portal also links to professional development tools offered by the ACS such as the ACS Salary Comparator that computes surveyed data to offer a realistic picture of chemists' salaries.

American Institute of Chemical Engineers

www.careerengineer.aiche.org

While the Career Resources center offered by the American Institute of Chemical Engineers (AIChE) offers the standard "Find a Job" and "Post a Job" functionalities of online job boards (including internships), a collection of additional resources enriches the user experience. A Career Development portal offers a collection of useful links, including salary resources and chemical engineering licensure information. A Networking portal provides resources and tools to get

"ChEnected" with industry insiders. A Mentor Center, available only to active AIChe members, allows job seekers to secure a mentor to help develop career-oriented connections.

American Society for Biochemistry and Molecular Biology

www.asbmb.org

The ASBMB (American Society for Biochemistry and Molecular Biology) provides a number of career resources for those interested in biochemistry. There are resources for interested parties at all ends of the spectrum. Helpful career options can be found in several sections titled "77 Things to do with a Biochemistry Degree," "Non-traditional Careers in Science," and "Research Positions and Fellowship Opportunities."

American Society of Clinical Oncology

www.asco.org/ascov2/Education+&+Training/Career+Resources

The ASCO, or American Society of Clinical Oncology offers services for both job seekers and employers within the numerous branches of oncology. Job seekers benefit from support services and the possibility of having face-to-face meetings with employers at the two-day Oncology Career Fair. Those searching for jobs through this portal can create an account with a searchable resume in only a few minutes. Advanced searches allow users to narrow postings by state, category, country, and level of education.

Genetics Society of America

careers.genetics-gsa.org/careerdev/

The GSA's (Genetics Society of America) career center offers a wide range of information for those in various stages of their careers, from getting started, finding job opportunities, and career advancement. It also features professional resume-writing services and resume review for all job levels, from entry level to executive. The Career Center also has a Career Coaching page where highly experienced coaches (all of whom are members of the International Coach Federation) from a variety of professional backgrounds work with clients to further their careers. The Career Center page also offers social networking/profile development, reference checking, and discounted test prep services.

Geochemical Society

jobs.geochemsoc.org

The Geochemical Society's career center provides services beginning with finding job opportunities, as well as planning and advancing your career. It also provides expert resume-writing services and critiques for all job levels, ranging from entry-level to executive resumes. Career coaching pages provide job seekers access to highly knowledgeable coaches (all members of the International Coach Federation) from diverse professional backgrounds to work with clients in advancing their careers. The career center page also provides social networking profile improvement, reference inspection, and low-cost test prep services.

Institute of Food Technologists

www.ift.org/careercenter

The Institute of Food Technologists (IFT) works to provide the global community with an abundant food supply. The career resources page allows visitors to seek information about the IFT's career fair, a free service where face-to-face interviews are available. They also have an eMentoring program where mentors and job seekers are connected. The career center also supplies professional development courses where users can access business skill development through the IFT's online classes. The IFT also offers a basic job board that provides insights and information to help those involved in the food science industry to advance their careers.

National Human Genome Research Institute

www.genome.gov/GenomicCareers/

Genomic Careers from the National Human Genome Research Institute (NHGRI) displays many resources for those seeking a job in the field of genomics. An orientation page welcomes visitors to the website and introduces them to genomics. Interactive videos of genomics professionals provide insight into various career segments. Job seekers may also browse through career profiles based on interest area, career category, and median income.

OilCareers

www.Oilcareers.org/ worldwide/

OilCareers prides itself on providing career-related services to the oil and gas industry. The job search tool offers career profiles in a number of categories. The Training page displays numerous courses, from short courses to full-time educational programs, as well as information about evening courses, distance learning, and oil and gas conferences. The Community page presents opinions and views of its membership. The site also provides a career advice and guidance portal to assist those looking for a job in the oil and gas industry as well as those who already have career in the industry. Some other resources on this page include a career advice report, salary checker, and interview advice.

Society of Environmental Toxicology and Chemistry

www.setac.org

The CareerCenter from SETAC (Society of Environmental Toxicology and Chemistry) is an online resource for connecting educational organizations, businesses, government agencies, and other industry employers. This resource is designed to help people to make their next employment connection. Job seekers can view openings, as well as access many other basic features like resuming posting and advanced searches. Support for candidates is available, complete with many frequently asked questions. If the FAQs do not satisfy potential questions, access to a customer service representative is available as well.

Society of Plastics Engineers

spe.4careersolutions.org

The Society of Plastics Engineers' (SPE) career resources page has a large volume of information relating to career searches and advancement, from choosing the right coach, negotiating an offer, and closing the deal. They also provide professional resume services and analysis for all job levels. The career coaching pages feature knowledgeable coaches (all of whom are members of the International Coach Federation) from a variety of professional backgrounds. Social networking profile development, reference checking, and discounted test prep services are also available.

Society of Toxicology

www.toxicology.org

The Society of Toxicology (SOT) provides a large number of career resources and development services related to toxicology. The job bank provides services for both employers and job seekers. Employers may post employment positions, search the extensive database, view resumes, and contact candidates. Job seekers may post resumes, search openings, view sample CVs and resumes. The organization's annual meeting offers an opportunity for candidates to connect with potential employers. Career development sessions from past meetings are all available online for public viewing. The SOT's Mentor Match, an online mentoring program, provides advice on career path selection and the search for balance between work and life.

Occupational Resources on the Web

Below is an alphabetized list of list of web sites that students and readers alike can turn to for further research and information about the particular occupations profiled. In selecting the following web sites, efforts have been made to identify sites of occupational interest.

Academy of Nutrition and Dietetics
120 South Riverside Plaza, Ste. 2000
Chicago, IL 60606-6995
http://www.eatright.org

American Academy of Clinical Toxicology
6728 Old McLean Village Drive
McLean, VA 22101
www.clintox.org

American Academy of Forensic Sciences
410 North 21st Street
Colorado Springs, CO 80904
www.aafs.org

American Association for Cancer Research
615 Chestnut Street, 17th Floor,
Philadelphia, PA 19106-4404
http://www.aacr.org/

American Association of Colleges of Pharmacy
1727 King Street
Alexandria, VA 22314
www.aacp.org

American Association of Petroleum Geologists
PO Box 979
Tulsa, OK 74101
www.aapg.org

American Board of Internal Medicine
10 Walnut Street, Suite 1700,
Philadelphia, PA 19106
http://www.abim.org/

American Board of Nuclear Medicine
4555 Forest Park Boulevard, Suite 119
St. Louis, MO 63108
www.abnm.org

American Board of Radiology
5441 E. Williams Circle
Tucson, AZ 85711-7412
http://www.theabr.org/

American Board of Toxicology
PO Box 30054
Raleigh, NC 27622-0054
www.abtox.org

American Chemistry Council
700 Second Street NE
Washington, DC 20002
www.americanchemistry.com

American Chemical Society
1155 Sixteenth Street NW
Washington, DC 20036
portal.acs.org

American Clinical Board of Nutrition
6855 Browntown Rd.
Front Royal, VA 22630
http://www.acbn.org

American College of Medical
  Toxicology
10645 N. Tatum Boulevard, Suite
  200-111
Phoenix, AZ 85028
www.acmt.net

American Fuel and Petrochemical
  Manufacturers
1667 K Street NW, Suite 700
Washington, DC 20006
www.afpm.org

American Genetic Association
2030 SE Marine Science Drive
Newport, OR 97365
Tel. 541-867-0334
www.theaga.org

American Geosciences Institute
4220 King Street
Alexandria, VA 22302
www.agiweb.org

American Institute of Chemical
  Engineers
3 Park Avenue

New York, NY 10016-5991
http://www.aiche.org/

American Petroleum Institute
1220 L Street NW
Washington, DC 20005-4070
www.api.org

American Pharmacist Association
2215 Constitution Avenue NW
Washington, DC 20037
www.pharmacist.com

American Society for Biochemistry
  and Molecular Biology
11200 Rockville Pike, Suite 302
Rockville, MD 20852-3110
http://www.asbmb.org/

American Society for Engineering
  Education
1818 N Street, NW, Suite 600
Washington, DC 20036-2479
http://www.asee.org/

American Society for Engineering
  Management
600 West Fourteenth Street
Rolla, MO 65409
www.asem.org

American Society of Clinical
  Oncology
2318 Mill Road, Suite 800
Alexandria, VA 22314
http://www.asco.org/

American Society of Health-System
  Pharmacists
7272 Wisconsin Avenue
Bethesda, MD 20814
www.ashp.org

American Society of Human Genetics
9650 Rockville Pike
Bethesda, MD 20814-3998
http://www.ashg.org

American Society of Perfumers
PO Box 1551
West Caldwell, NJ 07004
www.perfumers.org

Association of Professors of Human
and Medical Genetics
9650 Rockville Pike
Bethesda, MD 20814
www.aphmg.org

Biotechnology Industry Organization
1625 K Street NW, Suite 1100
Washington, DC 20006-1621
www.bio.org

CropLife America
1156 Fifteenth Street NW, Suite 400
Washington, DC 20005
www.croplifeamerica.org

Environmental Protection Agency
1200 Pennsylvania Avenue NW
Washington, DC 20460
www.epa.gov

Fragrance Foundation
545 Fifth Avenue, Suite 900
New York, NY 10017
www.fragrance.org

Fuel Cell and Hydrogen Energy
Association
1211 Connecticut Avenue NW, Suite
600
Washington, DC 20036
www.fchea.org

Genetics Society of America
9650 Rockville Pike
Bethesda, MD 20814-3998
www.genetics-gsa.org

Geochemical Society
1 Brookings Drive, CB 1169
St. Louis, MO 63130
www.geochemsoc.org

Human Factors and Ergonomics
Society
PO Box 1369
Santa Monica, CA 90406
www.hfes.org

Institute of Industrial Engineers
3577 Parkway Lane, Suite 200
Norcross, GA 30092
www.iienet2.org

International & American
Associations of Clinical
Nutritionists (IAACN)
15280 Addison Road, Ste. 130
Addison, TX 75001mailto:
http://www.iaacn.org

International Society of Automation
67 T. W. Alexander Drive
PO Box 12277
Research Triangle Park, NC 27709
www.isa.org

Joint Institute for the Study of the
Atmosphere and Ocean
University of Washington
3737 Brooklyn Avenue NE
Box 355672
Seattle, WA 98195-5672
www.jisao.washington.edu

Materials Research Society
506 Keystone Drive
Warrendale, PA 15086
www.mrs.org

National Center for Atmospheric
  Research
University Corporation for
  Atmospheric Research
PO Box 3000
Boulder, CO 80307-3000
www2.ucar.edu

National Center for Forensic Science
12354 Research Parkway
Orlando, Florida 32826
http://ncfs.ucf.edu/index.html

National Council of Examiners for
  Engineering and Surveying
280 Seneca Creek Road
Seneca, SC 29678
www.ncees.org

National Oceanic and Atmospheric
  Administration
1401 Constitution Avenue NW
Room 5128
Washington, DC 20230
www.noaa.gov

National Society of Professional
  Engineers
1420 King Street
Alexandria, VA 22314
www.nspe.org

Pacific Northwest National
  Laboratory
Radiochemical Science and
  Engineering Group
902 Battelle Boulevard

Richland, WA 99352
www.radiochemscieng.pnnl.gov

Radiochemistry Society
PO Box 3091
Richland, WA 99354
www.radiochemistry.org

Research Institute for Fragrance
  Materials
50 Tice Boulevard
Woodcliff Lake, NJ 07677
www.rifm.org

Society of Plastics Engineers
13 Church Hill Road
Newtown, CT 06470
www.4spe.org

Society of Surgical Oncology
85 W. Algonquin Road, Suite 550
Arlington Heights, IL 60005
http://www.surgonc.org/

Society of Toxicology
1821 Michael Faraday Drive, Suite
  300
Reston, VA 20190
www.toxicology.org

Technology Student Association
1914 Association Drive
Reston, VA 20191-1540
www.tsaweb.org

Nobel Prizes in Chemistry

1901	van't Hoff, Jacobus Henricus
1902	Fischer, Hermann Emil
1903	Arrhenius, Svante August
1904	Ramsay, Sir William
1905	Wilhelm Adolf von Baeyer, Johann Friedrich
1906	Moissan, Henri
1907	Buchner, Eduard
1908	Rutherford, Ernest
1909	Ostwald, Wilhelm
1910	Wallach, Otto
1911	Curie née Sklodowska, Marie
1912	Grignard, Victor
1912	Sabatier, Paul
1913	Werner, Alfred
1914	Richards, Theodore William
1915	Willstätter, Richard Martin
1918	Haber, Fritz
1920	Nernst, Walther Hermann
1921	Soddy, Frederick
1922	Aston, Francis William
1923	Pregl, Fritz
1925	Zsigmondy, Richard Adolf
1926	Svedberg, The (Theodor)
1927	Wieland, Heinrich Otto
1928	Reinhold Windaus, Adolf Otto
1929	Harden, Arthur
1929	August Simon von Euler-Chelpin, Hans Karl
1930	Fischer, Hans
1931	Bosch, Carl
1932	Langmuir, Irving
1934	Urey, Harold Clayton
1935	Joliot, Frédéric
1935	Joliot-Curie, Irène
1936	Wilhelmus Debye, Petrus (Peter) Josephus
1937	Haworth, Walter Norman
1937	Karrer, Paul
1938	Kuhn, Richard
1939	Johann Butenandt, Adolf Friedrich
1939	Ruzicka, Leopold
1943	de Hevesy, George
1944	Hahn, Otto
1945	Virtanen, Artturi Ilmari
1946	Sumner, James Batcheller
1946	Northrop, John Howard
1946	Stanley, Wendell Meredith
1947	Robinson, Sir Robert
1948	Kaurin Tiselius, Arne Wilhelm
1949	Giauque, William Francis
1950	Hermann Diels, Otto Paul
1951	McMillan, Edwin Mattison
1951	Seaborg, Glenn Theodore
1952	Porter Martin, Archer John
1952	Millington Synge, Richard Laurence
1953	Staudinger, Hermann
1954	Carl Pauling, Linus
1955	du Vigneaud, Vincent
1956	Hinshelwood, Sir Cyril Norman
1956	Semenov, Nikolay Nikolaevich

1957	Todd, Lord (Alexander R.)	1980	Sanger, Frederick
1958	Sanger, Frederick	1981	Fukui, Kenichi
1959	Heyrovsky, Jaroslav	1981	Hoffman, Roald
1960	Libby, Willard Frank	1982	Klug, Aaron
1961	Calvin, Melvin	1983	Taube, Henry
1962	Perutz, Max Ferdinand	1984	Merrifield, Robert Bruce
1962	Kendrew, John Cowdery	1985	Hauptman, Herbert A.
1963	Ziegler, Karl	1985	Karle, Jerome
1963	Natta, Guilio	1986	Herschbach, Dudley R.
1964	Hodgkin, Dorothy Crowfoot	1986	Lee, Yuan T.
		1986	Polanyi, John C.
1965	Woodward, Robert Burns	1987	Cram, Donald J.
1966	Mulliken, Robert S.	1987	Lehn, Jean-Marie
1967	Eigen, Manfred	1987	Pedersen, Charles J.
1967	Wreyford Norrish, Ronald George	1988	Deisenhofer, Johann
		1988	Huber, Robert
1967	Porter, George	1988	Michel, Hartmur
1968	Onsager, Lars	1989	Altman, Sidney
1969	Barton, Derek H. R.	1989	Cech, Thomas R.
1969	Hassel, Odd	1990	Corey, Elias James
1970	Leloir, Luis F.	1991	Ernst, Richard R.
1971	Herzberg, Gerhard	1992	Marcus, Rudolph A.
1972	Anfinsen, Christian B.	1993	Mullis, Kary B.
1972	Moore, Stanford	1993	Smith, Michael
1972	Stein, William H.	1994	Olah, George A.
1973	Fischer, Ernst Otto	1995	Crutzen, Paul J.
1973	Wilkinson, Geoffrey	1995	Molina, Mario J.
1974	Flory, Paul J.	1995	Rowland, F. Sherwood
1975	Cornforth, John Warcup	1996	Curl Jr., Robert F.
1975	Prelog Vladimir	1996	Kroto, Sir Harold W.
1976	Lipscomb, William N.	1996	Smalley, Richard E.
1977	Prigogine, Ilya	1997	Boyer, Paul D.
1978	Mitchell, Peter D.	1997	Walker, John E.
1979	Brown, Herbert C.	1997	Skou, Jens C.
1979	Wittig, Georg	1998	Kohn, Walter
1980	Berg, Paul	1998	Pople, John A.
1980	Gilbert, Walter		

1999	Zewail, Ahmed H.
2000	Heeger, Alan J.
2000	MacDiarmid, Alan G.
2000	Shirakawa, Hideki
2001	Knowles, William S.
2001	Noyori, Ryoji
2001	Sharpless, K. Barry
2002	Fenn, John B.
2002	Tanaka, Koichi
2002	Wüthrich, Kurt
2003	Agre, Peter
2003	MacKinnon, Roderick
2004	Ciechanover, Aaron
2004	Hershko, Avram
2004	Rose, Irwin
2005	Chauvin, Yves
2005	Grubbs, Robert H.

2005	Schrock, Richard R.
2006	Kornberg, Roger D.
2007	Ertl, Gerhard
2008	Shimomura, Osamu
2008	Chalfie, Martin
2008	Tsien, Roger Y
2009	Ramakrishnan, Venkatraman
2009	Steitz, Thomas A.
2009	Yonath, Ada E.
2010	Heck, Richard F.
2010	Negishi, Ei-ichi
2010	Suzuki, Akira
2011	Dan Shechtman
2012	Robert J. Lefkowitz
2012	Brian K. Kobilka

Indexes

Occupational Index

Index